Reader's Digest

OUR ISLAND HERITAGE

OUR ISLAND HERITAGE
was edited and designed by
The Reader's Digest Association Limited
London

First Edition
Copyright © 1988
The Reader's Digest Association Limited
Berkeley Square House
Berkeley Square
London W1X 6AB

Reprinted with amendments 1990

Copyright © 1988
Reader's Digest Services Pty. Limited
Sydney, Australia

Copyright © 1988
The Reader's Digest Association
South Africa (Pty.) Limited

Copyright © 1988
Reader's Digest Association
Far East Limited

Philippines Copyright © 1988
Reader's Digest Association
Far East Limited

ISBN 0 276 48944 6
Printed in Great Britain

Reader's Digest

OUR ISLAND HERITAGE

VOLUME THREE

The Industrial Age to the Present

Published by The Reader's Digest Association Limited
London • New York • Montreal • Sydney • Cape Town

VOLUME THREE

Contents

CHAPTERS

EPILOGUE

SOCIAL HISTORY SECTIONS

COLOUR SECTIONS

TIME CHART · PLACES TO SEE · INDEX

Part One: from Winston S. Churchill's
A History of the English-Speaking Peoples

CHAPTER 1
THE VICTORY PEACE

AFTER A GENERATION OF WARFARE peace had come to Europe. It was to be a long peace, disturbed by civil commotions and local campaigns, but flaring into no major blaze until the era of German expansion succeeded the age of French predominance. In the Napoleonic struggles Britain had played a heroic part. The task that had united and preoccupied her people was now at last accomplished. Henceforth they could bend their energies to developing the great resources of industrial and commercial skill which had accumulated in the island during the past half-century. But the busy world of trade and manufacture and the needs and aspirations of the mass of men, women, and children who toiled in its service were beyond the grasp of the country's leading statesmen on the morrow of Waterloo. Under the shock of the French Terror the English governing classes had closed their minds and their ranks to change.

The Tories, as we may call them, though not all would have acknowledged the name, were firmly in power. They had won the struggle against Napoleon with the support of a war cabinet drawn largely from their own party, and throughout the country they had innumerable allies among men of substance and independent mind. They embodied the tradition of resistance to the principles of Revolutionary France and the aggressive might of the Napoleonic empire. They regarded themselves as the defenders not only of the island, but of the almost bloodless aristocratic settlement achieved by the Revolution of 1688.

The principal figures in the Government were Lord Liverpool, Lord Castlereagh, and, after 1818, the Duke of Wellington. Liverpool was a man of conciliatory temper, a mild chief, and an easy colleague. He had held a variety of public offices almost continuously since the start of the war with France. In 1812 he became Prime Minister, and for fifteen years presided over the affairs of the realm with tact, patience, and laxity. Castlereagh was the architect of the coalition which gained the final victory and one of the principal authors of the treaties of peace. For home affairs he cared little, his cool, collected temperament was stiffened with disdain; he thought it beneath him to inform the public frankly of the Government's measures. Wellington's conception of politics was simple. He wished to unite all parties and imbue them with the duty of preserving the existing order.

The rest of the Cabinet were Tories of the deepest dye, such as the Lord Chancellor, Eldon; Addington, now Viscount Sidmouth, once Prime Minister and now at the Home Office; and Earl Bathurst, Colonial Secretary,

This illustration is taken from The Life and Adventures of Michael Armstrong the Factory Boy *by Frances Trollope, and shows hungry factory children scavenging for food in a pig-trough. The post-Waterloo politicians were slowly recognising the evils of the factory system and in 1819 Parliament passed a Factory Act forbidding the employment of children under the age of nine.*

Castlereagh, Marquis of Londonderry, (1769-1822) dominated British foreign politics in the years after the Napoleonic Wars. He initiated moderate terms for France at the Congress of Vienna and thus secured a lasting peace. This portrait by G. Dance can be seen in the National Portrait Gallery.

whom Lord Rosebery has described as "one of those strange children of our political system who fill the most dazzling offices with the most complete obscurity". These men had begun their political life under the threat of world revolution. Their sole aim in politics was an unyielding defence of the system they had always known. Their minds were rigid, and scarcely capable of grasping the changes pending in English society. They were the upholders of the landed interest in government, of the Protestant ascendancy in Ireland, and of Anglicanism at home. They were plain Tory politicians resolved to do as little as possible as well as they could.

The sea power, the financial strength, and the tenacity of Britain had defeated Napoleon. In the summer of 1815 Britain and Castlereagh stood at the head of Europe, and it was upon the terms of the European settlement to be concluded that the peace of generations depended. France must be rendered harmless for the future. An international structure must be raised high above the battlefields of nations, of theories and of class. The treaties that created the new Europe involved Britain in obligations she had never assumed before. She was a party to the settlement of the new frontiers of France, which deprived the restored Bourbons of what is now the Saarland and of parts of Savoy. France was reduced to the frontiers of 1789, and Prussia established as the chief power upon the River Rhine. The Allied army of occupation in northeastern France, which included thirty thousand British troops, was commanded by the Duke of Wellington. Although Tory opinion even in the day of triumph was fearful of continental commitments, Castlereagh resolved that Britain should not abandon the position of authority she had won during the war. Immune from popular passions, race hatreds, or any desire to trample on a fallen enemy, he foresaw the day when France would be necessary to the balance of Europe. With Wellington he stood between France and her vindictive foes. Unrestrained, Prussia, Austria, and Russia would have divided between them the states of Germany, imposed a harsh peace upon France, and fought each other over the partition of Poland. The moderating influence of Britain was the foundation of the peace of Europe.

In the eighteenth century the European powers had no regular organisation for consulting each other, and little conception of their common interests. The Revolution in France had united them against the common danger, and they were now determined to remain together to prevent a further outbreak. An alliance of the four Great Powers already existed, sworn to confer as occasion demanded upon the problems of Europe. This was now supplemented by a Holy Alliance between the three autocratic rulers on the Continent, the Emperors of Russia and Austria and the King of Prussia. Its main purpose was to intervene in any part of Europe where revolution appeared and instantly to suppress it.

This made small appeal to Castlereagh. He was opposed to any interference in the affairs of sovereign states, however small and whatever liberal complexions their governments might assume. Although caricatured as a reactionary at home, he was no friend to continental despotism. To him the quadruple alliance and the Congress at Vienna were merely pieces of diplomatic machinery for discussing European problems. On the other hand, the Austrian Chancellor Metternich and his colleagues regarded them as instruments for preserving the existing order. This divergence between the Great Powers was in part due to the fact that Britain had a Parliamentary

Government which represented, however imperfectly, a nation. Castle-reagh's European colleagues were the servants of absolute monarchs. Britain was a world power whose strength lay in her ranging commerce and in her command of the seas. Her trade flourished and multiplied independently of the reigning ideas in Europe. Moreover, her governing classes, long accustomed to public debate, did not share the absolutist dreams that inspired, and deluded, the courts of the autocrats.

In spite of these differences the Congress of Vienna stands as a monument to the success of classical diplomacy. No fewer than twenty-seven separate agreements were concluded during the first six months of 1815, in addition to the formidable final act of the Congress itself. Castlereagh was the genius of the conference. He reconciled opposing views, and his modest expectation that peace might be ensured for seven years was fulfilled more than fivefold. Indeed within three years of the signing of the peace treaty British troops had evacuated French territory, the war indemnity had been paid, and France was received as a respectable nation into the European Congress. Wellington, released from military duties in France, thereupon entered the Cabinet in the not inappropriate office of Master-General of the Ordnance.

At home the Government was faced with the delicate and perplexing task of economic reconstruction. For this its members were supremely unfitted. The dislocation caused by the end of the war and the novel problems posed by the advance of industry were beyond the power of these men to remedy or solve. Earlier than her neighbours Britain enjoyed the fruits and endured the rigours of the Industrial Revolution. At the same time the growing masses in her ill-built towns were often plunged into squalor and misery, the source of numerous and well-grounded discontents. Her technical lead

ELIZABETH FRY AT NEWGATE

Elizabeth Fry (1780–1845) was a member of a well-known family of Norfolk Quakers. Her first visit to Newgate prison in 1813, described here by Thomas Fowell Buxton, so appalled her that it ultimately led to pioneering reforms in prisons and convict ships.

About four years ago, Mrs Fry was induced to visit Newgate, by the representations of its state made by some persons of the Society of Friends.

She found the female side in a situation which no language can describe. Nearly three hundred women, sent there for every gradation of crime, some untried, and some under sentence of death, were crowded together in the two wards and two cells, which are now quite appropriated to the untried, and which are found quite inadequate to contain even this diminished number with any tolerable convenience. Here they saw their friends, and kept their multitudes of children; and they had no other place for cooking, washing, eating and sleeping.

They all slept on the floor; at times one hundred and twenty in one ward, without so much as a mat for bedding; and many of them were very nearly naked. She saw them openly drinking spirits; and her ears were offended by the most dreadful imprecations. Everything was filthy to excess, and the smell was quite disgusting. Everyone, even the Governor, was reluctant to go amongst them. He persuaded her to leave her watch in the office, telling her that his presence would not prevent its being torn from her! She saw enough to convince her that everything bad was going on. In short, in giving me this account, she repeatedly said, "All I tell thee, is a faint picture of the reality; the filth, the closeness of the rooms, the ferocious manners and expressions of the women towards each other, and the abandoned wickedness . . . are quite indescribable!"

Elizabeth Fry earned public acclaim for her dauntless visits to Newgate prison. In the idealised scene above, an artist shows her reading the Bible to convicts.

was due to the ingenuity and success of British inventors and men of business and to the fortunate proximity of her main coal and iron deposits to each other and to the coast. Supremacy at sea, the resources of the colonial empire, and the use of capital accumulated from its trade nourished the industrial movement. Steam engines were gradually harnessed to the whole field of contemporary industry. In engineering, accurate tools were perfected which brought a vast increase in output. The spinning of cotton was mechanised, and the factory system grew by degrees. The skilled man, self-employed, who had hitherto worked in his home, was steadily displaced. Machinery, the rise of population, and extensive changes in employment all presented a formidable social problem. The members of the Government were by background and upbringing largely unaware of the causes of the ills which had to be cured. In a society which was rapidly becoming industrial most of them represented the abiding landed interest. Incapable of carrying out even moderate reforms, they concentrated upon the one issue they understood, the defence of property.

Napoleon had closed the Continent to British commerce, and the answering British blockade had made things worse for industry at home. There was much unemployment in the industrial north and the Midlands. The "Luddite" riots of 1812 and 1813 against the use of machinery had exposed the complete absence of means of preserving public order. There was no coordination between the Home Office in London and the Justices of the Peace in the country. Disorder was in the end suppressed only by the tactful and efficient behaviour of the officers commanding the troops sent to put down the rioters. Often before in the eighteenth century low wages and lack of employment had caused widespread unrest, which had been fanned into riot whenever a succession of bad harvests made food dearer. But eighteenth-century riots were generally soon over. They were snuffed out by a few hangings and sentences of transportation to the colonies. The sore-pates who remained at home were more inclined to blame Nature for their woes than either the economic or political system. After Waterloo the public temper was very different. Extremist radical leaders came out of hiding and kept up a perpetual and growing agitation. Their organisations, which had been suppressed during the French Revolution, now appeared, and began to take the shape of a political movement, though as yet scarcely represented in the House of Commons.

In the radical view it was the Government alone, and not chance or Act of God, that was to blame for the misfortunes of the people. The Tory Cabinet in the face of such charges knew not what to do. It was no part of Tory philosophy to leave everything to be settled by the marketplace, to trust to good luck and ignore the bad. The Tories of the time recognised and sometimes gloried in the responsibility of the governing classes for the welfare of the whole nation. The tasks of government were well understood to be as Burke had defined them: "The public peace, the public safety, the public order, the public prosperity." It was the last of these that was now foremost. The trouble was that the Government, in the unprecedented conditions that confronted them, had no idea how to secure that prosperity. And even if they had hit upon a plan they possessed no experienced body of civil servants to put it into effect. As a result the only remedy for misery was private charity or the Poor Law.

It was a misfortune for Britain in these years that the Parliamentary

Opposition was at its weakest. A generation in the wilderness had demoralised the Whig Party, which had not been effectively in office since 1783. Among themselves the Whigs were deeply divided, and none of them had any better plans for postwar reconstruction than the Tories. Indeed, their interests were essentially the same. Like their rivals, they represented the landed class, and also the City of London. The only issues upon which they seriously quarrelled with the Government were Catholic Emancipation and the enfranchisement of the middle classes in the rising industrial towns. In the 1790s the Whigs had favoured the cause of Parliamentary Reform. It had been a useful stick with which to beat the administration of the younger Pitt. But they had been badly scared by the headlong course of events in France. Their leaders only gradually and reluctantly regained their reforming zeal. In the meantime, as Hazlitt put it, the two parties were like competing stagecoaches which splashed each other with mud but went by the same road to the same place. The radicals in Parliament were, however, too few to form an effective Opposition.

Men still looked to Parliament to cure the evils of the day. If Parliament did nothing, then the structure of Parliament must be changed. Agitation therefore turned from airing social discontents to demanding Parliamentary Reform. Huge meetings were held, advocating annual Parliaments and universal suffrage. But the tactics of the radicals were too much like those of the French Revolutionaries to gain support from the middle classes. Though still denied much weight in Parliament, the middle classes were bound by their fear of revolution to side in the last resort with the landed interest. The Cabinet was thoroughly perturbed. Habeas corpus was suspended, and legislation passed against the holding of seditious meetings. Throughout the country a fresh wave of demonstrations followed. A large body of men set out to march from Manchester to London to present a petition against the Government's measures, each carrying a blanket for his night's shelter. This march of the "Blanketeers" disturbed the authorities profoundly. The leaders were arrested and the rank and file dispersed.

These alarums and excursions revealed the gravity of conditions. Not only was there grinding poverty among the working population, but also a deep-rooted conflict between the manufacturing and agricultural classes. The economy of the country was dangerously out of balance. The war debt had reached alarming proportions. The fund-holders were worried at the instability of the national finances. In 1797 the country had gone off the gold standard (the system under which a government is obliged to exchange paper currency for gold), and the paper currency had seriously depreciated. In 1812 a Parliamentary committee advised returning to gold, but the Bank of England was strongly adverse and nothing was done. The income tax, introduced by Pitt to finance the war, was highly unpopular, especially among the industrial middle class. It took ten per cent of all incomes over a hundred and fifty pounds a year, and there were lower rates for smaller incomes. The yield in 1815 was fifteen million pounds, which was a large proportion of the Budget. Agriculture as well as industry quaked at the end of the war. Peace brought a slump in the prices fetched by crops, and landowners clamoured for protection against the importation of cheap foreign corn. This had been granted by the Corn Law of 1815, which excluded foreign wheat unless the domestic price per quarter rose above eighty shillings. The cost of bread went up, and the manufacturing classes

LANDLORD & TENANT.

Landowners in the early nineteenth century often showed little respect for those beneath them, as can be seen in this cartoon. They dominated Parliament and the 1815 Corn Laws were passed to protect their interests, irrespective of the hardship imposed on the poor by the subsequently high cost of bread.

THE CHANGING LANDSCAPE

AGRICULTURAL IMPROVEMENTS in the eighteenth century led to a transformation of the English landscape. Hedges and walls now separated fields from neighbouring properties, wasteland was brought into cultivation—no less than three million acres between 1760 and 1799—and careful attention was paid to paths, to drainage, to the planting of trees and to the building of canals. It was not only the landscapes that were improved, but houses also, and Georgian gentlefolk deliberately built their country houses where they could enjoy a beautiful prospect.

Not surprisingly, therefore, this was a time when the countryside was a favourite subject for English painters. John Constable, born in the year of the American Declaration of Independence, 1776, died in the year Victoria became Queen, 1837. One of his landscapes was first shown at the Royal Academy in 1802.

A very different but superb painter, J.M.W. Turner, whose impressionistic style was to influence so many later artists, was born in 1775 and lived on to the year of the Great Exhibition, 1851.

These were the years, too, of the great Romantic poets. William Wordsworth, particularly, explored Nature—not the "improved nature" of the planned landscape, but the wild nature of lakes and mountains, which, it was thought, had lessons to teach, and reminded people of their proper place within the universe.

The later Romantic poets were to write of a Nature that was cruel as well as kind, and in the late eighteenth and early nineteenth centuries there were writers who pointed to the darker side of rural and agricultural life, among them George Crabbe, whose picture of village life was starkly realistic. William Cobbett, Tory turned radical, complained that "when farmers become gentlemen, their labourers become slaves".

THE RAILWAYS *brought huge changes to the face of Britain. The Welwyn Viaduct, (above) designed by Lewis Cubitt in 1848, has forty arches and carries the railway tracks ninety feet above the River Maron in Hertfordshire. New machinery also left its mark upon the landscape. Steam engines, like the one below which is providing power for one of the new threshing machines, were put to work on the land. The "Open Field" system of farming now disappeared, and a patchwork of fields was created instead. Networks of roads, railways and canals threading through the countryside made these changes more apparent, and with this transformation of the landscape came a new delight in Nature, but at the same time, concern about its possible destruction. Poets and painters recorded detailed observations of the landscape, which had often been regarded as unworthy of notice.*

NATURE COULD BE CRUEL, *as when the poet, Percy Bysshe Shelley (1792–1822) was drowned in the Bay of Lerici, Italy. His friend, the poet George Gordon, Lord Byron (1788–1824) arranged a funeral cremation of the body after it was washed ashore. In the painting (above) by Louis Edouard Fournier, Byron (in a white scarf) watches the pyre. Shelley's ashes were later interred in the Protestant* cemetery at Rome, near the recent grave of the poet, John Keats (1795–1821). The commitment of the "Romantic" poets to emotional and intellectual freedom could produce marvellous poetry, but the problems of poverty, ill health and tragic personal relationships brought some of them to an early grave. William Wordsworth, the great Lake District poet, was an exception. He lived until he was eighty.

ROAD CONSTRUCTION *was improved to facilitate the transport of goods to and from industrial towns such as Leeds (above) shown from the tollgate on Rope Hill in 1840. Before the Industrial Revolution roads were little better than cart-tracks, cut up by the huge wheels of carriages. In the eighteenth century, surveyors like Thomas Telford and John Metcalf improved road surfaces by covering them with compacted stones, and straightened out some of the more dangerous bends and corners. But in 1827, John McAdam (1756–1836) became surveyor general of Britain's roads and introduced his effective methods of road-building, using compressed angular stones. Nearly one hundred years after his death, the stones were bound with asphalt or tar and became known as macadam roads.*

DELIGHT IN SIMPLE COUNTRY SCENES *was the hallmark of the Suffolk painter, John Constable. He wrote in a letter: "the sound of water escaping from mill dams, willows, old rotten planks, slimy posts and brickwork, I love such things . . . These scenes made me a painter and I am grateful." Constable rejected all traditional methods of landscape painting and sketched only what he actually saw. He* told a friend that he regarded his art as a branch of natural science. At first his works were unpopular and he was forced to turn to portraiture. It was in France that his art first gained recognition. At the Paris Salon of 1824 the French painter Eugene Delacroix praised his paintings and advised him to work on a larger scale. Pictured above is Constable's native district, East Bergholt, Suffolk.

had to raise wages to save their workers from hunger. The manufacturers in their turn got the income tax abolished, which helped them but imperilled the Budget. The Chancellor of the Exchequer, Nicholas Vansittart, struggled vainly with the chaos of a mounting deficit and an unstable currency.

In 1819 an incident took place which increased the unpopularity and quickened the fears of the Government. A meeting of protest was held at St Peter's Fields, in mid-Manchester, attended by over fifty thousand people. The local magistrates lost their heads, and, after reading the Riot Act, ordered the yeomanry to charge. Eleven people were killed, two of them women, and four hundred were injured. This "massacre of Peterloo", as it was called in ironic reference to the Battle of Waterloo, aroused widespread indignation, which was swelled still further when the Government took drastic steps to prevent the recurrence of disorder. Six Acts were passed regulating public meetings, empowering the magistrates to seize seditious literature, forbidding unauthorised drilling in military formations, imposing a heavy tax upon the press to restrict the circulation of radical newspapers, regulating the issue of warrants and the bringing of cases to trial.

The attack by the Government upon the traditional principles of English liberty aroused the conscience of the Whigs. They considered that "Peterloo" was no excuse for invading the rights of the subject. They demanded an inquiry. Liberty was at stake, and this was a struggle they well understood. When they were outvoted, however, they took their defeat with some equanimity, for they were as frightened as the Tories by the social unrest, especially when a small gang of plotters was arrested in Cato Street, off the Edgware Road, where they had met to plan to murder all the Cabinet Ministers at a dinner party and seize the Bank of England.

However, compared with most continental countries, Britain came lightly out of these years of disturbance. By the end of 1819 trade and harvests had improved. A commission under the chairmanship of Robert Peel, a young Tory politician who had been Chief Secretary for Ireland at the age of twenty-four, recommended a return to the gold standard. Peel brought in and carried a Bill embodying the principles of their report. Stabilisation of the currency was at last achieved. Though the landed interests suffered

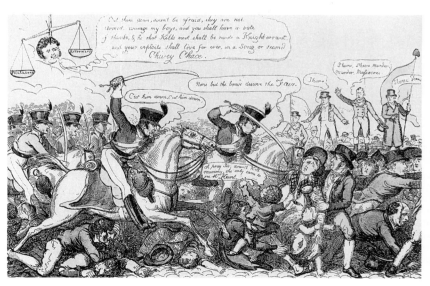

George Cruikshank, famous for his caricatures and illustrations of the novels of Charles Dickens, drew this cartoon of the "massacre of Peterloo". The Manchester magistrates, who ordered the action, received a letter of congratulation from the Home Secretary.

some hardship, not without raising their voices in complaint, it seemed that a corner had been turned.

Now, once again in English history, the personal affairs of the royal family exploded into public view. The republican influence of the French Revolution had left its mark on public opinion in most European countries, and the vices or incapacity of many monarchs made them easy targets for criticism and abuse. In England King George III had long been intermittently mad, and in 1810 the old King had finally sunk into incurable imbecility. He lived for another ten years, roaming the corridors of Windsor Castle with long white beard and purple dressing gown.

"Farmer George", as George III was called in his happier middle years, had become a popular figure. He had been the only person who had not lost his nerve at the time of the Gordon Riots, when a crazy Protestant mob, led by an unbalanced member of the aristocracy, reduced London to panic. He had endured the disasters of the American War of Independence. But though he commanded his people's affection he scarcely inspired their leaders' respect. He married a German princess, Queen Charlotte, who bore him a brood of sons, seven of whom grew to manhood. None of them added dignity or lustre to the royal house.

The atmosphere of the Court was like that of a minor German principality. All was stiff, narrow, fusty. The spirited lad who was to be first Regent and then George IV soon rebelled against his decorous mother and parsimonious father. A gift for facile friendship, often with dubious personages, alienated him still further from the home circle. He was early deprived of the companionship of his brothers, who were dispatched to Germany, there to receive a thorough Teutonic grounding. George, as heir to the throne, had to have an English background; and in the circle of his more intimate friends, Charles James Fox, Richard Sheridan, and Beau Brummel, he soon acquired the attributes of the eighteenth-century English gentleman—the arts of acquiring debts, of wearing fine clothes, and making good conversation. His natural intelligence and good taste went undisciplined and his talent for self-expression was frequently squandered in melodramatic emotion. Self-indulgence warped his judgment and frivolity marred his bearing. When pleasure clashed with royal duty it was usually pleasure that won.

In 1784 the Prince had fallen in love with Maria Fitzherbert, a commoner of obscure family. Her morals were impeccable and she would be content with nothing less than marriage. Under the Royal Marriages Act the union was illegal, and it was finally broken off, but not until some years after George had contracted a second, legal, and dynastic marriage.

At the bidding of his parents in 1795 he was wedded to Caroline of Brunswick, a noisy, flighty, and unattractive German princess. George was so appalled at the sight of his bride that he was drunk for the first twenty-four hours of his married life. A few days after his wedding he wrote his wife a letter absolving her from any further conjugal duties. However, a high-spirited, warm-hearted girl was born of their brief union, Princess Charlotte, who found her mother quite as unsatisfactory as her father. In 1814 George banned his wife from Court, and after an unseemly squabble she left England for a European tour, vowing to return to plague her husband when he should accede to the throne.

Princess Charlotte married Prince Leopold of Saxe-Coburg, later King of

Maria Fitzherbert's marriage to George, Prince of Wales in 1785 was declared illegal. The couple continued to live in Brighton where, in 1787, George commissioned the architect Henry Holland to design a "marine pavilion". The Royal Pavilion is now a distinctive part of our national heritage.

the Belgians, but in 1817 she died in childbirth. Her infant was stillborn. The Government were now perturbed about the problem of the succession. George's brothers were thoroughly unpopular; as Wellington said, "the damnedest millstone about the necks of any Government . . . they have personally insulted two-thirds of the gentlemen of England". They lacked not only charm, but lawful issue. But they were well aware that they had a cash value to the Government on the royal marriage market. Although already involved in long-standing relationships with women, in 1818 the obliging Dukes of Clarence and Kent did their royal duty—for a sum. The Duke of Kent made a German marriage and the offspring of this alliance was the future Queen Victoria.

The Prince of Wales had long played with the idea of divorcing his itinerant wife. But Liverpool's Government were apprehensive. The Prince's extravagance, his lavish architectural experiments at Brighton and Windsor, were already causing them anxiety and giving rise to hostile speeches in Parliament. The bench of bishops was opposed to any idea of divorce. But George was persistent. He got a commission appointed to inquire into the Princess's conduct. It posted to Italy to collect evidence from Caroline's unsavoury entourage. In July 1819 the Government received a report producing considerable circumstantial evidence against her. George was delighted, Liverpool and the Cabinet dismayed.

The Princess's chief legal adviser was Henry Brougham, the ablest of the younger Whigs. This witty, ambitious, and unscrupulous attorney entered into confidential relations with the Government, hoping for a compromise which would bring advancement to himself. But in January 1820 the mad old King died and the position of the new sovereign's consort had to be determined. The Cabinet presented George IV with a nervous note pointing out the difficulties of action. But now he was King. He warned them he could dismiss the lot, and threatened to retire to Hanover. The Whigs were as much alarmed as the Tories by the King's determination. They too feared the effect on public opinion outside Parliamentary and political circles. Whatever happened there would be a scandal which would bring the monarchy into dangerous disrepute.

Caroline now showed her hand. In April 1820 an open letter appeared in the London press, signed by her, and recounting her woes. The City of London was easily aroused in her favour, and the radicals promised her a warm reception. In June she landed, and drove amid stormy scenes of enthusiasm from Dover to London, her carriage hauled most of the way by exuberant supporters. Her arrival produced a tumult of agitation.

The Government reluctantly decided that they must go through with the business. A secret committee of the Lords was set up, and their report persuaded Liverpool to agree to introduce a Bill of Pains and Penalties if the Queen were proved guilty of adultery. Popular feeling against the conditions of England was now diverted into a national inquiry into the condition of the monarchy. The characters of the royal personages concerned came under merciless scrutiny. A well-organised campaign was launched on behalf of Queen Caroline, led by the City radicals, and, now that there was no turning back, by Brougham. Cheering crowds gathered every day outside her house in London. Politicians known to oppose her case were stoned in their carriages. In July the hearing of the charges was opened in Westminster Hall. In lengthy sessions the attorney general put

This portrait of Caroline of Brunswick by Sir Henry Lawrence can be seen in the National Portrait Gallery. George was persuaded to marry Caroline in 1795 in return for Parliament paying off his debts. The sight of her drove him into a drunken stupor for the first twenty-four hours of their marriage, and very soon afterwards they lived apart.

the case for the Government, producing unreliable Italian witnesses from Caroline's vagabond Court. The conflicting and sordid evidence of lackeys and chambermaids was displayed before the audience in Westminster Hall. Stories of keyholes, of indecorous costumes and gestures, regaled the public ear. The London press openly attacked the credibility of the witnesses with their broken Italianate English and their uninspiring appearance.

Brougham led the defence. With great effect he produced George's letter of 1796 absolving his wife from all marital obligations. It was not difficult to show that the conflicting evidence produced hardly justified the divorce clause in the Bill of Pains and Penalties. He boldly attacked the veiled personage behind the case, the King himself, malevolently referring to George's obesity in a wounding quotation from *Paradise Lost*:

> The other shape—
> If shape it could be called—that shape had none
> Distinguishable in member, joint or limb . . .
> What seemed its head
> The likeness of a kingly crown had on.

The peers thought the Queen guilty, but doubted the wisdom of divorce, and the Bill passed through their House by only nine votes, the Whigs voting against the Government. Their leader, Earl Grey, had declared his belief in the innocence of Caroline. The Cabinet now decided that there was small chance of forcing the Bill through the Commons. They withdrew it and the affair was dropped. The London mob rioted in joy. The windows of the Ministers' houses were broken. But the bubbling effervescence of the masses quickly subsided. Caroline was granted an annuity of £50,000, which she was not too proud to accept. One political result of the crisis was the resignation of George Canning, who had been on friendly terms with the Queen. This gifted pupil of Pitt had rejoined the administration in 1816 as President of the Board of Control, which supervised the Government of India. He had made his influence felt in other spheres as well, and his departure was a serious loss to the Cabinet.

Two more awkward scenes closed this regrettable story. In July 1821 George IV was crowned in pomp at Westminster Abbey. Caroline attempted to force her way into the Abbey, but was turned away. A month later she died. An attempt by the authorities to smuggle her coffin out of the country was frustrated and a triumphant and tumultuous funeral procession struggled through the City of London. This was the last victory that the radicals gained from the affair.

The agitation over the Queen had been essentially the expression of discontent. It marked the highest point of the radical movement in these postwar years. Towards the end of 1820, however, industry and trade revived and popular disturbances subsided. The mass of the country was instinctively royalist and the personal defects of the sovereign had little effect upon this deep-rooted tradition.

The Tory administration, however, which consisted largely of ageing reactionaries, had been gravely weakened. It was isolated from general opinion and badly in need of new recruits. The Whigs too had been forced to recognise their lack of popular backing, and the younger members saw that the "old and natural alliance between the Whigs and the people" was now in danger. They began henceforth to renew their interest in Parliamentary Reform, which soon became the question of the hour.

James Gillray was one of several cartoonists who made fun of George IV's size, extravagance and infidelities. For all his outward absurdities, George possessed great artistic taste. While he was Prince Regent he patronised, among others, the architect John Nash who had designed Regent's Park and much of the surrounding area, including the original Regent Street. He had also redesigned the Royal Pavilion, Brighton, at the Prince's request.

CHAPTER 2

CANNING AND THE DUKE

George Canning (1770-1827) was a brilliant Tory Foreign Secretary, the successor of Castlereagh. In 1827 he became Prime Minister, but his wit, his sarcasm and his belief in Catholic Emancipation had made him too many enemies. He resigned in failing health, after four months in office, and died soon afterwards.

URING THE TEN YEARS' REIGN of King George IV the old party groupings in politics were fast dissolving. The nineteenth century called for a fresh interpretation of the duties of government. New principles and doctrines were arising which were to break up the political parties and in the Victorian age reshape and recreate them. These developments took time, but already the party built up by the younger Pitt was feeling their stir and stress. Pitt had enlisted the growing mercantile and commercial interests of his day on the Tory side, and his policy of free trade and efficient administration had won over leaders of industry such as the fathers of Robert Peel and William Gladstone. But Pitt's tradition had faded during the years of war. Faithful disciples among the younger men strove to carry on his ideas, but his successors in office lacked his prestige and broad vision. Without skilful management an alliance between the landed gentry and the new merchant class was bound to collapse. The growers of corn and the employers of industrial labour had little in common, and conflict had been sharpening since the end of the war amid falling agricultural prices and weary bickering over the Corn Laws. Caroline's divorce had discredited and weakened the Government. Parties were not yet expected to work out and lay before the country ambitious programmes of action. But even to its friends Lord Liverpool's administration seemed to have no aim or purpose beyond preserving existing institutions.

The younger Tories, headed by George Canning and supported by William Huskisson, spokesman of the merchants, advocated a return to Pitt's policy of free trade. But even they were disunited. The issue of Catholic Emancipation was soon to confuse and split the Tory Party, and on this they were opposed by one of their own generation. Robert Peel during his six years in Ireland had successfully upheld the English ascendancy against heavy discontent and smouldering rebellion. By a mixture of coercion and adroit patronage he had imposed comparative quiet and orderliness. He had come home convinced that Catholic Emancipation would imperil not only Protestantism in Ireland but the entire political system at Westminster. Peel became Canning's rival for the future leadership of the Tories. Personalities added their complications. Brilliant, witty, effervescent, Canning had a gift for sarcasm which made him many enemies. His seniors thought him an intriguer, and when he resigned over the royal divorce in 1820 a Tory lord declared with relish, "Now we have got rid of those confounded men of genius." His political life seemed at an end. But then Fate took a hand. In August 1822 Castlereagh, his mind unhinged by overwork, cut his throat. Canning's experience in foreign affairs was now essential to the Government; he was appointed Foreign Secretary, and in this office he dominated English politics until his death five years later.

The Ministry had recently been joined by Peel at the Home Office and now Huskisson went to the Board of Trade. The Government thus had as many as three leading members in the Commons. (In 1815 three-quarters of the Cabinet had been in the Lords.) The following years saw a more enlightened period of Tory rule. Canning, Peel and Huskisson pursued bold policies which in many respects were in advance of those propounded by the Whigs. The penal code was reformed by Peel, and the London police force is his creation. Huskisson overhauled the tariff system, and continued Pitt's work in abolishing uneconomic taxes and revising the customs duties. Canning urged a scaling down of the duty on corn as the price rose at home. This was bound to bring conflict in the Tory ranks. He realised the political danger it would cause, and declared on one occasion, "We are on the brink of a great struggle between property and population. Such a struggle is only to be averted by the mildest and most liberal legislation." He was, however, a stubborn defender of the existing franchise. He believed that by farsighted commercial measures and a popular foreign policy the problems of Parliamentary Reform could be evaded. Length of years was not given him in which to perceive himself mistaken.

A crisis in Spain confronted Canning with his first task as Foreign Secretary. The popular elements which had led the struggle against Napoleon now revolted against the autocratic Bourbon government, formed a revolutionary junta, and proclaimed a constitution on the model of that set up in France in 1815. Canning had backed the Spanish national rising in 1808, and was naturally sympathetic, but Metternich and the Holy Alliance saw the revolt, which soon spread to the Bourbon kingdom of Naples, as a threat to the principle of monarchy. Austria and Russia were determined to act. An instrument lay ready to their hand. The ex-enemy, France, coveted respectability. Her restored Bourbon government feared the revolutionaries and offered to send a military expedition to Spain to recover for King Ferdinand his absolutist powers. As the whole tradition of British foreign politics was against intervention in the domestic affairs of other states, Canning would have nothing to do with it. There was great excitement in London. English volunteers went to Spain to serve in the defence forces of the Spanish "Liberals", a name which entered English politics from this Spanish revolt, while "Conservative" came to us from France. But Canning was equally against official intervention on the side of "Spanish Liberalism", and it was upon this that the Whigs attacked him. These heart-searchings in Britain made little difference to the outcome in Spain. The French expedition met with no serious resistance, and the Spanish Liberals retired to Cadiz and gave in.

A much larger issue now loomed beyond the European scene. Britain had little direct interest in the constitution of Spain, but for two centuries she had competed for the trade of Spain's colonies in South America. Their liberties were important to her. During the wars with Napoleon these colonies had enjoyed the taste of autonomy. They had no relish, when the Bourbons were restored in Madrid, for the revival of royal Spanish rule. Up and down the whole length of the Andes campaigns were fought for South American liberation. By Canning's time at the Foreign Office most of the republics that now figure on the map had come into separate if unstable existence. In the meanwhile British commerce with these regions had trebled in value since 1814. If France or the Holy Alliance sent troops across the Atlantic to subdue the rebels, all this was lost. The business elements in England, whose support Canning was keen to command, were acutely sensitive to the peril. He acted with decision. He urged the United States to join Britain in opposing European interference in the countries

As Home Secretary, Robert Peel founded the Metropolitan Police Force in 1829. Nicknamed "Peelers" or "Bobbies" after their founder, the members of this civilian organisation were employed not only to fight crime but also to preserve order in times of unrest, a role hitherto carried out by the army. The Metropolitan Police Force preceded the development of the county and borough forces that developed later in the century.

across the Atlantic. While the Americans meditated upon this proposal Canning made an approach to the French. France had no desire to start an overseas quarrel with Britain. She disclaimed the use of force in South America and forswore colonial ambitions there. Thus was the Holy Alliance checked. As Canning later declared in a triumphant phrase, he had "called the New World into existence to redress the balance of the Old".

The New World meanwhile had something of its own to say. The United States had already recognised the independence of the principal Latin-American republics. They did not want European reconquest and colonisation. President Monroe also had in mind Russian designs in the Pacific Ocean, for the Russians occupied Alaska, and the territorial claims of the Tsar stretched down the western coast of America to California, where his agents were active. Monroe however had in John Quincy Adams a Secretary of State who distrusted Canning, whom he earnestly thought to possess "a little too much wit for a Minister of State". He believed that the United States should act on their own initiative. As Adams noted in his diary, "It would be more candid, as well as more dignified, to avow our principles explicitly to Russia and France, than to come in as a cock-boat in the wake of the British man-of-war." Hence there was propounded on December 2, 1823, in the President's annual message to Congress, a purely American doctrine, the Monroe Doctrine, which has often since been voiced in transatlantic affairs. "The American continents," Monroe said, "by the free and independent condition they have assumed and maintain, are henceforth not to be considered as subjects for future colonisation by any European Powers . . . . We should consider any attempt on their part to extend their [political] system to any portion of this hemisphere as dangerous to our peace and safety."

Monroe's famous message conveyed a warning to Britain as well as to the authoritarian powers. Canning's private comment was short and to the point. "The avowed pretension of the United States," he wrote, "to put themselves at the head of the confederacy of all the Americas and to sway that confederacy against Europe (Great Britain included) is not a pretension identified with our interests, or one that we can countenance or tolerate. It is, however, a pretension which there is no use in contesting in the abstract, but we must not say anything that seems to admit the principle."

Soon afterwards Britain officially recognised the independence of the South American states. King George IV, who bore no love for republics, and many of Canning's colleagues in the Government, had strenuously opposed this step. Even now the King refused to read the Royal Speech containing the announcement. It was read for him by a reluctant Lord Chancellor. So Canning's view prevailed, and for the best part of a century the Royal Navy remained the stoutest guarantee of freedom in the Americas.

During the worst years of the Napoleonic wars Britain's greatest military effort had been launched in defence of Portugal. Now our oldest ally again called for assistance. Once more South America was involved. The Portuguese colony of Brazil had proclaimed its independence, but surprisingly accepted as its ruler a Portuguese prince. Canning recognised the new Empire of Brazil, and persuaded the Portuguese to do so. But affairs took a fresh turn. The King of Portugal died and his throne lay in dispute. His rightful heiress was the daughter of the Brazilian Emperor, eight years old, around whom the Liberal and constitutional forces rallied. But another claimant appeared in her absolutist uncle, who enjoyed the smiles of the Holy Alliance and the active support of Spain. It now seemed possible that the whole of Portugal might succumb to authoritarian intervention. Under the terms of the ancient alliance British troops were dispatched to the Tagus in December 1826. Canning declared his views to the House of Commons. The movement of troops was not intended, he said, "to prescribe constitutions, but to defend and preserve the independence of an ally". Our ambassador in Lisbon described the wild scenes when the ships of the Royal Navy were sighted in the Tagus. "No one is afraid to be a constitutionalist now . . . . England has spoken."

Another crisis had meanwhile erupted in the eastern Mediterranean. After four centuries of subjection to the Turks the Greeks broke into revolt, and in 1822 declared their independence. In England there was widespread enthusiasm for their cause. It appealed to the educated classes who had been brought up on the glories of Thermopylae and Salamis. Subscriptions were raised. Lord Byron and other British volunteers went to the aid of the Greeks. Before he met his death at Missolonghi Byron was deeply disillusioned. Not for the first or last time in the history of Greece a noble cause was nearly ruined by faction. With the aid of an army supplied by Mahomet Ali, the formidable Pasha of Egypt, the Sultan of Turkey was almost everywhere victorious. Unfortunately for the Greeks, the powers of Europe were themselves divided. The Greek revolt had split the Holy Alliance, Austria and Russia taking opposite sides. Canning feared that Russia would set up a client state in Greece, and exact her own price from the Turks. If Russia grew at Turkey's expense, British interests in the Middle East and in India would be put in jeopardy. Here lay the origins of the "Eastern Question", as it was called, which increasingly preoccupied and baffled the powers of Europe down to the First World War. After complicated negotiations, Britain, France, and Russia agreed in 1827 on terms to be put to the Turks. British and French squadrons were sent to Greek waters to enforce them. This was the last achievement of Canning's diplomacy. The next act in the Greek drama was played after his death.

This painting of "Greek Fugitives" by Sir Charles Eastlake gives a romanticised view of the Greek revolt against the Turks. There was great enthusiasm in England for the Greek cause and Lord Byron, poet and revolutionary, sailed for Missolonghi, where he helped to organise the insurgent forces and tried to settle quarrels between Greek leaders.

Canning's colleagues had become increasingly critical of the activities of their Foreign Secretary. Wellington was particularly disturbed by what he regarded as Canning's headlong courses. The two wings of the administration were only held together by the conciliatory character of the Prime Minister, and in February 1827 Liverpool had a stroke. A major political crisis followed. Who was now to lead the Government? The whole future of the Tories was at stake. Were they to go upon the road of Wellington or of Canning? The choice of Prime Minister still lay with the Crown, and George IV hesitated for a month before making his decision. The Whigs were divided among themselves. So it had to be one or other of the Tory wings. Many members of Liverpool's Cabinet, including Wellington and Eldon, declined to serve under Canning. On the other hand, Canning could command the support of a number of the leading Whigs. It soon became plain that no Government could be constructed which did not include Canning and his friends, and that Canning would accept all or nothing. His final argument convinced the King. "Sire," he said, "your father broke the domination of the Whigs. I hope your Majesty will not endure that of the Tories." "No," George IV replied, "I'll be damned if I do." In April 1827 Canning became Prime Minister, and for a brief hundred days held supreme political power.

Canning's Ministry signalled the coming dissolution of the eighteenth-century political system. He held office by courtesy of a section of the Whigs. The only able Tory leader in the House of Commons whom he had lost was Robert Peel. Peel resigned partly for personal reasons and partly because he knew that Canning was in favour of Catholic Emancipation. But the Opposition Tories and the diehard Whigs harassed the new Government. Had Canning been granted a longer spell of life the group he led might have founded a new political allegiance. But on August 8, after a short illness, Canning died. He was killed, like Castlereagh, by overwork.

Canning's death at a critical moment at home and abroad dislocated the political scene. A makeshift administration composed of his followers, his Whig allies, and a group of Tories struggled ineptly with the situation. Its leader was the lachrymose Lord Goderich, formerly Chancellor of the Exchequer. More than half the Tory Party, under Peel and Wellington, was in opposition. Quarrels among Whig and Tory members of the Government ruptured its unity. There had been a hitch in carrying out Canning's policy of non-intervention in Greece. Admiral Codrington, one of Nelson's captains, who had fought at Trafalgar and was now in command of the Allied squadron in Greek waters, had on his own initiative destroyed the entire Turkish fleet in the Bay of Navarino. There was alarm in England in case the Russians should take undue advantage of this victory. The battle, which meant much to the Greeks, was disapprovingly described in the King's Speech as an "untoward incident", and the victor narrowly escaped court-martial. The Government, rent by Whig intrigues, abruptly disappeared. Wellington and Peel were instructed to form an administration. This they did. Wellington became Prime Minister, with Peel as Home Secretary and Leader of the House of Commons. The old Tories were to fight one more action. It was a stubborn rearguard.

The political views of the new Government were simple—defence of existing institutions, conviction that they alone stood between order and chaos, determination to retreat only if pressed by overwhelming forces. Peel was one of the ablest ministers that Britain has seen. But his was an administrative mind. General ideas moved him only when they had seized the attention of the country and become inescapable political facts. The Government's first retreat was to carry an Opposition measure repealing Acts which nominally excluded the Nonconformists from office. After a long struggle they at last achieved political rights and equality. Not so the Catholics. Their Emancipation was not merely a matter of principle, but also an Imperial concern. The greatest failure of British government was in Ireland. Irish discontent had seriously weakened Britain's strategic position during the Napoleonic wars. The social and political monopoly of a Protestant minority, which had oppressed Irish life since the days of Cromwell, would not be tolerated indefinitely. British governments were perpetually threatened with revolution in Ireland. A main dividing line in politics after 1815 was upon this issue of Catholic Emancipation. It had sundered George Canning and his followers, together with the Whigs, from Wellington and Peel. A decision had been postponed from year to year by "gentlemen's agreements" among the English politicians. But the patience of the Irish was coming to its end. They were organising under Daniel O'Connell for vehement agitation against England. O'Connell was a land-lord and a lawyer. He believed in what later came to be called Home Rule for Ireland under the British Crown. Though not himself a revolutionary, O'Connell was a powerful and excitable orator, and his speeches nourished thoughts of violence.

A minor political incident in England fired the train. The leader of the Canningites, William Huskisson, had been forced out of the Government along with his followers, and Vesey Fitzgerald, an Irish Protestant land-owner, was promoted to one of the vacant ministerial posts. Appointment to office in those days involved submitting to the electorate at a by-election, and so a poll was due in County Clare. O'Connell stood as candidate, backed by the whole force of his organisation, the Catholic Association. He was of course debarred by existing legislation from taking a seat in Parliament, but in spite of the efforts of the local Protestant gentry he was triumphantly elected. Here was a test case. If the English Government

The threat of revolution in Ireland forced Wellington and Peel to carry Catholic Emancipation in 1829. They had hitherto opposed it. In this contemporary cartoon the "Emancipation Pudding" is carved up by the Irish leader, Daniel O'Connell, and the Pope, waited upon by Wellington and Peel. Catholic Emancipation meant that Roman Catholics could now sit in Parliament and hold any public office except the offices of Lord Chancellor of England and Lord Lieutenant of Ireland.

refused to enfranchise the Catholics there would be revolution in Ireland, and political disaster at home.

The Protestants in Ireland were thoroughly alarmed. They had nothing to gain from an Irish revolt. Political equality for the Catholics was a bitter draught for them to swallow, but if Emancipation was not conceded the whole land settlement would be in danger. In December the Chief Secretary for Ireland made the dangers clear to Peel. "I have little doubt that the peasantry of the south at present look forward to the period of O'Connell's expulsion from the House of Commons as the time of rising. But any occurrence in the interval which might appear to be adverse to the Roman Catholic body might precipitate this result." And one of the English Opposition in a letter described the view of the Irish Protestants: "I know from the most unquestionable authority that very many of the Orange Protestants in Ireland are now so entirely alarmed at their own position that they express in the most unqualified terms their earnest desire for any settlement of the question at issue on any terms."

As a general Wellington knew the hopelessness of attempting to repress a national rising. He had seen civil war at close quarters in Spain. He himself came from an Irish family and was familiar with the turbulent island. He used plain language to the House of Lords. "I am one of those who have probably passed a longer period of my life engaged in war than most men, and principally in civil war; and I must say this, that if I could avoid by any sacrifice whatever even one month of civil war in the country to which I was attached I would sacrifice my life in order to do it."

Wellington now felt able to take without qualm the line of expediency. Peel's position was more delicate. He felt justified in remaining in an administration which was about to introduce a measure he had opposed all his political life only if his presence were vital to its success. The fact that the Opposition could force Parliament to carry Catholic Emancipation did not weigh with him. They lacked the confidence of the Crown, and this was still indispensable. Wellington could not carry the measure without Peel, and the Whigs could not carry it without the King. This determined Peel. He resigned his High Tory seat at Oxford and bought himself in for Westbury. His offer to stand by Wellington finally persuaded George IV, who dreaded a Whig administration. Peel himself introduced the Bill for Catholic Emancipation into the House of Commons, and it was carried through Parliament in 1829 with comfortable majorities. Revolution in Ireland was averted. But the unity of the English Tories had received another blow. The "Old Guard", still powerful under the unreformed franchise, never forgave Peel and Wellington for deserting the principle of the Anglican monopoly of power in Great Britain. Toryism meant many different and even conflicting things to its followers, but the supremacy of Protestantism had long been one of its binding political beliefs.

Wellington's military view of politics had led him to overawe his critics by a characteristic challenge to a duel. Lord Winchilsea had overstepped the bounds of decorum in an attack upon the Prime Minister in the House of Lords, accusing Wellington of dishonesty. A full-dress challenge followed. The meeting took place in Battersea Fields. The Field Marshal, now aged sixty, was nonchalant, slow and deliberate in his movements. This was much more his line than smoothing the susceptibilities of politicians, or, as he once put it in a moment of complaint, "what gentlemen call their

When Lord Winchilsea accused the Duke of Wellington of dishonesty in the House of Lords, the "Iron Duke" responded in the way he knew best: he challenged him to a duel. Duelling was illegal but still undertaken mainly by aristocrats and army officers to settle a point of honour. Seconds were appointed on both sides to ensure that all the codes of conduct were observed.

feelings". Turning to his second, who was also his Secretary at War, he said, "Now then, Hardinge, look sharp and step out the ground. I have no time to waste. Damn it! don't stick him up so near the ditch. If I hit him he'll tumble in." Neither party was wounded and Winchilsea signed a paper withdrawing his insinuations. Later in the day Wellington called upon the King. "I have another subject to mention to your Majesty, personal to myself. I have been fighting a duel this morning." George graciously replied that he was glad of it; he had always been in favour of upholding the gentleman's code of honour. Politics, alas, are not always so easily managed.

The Duke's administration showed little sign of continuing its Liberal course. It was increasingly out of touch with political opinion, and the forces of Opposition were gathering. But upon the surface the atmosphere was calm. In June 1830 King George IV died, with a miniature of Mrs Fitzherbert round his neck. "The first gentleman of Europe" was not long mourned by his people. This once handsome man had grown so gross and corpulent that he was ashamed to show himself in public. His extravagance had become a mania, and his natural abilities were clouded by years of self-indulgence. Yet he was not in his conduct much worse than most contemporary men of fashion.

George IV was succeeded on the throne by his brother, William, the Duke of Clarence, the most eccentric and least obnoxious of the sons of George III. He had been brought up in the navy, and had passed a life of total obscurity, except for a brief and ludicrous interval when Canning had made him Lord High Admiral in 1827. For many years he had lived with an actress at Bushey Park. But in the end he too had had to do his duty and marry a German princess, Adelaide of Saxe-Meiningen. She proved to be a generous-hearted and acceptable Queen. Good nature and simplicity of mind were William IV's in equal measure. The gravest embarrassments he caused his ministers sprang from his tactlessness at public functions.

The royal pair were popular, although the diarist, Charles Greville, was not certain if the kingly wits would last. The Queen was not a beauty, but her quiet homeliness was a welcome change after the domestic life of George IV. The bluffness of the monarch was attractive to the lower orders, though

Queen Adelaide, a steadying influence on her husband, brought respectability to the Court. During the Reform Bill crisis, Adelaide became the people's scapegoat: her carriage was mobbed and her influence over William IV criticised. Later, as Queen Dowager, she became once again a favourite of the people.

once, when he spat out of the window of the State coach, a reproving voice from the crowd said, "George the Fourth would never have done that!" In any case, the life and manners of London society did not depend upon the example of the Court.

It had been expected that the new King might prefer a Whig administration. As Duke of Clarence he had been dismissed from the Admiralty by the Duke of Wellington. But on his accession William IV welcomed and retained the Duke. His reputation for fairness proved to be of political value. Wellington bore witness to it. "It is impossible for one man to have treated another man better or more kindly than the King did me from that day [his accession] to the day of his death. And yet it was also impossible for one man to have run another as hard as I did him as Lord High Admiral. But he showed no resentment of it."

"Sailor William" needed every ounce of fairness. There were heavy seas ahead. Revolution had again broken out in France. As the news swept across the Channel there were mutterings of a coming storm in England.

CHAPTER 3

REFORM AND FREE TRADE

I N 1830 THE LIBERAL FORCES IN EUROPE STIRRED AGAIN. The July Revolution in France set up a constitutional monarchy under King Louis Philippe, the son of the Revolutionary Philippe Egalité, who had voted for the death of his cousin, Louis XVI, and himself been guillotined later. Louis Philippe was a wiser and more honourable man than his father. He was to keep his uneasy throne for eighteen years, and he also kept his head.

Encouraged by events in Paris, the Belgians rebelled against the kingdom of the Netherlands, in which they had been incorporated by the peace treaties of 1815. Britain had played a big part in this arrangement. It had long been British policy to support the independence of the Low Countries, and the twentieth century needs no reminding of the great wars that have been fought with this as a leading cause. In 1815 an enlarged united Netherlands had seemed a promising experiment. After all, it at last realised the dreams of the first William of Orange. But the Dutch and Belgians were divided by language, religion, and commercial interests, and these barriers could not easily be overcome. The Belgians demanded autonomy, and then independence. Much diplomatic activity ensued before a peaceful solution was eventually found. Meanwhile, a wave of revolts spread across Germany into Poland. The Europe of Metternich and the Holy Alliance was severely shaken, though not yet overturned.

These agitations on the European continent, largely orderly in character and democratic in purpose, were much acclaimed in England. The Tory Government alone seemed suspicious and hostile. With some reason the Government feared that France might annex Belgium. Wellington was even suspected of intending to restore the kingdom of the Netherlands by armed force. This was not true. But the rumour was enough to inflame the hot tempers of the times. Poverty in the villages and on the farms had already led to rioting in parts of rural England. In the growing towns and cities industrial discontent was driving men of business and their workers into political action. Turmoil, upheaval, even revolution, seemed imminent. Instead there was a General Election.

At the polls the Whigs made gains, but the result was indecisive. The Whig leader was Earl Grey, a friend and disciple of Fox. It is given to few men to carry out late in life a great measure of reform which they have advocated without success for forty years. Such was to be Grey's achievement. He had held office briefly in the ministry of 1806. For the rest, since the early years of the younger Pitt he had been not only continuously out of office, but almost without expectation of ever winning it. Now his hour was at hand. Grey was a landowner who regarded politics as a social duty, and much preferred his country estates to Westminster. However, his judgment on home affairs was well directed. He and his colleagues perceived that the agitation which had shaken England since Waterloo issued from two quite separate sources—the middle classes, unrepresented, prosperous, respectable, influenced by the democratic ideas of the French Revolution, but deeply law-abiding in their hunger for political power; and on the other side a bitter and more revolutionary section of working men, smitten by the economic dislocation of war and its aftermath, prepared to talk of violence and perhaps even to use it. An alliance with the middle classes and a moderate extension of the franchise would suffice, at any rate for a time, and for this Grey prepared his plans. He had the support of Lord John Russell, son of the Duke of Bedford, who was a man of impulsive mind, with a high devotion to the cause of liberty in the abstract, whatever the practical consequences might be. With them stood Henry Brougham, fertile with modern ideas, and a friend of leading radicals and newspaper editors.

Earl Grey (1764-1845) had been the acknowledged leader of the Whig opposition since Charles James Fox's death in 1806. His opportunity to carry out major reforms came in 1830 when William IV invited him to form a government. This portrait of Earl Grey can be seen in the National Portrait Gallery.

Parliament met in November. There were some Tories who hoped that their leaders would do again what they had done over Catholic Emancipation and, after a rearguard action, reform the franchise themselves. But Wellington was adverse. To the House of Lords he said, "I have never read or heard of any measure . . . which can in any degree satisfy my mind that the state of the representation can be improved. . . . I am fully convinced that the country possesses at the present moment a legislature which answers all the good purposes of legislation, and this to a greater degree than any legislature ever has answered in any country whatever." When he sat down he turned to his Foreign Secretary, the Earl of Aberdeen. "I have not said too much, have I?" He received no direct answer, but in reporting the incident later the Foreign Secretary described Wellington's speech briefly: "He said that we were going out."

Wellington hoped that the Whigs were too disorganised to form a government, but his own party was even more disunited. Those who had followed Canning would have nothing more to do with the Tory "Old Guard", and now made common cause with the Whigs. A fortnight later the Tories were defeated and King William IV asked Grey to form a government. With one brief interval the Whigs had been out of office for nearly fifty years. Now at a bound they were at the summit of power.

They were confronted with an ugly scene. French threats to intervene in Belgium made it imperative but unpopular to increase the military estimates. Law and order were breaking down in the southern counties, and Lord Melbourne, the new Home Secretary, acted decisively. Over four hundred farm workers were sentenced to transportation. The radicals were indignant

PROTEST AND REFORM

THE YEARS AFTER THE END of the Napoleonic Wars were bleak for many families. Food prices were high and industrial unemployment increased. Not surprisingly, movements of radical protest arose, the most dramatic of them ending in the so-called Massacre of Peterloo. In 1819, hundreds of peaceful demonstrators had gathered in a square in Manchester, protesting for their right to vote. A sudden yeomanry charge killed a dozen and injured many more. A year later, a sinister plot to murder the entire Cabinet of Lord Liverpool's government and seize the Bank of England was discovered in London.

London crowds caused alarm in political circles by exuberantly supporting Queen Caroline against George IV when, in 1820, he was attempting to divorce her. Although the year was one of considerable protest, as industry revived and people were better off, disturbances subsided. As Cobbett said, it is impossible to "agitate a man on a full stomach." But protest had quickened again by the end of the decade.

The Whig government of Earl Grey, returned to power in 1830, carried through the Parliamentary Reform Act of 1832 in face of persistent opposition: it gave the vote to the middle classes, but it did not satisfy the militant radicals. In the years of economic depression which followed a financial crisis in 1836, two remarkable extra-parliamentary movements won much support—the Chartists, demanding among other things universal manhood suffrage and voting by ballot; and the Anti-Corn Law League, demanding the repeal of the Corn Laws which, it was claimed, increased food prices and created unemployment.

There were as many far-sighted and active reformers in the early nineteenth century as there have ever been in British history; among them were Lord Shaftesbury, reformer of laws on child labour, factories, lunacy and much else, and Elizabeth Fry, a Quaker who set out to reform prisons. But there was no drive for violent revolution.

PARLIAMENTARY REFORM *was a highly controversial issue. But population changes caused by industrial working patterns made reform essential. People had moved away from old rural communities to work in the new factory towns, and few of these had any representation in Parliament. Banners urging reform can be seen in the picture (above) of a hustings at Covent Garden in 1820.*

THE PEOPLE'S CHARTER *gave its name to th[e] political movement known as Chartism which demanded electoral reform. A petitio[n] was drawn up by a group of working me[n] and published in 1838. For the next ten year[s] there were meetings, rallies and petitions. I[n] the picture (below), members of Peel's newl[y] created police force can be seen at a Chartis[t] rally. A few Chartists favoured violence.*

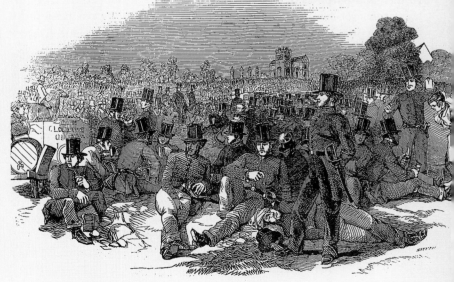

HE CO-OPERATIVE MOVEMENT *was master-min-
ed in Britain by the philanthropist, Robert
Owen (above). He established the mill com-
unity of New Lanark where he was man-
ger, and later owner, as a co-operative and
arted similar ventures in the United States
nd Ireland. Workers held shares in the mill
r factory in which they were employed and
ained a proportion of the profits. Owen
elieved that character was formed by circum-
ances and environment and wanted people
o be moulded along lines of goodness and
ecency at the earliest possible age. This doc-
ine was published in an influential pamphlet
ntitled* A New View of Society *in 1813. His
ter writings encouraged the growth of early
ade unionism.*

SALTAIRE MILL *and industrial settlement near
Bradford, West Yorkshire, survive to this day
virtually as they were when created by the
reformer, Titus Salt, in the 1870s. The huge
five-storey Italianate mill is the most impressive centrepiece of Salt's model village of spacious terraced houses near the River Aire. A
church, hospital, school and public baths complete the civic amenities in this well-planned
community (above).*

THE POLITICAL "ROBIN" DRIVEN BY THE SEVERITY OF THE
TIMES TO SEEK FOR GRAIN.

FREE TRADE IN CORN *was the battle cry of the
Anti-Corn Law League started by Richard
Cobden and John Bright in 1839. New Corn
Laws were passed in 1815 to protect the
interests of corn-growing landlords by controlling imports and exports of grain, thereby
keeping up the price of bread, and this
produced immediate protest. The political
"Robin" in the cartoon above represents the
Tory Prime Minister, Robert Peel, who
repealed the Corn Laws in 1846 when the
potato famine in Ireland made this measure
even more imperative than it had been. The
figure on the doorstep represents Cobden.*

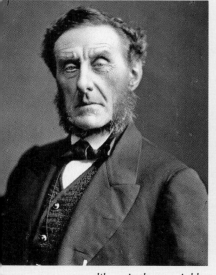

OCIAL REFORMERS *like Anthony Ashley
ooper, seventh Earl of Shaftesbury (1801–
5) improved conditions for the workers. An
.P. from 1826, he helped to introduce laws
at banned sweeps from using climbing boys*
(1840), *excluded women and children from
the mines* (1842) *and established the ten-hour
day for factory workers* (1847). *The photographs (above) are of Shaftesbury (left) and a
sweep called John Day (right).*

and disillusioned. Only Parliamentary Reform could save the Government.

A secret Cabinet committee was appointed to draft the scheme, and in March 1831 Lord John Russell rose in the House of Commons to move the first Reform Bill. Amid shouting and scornful laughter he read out to their holders a list of over a hundred and fifty "pocket" borough seats which it was proposed to abolish and replace with new constituencies for the unrepresented areas of the Metropolis, the industrial north, and the Midlands. To the Tories this was a violation of all they stood for, an affront to their deepest political convictions, a gross attack on the rights of property. A seat was a thing to be bought or sold like an estate, and a more uniform franchise savoured of an arithmetical conception of politics dangerously akin to French democracy. Many Whigs, too, who had expected a milder measure were at first dumbfounded by the breadth of Russell's proposals. They soon rallied to the Government when they saw the enthusiasm of the country, for the Whigs believed that Reform would forestall revolution. The Tories, on the other hand, feared that it was the first step on the road to cataclysm. To them, and indeed to many Whigs, English government meant the rule, and the duty to rule, of the landed classes in the interests of the community. A wider franchise would mean the beginning of the end of the old system of administration by influence and patronage. Could the King's Government be carried on in the absence of these twin pillars of authority? It was not altogether a vain question. After 1832 Britain was to see many unstable ministries before the pattern was changed by the rise of disciplined parties with central organisations and busy Whips.

Radical leaders were disappointed by what they conceived to be the moderation of the Bill, but in their various ways they supported it. There was not much in common between them. Jeremy Bentham and James Mill were philosophical advocates of democracy and middle-class education; William Cobbett was a vigorous, independent-minded journalist; Francis Place, the tailor of Charing Cross, and Thomas Attwood, the banker of Birmingham, were active political organisers. But they were all determined that the Bill should not be whittled away by compromise. Agitation spread through the country. A cataract of journals and newspapers appeared in support of the cause. To avoid the tax upon the press, a relic of the repressive legislation of 1819, weekly newsletters were posted.

In the House of Commons the Tories fought every inch of the way. The Government was by no means sure of its majority, and although a small block of Irish votes controlled by O'Connell, leader of the Emancipated Catholics, was cast for Grey, the Bill was defeated. A roar of hatred and disappointment swept the country. Grey asked the King for a dissolution, and William IV had the sense to realise that a refusal might mean revolution. The news caused uproar in the Lords, where a motion was introduced asking the King to reconsider his decision, but as the shouting rose from the benches and peers shook their fists across the floor of the House the thunder of cannon was heard as the King left St James's to come in person to pronounce the dissolution. In both Houses the Tories stormed. One of them, jumping to his feet in the Commons, shouted to the jubilant Whigs, "The next time you hear those guns they will be shotted, and take off some of your heads."

Excited elections were held on the single issue of Reform. It was the first time a mandate of this kind had been asked of the British people. They returned an unmistakable answer. The Tories were annihilated in the county constituencies and the Whigs and their allies gained a majority of a hundred and thirty-six in the House of Commons. When Parliament reassembled the battle was shifted to the House of Lords. Wellington rose again and again to put the case against Reform. "A democracy," he declared, "has never been established in any part of the world that it has not immediately declared war against property, against the payment of the public debt, and against all the principles of conservation, which are secured by, and are in fact the principal objects of the British Constitution as it now exists. Property and its possessors will become the common enemy." Most of his political experience had been gathered in Spain, and he was oppressed with memories of revolutionary juntas. Reform would break "the strength which is necessary to enable His Majesty to protect and keep in order his foreign dominions and to ensure the obedience of their inhabitants. We shall lose these colonies and foreign possessions, and with them our authority and influence abroad." On the night of October 7, 1831, the critical division took place. The peers were sharply divided, and it was twenty-one of the bishops in the Upper House who decided the issue; they were against Reform. Thus the Tories triumphed. The Bill was defeated and a new constitutional issue was raised—the peers against the people.

Next morning the newspapers, bordered in black, proclaimed the news. Rioting broke out in the Midlands; houses and property were burnt; there was wild disorder in Bristol. The associations of Reformers in the country, called Political Unions, strove to harness enthusiasm for the Bill and to steady the public temper. Meanwhile the Government persevered. In December Russell introduced the Bill for the third time, and the Commons carried it by a majority of two to one. In the following May it came again before the Lords. It was rejected by thirty-five votes. Grey realised that only extreme remedies would serve. He accordingly drove to Windsor and asked the King to create enough new peers to carry the Bill. The King refused and the Cabinet resigned. William IV asked Wellington and Peel to form

DEATH or LIBERTY! or Britannia & the Virtues of the Constitution in danger of Violation from the great Political Libertine, Radical Reform.

As this cartoon suggests, the landed classes at first saw the Reform Bill of 1831 as a measure to end their parliamentary patronage and influence. However, when the Bill was finally enacted in 1832 it enfranchised only the prosperous upper middle classes.

31

Lord Palmerston (1784-1865) was a major influence on the foreign policy of Britain during the first half of the nineteenth century. He resolutely safeguarded British interests abroad and his style was highly popular with the majority of people outside Parliament.

an administration to carry Reform as they had carried Catholic Emancipation, and thus avoid swamping the Lords. But Peel would not comply. Feeling in the country became menacing. Plans were made for strikes and a general refusal of taxes. Banners and placards appeared in the London streets with the caption "To Stop the Duke Go for Gold", and there was a run on the Bank of England. Radical leaders declared they would paralyse any Tory Government which came to power, and after a week the Duke admitted defeat. On the afternoon of May 18 Grey and Brougham called at St James's Palace. The King authorised them to draw up a list of persons who would be made peers and could be counted on to vote for the Whigs. At the same time his private secretary told the leading Tories of the King's decision and suggested that they could avoid such extremities by abstaining. When the Bill was again introduced the Opposition benches were practically empty. On this occasion the Bill was carried by an overwhelming majority, and became law on June 7, 1832.

The new electors and the radicals were not content to stop at extending the franchise, and during the next five years the younger politicians forced through an equally extensive reform of public administration. The Whigs became more and more uncomfortable, and Grey, feeling he had done enough, retired in 1834. The new leaders were Lord Melbourne and Lord John Russell. Russell was a Whig of the old school, sensitive to any invasion of political liberty and rights. He saw the need for further reforms in the sphere of government, but the broadening paths of democracy did not beckon him. Melbourne in his youth had held advanced opinions, but personal friendships and agreeable conversation mattered more to him than political issues. He accepted the office of Prime Minister with reluctance, genuinely wondering whether the honour was worthwhile. Once in power Melbourne's bland qualities helped to keep his divided team together. But his administration wore an eighteenth-century air in the midst of nineteenth-century' stress.

One of Melbourne's ablest colleagues was Lord Palmerston, who held the Foreign Office for nearly eleven years. Under the wise guidance of Lord Grey, Palmerston had secured a settlement of the Belgian problem which still endures. The Dutch and French were both persuaded to withdraw, and Prince Leopold of Saxe-Coburg was installed at Brussels as an independent sovereign. The neutrality of the country was guaranteed by international treaty. Thus was a pledge given which was to be redeemed with blood in 1914. Under Melbourne Palmerston did much as he pleased in foreign affairs. His leading beliefs were two: that British interests must everywhere be stoutly upheld, if necessary by a show of force, and that Liberal movements in the countries of Europe should be encouraged whenever it was within Britain's power to extend them sympathy or even aid. There was a jaunty forthright self-assurance about everything Palmerston did which often gave offence in the staider chancelleries of Europe and alarmed his more nervous colleagues. But his imperturbable spirit gradually won the admiration of the mass of his fellow countrymen. He was building up the popularity which was later to make him seem to many the embodiment of mid-Victorian confidence.

The Whig rank and file were perplexed and uncertain. Champions of political reform, they wavered and boggled at the sterner and more fateful issue of social reorganisation. In the past they had quarrelled with the

THE ROMANTIC VISION

In the nineteenth century, artists, poets and architects began to observe the world from a new, romantic perspective. They were also prepared to make a dramatic break with conventional attitudes and modes of behaviour.

"IN A SHOREHAM GARDEN" BY SAMUEL PALMER, VICTORIA AND ALBERT MUSEUM, LONDON

HAWORTH PARSONAGE, W. YORKS,
(above) was from 1820 the home of
probably the most talented, and ill-
fated, family in the history of British
literature. It was here that Emily,
Charlotte and Anne Brontë wrote
their first novels (Wuthering
Heights, Jane Eyre and Agnes Grey)
all being published in the same year,
1847. The following year Emily, and
their brother Branwell, died of
tuberculosis, then Anne died in
1849. Charlotte married her father's
curate in 1854, but died a few
months later. Their scholarly but
dictatorial father, Patrick Brontë,
whose study is shown (right) lived
on till 1861. The house is kept as a
museum to their lives and work.

THOMAS CHATTERTON, *shown here (above) in Henry Wallis's famous painting, which now hangs in the Tate Gallery, London, is remembered today not so much for his work, as for his unfulfilled promise. He committed suicide at the age of seventeen. Yet even by then he had displayed great brilliance in his poetry, plays, histories, and some extraordinary "medieval" writings, with which he deceived the experts.*

KEATS'S HOUSE, LONDON, *(right) was the home of John Keats, who later became the most famous of the Romantic poets. In the garden is the mulberry tree beneath which he is said to have sat and listened to the bird that inspired his "Ode to a Nightingale". Keats died in Rome in 1821.*

LORD BYRON, *seen here (left) in Albanian costume in a painting by Thomas Phillips, now in the National Portrait Gallery, London, was perhaps the most romantic poet of the Romantic age. Renowned as much for his scandalous love affairs as for his epic poetry, he was to die in 1824 while fighting for Greek freedom from the Turks.*

ABBOTSFORD, BORDERS, *(right) was built between 1811 and 1824 for Sir Walter Scott, one of the greatest storytellers of all time, and creator of those fine historical romances, The Waverley Novels.*

ST PANCRAS HOTEL AND STATION, LONDON, (above) was designed by Gilbert Scott, the leading architect of the Victorian Gothic revival. This painting, by John O'Connor, hangs in the Museum of London.

THE LAW COURTS, LONDON, (left) designed by George Street, are some of the most romantic Victorian neo-Gothic buildings. They seem, quite inappropriately, the ideal setting for medieval fairy tales.

CONSTITUTION ARCH, LONDON, (below) was commissioned from Decimus Burton in 1828. When a huge statue was placed upon it to the Duke of Wellington (who liked to see himself from the windows of his Apsley House!), Burton was so angry that he left £2000 to cover the cost of its removal. The present sculpture was added in 1912.

THE HOUSES OF PARLIAMENT, LONDON, were rebuilt by Charles Barry, after a fire. Work began in 1840, and the world-famous clock-tower housing Big Ben (above) was completed in 1858. Augustus Pugin, who designed the Gothic decoration, died in 1852, the same year that Queen Victoria opened Parliament from the splendid throne he had designed in the House of Lords (left).

37

"THE CHAIN PIER, BRIGHTON", (above) from the Tate Gallery, London, and "WILLY LOTT'S HOUSE", (left) from the Victoria and Albert Museum, London, are by John Constable, the greatest of Britain's East Anglian artists. "The Chain Pier" is a finished painting, for which Constable made a number of sketches in his determination to capture the most direct and realistic view he could of the subject. At that time this was a new approach to landscape, and it was to establish Constable as a major figure in international art. For this reason, sketches such as that of "Willy Lott's House", on the River Stour near his own home, are considered especially important.

"GRETA BRIDGE", by John Sell Cotman, (above) now hangs in the Castle Museum, Norwich. Cotman (1782–1842) was a leading artist in watercolours. He was a founder of the Norwich group of painters, which owed much to the Dutch tradition with which East Anglia has always had close links. However, he had his own distinctive style, foreshadowing that of Cézanne.

"THE FALL OF BABYLON", by John Martin, (right) was painted in 1819, when large visionary paintings with Biblical or literary import were very popular. Martin's style of romantic expression was especially admired on the Continent. His paintings, however, always appealed more to the imagination of writers, than to fellow painters.

"RAIN, STEAM AND SPEED", (below) by J.M.W. Turner, hangs in the National Gallery, London. It illustrates how "impressionistic" Turner's style was decades before the term was coined in France. His self-portrait (above) hangs in the Clore Gallery, part of the Tate Gallery, London, (left) which contains many of his pictures.

THE MENAI STRAITS, GWYNEDD, are still spanned by Thomas Telford's beautiful suspension bridge. It was opened in 1826, the final stage in the great engineer's last major public assignment: the opening up of a new route from Holyhead across North Wales — to ease the journey of Irish M.P.s to Westminster.

Tories over constitutional issues but all this was now dead and settled, and the problems and perils of the Industrial Revolution glowered across obsolete party alignments. With the passing of the Reform Bill the Whig Party had done its work. Its leaders neither liked nor understood the middle classes. They looked on radicalism as a fashionable creed to be held in undergraduate days and dropped on reaching maturity, and they perceived, uneasily and dimly, that they were being pushed from behind by mass agitation and organisation into strange and perilous paths.

Moreover, their hold on the country was by no means certain. Some quarter of a million voters had been added by the Reform Bill to the electorate, which now numbered nearly eight hundred thousand persons. This meant that about one adult male in six had the vote. However, they by no means gave their undivided support to the Whigs. The strange habit of British electors of voting against governments which give them the franchise now made itself felt, and it was with great difficulty that the Whig administrations preserved a majority with the help of O'Connell's Irish votes. Their only hope was to unite with the radicals, who, though few in Parliament, had the backing of the middle class and the press, and whose strength was not truly reflected in the number of seats they held. But the Whigs hesitated. One of the few who favoured such an alliance was "Radical Jack"—John Lambton, Earl of Durham, Grey's son-in-law. But his hot temper made him a prickly colleague. He soon left the Government, and later became absorbed in the problems of colonial government, greatly to the advantage of Canada and the whole Imperial connection. His early death removed all hope of domestic fusion between radicals and Whigs.

Nevertheless, the legislation and the commissions of these years were by no means unfruitful. The slaves in the West Indies were finally emancipated in 1833. For the first time in English history the Government made educational grants to religious societies. The Poor Law was reformed on lines that were considered highly advanced in administrative and intellectual circles, though they did not prove popular among those they were supposed to benefit. The first effective Factory Act was passed, though the long hours of work it permitted would horrify the twentieth century and did not satisfy the humanitarians of the time. The whole system of local government was reconstructed and the old local oligarchies abolished. Politics meanwhile centred on the position of the Established Church and the maintenance of order in Ireland, and it was their failure to deal with these issues and to balance their Budgets that in due course ruined the Whigs. Moreover, great forces were at work outside the House of Commons. A large mass of the country still remained unenfranchised. The relations of capital and labour had scarcely been touched by the hand of Parliament, and the activities of the early trade unions frightened the Government into oppressive measures. The most celebrated case was that of the Tolpuddle "Martyrs" of 1834, when six labourers from that Dorsetshire village of curious name were sentenced to transportation for the technical offence of "administering unlawful oaths" to members of their union. Public agitation eventually secured their pardon, but not until they had served two years in New South Wales. Unrest spread, and the Whigs were not the men to bridge the gulf which seemed to yawn between official political circles and the nation.

Sir Robert Peel, on the other hand, was not slow to adjust the Tories to the new times. A speedy reorganisation of their machinery was set on foot.

This medallion of the Anti-Slavery Society, which shows a supplicant negro in chains, was manufactured by the Wedgwood Pottery. The Act, emancipating all slaves in British territories, was finally passed in 1833.

"I presume," he declared in 1833, "the chief object of that party which is called Conservative will be to resist radicalism, to prevent those further encroachments of democratic influence which will be attempted as the natural consequence of the triumph already achieved." He made it clear that the Tories would support administrative changes which increased efficiency, but oppose any weakening of the traditional institutions of the State. A disciplined, purposeful, but not factious Opposition gradually took shape under his leadership. In the following year the party was heartened by a rousing election address which Peel had issued to his constituency. Peel showed considerable cleverness in revealing his desire to modify the whole position of the Established Church. The Nonconformist voters did not forget this in the coming years, for religion still counted in politics. As the great Acts of Reform succeeded each other, so further interests were antagonised and the Conservative sentiment in the country gradually rallied to Peel. In the elections of 1835 the Tories won a hundred seats, and for some months he presided over a minority Government. Then the Whigs returned, as divided among themselves as ever. The dangers of spasmodic and uncoordinated reform were borne in upon the middle classes by their fumbling leadership. The Whig coach was clattering down a twisting, unknown road, and many supporters alighted in the course of the journey.

In 1837 King William IV died. Humorous, tactless, pleasant, and unrespected, he had played his part in lowering esteem for the monarchy, and indeed the vices and eccentricities of the sons of George III had by this time almost destroyed its hold upon the hearts of the people. An assault on the institution

---

THE EMPLOYMENT OF CHILDREN

Young children were useful in factories because they could move easily between the machines, and were paid even less than adults. The exploitation of mill girls is described in the following extract from the Report of the Committee on Factory Children's Labour, 1832.

At what time in the morning did these girls go to the mills?

In the brisk time, for about six weeks, they have gone at three o'clock in the morning, and ended at ten, or nearly half past at night.

What intervals were allowed for rest or refreshment during those nineteen hours of labour?

Breakfast a quarter of an hour, and dinner half an hour, and drinking a quarter of an hour.

Was any of that time taken up in cleaning the machinery?

They generally had to do what they call dry down; sometimes this took the whole of the time at breakfast or drinking, and they were to get their dinner or breakfast as they could; if not, it was brought home.

Had you not great difficulty in awakening your children to this excessive labour?

Yes, in the early time we had to take them up asleep and shake them when we got them on the floor to dress them, before we could get them off to their work. . . .

Did this excessive term of labour occasion much cruelty as well?

Yes, with being so very much fatigued the strap was very frequently used. . . .

What was the wages in the short hours?

Three shillings a week each.

When they wrought those very long hours what did the children get?

Three shillings and sevenpence halfpenny.

This spinning factory of 1820 employed well-drilled little girls to attend to the reels of yarn.

which had played so great a part in the history of England appeared imminent, and there seemed few to defend it. The new sovereign was a maiden of eighteen. She had been brought up by a dutiful mother, who was shocked at the language and habits of the royal uncles, and had secluded her in Kensington Palace from both the Court and the nation. Her education was supervised by a German governess, with occasional examination by Church dignitaries, and a correspondence course on her future duties with her maternal uncle, King Leopold of Belgium. The country knew nothing of either her character or her virtues. "Few people," wrote Palmerston, "have had opportunities of forming a correct judgment of the Princess; but I incline to think that she will turn out to be a remarkable person, and gifted with a great deal of strength of character." He was right. On the eve of her accession the new Queen wrote in her diary: "Since it has pleased Providence to place me in this situation, I shall do my utmost to fulfil my duty towards my country; I am very young, and perhaps in many, though not in all things, inexperienced, but I am sure that very few have more real good will and more real desire to do what is fit and right than I have." It was a promise she was spaciously to fulfil.

Queen Victoria, who was crowned in 1838, had a great sense of duty and a strict moral code which was to set the pattern for nineteenth-century Britain. Victoria was the first sovereign to use Buckingham Palace as her London home.

By the time Queen Victoria came to the throne the Whigs had shot their bolt. The middle classes were fearful of unrest and beginning to vote for the Tories. Meanwhile Lord Melbourne, with grace and pleasantness, was doing nothing. On top of all this there appeared towards the end of the year the first signs of a great economic depression, and in May 1838 a group of working-class leaders published a "People's Charter". Chartism, as it was called, in which some historians discern the beginnings of Socialism, was the last despairing cry of poverty against the Machine Age. The Chartists, believing that an extension of the franchise would cure all their miseries, demanded annual Parliaments, universal male suffrage, equal electoral districts, the removal of the property qualification for membership of Parliament, the secret ballot, and the payment of members. Their only hope of success was to secure, as the radicals had done, the backing of a Parliamentary party and of the progressive middle classes. But they deliberately refused to bid for middle-class support. Their leaders quarrelled among themselves and affronted respectable people by threatening and irresponsible speeches. They had no funds, and no organisation such as the Labour Party was to find later in the trade unions. The few unions which then existed soon deserted the cause and the more prosperous artisans were lukewarm. For a time England was flooded with petitions and pamphlets, but whenever conditions improved the popular temper cooled, and no united national movement emerged as a permanent force. Agitation revived from time to time in the years that followed, culminating in the revolutionary year of 1848. But the whole muddled, well-intentioned business came to nothing.

Peel drew the right conclusions. He discerned, much more clearly than the Whigs, the causes of the unrest, and, though steadfast against radicalism, he believed that the remedy lay in efficient administration and an enlightened commercial policy. The younger Tories supported him, and like him were oppressed by the division of the country into "two nations", the rich and the poor, as portrayed in the novels of a young Jewish Member of Parliament called Benjamin Disraeli. A small group of Conservatives were already seeking an alliance with the working man against the middle classes.

In 1839 Melbourne offered to resign, but for another two years Victoria

Queen Victoria and Prince Albert on the day of their wedding in February 1840. They were to have nine children, who through their marriages linked the British royal house with those of Europe. Victoria's love for Albert was so strong that after his early death in 1861 she wore widow's weeds for the rest of her life.

kept him in office. His charm had captured her affections. He imparted to her much of his wisdom on men and affairs, without burdening her with his scepticism, and she refused to be separated from her beloved Prime Minister. In February of the following year a new figure entered upon the British scene. The Queen married her cousin, Prince Albert of Saxe-Coburg. The Prince was an upright, conscientious man with far-ranging interests and high ideals. He and the Queen enjoyed for twenty-one years, until his early death, a happy family life, which held up an example much in accord with the desires of her subjects. After the excesses of George IV and his brothers, the dignity and repute of the monarchy stood in need of restoration, and this was Victoria and Albert's achievement. At first the Prince found his presence in England resented. The political magnates would not let him take a seat in the House of Lords, they cut down his annual allowance, and he was not granted even the title of Prince Consort until 1857. Nevertheless the patronage which he earnestly extended to science, industry, and the arts, and to good causes of many kinds, gradually won him a wide measure of public respect. Eventually the party leaders in England learnt to value his advice, especially on foreign affairs, though they did not always pay heed to it. As permanent adviser to the Queen, on all issues laid before her, he played a scrupulous, disinterested part. Wise counsels from his uncle, King Leopold, and Baron Stockmar, his former tutor, taught him the role and duties of a constitutional sovereign. The Queen, a woman of strong mind, who had begun her reign as a vehement partisan of the Whigs, came to perceive that in public at least she must be impartial and place her trust in whichever minister could command a majority in the House of Commons, though this did not prevent her from entertaining vivid likes and dislikes for her chief servants, to which she gave vigorous expression in private letters. Together the Queen and the Prince thus set a new standard for the conduct of monarchy which has ever since been honourably observed.

Peel had given the Queen an impression of awkwardness and coldness of manner; but when at last in 1841 a General Election brought him to power, he won her confidence. His abilities now came into full play. He had absolute control of his Cabinet, himself introduced his Government's more important Budgets, and supervised the work of all departments, including that of William Gladstone at the Board of Trade. Tariffs were again reformed, customs duties reduced, and income tax was reimposed. These measures soon bore fruit. In 1843 trade began to revive, prosperity returned, and the demand for political reform was stilled. Once again the sky seemed clear at Westminster. But a storm was gathering in Ireland.

The immediate issue was the price of bread. To promote foreign commerce Peel had reduced import duties on everything except corn. Dear bread, however, meant either high wages or misery for the masses, and Peel gradually realised that cheap imported food could alone sustain the continued prosperity of the nation. Free Trade in corn seemed imperative, but the political obstacles were formidable. The Tory Party leant heavily on the votes of the landowners. Peace had brought cheaper corn from abroad, and the cry for protection had led in 1815 to a prohibition of the import of foreign grain except when the price in the home market was abnormally high. The repeal or modification of this and later Corn Laws now overclouded all other issues. The landowners were accused of using their power in Parliament to safeguard their interests at the expense of the rest of the community. The enmity of the manufacturers and industrialists sharpened the conflict, for the Corn Laws not only caused great distress to the working classes, but angered many employers. Protection in their view prevented them from building up new markets overseas and from competing on fair terms in old ones.

During the depression of 1838–42, an Anti-Corn Law League was formed at Manchester. It soon exerted a powerful influence on public opinion, and produced two remarkable leaders and organisers who became the free trade prophets of nineteenth-century England, Richard Cobden, a calico printer, and John Bright, a Quaker mill-owner. The movement was strongly supported. The new penny postage, introduced by Sir Rowland Hill in 1840, carried circulars and pamphlets cheaply all over the country. Meetings were held throughout the land. The propaganda was effective and novel: a few simple ideas hammered into the minds of audiences by picked lecturers and speakers. Never had there been such a shrewdly conducted agitation. Monster petitions were sent to Parliament. Cobden persuaded prosperous townspeople to buy forty-shilling freeholds in the country constituencies and thus secure a double vote. This so increased the number of Anti-Corn Law electors that the League started influencing Parliament from within.

Cobden and Bright's thundering speeches against the landed classes reverberated through the nation. Peel, like them, came from the middle class, and their arguments bit deeply into his mind. By 1843 Peel was determined to act. His position was very difficult, for some of his followers felt he had betrayed them once already over Catholic Emancipation. But he was sure of himself. Perhaps he believed that his personal ascendancy would carry the majority with him; but he needed time to convince his party, and time was denied him.

In August 1845 the potato crop failed in Ireland. Famine was imminent and Peel could wait no longer, but when he put his proposals to the Cabinet several of his colleagues revolted and in December he had to resign. The Whig leader Russell refused to form an administration, and Peel returned to office to face and conquer the onslaught of the Tory Protectionists. Their spokesman, the hitherto little-known Benjamin Disraeli, denounced him not so much for seeking to abolish the Corn Laws as for betraying his

PUNCH'S MONUMENT TO PEEL.

Bad harvests and the potato famine in Ireland finally forced Peel to recognise the arguments of the Anti-Corn Law League and to repeal the Corn Laws in 1846. His actions split the Tory Party, but provided cheap bread for the people and thus inspired this appreciative cartoon which appeared in Punch.

ROWLAND HILL AND THE PENNY POST

G.M. Trevelyan, in his English Social History, *describes the revolutionary changes brought about by improvements in communication, particularly by the penny post.*

The same decades that saw the rapid growth of the railway system and the electric telegraph, saw the triumph of the penny post, established by the unselfish and tireless efforts of Rowland Hill, supported by the popular demand, against the indifference of statesmen and the angry obstruction of the unreformed civil service. Prior to this great change, the poor who moved in search of work either inside the island or by emigration overseas, could seldom exchange news with those they

had left behind, owing to the heavy charge made for the receipt of letters. Rowland Hill's plan for a postal delivery prepaid by a cheap adhesive stamp, enabled the poor, for the first time, to communicate with the loved ones from whom they were separated. And since the business world found cheap postage a boon, and since it proved a great financial success after it had been forced upon the obdurate Post Office, the new method was soon imitated in every civilised country in the world. In this great reform the State had necessarily to be made the instrument, but the thought and the leadership had come from an individual, backed by public opinion.

The Penny Black stamp remained in use from May 6, 1840 to January 17, 1841.

position as head of a great party. If Peel, he declared, believed in the measure he should resign, as a large section of his party was traditionally pledged to oppose it. The wilful destruction of a great party by its leader was a political crime, for the true working of English politics depended on the balance of parties, and if a leader could not convince his colleagues he should withdraw. Thus Disraeli. But Peel maintained that his duty to the nation was higher than his duty to his party.

On June 25, 1846, with the help of Whig and Irish votes, the Corn Laws were repealed. Disraeli immediately had his revenge. Turmoil in Ireland destroyed Peel's Government, and by a vote on the same night the great ministry, one of the strongest of the century, came to an end. Peel had been the dominating force and personality in English politics since the passing of the great Reform Bill. Whether in Opposition or in office, he had towered above the scene. He was not a man of broad and ranging modes of thought, but he understood better than any of his contemporaries the needs of the country, and he had the outstanding courage to change his views in order to meet them. It is true that he split his party, but there are greater crimes than that. The age over which he presided was one of formidable industrial advance. It was the railway age. By 1848 some five thousand miles of railways had been built in the United Kingdom. Speed of transport and increasing output were the words of the day. Coal and iron production had doubled. Engineering was making great, though as yet hesitating, strides. Steps were being taken by enterprisers which were to make Britain the

THE IRISH POTATO FAMINE

This harrowing extract is taken from Arthur Bryant's book The English Saga.

The autumn of 1846 saw a climax to the suffering and misery of the Irish. The English harvest was bad, there was a world food shortage, and for the second season running the Irish potato crop, ravaged by disease, failed. Wheat and provision prices soared. The British Government, faced with the prospect of a whole nation starving, advanced ten million pounds to relieve distress and bought yellow maize from India to make broth.

It was in vain. By December over forty thousand were totally dependent on poor relief in County Roscommon alone, while the streets of Cork were thronged with five thousand homeless wretches in the last stages of famine. By February the number had doubled. Men, women and children filled their stomachs with cabbage leaves and turnip tops: hundreds died weekly in every rural union. In the remoter villages beyond even the feeble reach of the Government, the dead lay in the roads and ditches unburied.

In a letter that Christmas to the Duke of Wellington, a local Justice of the Peace described a visit to the district of Skibbereen. On reaching the village of South Reen with supplies of bread, he was surprised to find the hamlet apparently deserted.

"I entered some of the hovels to ascertain the cause, and the scenes that presented themselves were such as no tongue or pen can convey the slightest idea of. In the first, six famished and ghastly skeletons, to all appearances dead, were huddled in a corner on some filthy straw, their sole covering what seemed a ragged horsecloth. I approached with horror, and found by a low moaning they were alive. They were in fever—four children, a woman and what had once been a man."

In the course of one terrible winter it was believed that over a quarter of a million Irish peasants died of starvation. Within the next five years, during which the ravages of famine still continued in a milder form, her population declined by two and a half million, about a third. Of these more than a million perished of starvation and pestilence: the rest emigrated to America.

Starving Irish labourers and their families throng the gates of a workhouse in 1846, hoping for a meal.

greatest industrial power of the nineteenth-century world. The days of the landowning predominance were doomed. Free trade seemed essential to manufacture, and in manufacture Britain was entering upon her supremacy. All this Peel grasped. His Government set an example of initiative which both the Conservative and Liberal Parties honoured by imitation in the future. Of his own methods of government he once said, "The fact is, people like a certain degree of obstinacy and presumption in a Minister. They abuse him for dictation and arrogance, but they like being governed." High words perhaps, but they fitted the time.

Early in 1850, after he had watched with restraint and composure the totterings of his Whig successors, Peel fell from his horse while riding in Green Park and was fatally injured. So died one of the great shapers of British politics in the Victorian age.

CHAPTER 4

THE CRIMEAN WAR

Towards the middle of the nineteenth century political life in England was only slightly changed by the acceptance of the great Reform Bill. The Whigs were in power under Lord John Russell. His family had served the State since the days of Henry VII. Whatever novel agitations might spread among working men in the industrial towns, who as yet enjoyed few votes, the Whig leaders pursued their reasonable, moderate, and undemocratic courses. Lord John's Government, with a few upsets, survived for six years. It achieved little of lasting note, but it piloted Britain through a restless period when elsewhere in Europe thrones were overturned and revolutions multiplied.

The Tories for their part were irreconcilably split. The followers of Peel and Free Trade, who included in Aberdeen and Gladstone two future Prime Ministers, were content to let the Whigs bear the heat of the day. The Liberal Party, which would presently arise from the coalition of Whigs, Peelites, and radicals, was not yet foreseen. The opponents of the Peelites, the old Tories, were led by Lord Stanley, soon to be Lord Derby, whose forebears had played a role in the kingdom for even longer than the Russells. Derby was increasingly assisted in the House of Commons by his lieutenant Disraeli, whose reputation for brilliance was growing rather faster than his capacity for inspiring trust. It was Disraeli's gradual task over these years to persuade the Tories to abandon their fidelity to the Corn Law tariff and to work out a new and more broadly-based Conservative policy.

While party affairs at Westminster dwelt gently in flux, Europe succumbed to an anguished spasm. In February 1848 the French monarchy fell. The rule of King Louis Philippe had given prosperity to her middle classes, but it had appealed neither to staunch Republicans nor to the Bonapartists, who were still dazzled by the remembered glories of the Empire. A few days rioting sufficed to eject Louis Philippe, and a government of romantic outlook and Socialist complexion briefly took control. This in turn collapsed, and by the end of the year a Bonaparte had been elected President of France by an overwhelming majority. Thus, after half a lifetime spent in plotting, exile, and obscurity, Prince Louis Napoleon, nephew of the

Louis Napoleon Bonaparte (1808-1873), the nephew of Napoleon I, felt himself destined to revive dreams of French grandeur. In 1848, the French rid themselves of their "citizen king", Louis Philippe, and shortly afterwards they elected Louis Napoleon as President. In the year 1852, he became Napoleon III, their Emperor.

THE RAILWAY AGE

THE COMING OF THE RAILWAY seemed like a great divide, locally and nationally, in nineteenth-century Britain. "We who lived before railways and survive out of the ancient world," wrote the novelist William Thackeray, "are like father Noah and his family out of the Ark."

With the opening of the line linking Liverpool and Manchester in September 1830, the railway age began in earnest. This was the first line to rely entirely on steam locomotives and to carry a high proportion of passenger traffic. In technical terms the railway locomotive was the culminating triumph of the gospel of steam. The Iron Horse could carry loads and travel farther and faster than any horse had ever been able to do. Railways, therefore, meant the end of stagecoach travel, and eventually led to the failure of the canals, too, as systems of transport. George Stephenson, a self-made Northumberland engineer, whose locomotive the *Rocket* won railway trials between Liverpool and Manchester in 1830, was one of the first great railway builders, and father of Robert Stephenson, who helped to fashion the railway age.

Each feature of the railway—locomotive, track, station—has its own history. Critics thought of locomotives and their carriages as "monsters navigated by a tail of smoke and sulphur". Dickens considered them symbols both of change and death.

But the towering Doric arch built outside London's Euston station in the 1830s was perhaps the most vivid symbol of the importance the Victorians attached to the railway age. For during the years between 1825 and 1835 no less than fifty-four Railway Acts permitting railway building were passed, and if at the end of 1838 there were still only five hundred miles of track, seventeen years later eight thousand miles of rails were carrying passengers and freight about the country.

By the middle of the nineteenth century the Victorians could proudly claim that they had created a railway system.

MASSIVE EXCAVATION was essential for laying the railway tracks which, unlike roads, had to be level. Hills were blasted with dynamite causing numerous deaths in the armies of "navvies" (short for navigators, the humorous nickname given to canal workers) who worked on the railways. By 1847 there were a quarter of a million navvies employed on the railways. The engraving (above) shows one of the earliest cuttings – Olive Mount on the Liverpool and Manchester Railway in about 1828. The expansion of the railways made cheap travel readily available to all classes. In stagecoach days, the return fare between Manchester and London was £3.10s. In 1851, the railway offered a special fare of 5s. The Doric arch (right) at Euston was known as the Gate of the North. It was the terminus of the London and Birmingham Railway.

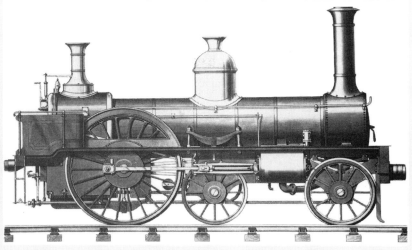

THE LONDON UNDERGROUND, *originally known as the Metropolitan, opened in 1863. The photograph (above) records the first trial trip taken by a group of VIPs, including William Gladstone (between the two men in white top hats in the centre), on May 24 at Edgware Road Station. In the same decade there was a great expansion of London's sewage system which, like the Underground, involved huge tunnelling operations and the diversion of London's rivers into pipes below ground. The "tube" network expanded steadily during the Victorian and Edwardian eras.*

EARLY LOCOMOTIVE STEAM ENGINES *relied on boilers containing huge tanks of water which produced the large amounts of steam required to generate power. George Stephenson, however, constructed a series of narrow copper tubes around which the flames from the fire box could pass freely. The Rocket was the first engine in which this revolutionary idea was used. However, technical change was rapid and the Rocket remained in use for only ten years. The picture (above) is of Stephenson's "A" type "long boiler" used on the London and North Western Railways.*

RAILWAY ARCHITECTURE *was influenced by the new technology. Liberal use was made of iron girders, supported on tall columns, and roofed over with glass. The first train-shed with arched iron ribs forming a high vault was at* Newcastle. *Iron and glass were used by I. K. Brunel for Paddington Station (1850) and by W. H. Barlow at St Pancras Station (1868). Many stations, like York (above), are extremely spectacular and remain unchanged.*

ISAMBARD KINGDOM BRUNEL (1806–59), *as the chief engineer to the Great Western Railway Company (1833–46), prepared the survey for the route between Bristol and London. While working on the project, he pioneered the broad gauge track to improve the comfort, safety and speed of rail travel, and he designed the Clifton suspension bridge. The Great Western Railway opened in 1841, and it was Brunel's vision of extending the railway across the Atlantic which led him into shipbuilding. In 1838 he designed the steamship, the Great Western, which made a record crossing from Bristol to New York. The photograph (above) shows Brunel at the Millwall shipyards in 1857, awaiting the launch of a steamship.*

great Emperor, came to power. He owed his position to the name he bore, to the ineptitude of his rivals, and to the fondness of the French for constitutional experiment. For more than twenty years this amiable, dreamy figure was to play a striking and not always ineffective part upon the European scene.

The peoples of Italy had also broken into revolt against both their own rulers and the Austrian occupiers of Lombardy and Venetia. High hopes were cherished that a united Italian nation might emerge from this commotion. Pope Pius IX, who was also the temporal ruler of Central Italy, was a liberal man of patriotic feeling. To him many of his fellow Italians looked up for guidance and inspiration. But his holy office forbade him to direct a purely national crusade against the Catholic power of Austria. His duty was to head a universal Church. Political leadership for Italy had to come from elsewhere. In the Italian provinces enthusiastic conspirators soon found that they could not hold their own against the organised forces of Austria and her allies. The Italian revolt ended in failure, but not without arousing a widespread sympathy in Britain, which was benevolently exercised when the next attempt at unity was made.

North of the Alps revolutionary nationalism was also stirring. The Austrian Chancellor, Metternich, who had dominated Central Europe for forty years, was forced to resign and this aged pillar of continental absolutism found refuge in an obscure hotel in the England of the Whigs. The Emperor was obliged to abdicate, leaving the Habsburg throne to a young Archduke, Francis Joseph, destined to live through many tribulations and witness the opening years of the First World War. Czechs, Poles, and Hungarians in turn all took up arms, and their gallant risings were eventually suppressed only with the help of the Tsar of Russia. In Germany itself the minor monarchs were thrown into disarray. A Parliament met at Frankfurt, and after lengthy debate offered the Crown of a united Germany to the King of Prussia. This sovereign and his military advisers preferred repressing revolutionaries to accepting favours from them, and the offer was declined. Little came of the events of 1848–49 in Germany, except a powerful impetus

This meeting on Kennington Common in April 1848 was the last large-scale demonstration in aid of Chartism. The Chartist proposals for electoral reform were too "radical" for the day, but over the next seventy years all but one of their demands – the demand for annual Parliaments – were realised.

to the idea of German unity, and a growing conviction that it could only be achieved with the backing of Prussian arms.

The turmoil in Europe was viewed in England with sympathetic interest, but it went unmatched by any comparable disturbance. The Chartist movement, for some time languishing, took fresh courage however. It was also stirred by a new economic crisis at home. There was half-hearted talk of revolution, but in the end it was decided to present a new petition to Parliament, reiterating all the old Chartist demands. A meeting was called in April 1848 on Kennington Common. From there the Chartist leaders proposed to lead an impressive march upon the Houses of Parliament. The Government took precautions. Troops were called out and special constables enrolled; but in the event no undue strain was placed upon their services. As Wellington remarked—still an imperturbable commander in chief at the age of seventy-eight—the English are "a very quiet people". This is especially so when it is raining. More spectators than Chartists assembled on that wet spring day at Kennington. When the police forbade the proposed march, the demonstrators quietly dispersed. Their petition was conveyed to the Commons in three cabs. Such was the measure of revolutionary feeling in London in 1848.

In the same year Thomas Babington Macaulay, who had been a minister of the Crown, published the first volumes of his *History of England*. This great work, with all its prejudiced opinions and errors of fact, provided the historical background for the sense of progress which was now inspiring Victorian Britain. In his opening chapter he wrote: "The history of our own country in the last hundred and sixty years is eminently the history of physical, moral, and intellectual improvement." This was a heartening note, and an even more shining future, Macaulay implied, lay before the United Kingdom. So indeed it did. His views were widely shared, and were soon given form in the Great Exhibition of 1851.

Prince Albert sponsored the idea. There had already been some small exhibitions of manufactures, in which he had taken an interest. Then, in 1849, after opening the new Albert Dock in Liverpool, the Prince, against considerable opposition, adopted with enthusiasm a plan for an exhibition on a far larger scale than had ever been seen before. It would display to the country and the world the progress achieved in every field. It would also be international, proclaiming the benefits of free trade between nations and looking forward to the universal peace which it was then supposed must inevitably result from the unhampered traffic in goods.

The Great Exhibition was opened in Hyde Park. Nineteen acres were devoted to the principal building, the Crystal Palace, designed by an expert glasshouse gardener, Joseph Paxton. Enclosing whole trees within its glass and iron structure, it was to be the marvel of the decade. In spite of prophecies of failure, the Exhibition was a triumphant success. Over a million people a month visited it during the six months of its opening. Nearly fourteen thousand exhibits of industrial skill and craft were shown, of which half were British. The Prince was vindicated, and the large profit made by the organisers was invested and put to learned and educational purposes. Queen Victoria described the opening day as "one of the greatest and most glorious in our lives". Her feelings were prompted by her delight that Prince Albert should have confounded his critics, ever ready to accuse him of meddling in national affairs, but there was more to it than that. The

The Great International Exhibition of 1851 was a showcase of Britain's industrial and manufacturing power. People from all over the country were encouraged to visit the Crystal Palace in London's Hyde Park.

THE GREAT EXHIBITION

A VISIT IN 1851 TO THE GREAT EXHIBITION at the Crystal Palace was counted as a landmark in the life of many nineteenth-century men and women. The great building itself was not the least of the exhibits on display. Built of glass and iron, and designed by Joseph Paxton, who was, surprisingly, not an architect but a landscape gardener, it was, in the words of a contemporary, "an outstanding sign of the mind of the age. . . . It could not have been imagined by the chivalry of the Middle Ages."

Designed, as Queen Victoria's husband, Prince Albert, put it, to reveal the state of knowledge and its application—particularly scientific knowledge—at that moment in the history of the world, its exhibits had been gathered from all parts of the globe. Yet although conceived as a universal exhibition, over half of the fourteen thousand exhibitors actually represented Great Britain and her colonies. In the words of Benjamin Disraeli, Great Britain was now "the workshop of the world."

There were to be many other international exhibitions on both sides of the Atlantic during the nineteenth century, but this was the *great* exhibition. Many of the objects on display would appear ugly to later generations, and there was argument at the time about the quality of the designs. But the Exhibition's enormous success and the money left over when it closed, enabled many future projects in both the arts and sciences to be financed—including the Victoria and Albert Museum and the Science Museum, sited in Exhibition Road.

There was undoubtedly a spirit of romance pervading Britain in 1851, as symbolised by the Exhibition and the Crystal Palace, but there was also a healthy understanding that prosperity was the fruit of hard work and invention. Competition between countries should be peaceful competition, however, not warlike struggle. To the rest of the civilised world Britain seemed to represent both peace and progress.

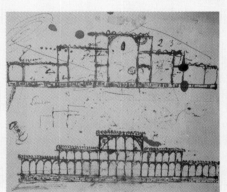

THE GREAT EXHIBITION (above) was opened by Queen Victoria with tremendous ceremony on May 1, 1851. The name, "Crystal Palace", was coined in the pages of Punch *magazine, and it perfectly suited the dazzling, fairy-like structure erected in Hyde Park. The blotting-paper sketches (left) made by the designer of the building, Joseph Paxton, show the essential features of his masterpiece. A later modification to the design was the enormous domed transept enabling a number of elm trees to be preserved by having them inside the building. The Crystal Palace was erected in less than six months, using standard component parts which merely needed to be assembled on arrival at the site.*

THE ROYAL COMMISSIONERS for the Exhibition had their group portrait (above) painted in 1851 by H. W. Philips. Joseph Paxton is seen pointing out a detail in the plans to Prince Albert, who was the Exhibition's originator and leading light. Opposite is the engineer, William Cubitt, who helped Paxton with his calculations, and behind him stands Charles Fox. The firm of Fox and Henderson, railway manufacturers, supplied the iron and steel girders and huge panes of glass used in the structure. The other men in the picture are members of the Royal Society of Arts. Initially, money for the building was raised by private subscription. Parliamentary support for the project was only given in January 1851.

THE BEST OF BRITISH ENGINEERING *was on display in the Hall of Invention (above). There were models of suspension bridges, a lighthouse and even a scale model of the entire Liverpool docks. Working machinery included a boiler house and immense steam pumps. Curiosities abounded, too. There was a machine for folding envelopes and a sportsman's knife with eighty blades. Cutlery, chinaware and ornaments (below) were also in abundance in the florid and elaborate style of the period. Outside the Exhibition many souvenirs were bought by the six million visitors, who came from all walks of life.*

THE CRYSTAL PALACE *was dismantled in October 1851, and moved to a site at Sydenham, South London. Paxton enlarged the building and turned it into a palace of leisure, rather than of work. Cast-iron street furniture created for the Exhibition was moved to London's streets. The gates which stand near the* Royal Albert Hall *were commissioned for the Exhibition from the sculptor, John Bell. Original cast-iron lampposts may be seen in Fleet Street, Trafalgar Square, and elsewhere in London. The photograph (above) shows the sad end of the celebrated building. It was destroyed by fire in November 1936.*

Queen paid many visits to the Crystal Palace, where her presence aroused in the scores of thousands of subjects with whom she mingled a deep loyalty and a sense of national pride. Prosperity, however unevenly its blessings fell, gave Britain a self-assurance that seemed worth more than social legislation. From mills and mines and factories flowed the wealth that was making life easier for the country. And this the country recognised.

The mid-century marks the summit of Britain's preponderance in industry. In another twenty years other nations had begun to cut down her lead. Until 1870 Britain had mined more than half the world's coal, and in that year foreign trade stood at a figure of nearly 700 millions sterling, as compared with 300 for the United States, 340 for France, and 300 for Germany. But the proportions were rapidly changing. Railways greatly assisted the growth of industry in Germany and America, where coal and iron resources were separated from each other by considerable distances. A challenge was also presented to British agriculture, now that prairie-grown American wheat could be carried to American ports by railroad and shipped across the ocean to European markets. Nevertheless there was no slowing down of industry in Britain. Textiles, the backbone of British exports, filled an insatiable demand in Asia, and the future of the mighty

AN ATTACK ON PUBLIC EXECUTIONS

Charles Dickens attacked many of the social evils of his day in his novels, and indirectly brought about reform. This letter to The Times, *written in 1849, refers to the execution of George and Maria Manning for murder.*

Sir,

I was a witness of the execution at Horsemonger-lane this morning. I went there with the intention of observing the crowd gathered to behold it, and I had excellent opportunities of doing so. . . . I believe that a sight so inconceivably awful as the wickedness and levity of the immense crowd collected at the execution this morning could be imagined by no man. The horrors of the gibbet and of the crime which brought the wretched murderers to it, faded in my mind before the atrocious bearing, looks and language, of the assembled spectators. . . .

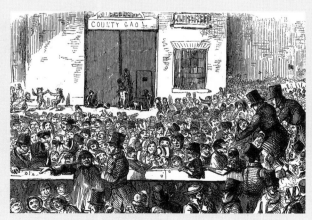

"The Great Moral Lesson at Horsemonger-lane" is the title of this engraving of the hanging witnessed by Charles Dickens.

When the day dawned, thieves, low prostitutes, ruffians, and vagabonds of every kind, flocked on to the ground, with every variety of offensive and foul behaviour. Fightings, faintings . . . brutal jokes, tumultuous demonstrations of indecent delight when swooning women were dragged out of the crowd by the police with their dresses disordered, gave a new zest to the general entertainment. When the sun rose brightly—as it did—it gilded thousands upon thousands of upturned faces, so inexpressibly odious in their brutal mirth or callousness, that a man had cause to feel ashamed of the shape he wore, and to shrink from himself, as fashioned in the image of the Devil.

When the two miserable creatures who attracted all this ghastly sight about them were turned quivering into the air, there was no more emotion, no more pity, no more thought that two immortal souls had gone to judgment, no more restraint in any of the previous obscenities than if the name of Christ had never been heard in the world, and there were no belief among men but that they perished like beasts.

I am solemnly convinced that nothing that ingenuity could devise to be done in this city . . . could work such ruin as one public execution, and I stand astounded and appalled by the wickedness it exhibits. I do not believe that any community can prosper where such a scene of horror and demoralisation as was enacted this morning outside Horsemonger-lane Gaol is presented at the very doors of good citizens, and is passed by, unknown or forgotten. And when, in our prayers and thanksgiving for the season, we are humbly expressing before God our desire to remove the moral evils of the land, I would ask your readers to consider if it is not a time to think of this one, and to root it out.

I am, Sir, your faithful servant,

Charles Dickens.

Devonshire Terrace, *Tuesday, Nov. 13.*

steel and engineering industries in the Midlands and North seemed assured for a long time to come.

Critics were not wanting of the age of mass production that was now taking shape. Charles Dickens in his novels revealed the plight of the poor, holding up to pity the conditions in which many of them dwelt and ridiculing the State institutions that crudely encompassed them. John Ruskin turned from the study of painting and architecture to modern social problems. Bad taste in manufacture, bad relations between employers and men, aroused his eloquent wrath. His was a voice that cried the way both to new movements in the arts and to Socialism in politics.

The threat of war, however, now began to darken the scene. Turkey had troubled the statesmen of Europe for many years. Preoccupation with the conflicts and intrigues of Court and harem had so distracted the Sultans at Constantinople and their chief advisers that the military empire which for three centuries had dominated the Eastern world from the Persian Gulf to Budapest, and from the Caspian to Algiers, seemed now on the edge of collapse. To whom then would fall the wide, fertile Turkish provinces in Europe and Asia? The urgency of this question was sharpened by the evident determination of Russia to seize the Danubian lands, Constantinople, and the Black Sea. England could not ignore the threat. The anxiety of the governing circles of England marched with a widespread and hearty dislike of the whole political system of which Nicholas I—the "o'ergrown Barbarian of the East", in Tennyson's phrase—was the principal prop. The contemporaries of Palmerston looked upon the police state of the Tsar as "the cornerstone of despotism in the world", a fatal obstacle to the great hopes which had sprung from the liberal revolutions of 1848.

Though the need to resist Russia was plain to most British observers, British diplomacy was confused about the best way of achieving its aims. For it was also necessary to keep an eye on the French, who had ambitions for extending their influence in the Levant. Canning had planned to head Russia off from southeast Europe by founding on the ruins of the Turkish Empire a bloc of small independent states. With such a programme of emancipation he had hoped to associate not only France, but Russia herself. The creation of the kingdom of Greece was the first and only result of his efforts. But twenty years had gone by and the ruling politicians of England had reversed his policy, and now attempted to check Russian expansion by the opposite method of propping up the decaying system of Turkish rule. In the execution of this plan the Government was much assisted by Stratford Canning, later Lord Stratford, the British ambassador at Constantinople. He was a cousin of George Canning, with a wider knowledge of Turkey than any other Englishman of his day. Proud, difficult, quick-tempered, he enjoyed immense authority with the Turks. He had no illusions about the character of the Ottoman Empire, but he hoped to induce the Sultan to make such reforms as would "retard the evil hour" when it would finally collapse. For years Stratford struggled with the laziness, corruption, and inefficiency of the Turkish administration. Whether he was wise to do so is another matter, since it was the very laxity of the regime that made it bearable by the subject peoples. Stratford however was unconvinced of this, and in 1852 he had little hope that the "evil hour" could be long delayed.

The immediate origin of the conflict which now came to a head between Turkey and Russia lay in Jerusalem, where the Greek Orthodox and Roman

John Ruskin (1819-1900), the writer, artist and reformer, is the subject of this portrait by George Richmond which can be seen in the National Portrait Gallery. Many of Ruskin's ideas for social reform, such as old age pensions, State education and the organisation of labour, eventually became realities.

Catholic Churches disputed the custody of certain shrines. The quarrel would have been unimportant had not the Tsar supported the Greek pretensions, and Louis Napoleon, now the Emperor Napoleon III, been anxious to please French Catholics by championing the Latins. After long negotiation the Tsar sent his envoy Menschikoff to Constantinople to revive his claims for a general protectorate over the Christians in the Turkish Empire. This, if granted, would have given Russia authority over the many millions of Romanians, Serbs, Bulgarians, Greeks, and Armenians within the Ottoman domains. The balance of power, which British governments always sought, would have been destroyed.

The electric telegraph, recently invented, only reached to Belgrade. Upon Stratford, much depended. He was the man on the spot, with considerable freedom from Cabinet control and with strong views on the Russian danger and the need to support Turkey. At home Lord Derby, after a brief spell in office, had been succeeded by Lord Aberdeen, who presided over a coalition Government of Whigs and Peelites, far from united in their opinions. The Prime Minister himself and his Foreign Secretary, Lord Clarendon, were hesitant and favoured appeasement. But Stratford could count on Palmerston, the most popular man in the Cabinet, and on the general hostility in England towards the Russians. He recommended the Turks to continue negotiations and not to take too stiff an attitude. But the Turks knew their man, and they knew that in the last resort the British fleet would protect Constantinople and stop Russia seizing the Straits. They accordingly rejected the Russian demands, and on June 2, 1853, the Russian attitude had become so menacing that the Cabinet ordered the British fleet to Besika Bay, outside the Dardanelles. Napoleon III, eager for British approval and support, agreed to provide a French squadron.

The fleet reached Besika Bay on June 13. In early July Russian troops crossed the River Pruth and entered Turkish Moldavia. The British Cabinet was still divided, and neither warned the Russians nor promised help to the Turks. The Turks ended the matter by rejecting an offer of mediation by a council of ambassadors.

War was still not certain. The Tsar, alarmed at Turkey's resistance, sought a compromise with the help of Austria, but by September Aberdeen and his Cabinet had become so suspicious that they rejected the offer. On October 4 the Sultan declared war on Russia, and soon attacked the Russians beyond the Danube. Such efforts as Aberdeen and Stratford could still make for peace were extinguished by a Russian onslaught against the Turkish fleet off Sinope, in the Black Sea. Indignation flared in England, where the action was denounced as a massacre. Palmerston resigned in December on a domestic issue, but his action was interpreted as a protest against the Government's vacillating Eastern policy, and Aberdeen was accused of cowardice. Thus England drifted into war. In February 1854 the Tsar recalled his ambassadors from London and Paris, and at the end of March the Crimean War began, with France and Britain as the allies of Turkey.

The operations were ill-planned and ill-conducted on both sides. With the exception of two minor naval expeditions to the Baltic and the White Sea, fighting was confined to southern Russia, where the great naval fort of Sebastopol, in the Black Sea, was selected as the main Allied objective, against the advice of the British commander, Lord Raglan. The necessity for this enterprise was questionable: the Turks had already driven the

Russians out of the Danube valley, there was little danger of an attack upon Constantinople, and it was folly to suppose that the capture of Sebastopol would make much impression on the vast resources of Russia. However, the British expeditionary force was encamped in Turkish territory and some use had to be made of it. The Allied fleet sailed close by Sebastopol harbour and ceremonial salutes were exchanged between the belligerents. A landing was made at the small town of Eupatoria, to the northwest. The Russian Governor declared that the armies might land, but according to regulations ought immediately to be placed in quarantine. Nobody took any notice of this precaution.

Sebastopol might have been entered by an immediate attack from the north, yet after an initial victory on the Alma in September 1854 the French commander, St Arnaud, who was a sick man and a political appointment, insisted on marching round to the south and beginning a formal siege. With this step Raglan reluctantly concurred; it was against his better judgment. The Russians were thus permitted to bring up reinforcements and strengthen the fortifications under the direction of the famous engineer Todleben. Unable to complete their investment of the town, the Allies had to beat off fresh Russian field armies which arrived from the interior. The British army, holding the exposed eastern wing of the lines, had twice to bear the brunt. At Balaclava in October the British cavalry distinguished themselves by two astonishing charges against overwhelming odds. The second of these was the celebrated charge of the Light Brigade, in which six hundred and seventy-three horsemen, led by Lord Cardigan, rode up the valley under heavy fire, imperturbably, as if taking part in a review, to attack the Russian batteries. They captured the guns, but only a third of the Brigade answered the first muster after the charge. Lord Cardigan calmly returned to the yacht on which he lived, had a bath, dined, drank a bottle of champagne, and went to bed. His Brigade had performed an inspiring feat of gallantry. But it was due, like much else in this war, to the blunders of commanders. Lord Raglan's orders had been badly expressed and were misunderstood by his subordinates. The Light Brigade had charged the wrong guns.

The camp of the 4th Light Dragoons in the Crimea. During this war, the British army failed to live up to the reputation it had won in the Napoleonic Wars. It was out of date and inefficient, bedevilled by inept commanders who still gained their commissions not on merit but with money, and by an inadequate, disorganised supply system.

William Russell, of The Times, *the first great war correspondent, reported on the appalling conditions and the blunders of the Crimean War. His powerful articles forced Englishmen at home to re-evaluate the organisation of the British army. His descriptions of the sufferings of the soldiers in the Crimea persuaded Secretary-at-War, Sidney Herbert, to ask Florence Nightingale to organise a hospital in Scutari.*

The Battle of Inkerman followed, fought in the mists of a November dawn. It was a desperate infantry action, in which the British soldier proved his courage and endurance. Russian casualties were nearly five times as many as those of the Allies. But Inkerman was not decisive. The Russians outnumbered the Allies by two to one, and it became plain that there was no hope of taking Sebastopol before the spring of 1855. Amid storms and blizzards the British army lay, without tents, huts, food, warm clothes, or the most elementary medical care. Cholera, dysentery, and malarial fever took their dreadful toll. Raglan's men had neither transport nor ambulances, and thousands were lost through cold and starvation because it did not occur to the Government of the greatest engineering country in the world to ease the movement of supplies from the port of Balaclava to the camp by laying down five miles of light railway. Nearly half a century of peace had dimmed the glory of the army which defeated Napoleon. Its great chief, Wellington, had died amid national mourning in 1852. During his long reign as commander in chief at the War Office nothing had changed since Waterloo. Nor could his successors in office see any need for reform. The conditions of service were intolerable; the administration was bad, the equipment scanty, the commanders of no outstanding ability. The French and British between them had fifty-six thousand troops in the Crimea in the terrible winter of 1854–55. Nearly fourteen thousand of them went to hospital, and many died for want of medical supplies. Most of these casualties were British. The French were better provided for, while the Russians perished in uncounted numbers on the long route marches through the snow southward to the Crimea.

Even the War Office was a little shaken by the incompetence and suffering. *The Times* sent out the first of all war correspondents, William Russell, and used his reports to start a national agitation against the Government. Aberdeen was assailed from every quarter, and when Parliament reassembled in January a motion was introduced by a Private Member to appoint a commission of inquiry into the state of the army before Sebastopol. It was carried by a majority so large that when the figures were announced they were greeted, not with the usual cheers, but with surprised silence, followed by derisive laughter. The Government had been condemned, as a contemporary wrote, "to the most ignominious end of any Cabinet in modern days". Aberdeen resigned, and was succeeded by Palmerston, who accepted the commission of inquiry. Palmerston did not at first command wide confidence, and it was at this moment that Disraeli wrote privately of him, "he is really an impostor, utterly exhausted, and at the best only ginger-beer and no champagne, and now an old painted pantaloon". Disraeli was wrong. Palmerston soon proved himself the man of the hour. The worst mistakes and muddles were cleared up, and at the War Office Sidney Herbert struggled manfully to reform the military administration.

By the summer of 1855 the Allied armies had been reinforced and were in good heart. An assault on Sebastopol was mounted in June, but it failed. This was too much for Raglan. Worn out by his responsibilities, he died on June 28. This disciple of Wellington, who had lost an arm at Waterloo, deserves a higher niche in military history than is sometimes accorded him. He was brave, loyal, and had the misfortune frequently to be right when others took the wrong decision.

The victory that should have been his due was won by his successor,

Sir James Simpson, in conjunction with the French Marshal Pélissier. In September Sebastopol at last fell. The futility of the plan of campaign was now revealed. It was impossible to invade Russia from the Crimea. What should the next move be? France by now had four times as many troops in the field as England, and Napoleon III was threatening to withdraw them. A peace party in Paris was making its views felt. Palmerston privately denounced this as "a cabal of stock-jobbing politicians", but he realised the war must stop. Threatened by an Austrian ultimatum, Russia agreed to terms, and in February 1856 a peace conference opened in Paris.

The Treaty of Paris, signed at the end of March, removed the immediate causes of the conflict, but provided no permanent settlement of the Eastern question. Russia surrendered her grip on the mouths of the Danube by abandoning southern Bessarabia; her claims to a protectorate over the Turkish Christians were set aside; the Dardanelles were closed to foreign ships of war, and Turkey's independence was guaranteed. Russia accepted the demilitarisation of the Black Sea, but only for the time being. Her expansion was checked, but she remained unappeased. Within twenty years Europe was nearly at war again over Russian ambitions in the Near East. The fundamental situation was unaltered: so long as Turkey was weak so long would her empire remain a temptation to Russian Imperialists.

With one exception few of the leading figures emerged from the Crimean War with enhanced reputations. Miss Florence Nightingale had been sent out in an official capacity by the Secretary-at-War, Sidney Herbert. She arrived at Scutari on the day before the Battle of Inkerman, and there organised the first base hospital of modern times. With few nurses and scanty equipment she reduced the death rate at Scutari from forty-two per hundred to twenty-two per thousand men. Her influence and example were far-reaching. The Red Cross movement, which started with the Geneva Convention of 1864, was the outcome of her work, as were great administrative reforms in civilian hospitals. She also favoured better girls' schools and devoted her attention to the founding of women's colleges. In an age of proud and domineering men she gave the women of the nineteenth century a new status, which revolutionised the social life of the country.

Florence Nightingale and her thirty-eight volunteer nurses revolutionised nursing methods by insisting on total cleanliness, which drastically reduced infection and thus lowered the death rate. Called "the lady with the lamp" by the wounded soldiers, Florence Nightingale was the founder of modern nursing and became the first woman to be awarded the British Order of Merit, in 1907.

CHAPTER 5

PALMERSTON

PALMERSTON, THOUGH NOW IN HIS SEVENTIES, presided over the English scene. With one short interval of Tory government, he was Prime Minister throughout the decade that began in 1855. Not long after the signing of peace with Russia he was confronted with another emergency which also arose in the East, in India, where suddenly there occurred a disturbing outbreak against British rule.

The causes of the Indian Mutiny lay deep in the past. India had been basking under the administration of the East India Company, with only a moderate degree of supervision from London. About the beginning of the nineteenth century a new generation of British administrators and soldiers appeared, austere, upright, Bible-reading men, who dreamt of Christianising and Europeanising the subcontinent. Hitherto the English, like the

Lord Palmerston (1784-1865), or "Old Pam" as he was affectionately known, believed that the British Constitution was the best in the world and that all countries could benefit from the lessons it provided.

Romans in the provinces of their empire, had a neutral policy on religion and no policy at all on Indian education. Regiments held parades in honour of Hindu deities, and Hindu and Muslim holidays were impartially and publicly observed. But in England respect for alien creeds gradually succumbed to the desire for proselytisation. For a time enlightened Hindu opinion seemed not unreceptive to elements of the Christian faith. *Suttee*, the burning of widows, *thuggee*, the strangling of travellers by fanatics who deemed it a religious duty, and female infanticide were suppressed. Largely owing to Macaulay, when he was a member of the governor-general's council, measures were taken to make English learning available to the higher-ranking Indians. All this however was unsettling, and played its part in the terrible events which now occurred.

A more immediate cause of the rising was a series of reverses suffered by the British. The Russian threat to India had begun to overhang the minds of Englishmen. It was in fact a gross exaggeration to suppose that Russian armies could have crossed the ranges of the Hindu-Kush in force and arrived in the Indus valley. But the menace seemed real at the time. When it was learnt that a small body of Russians had penetrated into the fringes of Afghanistan, a British expedition was dispatched in 1839 and a British candidate placed on the Afghan throne. The result was disaster. The country rose up in arms. In December 1841, under a promise of safe-conduct, the British garrison of some four thousand troops, accompanied by nearly three times as many women, children, and Afghan camp followers, began to withdraw through the snow and the mountain passes. The safe-conduct was violated, and only a handful of survivors reached India in the following January. A second expedition avenged the treachery in the following year, but the repute of European arms was deeply smitten and the massacre resounded throughout the peninsula.

Another defeat soon followed in the Punjab, the most northerly of the Indian provinces at that time. Here the warrior Sikhs, a reformed Hindu sect, forbidden to touch tobacco or cut their hair above the waist, had long held sway. Encouraged by the news from Afghanistan, and restless after the death of their great leader, Ranjit Singh, who had hitherto held them in check, they resolved to try their hand at invading the Company's territory. In 1845 they crossed the boundary, and were met and repulsed two hundred miles north of Delhi. The British installed a regency. Three years later the Sikhs tried to overthrow it. There was a desperate drawn battle deep within the province at Chilianwala, in which three British regiments lost their colours. Shortly afterwards the British forces redeemed their name and the Sikh army was destroyed. The Punjab was pacified by John and Henry Lawrence. These famous and splendidly resourceful brothers ruled with absolute power. They made landowners take a threefold oath: "Thou shalt not burn thy widow, thou shalt not kill thy daughters, thou shalt not bury alive thy lepers." They sent the Koh-i-noor diamond to Queen Victoria, and gained from the formidable warriors of the province an affection and loyalty for the British Crown which was to endure for nearly a century. Nevertheless, among the ill-disposed in other regions of India "Remember Chilianwala!" became a battle cry in the upheaval which was to come.

This was a period of confident expansion in India, generally undertaken by men on the spot and not always approved by opinion in Britain. Two other major annexations completed the extension of British rule. Possession of Sind, in the lower Indus valley, had been judged necessary to safeguard the command of the northwest coast. It was conquered by Sir Charles Napier, a veteran who had fought at Corunna. In England the magazine *Punch* commented sourly on this operation. It represented Napier as reporting the matter in a one-word telegram, "Peccavi" ("I have sinned"). Napier, unperturbed, proceeded to rule with absolute and benevolent power. He dealt with widow-burning by the simple expedient of placing a gibbet beside every pyre. "When men burn women alive we hang them," he said. Like the Punjab, Sind remained peaceful for many years. The other annexation was that of Oudh, on the borders of Bengal, where an Indian king had long oppressed his subjects. The Marquis of Dalhousie, appointed governor-general at the age of thirty-five, had no doubts about the benefits conferred on India by British rule and British skill. During his eight years of office he added principalities to the Company's dominion by applying what was called the "doctrine of lapse". This meant that when an Indian ruler died without an heir of his own blood his territory was forfeited. Adopted heirs were not allowed to inherit, though this had long been Hindu custom. In Oudh Dalhousie was more forthright. He bluntly declared that "the British Government would be guilty in the sight of God and man if it were any longer to aid in sustaining by its countenance an administration fraught with suffering to millions". He deposed the king and seized his province in 1856. Next year came the Mutiny, and much of the blame for provoking it was laid at Dalhousie's door.

Certainly a legacy of troubles confronted Dalhousie's successor, Lord Canning, most especially in the East India Company's Army of Bengal. This was largely composed of high-caste Hindus. This was bad for discipline. Brahmin privates would question the orders of NCOs of less exalted caste. The Company's British officers were often of poor quality and out of touch with their men, for the abler and more thrusting among them sought secondment to the more spacious fields of civil administration. There were grievances about pay and pensions. Other developments, unconnected with this military unrest, added their weight. By the 1850s railways, roads, posts, telegraphs, and schools were beginning to push their way across the countryside, and were thought by many Indians to threaten an ancient society whose inmost structure and spirit sprang from a rigid and unalterable caste system. If everyone used the same trains and the same schools, or

The British built a railway network in India which opened up the country and subsequently increased trade. This illustration shows an impressive railway station near Calcutta in 1867.

even the same roads, it was argued, how could caste survive? Indian monarchs were apprehensive and resentful of the recent annexations. Hatred smouldered at the repression of suttee. Unfounded stories spread that the Government intended to convert India forcibly to Christianity. The disasters in Afghanistan and the slaughter of the Sikh wars cast doubt on British invincibility. Then rumours began to flow that the cartridges for the new Enfield rifle were greased with the fat of pigs and cows, animals which Muslim and Hindu respectively were forbidden to eat. The cartridges had to be bitten before they could be inserted in the muzzle. Thus soldiers of both religions would be defiled. There was some truth in the story, for beef fat had been used in the London arsenal at Woolwich, though it was never used at the Indian factory at Dum-Dum, and as soon as the complaints began no tainted missiles were issued. Nevertheless the tale ran through the regiments in the spring of 1857 and there was much unrest. In April some cavalry troopers at Meerut were court-martialled and imprisoned for refusing to touch the cartridges, and on May 9 they were publicly stripped of their uniforms. Three regiments mutinied, killed their British officers, and marched on Delhi.

There was nothing at hand to stop them. South of the Punjab fewer than eleven full-strength battalions and ancillary forces, comprising in all about forty thousand British soldiers, were scattered across the vast peninsula, and even these were not on a war footing. The Indian troops outnumbered them by five to one and had most of the artillery. The hot weather had started, distances were great, transport was scarce, the authorities were unprepared. Nevertheless, when the British power was so weak, and India might have been plunged once again into the anarchy and bloodshed from which she had been gradually and painfully rescued, most of the populace remained aloof, and none of the leading Indian rulers joined the revolt. Of the three armies maintained by the East India Company only one, that of Bengal, was affected. Gurkhas from Nepal helped to quell the rising. The Punjab remained loyal, and its Sikhs and Muslims respected the colours and disarmed wavering regiments. The valley of the Ganges was the centre of the turmoil.

But at first all went with a rush. The magazine at Delhi was guarded by two British officers and six soldiers. They fought to the last, and when resistance was hopeless they blew it up. The mutineers killed every European in sight, seized the aged King of Delhi, now living in retirement as the Company's pensioner, and proclaimed him Mogul Emperor. The appeal failed and few Muslims rose to support it. For three weeks there was a pause, and then the mutiny spread. British officers would not believe in the disloyalty of their troops and many were murdered. Rightly perceiving that the key to the revolt lay in Delhi, the British mustered such forces as they could and seized the ridge overlooking the city. They were too few to make an assault, and for weeks in the height of summer three thousand troops, most of whom were British, held the fifty-foot eminence against an enemy twenty or thirty times their number. Early in August Brigadier Nicholson arrived with reinforcements from the Punjab, having marched nearly thirty miles a day for three weeks. Thus animated, the British attacked on September 14, and after six days' street-fighting, in which Nicholson was killed, the city fell. The king was sent to Burma. His two sons were taken prisoners, and shot after an attempt had been made to rescue them.

At Cawnpore, on the borders of Oudh, there was a horrible massacre. For twenty-one days nine hundred British and loyal Indians, nearly half of them women and children, were besieged and attacked by three thousand sepoys with the Nana Sahib, the dispossessed, adopted son of an Indian ruler, at their head. At length, on June 26, they were granted safe-conduct. As they were leaving by boat they were fired upon, and all the men were killed. Such women and children as survived the gunfire were cut to death with knives and the bodies thrown into a well. Two days later a relieving force under Sir Henry Havelock arrived. "Had any Christian bishop visited that scene of butchery when I saw it," wrote an eyewitness long afterwards, "I verily believe that he would have buckled on his sword." Here and elsewhere the British troops took horrible vengeance. Mutineers were blown from the mouths of cannon, sometimes with their bodies sewn up in the skins of cows and swine.

The rebels turned on Lucknow, the capital of Oudh. Here also there was a desperate struggle. Seventeen hundred troops, nearly half of them loyal sepoys, held the Residency, under Henry Lawrence, against sixty thousand rebels, for in Oudh, unlike most of India, the population joined the revolt. Food was short and there was much disease. On September 25 Havelock and his former battle comrade, James Outram, fought their way in, but were beset in their turn, Havelock dying of exhaustion a few days later. In November the siege was raised by Sir Colin Campbell, the new commander in chief appointed by Lord Palmerston. Campbell had seen service against Napoleon and had a distinguished record in the Crimean War. A fresh threat to Cawnpore compelled him to move on. Outram, reinforced, continued to hold out, and Lucknow was not finally liberated till the following March. No one knows what happened to the Nana Sahib. He disappeared forever into the Himalayan jungle.

Some twenty thousand Indian rebels attacked the city of Lucknow. This photograph shows the carnage inside the remains of what was once a grand imperial building.

Elsewhere the rising was more speedily crushed. Fighting, sporadic but often fierce, continued in the central provinces until the end of 1858, but on November 1 the Governor-General, "Clemency" Canning, derisively so-called for his mercifulness, proclaimed with truth that Queen Victoria was now sovereign of all India. Canning, a son of the renowned Foreign Secretary and Prime Minister, became the first Viceroy. The rule of the East India Company was abolished. This was the work of the short Conservative Government of Derby and Disraeli. Thus, after almost exactly a century, the advice which Clive had given to Pitt was accepted by the British Government. Henceforward there were to be no more annexations, no subsidiary treaties, no more civil wars. Religious toleration and equality before the law were promised to all. Indians for a generation and more were to look back on the Queen's Proclamation of 1858 as a Magna Carta.

The Indian Mutiny made, in some respects, a more lasting impact on England than the Crimean War. It paved the way for Empire. After it was over Britain gradually and consciously became a worldwide Imperial power.

But the scale of the Mutiny should not be exaggerated. Three-quarters of the troops remained loyal; barely a third of British territory was affected; the brunt of the outbreak was suppressed in the space of a few weeks. It was in no sense a national movement, or, as some later Indian writers have suggested, a patriotic struggle for freedom. The idea and ideal of the inhabitants of the subcontinent forming a single people and state was not to emerge for many years. But the easygoing ways of the eighteenth century were gone forever, and so were the missionary fervour and reforming zeal of the early Victorians and their predecessors. The English no longer looked on India as "home", or themselves as crusaders called to redeem the great multitudes. British administration became detached, impartial, efficient. Great progress was made and many material benefits were secured. The frontiers were guarded and the peace was kept. Starvation was subdued. The population vastly increased. The Indian Army, revived and reorganised, was to play a glorious part on Britain's side in two world wars. Nevertheless the atrocities and reprisals of the bloodstained months of the Mutiny left an enduring and bitter mark in the memory of both countries.

While these events unrolled in India the political scene in England remained confused. Peel's conversion to Free Trade had destroyed the party lines which he had done much to draw, and for twenty years governments of mixed complexion followed one another. Disraeli and Derby, having broken Peel, found that it took a long time to muster the remnant of the former Tory Protectionists into an effective political party. Rising men like Gladstone, who remained faithful to the Peel tradition, would have nothing to do with them, though on at least one occasion Disraeli tried hard to enlist Gladstone's cooperation. The Whigs, under Russell and Palmerston, felt that their main aims had already been accomplished. Palmerston was willing to make improvements in government, but large-scale changes were not to his mind. Russell hankered after a further measure of electoral reform, but that was the limit of his programme. Both conceived of themselves as guardians of the system that they had the fortune to head. In this attitude the two leaders, and Palmerston especially, were probably in harmony with mid-Victorian opinion. Radicalism in these years made little appeal to the voters. Prosperity was spreading through the land, and with it went a lull in the fiercer forms of political agitation.

Religion in its numerous varieties cast a soothing and uplifting influence on men's minds. More than half the population were regular attenders at church or chapel. Religious debate was earnest, sometimes acrimonious, but the contests it bred were verbal. Civil strife for the sake of religion was a thing of the past. When the Roman Catholic Church re-established its hierarchy of bishops in England there was vehement commotion and protest in London, but nothing amounting to riot.

The Church of England, earlier in the century, had been stirred from slumber by Evangelical zeal and the lofty ideas of the Oxford Movement. The Low Church and High Church parties, as they were called, strove eloquently for men's souls. The Church of Rome in England had also revived under the impulse of Catholic Emancipation, and was reinforced by the accession of a number of High Anglican clergy, including John Henry Newman, a profound and subtle thinker, later created a Cardinal.

Religious preoccupations were probably more widespread and deeply felt than at any time since the days of Cromwell. But thinking men were also disturbed by a new theory, long foreshadowed in the work of scientists, the theory of evolution. It was given classic expression in *The Origin of Species*, published by Charles Darwin in 1859. This book provoked doubt and perplexity among those who could no longer take literally the Biblical account of creation. But the theory of evolution, and its emphasis on the survival of the fittest in the history of life upon the globe, was a powerful

THE OXFORD DEBATE ON CHARLES DARWIN'S *ON THE ORIGIN OF SPECIES*

Charles Darwin's theories about evolution contradicted the story of the world's creation as it is recounted in Genesis. In 1860, the clergy confronted the scientists at Oxford. This account is taken from Alan Moorehead's biography, Darwin and the Beagle.

The clergy arrived at the meeting in strength; they were led by the formidable figure of Samuel Wilberforce, the Bishop of Oxford, a man whose impassioned eloquence was a little too glib for some people (he was known as "Soapy Sam"), but whose influence was very great indeed. Wilberforce announced beforehand that he was out to "smash Darwin". He was supported by the anatomist Richard Owen, who was a rabid anti-Darwinist, and who probably supplied the Bishop with scientific ammunition for his speech. Darwin was ill and could not come, but his old teacher, Professor Henslow, was in the chair, and he had two ardent champions in T.H. Huxley and the botanist Joseph Hooker.

By now Wilberforce had entered the hall with his attendant clergy about him, and he created something of a stir

Charles Darwin went on to publish The Descent of Man *in 1871. This renewed the public furore, and led to cartoons of the biologist portrayed as an ape.*

with his priestly clothes and his air of confident episcopal authority. Henslow called on him to speak, and he plunged at once with a fine flow of words into ridicule of Darwin's "Casual theory". Where were the proofs? Darwin was merely expressing sensational opinions, and they went flatly against the divine revelation of the Bible. This was no more than had been expected, but the Bishop on rising to the height of his peroration went too far. He turned to Huxley, who was sitting on the platform—an arresting figure in his top coat, with his high wing collar and his leonine black hair—and demanded to know if it was through his grandmother or his grandfather that he claimed to be descended from the apes.

It was not really the moment for heavy sarcasm, and Huxley was not a man to provoke lightly. Now when he heard how ignorantly the Bishop presented his case, ending with his "insolent question", he said in an undertone, "The Lord hath delivered him into my hands." He would certainly prefer, he said, to be descended from an ape rather than from a man like Wilberforce who prostituted the gifts of culture and eloquence to the service of prejudice and falsehood. . . .

INDUSTRIAL CITIES

In 1837, when Victoria came to the throne, there were six cities outside London with a population of a hundred thousand or more: in 1800 there had been none. By 1891 there were twenty-three in England and Wales alone, and two of the greatest, sharply contrasting with each other, were in Scotland: Edinburgh, the "Athens of the North", and Glasgow, a Victorian city of commerce and industry.

Industrial cities were thought of as a new kind of social phenomenon. There had been great capital cities before, of which London was the biggest in the world, and great seaports, like Bristol and Liverpool; but the city of workshops, factories, railways—and smoke—was described in the year 1840 as "a system of life constructed according to new principles".

It was certainly a more socially segregated city than the older and smaller cities of the pre-industrial world. Disraeli wrote of "two nations"—the rich and the poor—dwelling side by side within the same city, and another writer declared, "a hovel in one of the suburbs which they know least would be as strange to most Londoners as a village in the African forests".

Clergymen and doctors were links between the two nations, although the claims of religion were more difficult to establish in the city than they were in the village, and conditions of public health varied notoriously between one part of a city and another.

Industrial cities shared many problems, but no two cities handled their difficulties alike. In particular, there was a sharp contrast, drawn by the Victorians themselves, between Manchester and Birmingham. The former city expanded hugely in the 1840s, with much-publicised class divisions, but in Birmingham there were many small workshops and it was considerably easier for working men to become employers. Moreover, Manchester depended on steam power long before a similar state of affairs came into existence in Birmingham.

LARGE NUMBERS OF PEOPLE *were crowded into terraces in city centres near their places of work. In Sheffield, shown above in a watercolour by William Ibbitt in 1854, this meant living in the smoky pollution of the blast furnaces used for turning iron into cutlery steel. The process involved keeping the furnaces at white-heat for eight or nine days at a time. The artisans' houses were built "back to back" round a courtyard in which a single tap supplied water on certain days of the week, and a single earth closet served the needs of the twenty or more families. The population of Sheffield was one hundred and thirty-five thousand in 1850, three times that of 1800. By 1900 it had tripled again.*

THE WORKHOUSE *was the last resort for the elderly, disabled and unemployed. The inmates were given a subsistence diet of gruel, bread and cheese in order to deter most people from seeking admittance. This rare Victorian picture of a workhouse, "Eventide" (above) is by Sir Hubert von Herkomer and can be seen in the Walker Art Gallery, Liverpool. It was painted in 1878 from observations made at the Westminster Workhouse in London.*

URBAN BUILDING *reached unprecedented proportions in the nineteenth century. Many workers' houses were jerrybuilt, but organisations like the Society for Improving the Conditions of the Labouring Classes designed model cottages. In 1875, however, the Artisans' and Labourers' Dwellings Improvements Act allowed local councils to clear slums and to* embark *on schemes of urban redevelopment. Birmingham, following in the wake of Glasgow, had a most imaginative scheme. There were large numbers of new shops and places of entertainment and leisure. The drawing (above) appeared in* The Graphic *magazine in 1886 to illustrate the improvements in the centre of Birmingham.*

QUALID TENEMENTS *huddle beneath the railway in this engraving (above) by the French rtist, Gustave Doré (1832–83). Entitled "Over London by Rail", it shows the overrowding, pollution and monotony that, togeher with poor sanitation, encouraged the* rapid spread of disease. The dullness of both factory and home life could lead to exhaustion, despair and drunkenness among the work force who lived in these nightmarish social conditions, and upon whom much of Victorian industry relied.*

MUNICIPAL REFORMER *Joseph Chamberlain (above), nicknamed "the gas-and-water Socialist" for his pioneering efforts in Birmingham. At sixteen he entered his father's shoemaking business and two years later joined his cousin's hardware firm in Birmingham. As Mayor of Birmingham (1873–75) he enabled the Council to buy the gas and waterworks, clear slums and build new streets, the most famous of which was Corporation Street. There were fine civic buildings, a free library and art gallery.*

adjunct to mid-Victorian optimism. It lent fresh force to the belief in the forward march of mankind.

Palmerston seemed to his fellow-countrymen the embodiment of their own healthy hopes. He had lost none of his old vigour in chastising foreign governments, and his patriotic sentiments appealed to the self-confidence of the nation. They did not always appeal to the Queen and Prince Albert, who resented his habit of sending off sharply worded dispatches without consulting them. But it was Palmerston's desire, for all his strong language and sometimes hasty action, to keep the general peace in Europe. For this reason the Liberal movements in foreign countries which engaged his sympathy also sometimes gave him reason for anxiety.

The greatest of the European movements in these years was the cause of Italian unity. This long-cherished dream of the Italian peoples was at last realised, though only partially, in 1859 and 1860. As one small Italian state after another cast out their alien rulers, and merged under a single monarchy, widespread enthusiasm was aroused in England. Garibaldi and his thousand volunteers, who overturned the detested Bourbon government in Sicily and Naples with singular dash and speed, were acclaimed as heroes in London. These bold events were welcome to Palmerston and his Foreign Secretary, Russell, but non-intervention was still their policy.

In home politics meanwhile a sublime complacency enveloped the Government. Palmerston, like Melbourne before him, did not believe in too much legislation. Good humour and common sense distinguished him. As the novelist Trollope well said, he was "a statesman for the moment. Whatever was not wanted now, whatever was not practicable now, he drove quite out of his mind." This practical outlook found no favour among the younger and more thrusting members of the House of Commons. Disraeli, chafing on the Opposition benches, vented his scorn and irritation on this last of the eighteenth-century politicians. "His external system," he once told the House, "is turbulent and aggressive that his rule at home may be tranquil and unassailed. Hence arise excessive expenditure, heavy taxation, and the stoppage of all social improvement. His scheme of conduct is so devoid of all political principle that when forced to appeal to the people his only claim to their confidence is his name." Peel's disciples and followers were no less despairing and powerless. So long as leadership remained in the hands of Palmerston, Russell, and the Whig nobility there could be little hope of advance towards the Liberalism of which they dreamt.

The Tories were little better off. Their nominal head was Lord Derby, who could be brilliant in debate, but was apt to regard politics as an unpleasant duty imposed upon the members of his class. His real interest lay in horse-racing, and he also produced an excellent translation of Homer. Disraeli had become the leader of his party in the House of Commons. His struggle for power was hard and uphill. A Jew at the head of a phalanx of country gentlemen was an unusual sight in English politics. After the repeal of the Corn Laws protection was not only dead, but, as Disraeli himself said, damned, and he and Derby had agreed to discard it as a party principle. But the search for a new theme was long, painful, and frustrating. Meanwhile, he had to play the part of Derby's lieutenant, and their spells of office in 1852 and 1858 were brief and uneventful. Disraeli more than once sought an alliance with the radicals, and promised them that he would oppose armaments and an aggressive foreign policy. Colonies, he even declared, were "a millstone round our necks". But their chief spokesman, John Bright, was under no illusions. The shrewd Quaker was not to be caught. "Mr Disraeli," he said, "is a man who does what may be called the conjuring for his party. He is what among a tribe of Red Indians would be called the mystery-man." And that was the end of that. Thus foiled, Disraeli returned to his attack on the Whigs. He was convinced that the only way to destroy them was by extending the franchise yet further so as to embrace the respectable artisans and counter the hostility of the middle classes. In his youth he had dreamt of uniting the two nations, the rich and the poor, and the 1850s saw the slow emergence of a practical doctrine of Tory democracy. But Disraeli's idea took time to find acceptance.

Standing apart both from the Whigs and Derby's Tories were the Peelites, of whom the most notable was William Gladstone. He too was in search of a new theme. The son of a rich Liverpool merchant with slave-owning interests in the West Indies, Gladstone came from the same class as his old leader, and believed, like him, in the new arguments for Free Trade. Though admired as an administrator and an orator, his contemporaries considered him wanting in judgment and principle, but in fact he was awaking to the political potentialities of the English middle class. Despite his preoccupations with theology, he comprehended the minds of the new voters better than his colleagues and understood the workings of party better than Peel. "Oxford on the surface, but Liverpool underneath"—such was a contemporary judgment. But his progress was slow. Chancellor of the Exchequer at the beginning of the Crimean War, he then faded into Opposition.

In 1859, aged nearly fifty, Gladstone joined the Whigs and his long pilgrimage into the Liberal camp was over. His decision was made on an issue of foreign policy, but he again concentrated on finance. As Chancellor of the Exchequer under Palmerston his golden period began—great Budget speeches in the House of Commons, a superb handling of administrative detail, a commercial treaty with France, which opened a new era in Free Trade, and demands for retrenchment in military affairs, which brought him into conflict with his Prime Minister. His finance was a remarkable success. Three brilliant Budgets reduced taxation. Trade was rapidly expanding, and it was soon apparent who would succeed eventually to the leadership of the party. In 1865, in his eighty-first year, Palmerston died. "Gladstone," he declared in his last days, "will soon have it all his own way, and whenever he gets my place we shall have strange doings." The old Whig was right. The eighteenth century died with him. The later Victorian age demanded a new leader, and at long last he had arrived. But the Whigs still hesitated. Gladstone, like Disraeli, wanted to extend the franchise to large sections of the working classes: he was anxious to capture the votes of the new electorate. He prevailed upon the Government, now headed by Russell, to put forward a Reform Bill, but it was defeated on an amendment and the Cabinet resigned. Minority administrations under Derby and Disraeli followed, which lasted for two and a half years.

Disraeli now seized his chance. He introduced a fresh Reform Bill in 1867, which he skilfully adapted to meet the wishes of the House. There was a redistribution of seats in favour of the large industrial towns, and nearly a million new voters were added to an existing electorate of about the same number. The Tories were nervous at this startling advance from their original plan. In many towns the working classes would now be in

This Punch *cartoon records the successful enactment of the second Reform Bill of 1867 during the third term of Lord Derby's Conservative government. As Chancellor of the Exchequer, Benjamin Disraeli had been largely responsible for the introduction and successful outcome of the Bill, but the magazine's namesake regards him with scepticism. Almost one million new voters were enfranchised by the Act, mainly from the industrial towns, but despite this Disraeli and the Tories failed to win the election of 1868.*

the majority at elections. Derby called it "a leap in the dark", and even the radicals were anxious about how the uneducated masses would behave. But this immediately became clear. The carrying of the second Reform Bill so soon after the death of Palmerston opened a new era in English politics. New issues and new methods began to emerge. In February 1868 Derby resigned from the leadership of the party and Disraeli was at last Prime Minister—as he put it, "at the top of the greasy pole". He had to hold a General Election. The new voters gave their overwhelming support to his opponents, and Gladstone, now leader of the Liberal Party, formed the strongest administration that England had seen since the days of Peel.

CHAPTER 6

THE MIGRATION OF THE PEOPLES

O CCUPATION OF THE EMPTY LANDS of the globe was vehemently accelerated by the fall of Napoleon. The long struggle against France had stifled or arrested the expansion of the English-speaking peoples, and the ships and the men who might have founded the second British Empire had been consumed in twenty years of world war. There had been no time for dreams of emigration, and no men to spare if it had been possible. Suddenly all this was changed by the decision at Waterloo. Once again the oceans were free. No enemies threatened in Europe. Fares were cheap and transport was plentiful. The result was the most spectacular migration of human beings of which history has yet had record and a vast enrichment of the trade and industry of Great Britain.

During the years following the 1846 Irish potato famine many Irish people were forced to emigrate to the United States of America. They travelled cheaply, often taking little with them except a bitter hatred of the English.

Of course the process took time to gather way. But the road had been pointed by the grim convict settlements in Australia, by the loyalists from the United States who had moved to Canada, and by traders, explorers, missionaries, and whalers all over the temperate zones of the earth. News began to spread among the masses that fertile, unoccupied and habitable lands still existed, in which white men could dwell in peace and liberty, and perhaps could even better themselves. The increasing population of Great Britain added to the pressure. In 1801 it was about eleven million. Thirty years later it was sixteen million, and by 1871 it was ten million more. Fewer people died at birth or in early childhood. The numbers grew, and the flow began: in the 1820s a quarter of a million emigrants, in the 1830s half a million, by the middle of the century a million and a half, until sixty-five years after Waterloo no fewer than eight million people had left the British Isles.

The motives, methods, and characters of the movement were very different from those which had sustained the plantations of the seventeenth century. Famine drove at least a million Irishmen to the United States and elsewhere. Gold lured hardy fortune-hunters to Australia, and to the bleak recesses of Canada, where they discovered a more practical if less respectable El Dorado than had dazzled the Elizabethan adventurers. Hunger for land and for the profits of the wool trade beckoned the more sober and well-to-do. All this was largely accomplished in the face of official indifference and sometimes of hostility. The American War of Independence had convinced most of the ruling classes in Britain that colonies were undesirable possessions. The Government was interested in strategic bases, but the sooner these new lands became completely independent the better and cheaper for the taxpayer in England. Anyway, Greece was more interesting news than New Zealand, and the educated public were much more concerned about the slave trade than the squalors of the emigrant ships. Thus, as in India, the Second British Empire was founded almost by accident, and with small encouragement from any of the main political parties.

Of the new territories Canada was the most familiar and the nearest to the United Kingdom. Her Maritime Provinces had long sent timber to Britain, and rather than return with empty holds the shipowners were content to transport emigrants for a moderate fare. Once they landed, however, the difficulties and the distances were very great. The Maritime Provinces lived a life very much of their own, and many emigrants chose to push on into Lower Canada, or, as it is now called, the Province of Quebec. Pitt in 1791 had sought to solve the racial problems of Canada by dividing her into two parts. In Lower Canada the French were deeply rooted, a compact, alien community, untouched by the democratic ideas of liberal or revolutionary Europe, and holding stubbornly to their own traditions and language. Beyond them, to the northwest, lay Upper Canada, the modern Province of Ontario, settled by some of the sixty thousand Englishmen who had left the United States towards the end of the eighteenth century rather than live under the American republic. These proud folk had out of devotion to the British Throne abandoned most of their possessions, and been rewarded with the unremunerative but honourable title of United Empire Loyalists. The Mohawk tribe, inspired by the same sentiments, had journeyed with them. They had hacked a living space out of the forests, and dwelt lonely and remote, cut off from Lower Canada by the rapids of the St Lawrence, and watchful against incursions from the United States. Then there was a vast emptiness till one reached a few posts on the Pacific which traded their wares to China.

These communities, so different in tradition, character, and race, had been rallied into temporary unity by invasion from the United States. French, English, and native Indians fought against the Americans, and repulsed them in the three-year struggle between 1812 and 1814. Then trouble began. The French in Lower Canada feared that the immigrants

This illustration of Fort Garry in about 1821 shows one of the fur-trading posts of the Hudson's Bay Company. The influx of European immigrants was a growing problem for the Company, as new agricultural settlers encroached upon the traditional hunting lands.

would outnumber and dominate them. The Loyalists in Upper Canada welcomed new settlers who would increase the price of land but were reluctant to treat them as equals. Moreover, the two Provinces started to quarrel with each other over taxes. Differences over religion added to the irritations. French politicians made vehement speeches, and the Assembly in Lower Canada began to behave like the legislatures of the American colonies, refusing to vote money for the salaries of royal judges and permanent officials. In Upper Canada the new settlers struggled for political equality with the Loyalists. Liberals wanted to make the executive responsible to the Assembly and talked wildly of leaving the Empire.

In 1837 both Provinces rebelled, Lower Canada for a month and Upper Canada for a week. There were mobs, firing by troops, shifty compromises, and a very few executions. Everything was on a small scale, but it made the British Government realise that Canadian affairs required attention. The Whig leaders in London were wiser than George III. They perceived that a tiny minority of insurgents could lead to great troubles, and in 1838 Lord Durham was sent to investigate, assisted by Edward Gibbon Wakefield. His instructions were vague and simple, "To put things right", and meanwhile the Canadian Constitution was suspended by Act of Parliament. Durham was a radical, brilliant, decisive, and hot-tempered. Wakefield was an active theorist on Imperial affairs whose misconduct with a couple of heiresses had earned him a prison sentence and compelled him to spend the rest of his public life behind the scenes. Durham stayed only a few months. His high-handed conduct in dealing with disaffected Canadians aroused much criticism. However, he produced a famous report in which he diagnosed and proclaimed the root causes of the trouble and advocated responsible government, carried on by ministers commanding the confidence of the popular Assembly, a united Canada, and planned settlement of the unoccupied lands. These recommendations were largely put into effect by the Canada Act of 1840, which was the work of Lord John Russell.

Thereafter Canada's progress was swift and peaceful. Her population had risen from about half a million in 1815 to a million and a quarter in 1838. A regular steamship service with the British Isles and cheap transatlantic postage were established in the same year. There were doubts in England at the novel idea of allowing colonial Assemblies to choose and eject their own ministers, but the appointment of Durham's son-in-law, Lord Elgin, as Governor-General in 1847 was decisive. Elgin believed, like Durham, that the Governor should represent the sovereign and remain in the background of politics. He appointed and dismissed ministers according to the wishes of the Assembly. For this he was blamed or applauded, and even pelted with eggs and stones, according to how it pleased or angered either side. But when he laid down his office seven years later the principle had been firmly accepted by Canadians of all persuasions that popular power must march with popular responsibility. There was hardly any talk now of leaving the Empire or dividing Canada into separate and sovereign units or joining the American republic. On the contrary, the Oregon Treaty with the United States in 1846 extended the 49th parallel right across the continent as a boundary between the two countries and gave the whole of Vancouver Island to Great Britain.

In the mid-century a movement for the federation of all the Canadian provinces began to grow. The recent Civil War in the United States between

An early "Beaver" stamp designed by Sir Sandford Fleming shows two objects of significance to the young Dominion of Canada which was formed in 1867: the beaver and the British crown.

the North and South, helped to convince Canadians that all was not perfect in their neighbours' Constitution, and the victory of the North also aroused their fears that the exultant Union might be tempted to extend its borders farther still. Canada had already turned her gaze westward. Between the Province of Ontario and the Rocky Mountains lay a thousand miles of territory, uninhabited save by a few settlers in Manitoba, a roaming-place for Indians, trappers, and wild animals. Discharged soldiers from the Civil War had already made armed raids across the border, and Congress had declared itself powerless to arrest them. Might not the Americans even establish a kind of squatters' right to the prairies? The soil was believed to be fertile and was said to offer a living for white men. No one ruled over it except the Hudson's Bay Company, and the Company, believing that agriculture would imperil its fur trade, was both hostile to settlers and jealous of its own authority. In 1856, however, the discovery of gold on the Fraser River had precipitated a rush of fortune hunters to the Pacific coast. The Company's officials had proved powerless to control the turmoil, and the Government in London had been compelled to extend the royal sovereignty to this distant shore. Thus was born the Crown colony of British Columbia, which soon united with the island of Vancouver and demanded and obtained self-rule. But between it and Ontario lay a no-man's-land, and something must be done if it was not to fall into the hands of the United States.

These considerations prompted the British North America Act of 1867, which created the first of the self-governing British Dominions beyond the seas. The Provinces of Ontario, Quebec, New Brunswick, and Nova Scotia were the founding members. They adopted a federal constitution. All powers not expressly reserved to the Provinces of Canada were assumed by the central Government: the Governor-General, representing the monarch, ruled through ministers drawn from the majority in her Canadian House of Commons, and Members of the House were elected in numbers proportionate to the population they represented. Thus the way was made easy for the absorption of new territories, and on the eve of her railway age and westward expansion the political stability of Canada was assured.

When the Parliament of the new Dominion first met, its chief anxiety was about the western lands. Its members looked to the future, and it is convenient here to chart the results of their foresight. The obvious, immediate step was to buy out the Hudson's Bay Company. The Company kept its trading rights, and indeed retains them to this day, but it surrendered its territorial sovereignty to the Crown. The process was not accomplished without bloodshed. There was a brief revolt in Manitoba, where Indian half-breeds thought that their freedom was endangered, but order was soon restored. Manitoba became a Province of the Dominion in 1870, and in the next year British Columbia was also admitted. By themselves however these constitutional steps would not have sufficed to bind the broad stretches of Canada together. The challenging task that faced the Dominion was to settle and develop her empty western lands before the immigrant tide from America could flood across the 49th parallel. The answer was a promise to build a transcontinental railway.

It proved difficult to fulfil. Capital was scarce, investors were timid, politics were tangled, and much of the country was unknown. At length however a Scotsman, Lord Strathcona, carried out the plan. Helped by

This illustration is from Uncle Tom's Cabin *by Harriet Beecher Stowe, a novel that helped stir the conscience of Americans on the question of slavery. After the victory of the North in the American Civil War, slavery was brought to an end in the United States.*

This railway engine of 1876 was built to the standard Canadian Pacific Railway design. Regular service between Montreal and Port Moody began in June 1886 and trains consisted of a sleeping car, dining car, first-class coach and two colonist cars.

Cape Town was the capital city of the Dutch Cape of Good Hope Colony until the British finally took over in 1814. The city, which lies at the bottom of Table Mountain, was founded in 1652 by Jan van Riebeek as a supply depot for the Dutch East India Company.

government funds, the work was finished in five years, and the Canadian Pacific Railway was opened in 1885. Other lines sprang up, and corn, soon counted in millions of bushels a year, began to flow in from the prairies. Canada had become a nation, and shining prospects lay before her.

South Africa, unlike America, had scanty attractions for the early colonists and explorers. As the halfway house to the Indies, many broke their voyage there, but few cared to stay. The Gulf of St Lawrence made it easy to reach the interior of Canada, but the coastline of South Africa, short of natural harbours and navigable rivers, mostly consisted of cliffs and sandhills washed by strong currents and stormy seas. Inland a succession of mountain ranges, running parallel to the coast, barred the way. Few lands have been more difficult for Europeans to enter.

In the seventeenth century the fleets of the Dutch East India Company, sailing for the Indies or returning home to Amsterdam and Rotterdam, were the most frequent visitors to the Cape. The establishment of a permanent settlement was discussed, but nothing was done till 1652, when, at the height of their power, the Dutch sent Jan van Riebeek, a young ship's surgeon, with three ships to take possession of Table Bay. Colonisation was no part of the plan: they merely wanted to found a port of call for the Company's ships.

The change came at the turn of the seventeenth century, under the governorship of Simon van der Stel and his son William Adriaan. They encouraged settlers to come out from Holland and take up grants of land, and by 1707 there were over fifteen hundred free burghers. Not all were Dutch; many were Huguenots, Germans, or Swedes, driven into exile by religious persecution; but the Dutch gradually assimilated them. The little community was served and sustained by a local population of negro slaves.

Throughout the eighteenth century the colony prospered and grew. By the end of the century the population numbered about fifteen thousand, and there were three areas of settlement. Cape Town, or "Little Paris" as the settlers called it, was a town and port of five thousand inhabitants, and the Company's headquarters. The agricultural coast-belt near the Cape peninsula offered the farmers a limited prosperity, and life was easy, though primitive. Finally there was the inland plateau and remoter coast-belt, where dwelt the frontiersmen, restless, hard, self-reliant, narrow-minded, isolated from society, and impatient of the restraints of civilised government.

But Napoleon's wars ruined the Dutch trade, swept the Dutch ships from the seas, and overthrew the Dutch state. Holland had no longer the power

to protect her possessions, and when the Dutch were defeated by the French and the puppet-state of the Batavian Republic was established, the British seized Cape Colony as enemy territory. It was finally ceded to them under the peace settlement of 1814.

At first they met with no great hostility. There was no deliberate policy of Anglicisation, and the Cape kept most of its Dutch customs and traditions. The British dealt forcefully with the frontiers, where the settlers were in contact and conflict with a great southward migration of the Bantu peoples from Central Africa. Fighting between the Dutch and the natives had broken out in 1779. Thus began a long succession of local wars, lasting for a hundred years, in which the settlers, scattered in isolated farms over vast stretches of country, found it difficult to defend themselves.

The British decided that the only way to secure the eastern boundary, the Fish River, was to colonise the border with British settlers, and between 1820 and 1821 nearly five thousand of them were brought out from Great Britain. This emigration coincided with a change of policy. Convinced that South Africa was now destined to become a permanent part of the British Empire, the Government resolved to make it as English as they could. English began to replace Dutch as the official language. In 1828 the judicial system was remodelled on the English pattern, and the English began to dominate the churches and the schools. Thus was born a division which Canada had surmounted. With the same religion and kindred political and social traditions, British and Boers nevertheless plunged into racial strife. British methods of government created among the Boers a more bitter antagonism than in any other Imperial country except Ireland.

Anglicisation was not only ill-conceived, it was unsuccessful. The English were to discover, as the Spaniards had learnt in the sixteenth century, that no race has ever clung more tenaciously to its own culture and institutions than the Dutch, and the only result of the new policy was to harden differences of opinion, especially on the native question. At this time there was much enthusiasm in England for good works, and English missionaries had been active in South Africa since the early years of the century. The missionaries believed and preached that black men were the equals of white men; the settlers regarded the natives primarily as farmhands and wanted to control them as strictly as possible. When the missionaries got slavery abolished in 1833 the settlers were indignant at such interference, which meant a scarcity of labour, and a weakening of their authority and prestige.

The first crisis came in 1834. The settlement of the Fish River area brought no security, and hordes of Bantu swept over the frontier, laying waste the country and destroying the farms. The Governor, Sir Benjamin D'Urban, drove them back, and to prevent another attack he annexed the territory between the Rivers Keiskamma and Kei, expelled the native raiders, and compensated the settlers by offering them land in this new province, which was named after Queen Adelaide. This roused the missionaries, and they persuaded the Colonial Secretary, Lord Glenelg, to repudiate D'Urban and abandon the new province. The settlers lost all compensation, and insult was added to injury when it became known that Glenelg considered that the natives had ample justification for the war into which they had rushed. Thus was provoked the Great Trek.

In small parties, accompanied by their women and children and driving their cattle before them, about five thousand Boers set out into the unknown,

The Great Trek of the Boers (1836-37) was undertaken to escape British domination in the Cape Colony. The interior was difficult to traverse, as shown in this illustration, and the Trekkers were attacked by Zulus. An eleven-year-old boy on the Trek was later to become the Boer President, Paul Kruger.

like the Children of Israel seeking the Promised Land. They were soon followed by many others. Some journeyed over a thousand miles to the banks of the Limpopo, attacked by the Matabele and the Zulu, enduring thirst and famine; yet in the unyielding spirit of their Calvinist religion they marched on. The Great Trek was one of the remarkable feats of the nineteenth century, and its purpose was to shake off British rule forever.

For long their fortunes looked dark. It was the time of the Mfecane, the "crushing" of the other native tribes by the military empire of the Zulus under Chaka and his successor Dingaan. The Zulu massacre of thousands of natives gave the Boers room to move, but they moved in great peril. In many lonely places within the laager of their ox-wagons they faced the wild onslaught of the Zulu warriors, and not until December 1838 did they crush Dingaan's forces in a great battle at Blood River. After their victory they established the Republic of Natal around the little town of Pietermaritzburg, with Andries Pretorius as its first president.

Their freedom was brief. The British refused to recognise the Republic, and after a short struggle in 1845 made it a province of Cape Colony. There remained the Voortrekkers on the plateau farther west, now reinforced by many refugees from Natal. Here too the British intervened. In the year 1848 Sir Harry Smith, a brave and energetic soldier who had served under Wellington, annexed the country between the Orange and the Vaal Rivers, defeated Pretorius at Boomplaats, and left only scattered Boer settlements across the Vaal outside the Colony.

Soon afterwards there was trouble with the tribes beyond the Orange River, and in particular with the Basuto. In Natal the problem had been met by creating native reserves and re-establishing the old tribal hierarchies under the indirect supervision of the Government. But the Government in London did not care to extend its responsibilities, and in 1852 it recognised the independence of the Transvaal settlers. Two years later, in accordance with the Convention of Bloemfontein, the British withdrew from beyond the Orange River and the Orange Free State was formed. Political dissolution went farther: both Queen Adelaide Province and Natal were made into separate colonies administered directly by the Colonial Office. The old colony of the Cape meanwhile prospered, as the production of wool increased by leaps and bounds, and in 1853 an Order in Council established representative institutions in the colony, with a Parliament in Cape Town, though without the grant of full responsible government. Here we may leave South African history for a spell of uneasy peace.

CHAPTER 7

AUSTRALIA AND NEW ZEALAND

AUSTRALIA HAS A LONG HISTORY in the realms of human imagination. From the days of Herodotus mankind has had its legends of distant lands, seen for a moment on the horizon, inhabited by strange monsters and rich with the fabulous wealth of Solomon's Ophir and Tarshish. The wonder-loving age of the sixteenth century delighted in such tales, and men who made the long voyage to the East round the Cape of Good Hope talked mysteriously of the islands of King Solomon. How the ships of the King of Israel in the tenth century before Christ could have reached the South Pacific Ocean is beyond conjecture. But the geographers and navigators of the Renaissance conceived themselves to be inspired by Biblical example. In the sixteenth-century maps of the Dieppe cartographers a great southern continent, "Java la Grande", is marked in the Pacific. In 1568 Alvaro de Mendaña and Pedro Sarmiento de Gamboa discovered what they called the Solomon Islands. The name they gave them shows the strength of the belief. Yet the sixteenth century had ended before landfall was made in Australia by Europeans, and the men who found it were hardheaded, unromantic Dutch traders.

Their voyages to Java and Sumatra brought the Dutch close to the northern shores of the newest continent, but despite Tasman's great expedition in 1642 they avoided it when they could. They knew it was an evil coast on which their vessels crossing the Indian Ocean were too often driven by adverse winds. The extent of the continent was not accurately known until the middle of the eighteenth century, when Captain James Cook made three voyages between 1768 and 1779, in which he circumnavigated New Zealand, sighted the great Antarctic icefields, discovered the Friendly Islands, the New Hebrides, New Caledonia, and Hawaii, and charted the eastern coastline of Australia.

Cook was a surveyor trained in the Royal Navy. His reports were official, accurate, and detailed. His news reached Britain at a timely moment. English convicts had long been transported to America, but since the War of Independence the Government had nowhere to send them. Why not to the new continent? In January 1788 seven hundred and seventeen convicts were anchored in Botany Bay. A hundred and ninety-eight were women. The Bay had been so named by Sir Joseph Banks, a distinguished amateur of science, who accompanied Cook on one of his voyages. The convicts were soon moved a few miles north to Port Jackson, within the magnificent expanse of Sydney Harbour. Famine crouched above the settlement, and for long the colony could not supply all its own food. Without training, capital, or the desire to work, the forgers and thieves, poachers and Irish rebels, criminals and political exiles, had neither the will nor the ability to fit themselves to the new land. "The convict barracks of New South Wales," wrote an Australian governor, "remind me of the monasteries of Spain. They contain a population of consumers who produce nothing." The region had been named by Captain Cook after South Wales. He thought he had detected a resemblance in coastline. But hard-working Wales and its Antipodean namesake had very little else in common at the time.

There were of course a few free settlers from the first, but the full migratory wave did not reach Australia till the 1820s. Driven by the postwar distress in Great Britain and attracted by the discovery of rich pasture in the hinterland of New South Wales, English-speaking emigrants began to trickle into the empty subcontinent and rapidly transformed the character and life of the early communities. The population changed from about fifteen thousand convicts and twenty-one thousand free settlers in 1828 to twenty-seven thousand convicts and over a hundred thousand free settlers in 1841. Free men soon demanded, and got, free government. Transportation to New South Wales was finally abolished in 1840, and two years later a Legislative Council was set up.

Wool founded the prosperity of the country. In 1797 a retired army

Captain James Cook (1728-79) first dropped anchor in Australia on April 28, 1770, in a bay so rich and fertile that it became known as Botany Bay. Captain Cook later met his death in Hawaii, killed by natives who then gave him a ceremonial burial.

Transportation of convicts to Australia began in 1778. The sentence was often imposed for minor offences such as stealing. During the thirteen-thousand-mile voyage, convicts were locked up in the ships' holds and only allowed up on deck for air for a short period each day. The picture shows a typical hold on HMS Success.

Life for convicts in Australia was hard. They provided cheap labour for the colonists and, working in organised, guarded chain gangs, they built many of the country's towns and roads. Some convicts were also assigned as servants and labourers to a "master".

officer, John MacArthur, had obtained a few merino sheep from the Cape of Good Hope, and his breeding experiments in due course established the famous Australian flocks. The turning-point had been the discovery of the Bathurst Plains, beyond the Blue Mountains. Here and to the south of Sydney, and on the Darling Downs to the north, were great sheep-runs, mile after mile of lonely grazing land, inhabited only by a few shepherds and thousands upon thousands of silent, soft-footed sheep moving even farther into the interior. The flocks multiplied swiftly: by 1850 there were more than sixteen million sheep in Australia. The wool trade for the year was worth nearly two million pounds in sterling.

The British Government however distrusted sheep-farming. Not only did it claim that all land under British rule was Crown property, but the Colonial Office was much influenced by Gibbon Wakefield's advocacy of systematic colonisation. Wakefield maintained that to allow individuals to spread haphazard into the interior would hinder administration and reduce the value of land already settled. His theories had much to commend them, but were quite unsuited to Australia. A series of Land Acts, designed to make land more difficult to obtain by enforcing a minimum of price, soon broke down. "Squatters", who needed thousands of acres for their sheep-runs and neither could nor would pay a pound, or even five shillings, for their grazing, struck out into the emptiness and took what they wanted, arguing with force that the land belonged to the people of the colony and that they should be given every facility to occupy it. The Colonial Office surrendered to the pressure of events, and in 1847 the British Government authorised the granting of pastoral leases for a term of years, at the end of which the squatter was to have the right to purchase the land at its unimproved value.

Long before 1850 the settlement of other parts of Australia had begun. The first to be made was in the island of Tasmania, or Van Diemen's Land as it was then called; at Hobart in 1804, and two years later at Launceston. Like New South Wales, Tasmania at first encountered many difficulties. The penal settlements at Macquarie Harbour and Port Arthur had evil reputations; rule was by terror and the labour-gang, and many convicts escaped and lived by bushranging, attacking lonely houses at night, and raiding stock-farms when the men were away. Unlike the rest of Australia, where the aboriginal inhabitants, few in number, scattered over vast areas, and, very primitive, scarcely resisted the white settlers, Tasmania had aborigines who were fairly numerous and comparatively advanced. Their

Port Arthur was one of the most notorious penal settlements in Australia. Rigid punishments were needed to maintain control, and vicious floggings and many hangings took place.

defeat was inevitable; their end was tragic. The Tasmanian tribes were extinct by the beginning of the twentieth century.

Tasmania developed in much the same way as New South Wales, and had become a separate colony in 1824. Prosperity came from wool and whaling, and brought a solid upsurge in population. In 1820 there were six thousand five hundred settlers, mostly convicts; twenty years later the population numbered sixty-eight thousand and was mostly free. An elected Legislative Council was granted in 1850, and the abolition of transportation in 1853 placed Tasmania on an equal footing with New South Wales.

From Tasmania a settlement was made at Port Phillip in 1835. At first it was administered by New South Wales, but the settlers quickly demanded independence, and in 1848 they withdrew all other candidates for the Legislative Council and elected Earl Grey, Secretary of State for the Colonies, as "Member for Melbourne". The move succeeded: within a few months the Colonial Office agreed to the separation, and in 1851 the new colony of Victoria, complete with representative institutions, was established, with its capital at Melbourne. The Queen gave her name to this offshoot of the English-speaking peoples. Its capital commemorates the Whig Prime Minister whom she had found the most agreeable of her advisers.

The third offspring of New South Wales was Queensland. It grew up round the town of Brisbane, but developed more slowly and did not become a separate colony until 1859. By then two other settlements had arisen on the Australian coasts. In 1834 a body known as "the Colonisation Commissioners for South Australia" had been set up in London, and two years later the first settlers landed near Adelaide. The city was named after William IV's Queen. South Australia was never a convict settlement. It was organised by a group of men under the influence of Gibbon Wakefield, whose elaborate theories were now put into practice. On the whole they succeeded, though a system of dual control by which responsibility was divided between the Government and the Colonisation, or Land, Commissioners gave so much trouble that the Commissioners were abolished in 1842. Within seven years the colony numbered fifty-two thousand inhabitants, and had been enriched by the discovery of copper deposits.

The other colony, Western Australia, had a very different history. Founded in 1829, it nearly died at birth. With much less fertile soil than the eastern colonies and separated from them by vast and uninhabitable desert, it suffered greatly from lack of labour. Convicts, which the other colonies deemed an obstacle to progress, seemed the only solution, and the British Government eagerly accepted an invitation to send some out to Perth. Thus resuscitated, the population trebled within the next ten years, but Western Australia did not obtain representative institutions until 1870, after the convict settlement had been abolished, nor full self-government till 1890.

Meanwhile, in 1848 gold had been discovered in California, and among the prospectors who crossed the Pacific to try their luck was a certain Edward Hargraves. A few months of digging brought him small success, but he noticed that the gold-bearing rocks of California resembled those near Bathurst, in New South Wales. He returned to Australia early in 1851 to test his theory. The first pans of earth proved him right. News of the discovery leaked out, and within a few weeks the Australian Gold Rush had begun in earnest.

The gold fever swept the eastern colonies. The whole of Australia seemed

"Bushmen" was the name given to the Australian frontiersmen who explored the interior of the country. As they moved away from the coastline in their ox-drawn carts, they soon discovered that much of the land was both arid and inhospitable. Some of them became folk heroes.

Gold-diggers at work in New South Wales. Some Australians already had experience of panning for gold from the earlier Californian gold rush.

to be on the move, marching out to Bathurst, Ballarat, or Bendigo, with picks and shovels on their shoulders, pots and basins round their waists, an excited, feverish crowd, pouring into mining towns that had sprung up overnight, fully equipped with gambling saloons, bars and brothels. The Victorian goldfields soon had a population of nearly 100,000. Not all were "diggers", as the miners came to be called, and the hotel-keepers, store-keepers, prostitutes, and other toilers usually fared best. A penniless lollipop-seller made £6,000 a year by opening a public house on the road to Ballarat. When the miners flocked back to Melbourne or Sydney their money vanished in crazy extravagance and ostentation. Men lit their pipes with bank notes, so the stories ran. When fortunes could be made and lost overnight there seemed no point in steady employment. Squatters lost their shepherds, business houses their clerks, ships their crews. Early in 1852 there were only two policemen left in Melbourne; more than fifty had gone off to the goldfields. Wages doubled and trebled; prices rose fantastically, and the values of land changed with bewildering rapidity. The other colonies lost great numbers of men to the goldfields. In a single year 95,000 immigrants entered Victoria; in five months 4,000 men out of a total population of 50,000 left Tasmania for Victoria.

Keeping the peace, settling disputed claims, providing transport, housing, and enough food to stop famine was a grievous burden for the new administration at Melbourne, most of whose staff had also deserted to the goldfields. For some time there were no more than forty-four soldiers in the whole of Victoria, and in 1853 fifty policemen had to be sent out from London. The diggers probably enjoyed the turbulence they created in the mining towns, but they had a serious grievance against the Government. As with the squatters, the Crown claimed ownership of the land, and demanded a licence fee. The fee was fiercely resented and very difficult to collect. On November 30, 1854, a search for unlicensed miners caused a riot. Led by one Peter Lalor, the diggers began to drill, and build a stockade. The local military commander, Captain Thomas, acted with speed. He determined to attack before the movement spread. With three hundred men, mainly soldiers, he carried the stockade with a bayonet charge, killing thirty rebels and capturing over a hundred and twenty.

Thus ended what might have become a serious rebellion. Licence fees were soon afterwards abolished and replaced by an export duty on gold. The miners were given the franchise and peace was restored. In the next few years independent diggers were replaced by mining companies, which alone had the resources to carry on underground work. Much the same happened in New South Wales, the only other colony where gold was discovered at this time. Between 1851 and 1861 £124,000,000 worth of it was raised. A more permanent enrichment was the increase in Australian population, which now rose to over a million.

Wool and agriculture at first were deeply smitten by the rush for gold, but Australia gained in the end. The squatter prospered by the establishment of better roads and more railways. Food was needed, and over a million acres were soon under cultivation. The economy of the country, hitherto far too dependent on wool, thus achieved a balance.

The political repercussions were far-reaching. The increase of population, trade, and revenue made it imperative to reform the makeshift constitutions. Between 1855 and 1859 two-chamber Parliaments, elected by popular vote

With the growing prosperity of Australia, banks were soon established. The Australian Joint Stock Bank, shown in this illustration, was one of the two banks in the town of Gulgong, New South Wales, in 1872.

and with ministers responsible to the Lower House, were introduced in all the Antipodean states except Western Australia, where, as already related, self-government came later.

Australia, as we now know it, was born in 1901 by the association of the colonies in a Commonwealth, with a new capital at Canberra. Federation came late and slowly to the southern continent, for the lively, various, widely separated settlements cherished their own self-rule. Even today most of the Australian population dwells in the settlements founded in the nineteenth century. The heart of the country, over a million square miles in extent, has attracted delvers after metals and ranchers of cattle, but it remains largely uninhabited.

Twelve hundred miles to the east of Australia lie the islands of New Zealand. Here, long before they were discovered by Europeans, a Polynesian warrior race, the Maoris, had sailed across the Pacific from the northeast and established a civilisation notable for the brilliance of its art and the strength of its military system. When Captain Cook visited them towards the end of the eighteenth century he judged that they numbered about a hundred thousand. This was probably an over-estimate, but here neverthe-less was a first formidable obstacle to European colonisation, a cultured people long in possession of the land, independent in spirit and skilled in warfare. Soon after Cook's discovery a small English community gained a footing in the Bay of Islands in the far north, but they were mostly whalers and sealers, shipwrecked mariners, and a few escaped convicts from Australia, enduring a lonely, precarious, and somewhat disreputable existence. They were tolerated by the Maori chiefs, whom they supplied with firearms. They constituted no great threat to Maori life or lands. Resistance to English colonisation was fortified by the arrival of Christian missionaries. In 1814 the Reverend Samuel Marsden set up a mission station in this same Bay of Islands. He was joined by other clerics, and Christianity quickly gained a large ascendancy over the Maoris. The missionaries struggled to defeat the power of the traders, and for many years they opposed, in the interests of the Maoris, all schemes for admitting English immigrants. For a time they succeeded, and the Australian colonies had been established for half a century before the first official English settlement was founded in New Zealand. A move to colonise the islands had neverthe-less long been afoot in London, impelled by a group of men around Gibbon Wakefield, who had already so markedly influenced the future of Canada and Australia. But the Government was hostile. The missionaries denounced the project as disastrous to the natives, and the Colonial Office refused to sanction its plans.

Wakefield however was resolute, and in 1838 his New Zealand Associ-ation formed a private joint-stock company for the colonisation of the country, and a year later dispatched an expedition under his younger brother. Over a thousand settlers went with them, and they founded the site of Wellington in the North Island.

News that France was contemplating the annexation of New Zealand compelled the British Government to act. Instead of sanctioning Wakefield's expedition they sent out a man-of-war, under the command of Captain Hobson, to treat with the Maoris. In February 1840 Hobson concluded the Treaty of Waitangi with the Maori chiefs. By this the Maoris ceded to Great Britain all the rights and the powers of sovereignty in return for

The Wakefield colonists brought these "V" huts with them from England. The huts became their first homes in Christchurch, New Zealand.

Dairy farming in New Zealand was established by the early colonists and thrives to this day. This photograph, taken in about 1890, illustrates just how difficult the conditions could be.

confirmation in "the full, exclusive possession of their lands and estates".

Then, but not till then, the Company received official recognition. Two powers were thus established, the Governor at Auckland at the top of the North Island, which Hobson had chosen as the capital, and the company at Wellington. They championed different interests and opposing policies. The Company wanted land, as much and as soon as possible. The treaty and the Colonial Office said it belonged to the Maoris. The two authorities struggled and bickered throughout the forties. In 1843 Joseph Somes, Governor of the Company, wrote to the Colonial Secretary: "We have always had very serious doubts whether the Treaty of Waitangi, made with naked savages by a consul invested with no plenipotentiary powers, without ratification by the Crown, could be treated by lawyers as anything but a praiseworthy device for amusing and pacifying savages for the moment." The "naked savages" however were not to be caught. The treaty with Hobson clearly distinguished between the shadow of sovereignty, which they surrendered, and the substance of property, which they retained. If they lost their land, their tribal life would be extinguished. The ingenuity of their laws exasperated settlers who had innocently purchased land and found themselves denied possession because the tribe's inalienable rights over the soil were unaffected by private bargains. Nevertheless by 1859 the settlers had occupied seven million acres in the North Island and over thirty-two million acres in the South, where the Maoris were fewer.

The result was the Maori wars, a series of intermittent local conflicts lasting from 1843 to 1869. By the middle of the 1860s twenty thousand troops were engaged. The fanatical cult of the Hauhans and the skill of Te Kooti, a guerrilla leader of genius, taxed all the resources of the colony. The Maoris fought magnificently, and the admiration of the regular officers for their opponents sharpened their dislike of the settlers. But by 1869 the force of the movement was spent and the risings were defeated. Thereafter the enlightened policy of Sir Donald MacLean, the Minister for Native Affairs, produced a great improvement. The settlers gained some security of tenure. The Maoris realised that the British had come to stay. A series of Native Land Acts, passed in the sixties, protected them against extermination; in 1867 they secured direct representation in the New Zealand legislature, and after declining to 37,000 souls in 1871 by the 1951 census they numbered nearly 100,000.

Despite these years of strife the colony continued to expand. Wakefield, anxious to overcome the opposition of the missionaries, ingeniously persuaded both the Free Church of Scotland and the Church of England to cooperate in establishing two new settlements. These, at Otago and Canterbury, were remarkable applications of his theories. Both were in the South Island, and from 1860 until 1906 it was the South Island, prosperous and comparatively immune from the Maori wars, which contained most of the population. By 1868 the British numbered only about a quarter of a million; twelve years later there were nearly twice as many.

Peace brought prosperity. Great flocks of sheep were reared on the famous Canterbury Plains of the South Island, and a native Corriedale crossbreed was evolved. In the 1860s gold was found in Otago and Canterbury and there was a temporary boom. The Australian gold discoveries and the swift rise in prices in Melbourne and Sydney gave agriculture a flying start. Despite a depression in the eighties, the prosperity of New Zealand continued to grow. The invention of the refrigerator enabled the colony to compete with European and English producers thirteen thousand miles away. The cooperative movement, especially in dairy-farming, helped small farmers with little capital to build up an industry of remarkable magnitude, and the Dominion of New Zealand soon possessed the highest external trade in proportion to its numbers of any nation in the world.

New Zealand's political development was no less rapid. Founded in the days of the Durham Report and the first experiments with colonial self-government in Canada, she obtained by the Constitution Act of 1852 a broad measure of independence. Inland travel was so difficult, however, that until late in the nineteenth century the colony remained a number of small, scattered settlements, all differing in the circumstances of their foundation and the character of their interests. This was recognised in the Constitution Act, which set up a number of provincial councils on a democratic basis, each of which was, to a considerable extent, independent of the General Assembly.

Conflict between the provincial assemblies and the central administration troubled New Zealand politics for twenty years. Some provinces were wealthy, others less so. Otago and Canterbury, stimulated by the discovery of gold, became rich and prosperous, while the settlers in the North Island, harassed by the Maori wars, grew more and more impoverished. At one time Otago and Canterbury wanted to secede. Reform came in 1875, when the Constitution was modified, the provinces were abolished, local administration was placed in the hands of county councils, and the powers of the central Government were greatly increased. Thus, on a smaller scale, New Zealand faced and mastered all the problems of federal government thirty years before Australia did. Indeed her political vitality is no less astonishing than her economic vigour. The tradition and prejudices of the past weighed less heavily than in the older countries. Many of the reforms introduced into Great Britain by the Liberal Government of 1906, and then regarded as extreme innovations, had already been accepted by New Zealand. Industrial arbitration, old-age pensions, factory legislation, State insurance and medical service, all achieved between 1890 and the outbreak of the First World War, testified to the survival and fertility even in the remote and unfamiliar islands of the Pacific, of the British political genius.

The invention of refrigeration in the early nineteenth century revolutionised the meat and dairy businesses in New Zealand. For the first time, products could be exported.

CHAPTER 8

GLADSTONE AND DISRAELI

FROM 1868 TO 1885 WE HAVE A LONG, connected, and progressive period in British history—the Prime Ministerships of Gladstone and Disraeli. For nearly twenty years no one effectively disputed the leadership of these two great Parliamentarians, and until Disraeli died in 1881 the political scene was dominated by a personal duel on a grand scale. Both men were at the height of their powers, and their oratory gripped and focused public attention on the proceedings of the House of Commons. Every thrust and parry was discussed throughout the country. The political differences between them were no wider than is usual in a two-party system, but what gave the conflict its edge and produced a deep-rooted antagonism was

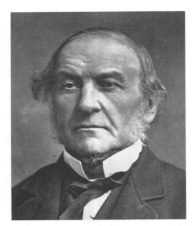

William Ewart Gladstone (1809–98) became Liberal Prime Minister in 1868. His first government introduced many overdue reforms: Acts designed to protect Irish tenants, and to establish national education in England and the use of the secret ballot in parliamentary elections.

their utter dissimilarity in character and temperament. "That unprincipled maniac, Gladstone," wrote Disraeli, ". . . extraordinary mixture of envy, vindictiveness, hypocrisy, and superstition; and with one commanding characteristic—whether preaching, praying, speechifying, or scribbling— never a gentleman!" Gladstone's judgment on his rival was no less sharp. His doctrine was ". . . false, but the man more false than his doctrine . . . . He weakened the Crown by approving its unconstitutional leanings, and the Constitution by offering any price for democratic popularity." Thus they faced each other across the dispatch boxes of the House of Commons: Gladstone's commanding voice, his hawklike eyes, his power to move the emotions, against Disraeli's romantic air and polished eloquence.

When Gladstone became Prime Minister in 1868, he was deemed a careful and parsimonious administrator who had become a sound Liberal reformer. But this was only one side of his genius. What gradually made him the most controversial figure of the century was his gift of rousing moral indignation in the electorate. In two great crusades on the Balkans and on Ireland his dominant theme was that conscience and the moral law must govern political decisions. Such a demand, strenuously voiced, was open to the charge of hypocrisy when, as so often happened, Gladstone's policy obviously coincided with the wellbeing of the Liberal Party. But the charge was false. He was willing to break his party rather than deny his conscience. Soon after his conversion to Home Rule for Ireland he said to his lieutenant, Sir William Harcourt, "I am prepared to go forward without anybody." It was a spirit which was to split the Liberals, but it won him a place in the hearts of his followers of which Britain has never seen the like.

To face Gladstone, Disraeli needed all the courage and quickness of wit with which he had been so generously endowed. Many Tories disliked and distrusted his reforming views, but he handled his colleagues with a rare skill. He has never been surpassed in the art of party management. He never became wholly assimilated to English ways of life, and it was this detachment that probably enabled him to diagnose and assess the deeper political currents of his age. Large sections of the working classes were held to Church, Crown, Empire, and aristocracy by practical interests which could be turned to party advantage. Or so he saw it. Long handicapped by his own party, he led it in the end to an electoral triumph, and achieved for a period the power he had always desired.

Nothing created more bitterness between them than Gladstone's conviction that Disraeli had captured the Queen for the Conservative Party and endangered the Constitution by an unscrupulous use of his personal charm. When Gladstone became Prime Minister Victoria was still in mourning and semi-retirement for Prince Albert, who had died in 1861. She deeply resented Gladstone's attempts to bring the monarchy back into public life. And he, though always respectful, was incapable of infusing any kind of warmth into his relationship with her. She once said, according to report, that he addressed her like a public meeting. Disraeli did not make the same mistake. He wooed her from the loneliness and apathy which engulfed her after Albert's death, and flattered her desire to share in the formulation of policy. At the height of one crisis in 1877, he ended a report on the various views of the Cabinet with the following words: "The seventh policy is that of Your Majesty, which will be introduced and enforced to his utmost by the Prime Minister." Victoria found this irresistible. She complained that

This Punch cartoon was captioned "Empress and Earl: or One Good Turn Deserves Another". A great favourite of Victoria's, Disraeli was raised to the peerage in 1876 and became Lord Beaconsfield.

Gladstone, when in office, never told her anything, and she detested the growing radicalism of his party. But in fact little harm was done; Gladstone was careful to keep the person of the Queen out of political discussion and none of their disagreements was known to the public. He grumbled that "the Queen is enough to kill any man", but he served her patiently, if not with understanding, while, in spite of her occasional leanings, Victoria remained a constitutional monarch.

Gladstone said that his Cabinet of 1868 to 1874 was "one of the best instruments for government that ever was constructed". Driven by his boundless energy, it put into effect a long-delayed avalanche of reforms. This was the golden age when Liberalism was still an aggressive, unshackling force, seeking out and destroying the last relics of eighteenth-century government. The Civil Service, the army, the universities, and the law were all attacked and the grip of the old landed interest began to crumble. The power of what the radical James Mill had called the "sinister interests" shrivelled bit by bit as the public service was gradually but remorselessly thrown open to talent and industry. Freedom was the keynote, *laissez-faire* the method; no undue extension of Government authority was needed; and the middle class at last acquired a share in the political sphere equal to its economic power.

Gladstone came in on the flood; a decisive electoral victory and a country ready for reform gave him his opportunity. The scale and scope of his policy, directed at a series of obvious abuses, was such that radicals, moderate Liberals, and even Whigs were brought together in agreement. He began with Ireland. "My mission," he had said when the summons from the Queen reached him at his country home in Hawarden, "is to pacify Ireland", and, in spite of bitter opposition and in defiance of his own early principles, which had been to defend property and the Anglican faith, he carried, in 1869, the disestablishment of the Protestant Church of Ireland. This was followed next year by a Land Act which attempted to protect tenants from unfair eviction. But Ireland was not so easily to be pacified.

In England the Government found no lack of work to do. After the Electoral Reform of 1867, Robert Lowe, the Chancellor of the Exchequer, had said that "We must educate our masters." Voters ought to know at least how to read and write, and have opened to them the paths to higher knowledge. A national system of primary schools was launched by W. E. Forster's Education Act of 1870, blurred though it was, like all education measures for some decades to come, by sectarian passion and controversy. At the same time, patronage was finally destroyed in the home Civil Service. Entrance to the new administrative class was henceforth possible only through a competitive examination. Ability, not wealth or family connection, was now the means to advance. In the following year the universities were thrown open to Roman Catholics, Jews, Dissenters, and young men of no belief. The ancient intricacies of the judicial system, so long a nightmare to litigants and a feeding ground for lawyers, were simplified and modernised by the fusion of courts of law and equity. A single Supreme Court was set up, with appropriate divisions, and procedure and methods of appeal were made uniform. All this was accompanied by a generally sound administration, and, what was perhaps closest to Gladstone's own heart, a policy of economy and low taxation.

In 1871 Prussia crushed Napoleon III in the Franco-Prussian War, and

This "Ragged School" in Lambeth was for children, and sometimes adults, who were unable to gain admission into a charity school. Open on Sunday evenings, it taught mainly the principles of morality and religion. "Ragged Schools" were run by anyone who could offer a modicum of instruction, and in Windsor a chimney sweep set up such a school. They were sometimes highly effective institutions.

Until Edward Cardwell's army reforms of 1868-71, military discipline had been maintained mainly by the lash, the "cat-o-nine-tails" whose ends were knotted to tear the victim's back. Punishment was usually attended by an officer and a regimental doctor.

the Iron Chancellor, Bismarck, united the German states under Prussian rule. The Prussian victories administered a shock to military and civilian opinion. During the decade ending in 1870 the Royal Navy had been powerfully re-equipped with iron-clad steamships which mounted rifled guns firing shell instead of shot. At sea the age of wood and sail was at long last over. But on land the regular British army remained by continental standards a negligible quantity. The sufferings and disgraces of the Crimea had made it evident that the great Duke of Wellington's practices, in the hands of lesser men, had broken down. The reforms were carried out by Gladstone's Secretary of State, Edward Cardwell. The Commander in Chief, the Duke of Cambridge, was opposed to any reform whatever, and the first step was taken when the Queen, with considerable reluctance, signed an Order in Council subordinating him to the Secretary of State. Flogging was abolished. An Enlistment Act introduced short service, which would create an efficient reserve. Then Cardwell went further, and the purchase of commissions was prohibited. The War Office was overhauled. The infantry were rearmed with the Martini-Henry rifle, and the regimental system was completely reorganised on a county basis.

All this was achieved in the space of six brilliant, crowded years, and then, as so often happens in English history, the pendulum swung back. Great reforms offend great interests. The Anglicans were hit by several measures; the Nonconformists found little to please them in the Education Act. The army and the Court resented Cardwell's onslaught. The working classes were offered little to attract them apart from a Ballot Act which allowed them to exercise the newly won franchise in secret and without intimidation. An unsuccessful Licensing Bill, prompted by the Temperance wing of the Liberal Party, founded an alliance between the brewers and the Conservative Party. Gladstone was soon to complain that he had been borne down from power "in a torrent of gin and beer". Disraeli, now at the height of his oratorical powers, painted this portrait of the Ministry: "Her Majesty's new ministers proceeded in their career like a body of men under the influence of some deleterious drug. . . . As time advanced it was not difficult to perceive that extravagance was being substituted for energy by the Government. The unnatural stimulus was subsiding. Their paroxysms ended in prostration. Some took refuge in melancholy, and their eminent chief alternated between a menace and a sigh. As I sat opposite the Treasury Bench the ministers reminded me of one of those marine landscapes not very unusual on the coasts of South America. You behold a range of exhausted volcanoes. Not a flame flickers on a single pallid crest. But the situation is still dangerous. There are occasional earthquakes, and ever and anon the dark rumbling of the sea."

Gladstone's first Government stands high in British history; but there were few fresh Liberal ideals to expound when Parliament was dissolved in 1874. He fought the election on a proposal to abolish the income tax, which then stood at three pence in the pound. But the country was now against him and he lost. He went into semi-retirement, believing that the great reforming work of Liberalism had been completed. Most of his Whig friends agreed. They were wrong. The "Grand Old Man" was soon to return to politics, and return amid a storm which would rend and disrupt the loyalties and traditions of English public life in a manner far more drastic than any of them yet conceived.

Now, however, while his great adversary devoted his leisure to felling trees at Hawarden and writing articles about Homer, Disraeli seized his chance. He had long waited for supreme power. For twenty-six years he had been the leader of the Conservative Party in the House of Commons, and now he was in his seventieth year. His physique had never been robust, and his last years, made lonely by the death of his wife, were plagued by gout and other ailments. "Power—it has come to me too late. There were days when, on waking, I felt I could move dynasties and governments; but that has passed away." But at first Disraeli was brilliantly successful.

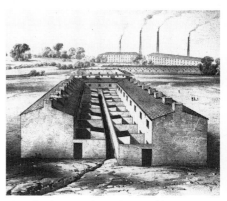

This illustration, from the Health in Towns Commission's First Report on Preston in 1844, shows back-to-back cottages with an open drain running between. The Public Health Act of 1848 resulted from such reports on the nation's appalling housing and sanitation.

He concentrated on social reform and on a new conception of the Empire, and both prongs of attack struck Gladstone at his weakest points. The Empire had never aroused his interest, and though passionate in defence of the political rights of the working class he cared little for their material claims. Disraeli, on the other hand, had proclaimed that "the first consideration of a minister should be the health of the people". Liberals tried to laugh this off as a "policy of sewage". In his first full session after reaching office Disraeli proceeded to redeem his pledge. He was fortunate in his colleagues, among whom the Home Secretary, Richard Cross, was outstanding in ability. A Trade Union Act gave the unions almost complete freedom of action, an Artisans' Dwelling Act was the first measure to tackle the housing problem, a Sale of Food and Drugs Act and a Public Health Act at last established sanitary law on a sound footing. Disraeli succeeded in persuading much of the Conservative Party not only that the real needs of the electorate included healthier conditions of life, better homes, and freedom to organise in the world of industry, but also that the Conservative Party was perfectly well fitted to provide them. Well might Alexander Macdonald, the miners' leader, declare that "The Conservative Party have done more for the working classes in five years than the Liberals have in fifty." William Gladstone had provided the administrative basis for these great developments, but Benjamin Disraeli took the first considerable steps in promoting social welfare.

The second part of the new Conservative programme, Imperialism, had also been launched before Disraeli came to power. Gladstone's passion for economy in all things military, and his indifference to the Empire jarred on a public which was growing ever more conscious of British Imperial glory. Disraeli's appeal was perfectly tuned to the new mood.

"Self-government, in my opinion," he said of the colonies, "when it was conceded, ought to have been conceded as part of a great policy of Imperial consolidation. It ought to have been accompanied by an Imperial tariff, by securities for the people of England for the enjoyment of the unappropriated lands which belonged to the Sovereign as their trustee, and by a military code which should have precisely defined the means and the responsibilities by which the colonies should be defended, and by which, if necessary, this country should call for aid from the colonies themselves. It ought, further, to have been accompanied by the institution of some representative council in the Metropolis which would have brought the colonies into constant and continuous relations with the home Government. All this however was omitted because those who advised that policy—and I believe their convictions were sincere—looked upon the colonies of England, looked even upon our connection with India, as a burden upon this country; viewing everything in its financial aspect, and totally passing by those moral and political

PUBLIC HEALTH

THE PROBLEMS OF PUBLIC HEALTH within Britain were first taken seriously with the rise in the population of the cities. Statistics collected during the 1830s and 1840s showed that the death rates varied significantly between one part of a city and another. To social reformers it seemed that it should be possible to raise health care to a uniformly high standard.

The energetic administrator Edwin Chadwick led a crusade for better conditions. Putting their trust in what they called "the Sanitary Idea", he and his supporters demanded that a cleaner water supply be made available to all, with more soap as well as more water, lavatories, both public and private, and efficient drainage and sewage systems.

Charles Kingsley, who wrote movingly of young chimney sweeps in *The Water Babies*, and George Eliot, whose novel *Middlemarch* brought public attention to the need for changes in medical practice, were among the advocates of reform.

Little was known about the cause of diseases, either of those which seemed to be always there, like typhus or tuberculosis, or of those which came in alarming epidemics, like cholera. Bacteria were not identified, and there were few effective medical remedies. Yet the efforts of the reformers improved the environment and prevented death rates from increasing.

The first national Public Health Act was passed in 1848, setting up local Boards of Health. London, however, was omitted, but in 1869 a further Act divided the entire country into districts. In these new districts, medical officers were worked extremely hard, being responsible for inspecting drains, rivers, factories, refuse pits and rubbish dumps in a genuine effort to eliminate possible health hazards. Insanitary housing continued to pose serious problems, however, until after 1919, when a Housing Act provided government subsidies to encourage the building of workers' houses by local authorities.

PROPER DRAINAGE AND FRESH WATER *did more to prevent disease than any medical discovery in the nineteenth century. The photograph above, taken in 1862, shows the building of London's eighty-three miles of sewers. Joseph Bazalgette, the civil engineer who designed the system, can be seen standing at the top right on the skyline. Until the 1860s, sewage was discharged directly into the Thames, where it* contaminated the water supply. Threats of dangerous outbreaks of disease, particularly cholera, prompted government action. There were fortunately some vigorous administrators such as Edwin Chadwick (below). He was Secretary to the Poor Law Commission, and in 1842 published a report on The Sanitary Conditions of the Labouring Population, which had far-reaching results.

FOOD ADULTERATION *was rife. Reports published in 1820 and 1848 contained shocking evidence of bakers adding stone and plaster to bread, grocers pouring fine sand into sugar (above) and substituting sloe, elder, beech and hawthorn leaves for tea.*

MICROBES, *portrayed by a* Punch *cartoonist in this representation of a drop of dirty water seen through a microscope, began to be examined by Victorian scientists. In the nineteenth century, Louis Pasteur, the French microbiologist, developed vaccines against anthrax, chickenpox and rabies. An English doctor, John Snow, investigating the source of cholera in the London epidemic of 1854, traced it to a well in Broad Street, Soho.*

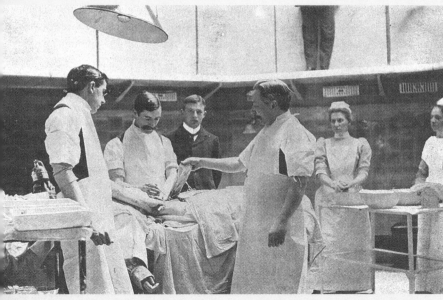

ADVANCES IN SURGERY *included the first use of general anaesthetics in 1846 and the introduction of antiseptic methods. In 1865, the surgeon Joseph Lister operated successfully on a boy who had fractured both legs. Lister used carbolic acid as disinfectant, and the wound* healed rapidly. Later, surgeons created an aseptic operating environment, as in this early twentieth-century photograph (above). However, surgery was still dangerous, as the presence of a clergyman to deliver the last rites, should the patient die, indicates.

FLUSHABLE LAVATORIES *disposed of waste matter by means of glazed earthenware pipes which prevented fresh-water pollution. This model, the Deluge Washdown Pedestal (above) cost £10.00, possibly a year's income for a working-class man. The first public lavatories were used at the Great Exhibition.*

As this Punch *cartoon shows, the Suez Canal opened up the route to India, and Disraeli's purchase of Khedive Ismail's shares made Britain the largest stockholder. The Canal, planned by the French engineer Ferdinand de Lesseps, connects the Mediterranean Sea with the Red Sea, via the Gulf of Suez.*

considerations which make nations great, and by the influence of which alone men are distinguished from animals."

First, the route to India was safeguarded. The Suez Canal had been open for six years, and had transformed the strategic position of Great Britain. No longer was the Cape of Good Hope the key to the route to India and the Far East. The Foreign Office had been curiously slow to appreciate this obvious fact and had missed more than one opportunity to control the waterway. Now, in 1875 Disraeli, on behalf of the British Government, bought, for four million pounds, the shares of the bankrupt Egyptian Khedive Ismail in the Canal—nearly half the total issue. A possible threat to British naval supremacy was thereby removed, and—of fateful importance for the future—Britain was inexorably drawn into Egyptian politics. In the following year Queen Victoria, to her great pleasure, was proclaimed Empress of India. Such a stroke would never have occurred to Gladstone. But Disraeli's oriental, almost mystical, approach to Empire, his emphasis on Imperial symbols, his belief in the importance of outward display, gave his policy an imaginative colour. His purpose was to make those colonies which he had once condemned as "a millstone round our necks" sparkle like diamonds. New storms in Europe, however, distracted attention from this glittering prospect.

In 1876 the eastern question erupted anew. The Crimean War had been mismanaged by the soldiers, and at the peace the diplomats had done no better. Most of the Balkans still remained under Turkish rule, and all attempts to improve the Ottoman administration of Christian provinces had foundered on the obstinacy of the Sultan and the magnitude of the task. Slavs, Romanians and Greeks were united in their detestation of the Turk. Revolt offered little hope of permanent success, and they had long looked to the Tsar of Russia as their potential liberator. Here was a fine dilemma for the British Government. The possibility of creating independent Balkan states, in spite of Canning's example in the small Greek kingdom, was not yet seriously contemplated. The nice choice appeared to lie between bolstering Turkish power and allowing Russian influence to move through the Balkans and into the Mediterranean by way of Constantinople. The threat had long been present, and the insurrection which now occurred confronted Disraeli with the most difficult and dangerous situation for Great Britain since the Napoleonic wars.

Rebellion broke out in Bosnia and Herzegovina. Germany, Austria, and Russia, united in the League of Three Emperors, proposed that Turkey should be coerced into making serious reforms. Disraeli resisted these plans, and to emphasise British support of Turkey a fleet was dispatched to the Dardanelles. But these diplomatic manoeuvres were soon overtaken by the news of terrible Turkish atrocities in Bulgaria. In reply to a Parliamentary question in July, Disraeli, handicapped by faulty reports from his ambassador at Constantinople, took leave to doubt whether "torture has been practised on a great scale among an oriental people who seldom, I believe, resort to torture, but generally terminate their connection with culprits in a more expeditious manner." This tone of persiflage fanned into fierce and furious activity the profound moral feeling which was always simmering just below the surface of Gladstone's mind.

In a famous pamphlet, *The Bulgarian Horrors and the Question of the East*, Gladstone delivered his onslaught on the Turks and Disraeli's

The British Fleet on the way to the Dardanelles in 1878 to support the Turks. The magnificent fighting ships seen here under full sail are, from left to right, HMS Salamis, Ruby, Rupert, Research, Temeraire, Swiftsure, Sultan, *and* Agincourt.

Government. "Let the Turks now carry away their abuses in the only possible manner, namely, by carrying off themselves. Their Zaptiehs and their Mudirs, their Bimbashis and their Yuzbachis, their Kaimakams and their Pashas, one and all, bag and baggage, shall, I hope, clear out from the province they have desolated and profaned. This thorough riddance, this most blessed deliverance, is the only reparation we can make to the memory of those heaps on heaps of dead; to the violated purity alike of matron, of maiden, and of child. . . . There is not a criminal in a European gaol, there is not a cannibal in the South Sea Islands, whose indignation would not arise and overboil at the recital of that which has been done, which has too late been examined, but which remains unavenged; which has left behind all the foul and all the fierce passions that produced it, and which may again spring up in another more murderous harvest, from the soil soaked and reeking with blood, and in the air tainted with every imaginable deed of crime and shame. . . . No Government ever has so sinned; none has proved itself so incorrigible in sin or—which is the same— so impotent for reformation." After this broadside, relations between the two great men became so strained that Lord Beaconsfield (as Disraeli now was) publicly described Gladstone as worse than any Bulgarian horror.

At the end of the year a conference of the Great Powers was held in Constantinople at which Lord Salisbury, as the British representative, displayed for the first time his diplomatic talents. Salisbury was the direct descendant of Queen Elizabeth's great servant. Over a period of twenty years he had been highly critical of his chief. He had joined Disraeli's Government only after much heart-searching. But in office gradually the two men grew together. Salisbury's caustic, far-ranging common sense supplemented Disraeli's darting vision. As Secretary of State for India, and later at the Foreign Office, Salisbury established himself as the next predestined Tory leader. At Constantinople a programme of reform for Turkey was drawn up, but the Turks, sustained in part by a belief that Salisbury's zeal for reform did not entirely reflect the views of the British Cabinet, rejected it. The delegates returned to their capitals and Europe waited for war to break out between Russia and Turkey. When it came, in the summer of 1877, the mood of the country quickly changed. Gladstone, whose onslaught on the Turks had at first carried all before it, was now castigated as a pro-Russian. Feeling rose as, month after month, in spite of heroic Turkish resistance, the mass of Russian troops moved ponderously towards the Dardanelles. At last, in January 1878, they stood before the walls of Constantinople. Public opinion reached fever-point. The music-hall song of the hour was:

"We don't want to fight, but by jingo if we do
We've got the ships, we've got the men, we've got the money too!
We've fought the Bear before, and while we're Britons true
The Russians shall not have Constantinople."

In February, after considerable prevarication, a fleet of British ironclads steamed into the Golden Horn. They lay in the Sea of Marmara, opposite the Russian army, for six uneasy months of truce; the whale, as Bismarck said, facing the elephant.

In March Turkey and Russia signed the Treaty of San Stefano. It gave Russia effective control of the Balkans, and was obviously unacceptable to the other Great Powers. War again seemed likely and Lord Salisbury immediately set about summoning a conference of Great Powers. They met at the Congress of Berlin in June and July. Business was dominated by the Austrian Andrassy, Beaconsfield, Bismarck, and the Russian Minister Gortchakov, a quartet whose combined diplomatic talents would have been difficult to match. The result was that Russia gave up much of what she had momentarily gained at San Stefano. She extended her territories to the mouths of the Danube, but of the big Bulgaria which she had planned to dominate only one part was granted practical independence. The rest was returned to the Sultan. Austria-Hungary, as we must now call the Habsburg Empire, secured the right to occupy and administer Bosnia-Herzegovina. Great Britain received Cyprus and guaranteed the territorial integrity of Turkey-in-Asia in return for yet another pledge by the Sultan to introduce proper reforms. Beaconsfield returned from Berlin claiming that he had brought "peace with honour". He had indeed averted war, and for the moment, Russia, blocked in the Balkans, turned her gaze away from Europe to the Far East. The arrangements at Berlin have been much criticised for laying the trail to the war of 1914, but the Eastern Question, as it was then posed before the nations, was virtually insoluble. No settlement could have been more than a temporary one, and the Congress of Berlin in fact ensured the peace of Europe for thirty-six years.

The following weeks saw the zenith of Beaconsfield's career. But fortune soon ceased to smile upon him. Thrusting policies in South Africa and Afghanistan led, in 1879, to the destruction of a British battalion by the Zulus at Isandhlwana and the massacre of the Legation staff at Kabul. These minor disasters, though promptly avenged, lent fresh point to Gladstone's vehement assault upon the Government, an assault which reached its climax in the autumn of 1879 with his Midlothian Campaign, when he denounced a "vigorous, that is to say a narrow, restless, blustering, and self-assertive foreign policy . . . appealing to the self-love and pride of the community." He argued that Britain should pursue the path of morality and justice, free from the taint of self-interest. Her aims should be self-government for subject peoples and the promotion of a true Concert of Europe. "Remember," he said at Dalkeith, "that the sanctity of life in the hill villages of Afghanistan among the winter snows is as inviolable in the eye of Almighty God as can be your own." This appeal to morality infuriated the Conservatives, who based their case on the importance of defending and forwarding British interests and responsibilities wherever they might lie. They maintained that Beaconsfield's policy had raised national power and prestige to new heights.

"HUMPTY-DUMPTY"!

In this cartoon from Punch, Disraeli props up the Sultan of Turkey, aided by Britain's latest acquisition, Cyprus. Disraeli was constantly exercised by the "Eastern Question", the collective term used to describe the problems in southeastern Europe, caused by the weakness of the Ottoman Turkish Empire and the rivalry of its warring successors.

But the force of Gladstone's oratory was too much for the exhausted Ministry. Moreover, their last years in office coincided with the onset of an economic depression, serious enough for industry but ruinous for agriculture. When Beaconsfield dissolved in March 1880, the electoral result was decisive; the Queen was forced to accept as Prime Minister for a second time the man whom she described in a letter to her private secretary as "that *half-mad firebrand* who would soon ruin everything".

While the duel between Disraeli and Gladstone held the centre of the stage, far-reaching movements were taking shape below the surface of Parliamentary policies. The emergence of a mass electorate called for a new kind of political technique. Two things were required: a party policy which would persuade the electors to vote, and an efficient organisation to make sure that they did so. Disraeli produced both a policy and an organisation. The Conservative Central Office was established and a network of local associations was set up. The transition was remarkably smooth and although there were to be storms in the early 1880s the system created by Disraeli still largely remains at the present time.

In the Liberal camp the situation was very different. Gladstone's coolness and Whig hostility prevented the building of a centralised party organisation. The impulse and impetus came not from the centre, but through the provinces. In 1873 Joseph Chamberlain had become Mayor of Birmingham. Aided by a most able political adviser, Schnadhorst, he built up a party machine which, although based on popular participation, his enemies quickly condemned as a "caucus". A policy of "Municipal Socialism" brought great benefits to Birmingham in the shape of public utilities, slum clearance, and other civic amenities. The movement spread to other towns and cities, and a National Liberal Federation was born. The aim of its promoters was to make the Federation the Parliament of the Liberal movement, which would work out a radical programme and eventually replace the Whigs by a new set of leaders drawn from its own ranks. This was a novel phenomenon. Unlike Chartism and the anti-Corn Law League, movements for reform need no longer operate on the fringe of party. Radicalism was now powerful enough to make a bid for control.

At the election Chamberlain and his followers put forward a programme of reform which was unacceptable to the Whigs, and indeed to Gladstone. Their success exposed and proclaimed the wide changes which the new franchise had wrought in the structure of the party system.

Gladstone and Disraeli had done much to bridge the gap between aristocratic rule and democracy. They both believed that governments should be active, and the statute books for the years between 1868 and 1876 bulge with reforming measures. Elections gradually became a judgment on what the Government of the day had accomplished and an assessment of the promises made by the two parties. By 1880 they were being fought with techniques which differ very little from those used today. Gladstone's Midlothian Campaign, the first broad appeal to the people by a potential Prime Minister, underlined the change. It shocked the Queen that he should make a speech about foreign policy from a railway carriage window, but her protest echoed an age that had already passed.

Beaconsfield died a year later. His great task, taken on almost single-handed, had been to lead the Conservative Party out of the despair of the period after 1846, to persuade it to face the inevitability of democracy, and

Gladstone's politics sprang from his sense of Christian mission. He believed that by holding high the lamps of sound finance and just foreign policy, he could safely guide home his boatload of social reforms.

THE VICTORIAN HOME

A FAVOURITE THEME OF VICTORIAN LIFE was, "Home, sweet home". The Englishman's home, be it cottage or palace, was deemed his castle, and in theory a place of domestic peace, removed from the pressing cares of the world. In reality, it was often far from this ideal. Families were large and the number of children placed considerable burdens on women, and perhaps on children, too, for they were expected to be seen and not heard. Women, of course, were expected to obey their husbands virtually without question, and this could create tensions.

While it is impossible to generalise about all aspects of Victorian domestic life, it can safely be said that an essential difference existed between those homes where there were domestic servants and those where there were not. During the twenty years after the Great Exhibition of 1851, the number of domestic servants increased by sixty per cent. In the great households they were organised hierarchically, "upstairs and downstairs", and it was the servants who maintained the arduous routines of the house. In small households, and the less wealthy ones, there might be only one maid-of-all-work.

With or without servants it was not easy for Victorians to make their homes as comfortable as they would have liked, for labour-saving devices were few. The houses were smoky and draughty and sanitation could be a nightmare.

In spite of these difficulties, however, the number of belongings and furnishings crammed into houses increased to unprecedented proportions during the Victorian years. There was a great deal of clutter, although by the end of the era there were signs of a reaction. Victorians attached great importance to gardens, where home-owners spent much of their time, and this trend has continued into the present century.

SOLID, SPACIOUS HOUSES or villas like the house above, built in 1868, proliferated on the outskirts of towns. Within the towns, long terraces of narrow houses stretched away from the new railway stations. Building styles ranged from the neo-Gothic to the rustic and later to the so-called Queen Anne. In poorer homes, the kitchen was the hub of the house. Meals were eaten at the kitchen table, children played on the floor and on Fridays each member of the family took a turn in the tin bath. Most such homes had a parlour, used on special occasions, in which there might be a piano and bookcase.

GAMES ROOMS in Victorian times were used for billiards, snooker, backgammon and smoking. The billiard table (above), at Osborne House, was designed by Prince Albert.

THE VICTORIAN NURSERY was the domain of those who should be seen but not heard, such as these two small girls (above) photographed in 1862. Queen Victoria had eight of her nine children within thirteen years, and families with more than ten children were common. The Queen set the fashion for the unemotional upbringing often favoured by the British upper classes. Children were brought up by nannies, nursery maids and governesses before being sent away to public schools.

UPSTAIRS *was where the master and his family lived. William Powell Frith, who painted "Many Happy Returns of the Day" (above) in 1856, used his daughter as a model for the birthday girl, and included a portrait of himself sitting at the head of the table. The picture can be seen in Harrogate Art Gallery. The dining-room furniture is typical of the period. Curtains and carpets are thick and abundant, the walls are hung with pictures in elaborate frames and the table legs, like human legs, are decorously hidden by cloth.*

DOWNSTAIRS *was the basement where the servants who cooked, looked after the children, cleaned, gardened, and ran the stables, had their servants' hall. Some labour-saving devices were invented in Victorian times, but were more costly than the minimal wages given to servants (left). The cook ruled the roost, while the housemaid, the worst paid, worked hardest. Wages usually included two sets of uniforms. Time off was limited, and restrictions such as "no followers" were often imposed.*

to endow it with the policies which would meet the new conditions. That he was successful is a remarkable indication of his skill in all matters related to party. He made the Conservatives a great force in democratic politics. The large-scale two-party system begins with him. Tory democracy—working men by hundreds of thousands who voted Conservative—became the dominant factor. The extension of the franchise which had hitherto threatened to engulf the past bore it proudly forward. Whereas the Whigs vanished from the scene, the Tories, though they were slow to realise it, sprang into renewed life and power with a fair future before them. Such was the work of Disraeli, for which his name will be duly honoured.

CHAPTER 9

HOME RULE FOR IRELAND

W HEN GLADSTONE IN 1880 BECAME PRIME MINISTER for the second time expectation stood high. A triumphant election campaign had given him a majority of a hundred and thirty-seven over his Conservative opponents. But almost as soon as the House assembled the Speaker remarked that Gladstone had "a difficult team to drive". So it was to prove. Few periods of office have been more disappointing.

The main fault lay in the composition of the Liberal Party. For long it had prided itself upon the strength afforded by diversity, but it soon began to find that the divisions between Whig and radical, right and left, were unbridgeable. In the first Gladstone Government there had been little discord. But now the old Whig faction thought that reform had gone far enough, and Gladstone himself had some sympathy with them. He disliked intensely the methods of the radical caucus and scorned their policies of social and economic reform. "Their pet idea," he wrote, "is what they call construction—that is to say, taking into the hands of the State the business of the individual man." Moreover he found the Whigs much better company than radical newcomers like Joseph Chamberlain. Gladstone never lost his conviction that the natural leaders of the Liberal cause were a small, leisured, cultured aristocracy.

When it came to forming his Cabinet he had to conciliate these same Whigs. The Marquis of Hartington, who had led the party in the Commons during his chief's retirement, had never been happy about Gladstone's onslaught on Disraeli's Eastern policy. He and his friends were fearful of the direction that the Prime Minister's mind and energy were next likely to take. In the upshot only one radical, Chamberlain, was admitted to the Cabinet, and to him was assigned what was then a lowly office, the Presidency of the Board of Trade. This was Gladstone's first great error. Not only was a Whig Cabinet profoundly unsuited to a time when the Liberal Party was becoming more and more radical, but its leader was to find himself in direct clash and conflict with his own colleagues on the main political, Imperial and foreign issues of the day, and above all on Ireland. A Cabinet with such deep cleavages was unlikely to prove an effective instrument of government. John Morley, Gladstone's biographer, wrote that it was not only a coalition, but "a coalition of that vexatious kind where those who happened not to agree sometimes seemed to be almost as

Even after Gladstone's Land Act of 1870, the position of the Irish tenant was precarious and evictions were commonplace. This illustration shows soldiers escorting an eviction party with a battering-ram. The evicted family stand, surrounded by their meagre possessions.

well pleased with contention as with harmony". Over this towered the Grand Old Man, as he was already considered in his seventy-first year, his force and energy undimmed, his passions and enthusiasms growing more intense with every year that passed.

But the Liberals, or rather the Whigs, were not alone in their troubles and anxieties. Shocked by the onset of democracy and its threat to old, established interests, the Tory leaders proceeded to forget the lessons which Disraeli had tried so long to teach them. Their leader in the Commons was Sir Stafford Northcote, who had once been Gladstone's private secretary and still stood in awe of the great man. His companions on the front bench clung desperately to the faith, practice, and timidity of their youth. Into the breach stepped a small but extremely able group whose prowess at Parliamentary guerrilla fighting has rarely been equalled, the "Fourth Party" —Lord Randolph Churchill, A. J. Balfour, Sir Henry Drummond Wolff, and John Gorst. They teased and taunted Gladstone without mercy or respect. But Lord Randolph, who quickly rose to special prominence, reserved his fiercest criticism for the leaders of his own side. In a letter to *The Times* he charged them with "a series of neglected opportunities, pusillanimity, combativeness at wrong moments, vacillation, dread of responsibility, repression and discouragement of hard-working followers, collusions with the Government, hankerings after coalitions, jealousies, commonplaces, want of perception". His denunciations were not confined to Parliament. With the motto "Trust the People" and the slogan "Tory Democracy" he appealed to the rank and file over the heads of their nominal leaders. So dramatic was his success that his power soon became almost as strong as Salisbury's.

These were strange years for party warfare. The upsurge of the new forces, radicalism and Tory democracy, was playing havoc with the old Parliamentary system. Chamberlain and Lord Randolph, though sometimes in bitter disagreement, had far more in common than they had with their own leaders. The confusion was not to be resolved until Gladstone, using Home Rule for Ireland like an axe, divided the political world by forcing men to make a clear and sharp decision about a single great proposal.

Meanwhile, the Liberals fell heirs to a set of Imperial complications which involved them in enterprises hateful to their anti-Imperialist sentiments. One of their first troubles sprang from South Africa. There the Boer Republic of the Transvaal had long been in difficulties, threatened by bankruptcy and disorders within and by the Zulu warrior kingdom upon its eastern border. To save it from possible extinction, Disraeli's Government had annexed it, an action which at first met with little protest. But now a fierce desire for renewed independence began to stir among the Transvaal Boers, and they looked for an opportunity to throw off British rule. As soon as British arms had finally quelled the Zulus in 1897 they felt safe enough to seize their chance. It was perhaps natural that they should expect their freedom from a Liberal Government. Gladstone had denounced the annexation of the Transvaal, but a powerful section of his party favoured the African natives more than the Boers. He himself was convinced that federation of all the white communities was the only solution for the South African puzzle, and he refused to make any immediate change. At the end of 1880 the Boers revolted and a small British force was cut to pieces at Majuba Hill. There was available in South Africa a force large enough to

Lord Randolph Churchill (1849-95) became the leader of the "Fourth Party", which advocated popular conservatism. He was a brilliant though sometimes erratic politician, who was famous for his sharp oratory. He married the American socialite and writer, Jennie Jerome, who in 1874 gave him a son, named Winston Churchill.

The Zulu War witnessed many acts of bravery. The Zulu warriors, called "impi", moved stealthily, fought bravely and had superior numbers to the British, but they were defeated by an army which had both cavalry and guns.

crush the Boers, but Gladstone declined to bow to the outcry for retaliation and continued with the negotiations that had already been underway at the time of Majuba. The outcome was the Pretoria Convention of 1881, which, modified in 1884, gave virtual independence to the Transvaal. This application of Liberal principles provided the foundation of Boer power in South Africa. All might have gone more smoothly in the future but for two developments. Immensely rich goldfields were discovered on the Rand and a large, bustling cosmopolitan mining community was suddenly planted in the midst of the Boer farmers' Republic. Meanwhile at Cape Town, Cecil Rhodes had entered politics, resolved to create a vast, all-embracing South African dominion, and endowed by nature with the energy that often makes dreams come true. From these events sprang consequences which have yet to run their course.

Also, as Gladstone had foreseen at the time, Disraeli's purchase of shares in the Suez Canal, brilliant stroke though it was, now brought all the problems of Egypt in its wake. When he took office, Egypt, nominally ruled by the Khedive, was in effect under Anglo-French control. The Khedive had

THE CUP FINAL OF 1882

Empire builders prided themselves on their bodily strength. One of the lasting legacies of Victorian England is the game of football, which developed in the public schools and was gradually refined into the game as played today. The Football Association was founded in 1863 and the FA Cup was first awarded in 1871. These extracts from the Blackburn Times *give a flavour of the 1882 Cup Final between a team of Old Etonians and Blackburn Rovers, who were a comparatively new football team from the north of England.*

With fine weather and the prospect of an exciting contest, it was to be expected that a large number of persons would be attracted to Kennington Oval, on Saturday afternoon, and the expectation was realised, as the attendance was swollen to 6,000 about three o'clock. There was a considerable body of the Rovers' supporters in attendance, the two special trains from East Lancashire in the early hours of the morning having brought about 700 persons, while 200 others had made the journey on the previous day.

Some of the Old Etonians first appeared within the enclosure, and were soon followed by the main body of the Rovers, while the majority of the Eton men, followed by the two captains, did not leave the dressing room until some minutes later.

When the cheering which greeted the advent of the rival captains had subsided, the toss for choice of goals was made, and the Rovers' chief was unfortunate in losing. The Etonians chose to play with the wind in their favour and the sun at their backs. The ball was "kicked off" at eight minutes past three.

There was a marked contrast in the style of play of the rival teams and to Blackburn spectators the game revealed features unusual in the north. While the Rovers worked their way towards their opponents' goal by passing, the Etonians did so by rushes, the player securing the ball at the start retaining possession of it until robbed or checked, and his partner bearing him company to render assistance when opposition appeared. The Etonians indulged in none of the dribbling or dodging which forms a pleasing part of the famous Lancashire team's play, reliance being placed instead on the weight and speed of the forwards. . . .

As the time for play gradually shortened, the supporters of the Rovers, who were one goal down, became less confident, and there were shouts from the grandstand of "Play up Blackburn", to which admirers of their opponents responded by cries of "E-e-ton". But there was ominous silence amongst the Lancashire spectators. For nearly twenty minutes before the close the Etonians were practically penned in their own quarters, and the Rovers were constantly striving to score, but only to be disappointed by seeing the ball go over the line on the wrong side of the posts or to be stopped by the goalkeeper. The desperate struggle was continued until the referee's whistle signalled the expiration of time, and the Etonians were hailed the victors by one goal to none.

After their defeat by the Old Etonians in 1882, the Blackburn Rovers won the English Football Cup three times in succession. The photograph shows the victorious Blackburn Rovers team.

only temporarily been saved from bankruptcy by selling his Canal shares. Soon French and British Debt Commissioners were appointed to take charge of his finances, and of much else too. At the end of 1881, however, Anglo-French control was shattered by a nationalist revolt led by Colonel Arabi Pasha. It was backed by the army and rapidly swept through the whole country. On June 11, 1882, fifty Europeans were killed in riots in Alexandria, and Arabi began to fortify the city in such a way as to threaten British ships in the harbour. Hence, exactly a month later, and after warning had been given, the forts were bombarded and the guns silenced. A few days later, the Cabinet decided to dispatch an army under Sir Garnet Wolseley to Egypt. The decision was crowned by military success, and Arabi's army was decisively defeated at Tel-el-Kebir on September 13. Gladstone delighted in the victory, but was troubled in his conscience. The Liberal instinct was now to withdraw, but Egypt could not be left a vacuum. To annex her, though logical and expected by the other powers of Europe, was repugnant to the Liberal conscience. Gladstone therefore chose the worst of both worlds. The odium of occupation remained on the British, but much authority continued to be exercised by the Commissioners of the Debt, a state of affairs which allowed all the major European powers to interfere. Nevertheless, after Evelyn Baring became Consul-General in 1883, and in effect ruler of the country, a new era opened of much-needed reform.

Intervention in Egypt led to an even more perplexing entanglement in the Sudan. This huge territory, more than a thousand miles deep, stretched along the torrid banks of the Nile from the borders of Egypt down almost to the equator. It formed a part of the Khedive's realm, and in spite of the efforts of British advisers it was woefully misgoverned by Pashas from Cairo. In 1882 the Sudanese rebelled against the Egyptians. They were led by the Mahdi, a Muslim fanatic who quickly destroyed an Egyptian army, and was soon in control of most of the Sudan. Gladstone spoke of the Sudanese as "a people rightly struggling to be free". This was a highly flattering way of describing the Mahdi's forces, whose blood-lust spread terror everywhere in their advance. Either the Sudan must be reconquered or it must be evacuated, and the Government in London chose evacuation. With this the Egyptians had to concur. At the end of 1883 the decision was made to withdraw their outlying garrisons scattered far to the south, for which Britain, as tutor to the Egyptian army, had a general responsibility. To make the decision was easy; to carry it out more difficult. But on January 14, 1884, General Charles Gordon, who had achieved fame in the Chinese wars of 1863, left London charged with the task of evacuation.

Gordon had himself served in the Sudan, and had played a notable part in attempts to suppress the slave trade. He also had a conscience. It was to cost him his life. He arrived in Khartoum in February, and once there he judged that it would be wrong to abandon the country to the mercy of the Mahdi's dervishes. He accordingly asked for reinforcements and put forward plans for counterattack. In London the Government were taken aback by this change of front. Gordon's strength of will, often capricious in its expression, was pitted against Gladstone's determination not to be involved in fresh colonial adventures. Lord Randolph Churchill was the first to raise in the House of Commons the problem of Gordon's personal safety. In March he put a blunt question to the Government. "Are they going to remain indifferent," he asked, "to the fate of the one man on whom they

Major General "Chinese" Gordon (1833-85), so nicknamed for his successes in China, was a man of action and of strong religious beliefs. But he had a fatal conviction of his own infallibility.

have counted to extricate them from their dilemmas, to leave him to shift for himself, and not to make a single effort on his behalf?" Lord Randolph was met with evasive replies. Help for Gordon was to be long in coming, in spite of his urgent appeals, which were backed by dispatches from Baring in Cairo and by the advice of the foremost Imperial soldier of the age, Lord Wolseley. By May, Gordon was cut off in Khartoum. Meanwhile the Cabinet, still insistent on the policy of "scuttling out", as Lord Salisbury called it, refused to dispatch a relieving army.

Throughout the spring and summer public opinion in England mounted, and large meetings were held demanding that Gordon must be saved. His stern religious faith, his assaults on slavery, his charitable work for the children of the poor, as well as his military prowess, had made him a heroic figure. Eventually, upon the insistence of Lord Hartington, then Secretary of State for War, the Government were induced to act. In September Wolseley hastened to Cairo, and in less than a month he had assembled a striking force of ten thousand men. He knew that a rapid foray against the massed spearmen of the Mahdi would accomplish nothing. A campaign of six months, soundly based, was the fastest he could hope for. In October he set out from the borders of Egypt upon the eight-hundred-mile advance to Khartoum. Much of his way lay through uncharted reaches of the Nile; rapids and cataracts abounded, and the heat was heavy and wearisome. In the Northern Sudan the River Nile describes an immense bend to the east.

Wolseley was aware that time was fatally short. He felt the eyes and anxieties of England focused upon Gordon and himself, and on the distance that lay between them. His main strength must proceed steadily upriver until, all cataracts surmounted, they would be poised for a swoop upon Khartoum. In the meantime he detached the Camel Corps under Sir Herbert Stewart to cut across a hundred and fifty miles of desert and rejoin the Nile to the north of Gordon's capital. Starting on December 30, Stewart acted with resolution, but at Abu Klea, on January 17, a hundred and twenty miles short of his goal, he was attacked by a dervish host. His column of fewer than two thousand men confronted an enemy at least five times as numerous. Under a desperate onset the British square was broken by the Mahdi's fanatical hordes, but the battle was won. Two days later, amid constant harassments, Stewart's advanced troops reached the Nile, but he had been mortally wounded. His successor inherited a perilous situation. There was a tragic but unavoidable delay while reconnaissances were made and the wounded tended. On January 24 a force of twenty-six British and two hundred and forty Sudanese sailed south on two steamers, assailed by dervish musketry fire from the banks. On the twenty-eighth they reached Khartoum. It was too late. Gordon's flag no longer flew over the Residency. He was dead; the city had fallen two days before, after a prodigious display of valour by its defender. He had fallen alone, unsuccoured by his own countrymen. In the eyes of perhaps half the nation Gladstone was a murderer. The Queen was so distressed that she made her own feelings clear to him in an open telegram. Gordon became a national martyr. It was true that he had disobeyed his orders, as indeed he admitted in his journal, but the fact remained that the Cabinet which had sent him out had then virtually abandoned him. As Gladstone later confessed, the Government had sent a "hero of heroes" to Khartoum with all the defects and virtues of his type and they had paid the penalty. The rescuing force retired to Egypt. Thirteen years went by before Gordon was avenged.

The position of the Liberal Party had been equally shaken by its activities at home. While the nation thought only of Gordon, the Government was pressing ahead with its one considerable piece of legislation, a Reform Bill which completed the work of democratising the franchise. Almost every adult male was given a vote. Another Act abolished the remaining small boroughs and, with a few exceptions, divided the country into single-member constituencies. All this was a logical extension of the Act of 1867, but it exacerbated an already difficult situation. Single-member constituencies stopped the old practice of running a Whig and a radical in harness. The radicals were quick to press their advantage. Chamberlain had made onslaught after onslaught on the class who "toil not, neither do they spin", and he now switched his main attack from town to country. The Whigs could not ignore the challenge; the division between them and the radicals was too deep and fundamental for them ever to work together again.

Further speculation about the future of English politics was now abruptly cut short by the announcement of Gladstone's conversion to the policy of Home Rule. To comprehend the significance and impact of this event we must look back upon the melancholy story of Ireland. In the years since the Great Famine of the 1840s Ireland had continued in her misery. Her peasants, especially in the west, lived in a state of extreme poverty and degradation. General Gordon had thus described them some time before in a letter to *The Times*: "I must say, from all accounts and from my own observation, that the state of our fellow countrymen in the parts I have named is worse than that of any people in the world." They were "living on the verge of starvation in places in which we would not keep our cattle". Ireland was a poor country, and in spite of famine and emigration she was still over-populated. But these misfortunes were greatly aggravated by the policies of the English Government. The Irish peasant was crushed by a land system which he hated not only because it put almost absolute power into the hands of the landlord, but also because it rested on the expropriation of land which he considered, by right, to belong to him. It was not just a matter of material poverty, of life passed in a one-roomed hut on a diet of potatoes. He felt he had been robbed of his heritage. For most of the nineteenth century the English answer was to ignore the hate and crush the crime which it produced. In the forty years before 1870 forty-two Coercion Acts were passed. During the same period there was not a single statute to protect the Irish peasant from eviction and rack-renting. This was deliberate; the aim was to make the Irish peasant a day-labourer after the English pattern. But Ireland was not England; the Irish peasant clung to his land; he used every means in his power to defeat the alien landlords.

It must not be supposed that the Irish picture can be seen from Britain entirely in black and white. The landlords were mostly colonists from England and of long standing; they believed themselves to be, and in many ways were, a civilising influence in a primitive country. They had often had to fight for their lives and their property. The deep hold of the Roman Catholic Church on a superstitious peasantry had tended on political as well as religious grounds to be hostile to England. Ireland more than once had threatened to become a steppingstone to the invasion of Britain from the Continent. The assassination of landlords and other acts of terrorism

"WHERE'S THE (IRISH) POLICE?"

CHIEF CONSTABLE. "H'm!—shooting landlords!—wrecking private property!—burning stores!—seizing arms!—breaking heads!—murder and intimidation!—'Pon my word, if they go much further I must really——DO SOMETHING!!!"

In the 1870s bad harvests led to outbreaks of Irish unrest, known as the Fenian outrages. The name "Fenian" comes from Fianna, *meaning heroic Irish warriors. There was sympathy for the rioters' cause, even among the Irish police.*

IRELAND'S EYE.

THE FATHER OF A CAUSE.

Isaac Butt was the father of the Irish Home Rule League, which won over fifty seats in Parliament in the 1874 election. In this contemporary cartoon Butt is seen shaking the parliamentary rattle for "baby" Home Rule.

had contributed to a general acceptance in England of the landlord's case. It was hard to grasp that the vicious circle of unrest, repression, and rebellion could only be broken by remedying fundamental grievances.

From the moment when he first took office as Prime Minister, Gladstone made Irish affairs his special concern until at last they came to dominate his mind to the exclusion of almost everything else. His crusade for Ireland, for such it was, faced formidable opposition. English political society had little sympathy for Irish problems, and indeed many of its leading figures were members of the Irish aristocracy. In his first Ministry, Gladstone had dealt successfully with the Irish dislike of an alien Church by disestablishing the Protestant Church of Ireland. His second measure, a Land Act to prevent uncompensated eviction, had been passed in 1870, but proved a failure. Ten more years went by before he became convinced that the Irish peasant had to be given real security in the tenure of his land.

In 1870 Isaac Butt had founded the Home Rule League. It aimed to achieve Home Rule by peaceful, constitutional methods, and its able, courteous leader put his faith in the persuasive processes of House of Commons debate. But there was no response to his cause in England and no confidence in his methods in Ireland and effective leadership of the movement soon passed into the hands of Charles Stewart Parnell, who was a landlord, a Protestant, and a newcomer to Parliament. From his mother, the daughter of an American admiral who had won distinction fighting the British, he had acquired a hatred for English ways and institutions. A patrician in the Irish party, he was a born leader, with a power of discipline and a tactical skill that soon converted Home Rule from a debating topic into the supreme question of the hour. Ruthless in pressing his cause, and defiant of the traditions of the House of Commons, he swiftly gained such a position that an English politician said that "dealing with him was like dealing with a foreign power".

The root of Parnell's success was the junction of the Home Rule cause with a fresh outburst of peasant agitation. A grave fall in world crop prices in the late seventies and a series of bad harvests accelerated the number of evictions as the impoverished peasants failed to pay their rents. This process was just beginning when, in 1877, Michael Davitt came out of prison after serving a seven-year sentence for treason. Davitt was a remarkable man who, in his love for Ireland and warm human sympathies, made a sharp contrast with Parnell. It was Davitt's belief that Home Rule and the land question could not be separated, and, in spite of opposition from the extreme Irish Nationalists, he successfully founded the Land League in 1879. Its objects were the reduction of rack rents and the promotion of peasant ownership of the land. Davitt had previously assured himself of the material backing of the Irish in America. When Parnell declared his support for the League, the land hunger of the peasant, the political demand for Home Rule, and the hatred of American emigrants for their unforgotten oppressors were at last brought together in a formidable alliance.

The Gladstone Government's first answer was to promote an interim Compensation for Disturbance Bill. When this was rejected by the House of Lords in August 1880, Ireland was quick to reply with terror. In the last quarter of the year nearly two thousand outrages were committed. A new weapon appeared when Parnell advised his followers to make life unbearable for anyone who violated peasant law and custom "by isolating him from his kind as if he were a leper of old". One of the first victims was a land agent, Captain Boycott, whose name has passed into the English language. This was the period of the Land League's greatest success. Funds were pouring in from America and Australia, and, since the League effectively controlled more of Ireland than did the authorities in Dublin Castle, evictions almost ceased.

The Government then decided both to strike at terrorism and to reform the land laws. In March 1881 a sweeping Coercion Act gave to the Irish Viceroy the power, in the writer Viscount Morley's phrase, "to lock up anybody he pleased and to detain him for as long as he pleased". It was during the debate on the Coercion Bill that the climax came in Parnell's policy of obstruction. His aim in the House of Commons had been to bring government to a standstill by exploiting the fact that Parliamentary procedure rested on custom rather than rules. From January 31 until February 2 the House sat continuously for forty-one hours, and the end came only when the Speaker took the arbitrary step of "putting the Question that the House should now adjourn". Subsequently a resolution introducing the Closure was passed, thus making the first great breach in the traditional methods of carrying through Parliamentary business.

The Coercion Act was followed immediately by a Land Act which conceded almost everything that the Irish had demanded. The Act was based on the "three Fs"—Fair Rents to be decided by a tribunal, Fixity of Tenure for all who paid their rents, and Free Sale by the tenant. This was far more generous than anything the Irish had expected, but Parnell, driven by Irish-American extremists and by his belief that even greater concessions could be extracted from Gladstone, set out to obstruct the working of the new Land Courts. The Government had no alternative, under the Coercion Act, but to arrest him. This it did in October. He was asked who would take his place. His reply was "Captain Moonlight". His prophecy was justified. Crime and murder multiplied, and by the spring of 1882 Gladstone was convinced that the policy of coercion had failed.

At the same time Parnell was anxious for release. As the extremists in Ireland were gaining ground it was vital for him to reassert his authority as leader. In April therefore what was called the "Kilmainham Treaty" was concluded, based on the understanding that Parnell would use his influence to end terror in return for an Arrears Bill which would aid those tenants who, because they owed rent, had been unable to take advantage of the Land Act. W. E. Forster, Chief Secretary for Ireland and advocate of coercion, and the Viceroy, Lord Cowper, resigned. They were replaced by Lord Frederick Cavendish and Lord Spencer. On May 2, Parnell was released, and it seemed that at last there was some likelihood of peace. But these bright prospects were destroyed by a terrible event. On May 6 Lord Frederick Cavendish landed in Dublin. A few hours after his arrival he was walking in Phoenix Park with his under-secretary, Burke, when both men were stabbed to death. The murderers were a group called the Invincibles. The English nation was shocked, and all hope of any immediate conciliation was quenched. Gladstone did what he could to salvage a little from the wreck of his policy. He was now convinced that Parnell was a restraining influence in Ireland and that the only hope of any lasting success was to cooperate with him. Parnell, for his part, was content to bide his time, and for three years Ireland was relatively quiet and peaceful.

This photograph of Charles Stewart Parnell (1846–91) was taken in c.1886. Parnell became known as the "uncrowned king" of Ireland through his fight for Irish Home Rule. In 1879 Michael Davitt persuaded him to become president of the Irish National Land League. His obstructive tactics in Parliament upset Gladstone, but the strength of his support in Ireland led to the Irish Land Act of 1881, and soon converted Gladstone to Home Rule.

The Illustrated Police News shows portraits of those responsible for the murder of Cavendish and Burke in 1883. They were members of the "Invincibles", a terrorist splinter group of the Fenian Society. Of those arrested, five were hanged. Parnell was accused of being one of those involved in the plot but he was later vindicated by a parliamentary commission.

Thus we return to the year 1885. On June 8 the Government was defeated on an amendment to the Budget, and Gladstone promptly resigned. Dissension and division in the Liberal Party had done their work, but a more direct cause was that the Irish Members voted with the Conservative Opposition. Lord Randolph Churchill had given Parnell to understand that a Conservative Government would discontinue coercion, and this was enough to swing Irish support. After some hesitation and difficulty Lord Salisbury formed a Government which was in a minority in the House of Commons. Lord Randolph took office as Secretary for India, and a most significant appointment was that of the Earl of Carnarvon as Viceroy of Ireland. It was well-known that Carnarvon favoured a policy of Home Rule, and when on August 1 he met Parnell in a house in Grosvenor Square, he left Parnell with the impression that the Government was contemplating a Home Rule measure. With an election approaching, Parnell had to make his choice. Through his mistress, Kitty O'Shea, who acted as intermediary, he made known to Gladstone the nature of the Conservative approach. Gladstone replied, "It is right I should say that into any counter-bidding of any sort against Lord Randolph Churchill, I for one cannot enter." The truth was that at this time Gladstone had already been converted to Home Rule, but was not prepared to bargain with Parnell, preferring to hold his hand and leave the next move to Salisbury.

When the election came in November, Parnell, unable to extract a clear promise of support from Gladstone, ordered the Irish in Britain to vote Conservative. The result could not have been more unfortunate. In the new House of Commons the Liberal majority over the Conservatives fell to eighty-six. But Parnell had realised his dream. His followers, their ranks swollen by the operation of the Reform Act in the Irish counties, also numbered eighty-six. The position was exactly what Salisbury had described as "low-water mark—*i.e.* Tories + Parnellites = Liberals".

In these circumstances Gladstone continued to hope that the Parnellite-Conservative alliance would hold fast and that Home Rule would pass as an agreed measure without undue opposition from the House of Lords. Precedents like Catholic Emancipation, the Repeal of the Corn Laws, and the second Reform Act were much in his mind. On December 20 he wrote, "I feel sure the question can only be dealt with by a Government, and I desire specially on grounds of public policy that it should be dealt with by the present Government." The Conservatives treated this with contempt. A few days earlier the political situation had been transformed by the public disclosure of Gladstone's views on Home Rule by his son, Herbert. The "Hawarden Kite", as it came to be called, immediately brought to the surface all those forces which had been struggling, hidden from public view, in the political depths. The split in the Liberal Party which Gladstone had been so anxious to avoid became a reality. The Whigs, already alienated by the growing power of radicalism, were solid against Home Rule. The attitude of the Conservatives hardened as they sensed the advantages they would gain from Gladstone's dramatic conversion. A possible alliance between them and the Whigs was already in the air. For Parnell the outcome was a disaster. His support had made the Conservatives a present of thirty seats. It proved to be a gift to the enemy.

It is doubtful whether there had ever been substance in Gladstone's hopes. Carnarvon represented himself and not his party or the Cabinet. Salisbury,

DAYS OF EMPIRE

Britain's Empire in the nineteenth century was vast and variegated. It included countries largely settled by Britons and countries with well-established native rulers. To the mother country, its Empire offered responsibility, opportunity, and—as at the Diamond Jubilee—an occasional excuse for imperial ceremonial and self-congratulation.

"THE QUEEN'S DIAMOND JUBILEE, 1897" BY A.C. GOW,
GUILDHALL ART GALLERY, LONDON

"THE LAST OF ENGLAND", by Ford Madox Brown, (left) from the Birmingham City Art Gallery, is the most famous of the many paintings on the theme of emigration. The models for the two figures were the artist and his wife (who was only fifteen when they married), its inspiration the departure of one of the artist's friends to Australia in 1852. The three contemporary paintings, (above) by less famous artists, are of South Australia, South Africa, and New Zealand. They convey something of the Victorian vision of the adventure of faraway places—and of the desperate discomfort of those who dared to take their families there. South Australia was founded in 1836, as the first state in Australia to be colonised originally by free men and not by convicts. The British occupied the Cape in South Africa in 1795, and later spread northward. The first major colonisation of New Zealand began in the year 1839.

"THE BALL ON SHIPBOARD", (above) by the distinguished French artist, James Tissot, illustrates the more glamorous side of Victorian imperial travel. Tissot settled in London from 1871 to 1882, and specialised in paintings of elegant society.

THE SS GREAT BRITAIN, (left) now docked at Bristol, the same port from which she was launched in 1843, was the first propeller-driven iron ship to cross the Atlantic. Built by the great engineer, Isambard Kingdom Brunel, she revolutionised sea travel at a time when the administration of the Empire depended as much on safe fast liners as it did on warships. The contemporary print (below) shows the great ship under steam and sail.

BATEMAN'S, E. SUSSEX, (top) was the home of Rudyard Kipling, whose portrait (above) by Burne-Jones can be seen at the National Portrait Gallery, London. Rudyard Kipling is now recognised not just as an imperial propagandist, but also as a great English writer.

THE DURBAR ROOM, OSBORNE HOUSE, ISLE OF WIGHT, (right) was built to hold Queen Victoria's gifts from India, the country she most treasured, but never visited. Her finest gift, however, the Koh-i-noor diamond, is in the Tower of London, in the crown of Queen Elizabeth, the Queen Mother (above). It is said to bring ill-fortune to any man, but good luck to any woman, who wears it.

THE VICTORIA MEMORIAL, CALCUTTA, INDIA, (above) was built to house the relics and art of almost three hundred years of British influence in India. A potent symbol of imperial power, it was designed by Lord Curzon, ironically almost at the moment of that empire's decline. The painting (left) of an imperial Durbar records the very successful use made by the British of Indian ceremonial to confirm their control over the subcontinent.

NEW DELHI, INDIA, formally succeeded Calcutta as the capital of India in 1911, and Edwin Lutyens and Herbert Baker set out to build a city that would combine the best of British and Indian styles. Between them they created an extraordinarily brilliant memorial to British rule, though their two greatest buildings failed to match each other. Baker built the government offices, the Secretariat (above), and Lutyens the Viceroy's Palace (right), a magnificent blending of East and West. The relationship between these key buildings was similar in layout to that of the Royal Naval College and the Queen's House at Greenwich, but sadly Baker decided to build the Secretariat on a platform which partly blocked the view of the Viceroy's Palace. Lutyens protested, but wryly had to admit that on this issue, great architect though he was, he had met his Bakerloo.

THE NATURAL HISTORY MUSEUM, LONDON, *(right) was opened in 1880 as a home for exhibits brought back to Britain by travellers, explorers and scientists of the Victorian age. Its architect, Alfred Waterhouse, created a cathedral out of terracotta and glass, supported, as can be seen from the entrance hall (above), by a massive iron structure.*

"GIANT PROTEA" (left) was painted in South Africa by the nineteenth-century traveller, Marianne North. Her botanical paintings are on display in their own gallery in Kew Gardens, Greater London.

*"GENERAL GORDON'S LAST STAND",
(above) by W.G. Joy, now hangs in
the Gordon Boys' School, Woking,
Surrey. This picture of the popular
Christian general, fearless in the
face of native fury, very much
reflected the Victorian view of the
imperial role of Britain.*

*LEIGHTON HOUSE, LONDON, was built
by the painter, Lord Leighton to
house his collection of treasures,
mostly from the Middle East. The
Arab Hall (right) has fourteenth-
century Persian tiles, damascene
stained-glass windows and a frieze
by the illustrator, Walter Crane.*

*THE CRYSTAL PALACE (below), in its
vast size and its revolutionary use
of materials, matched the pride and
splendour of the Great Exhibition
for which it was designed in 1851.
The palace was later moved to
Sydenham, where it was destroyed
by fire in 1936. The chair made by
Henry Eyles of Bath, (bottom right)
now in the Victoria and Albert
Museum, London, was exhibited in
1851. It carries a portrait of the
Prince Consort, who was very largely responsible for the success of
the Exhibition.*

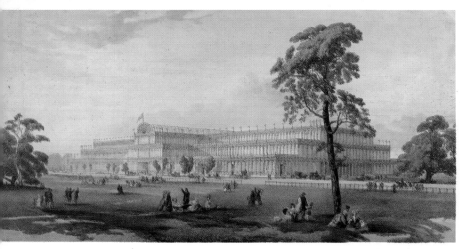

111

THE ALBERT MEMORIAL, LONDON,
stands in Kensington Gardens on
the site once occupied by the Crystal
Palace. It was designed by Gilbert
Scott in the style of a medieval
shrine to the memory of Prince
Albert, the Prince Consort, and to
the imperial and scientific achievements of Britain in the nineteenth
century. It stands, too, as perhaps
the best known, though hardly the
most admired, example of Victorian
Gothic architecture.

for his part, was naturally content to have the Irish vote in a critical election, but his Protestantism, his belief in the Union, his loyalty to the Irish landowners, were all far too strong for him ever to have seriously considered Home Rule. No leader has ever had less of the temperament of a Peel or a Gladstone. Enthusiasm of the kind that splits parties was quite outside Salisbury's nature.

By Christmas 1885 the die was cast. Carnarvon resigned in the New Year, and on January 26, Salisbury's Government announced that it would introduce a Coercion Bill of the most stringent kind. Without hesitation, almost without consultation with his colleagues, Gladstone brought about its defeat on an amendment to the Queen's Speech. There was no doubt that the new Government would be a Home Rule Government, and several leading Whigs refused to join. This was probably inevitable, but Gladstone destroyed any remaining hope of success by his treatment of Chamberlain. In the eyes of the country Chamberlain now stood next to his leader in the Liberal Party. But Gladstone refused him the Colonial Office, and sent him to the Local Government Board. Chamberlain was opposed to any large scheme of Irish self-government, and it would have needed all Gladstone's tact and persuasion to win him over. Gladstone made no attempt to do so. Chamberlain was not consulted in the preparation of the Home Rule Bill, and his own scheme for local government reform was ignored. He resigned on March 26, to become Gladstone's most formidable foe.

The Home Rule Bill was introduced by Gladstone into the Commons on April 8, 1886, in a speech which lasted for three and a half hours. He put the case for Home Rule as one of justice for Ireland and freedom for her people. It was an outstanding performance, even for Gladstone. But his sudden conversion to the new policy, his dependence upon the Irish vote for continuance in office, and the bitter memories of Irish crimes combined to deepen the fears and prejudices of his opponents. The emotions of race, religion, class, and economic interest all obscured the Liberal arguments. Fire evoked fire. Gladstone's deep moral feeling found its answer on the other side. He had embarked on a sudden, destructive crusade.

The Bill was defeated on the second reading two months after its introduction. Ninety-three Liberals voted against the Government. Gladstone had a difficult decision to make. He could resign or dissolve. He chose the latter course and fought the election on the single issue of Home Rule. His zeal, enthusiasm, and energy were not enough to overcome the mighty forces arrayed against him. The new House contained three hundred and sixteen Conservatives and seventy-eight Liberal Unionists, against a hundred and ninety-one Gladstonians and eighty-five Parnellites. Gladstone resigned immediately, and Salisbury again took office.

The long period of Liberal-Whig predominance was over. It had been brought to an end by Whig distaste for social reform and by Gladstone's precipitate conversion to Home Rule. The outlook for the Liberal Party was dark. In committing itself to a policy which was electorally unpopular in England it had not only shed its Right Wing, but also the man who had been by far the most outstanding of its young, reforming leaders. The turn of the wheel had brought fortune to the Conservatives, who apart from one short spell were to remain in power for twenty years. The opponents whom they had feared as the irresistible instruments of democracy had delivered themselves into their hands.

THE IRISH BILL REJECTED.

THE DIVISION ON THE SECOND READING.

MAJORITY AGAINST THE BILL, 30.

SCENES IN THE HOUSE.

EXPECTED RESIGNATION OF THE GOVERNMENT.

These were the headlines in the Irish Times *on June 8, 1886, when the Home Rule Bill was finally defeated. The result was received with cheers from the Conservative benches which were followed by further cheers for Gladstone, from the Irish Members who had fought so hard for Irish Home Rule. Nevertheless, Gladstone resigned.*

CHAPTER 10

LORD SALISBURY'S GOVERNMENTS

This satirical cartoon is captioned "Salisbury Sisyphus". In Greek mythology, Sisyphus was condemned by Zeus forever to roll a huge stone up a hill in Hades, only to find it roll down again on nearing the top. For Salisbury, the problems in Ireland were to remain throughout his three terms of office, and his policy of firm government to combat lawlessness was not the solution.

IT WAS NOT IMMEDIATELY PERCEIVED in the summer of 1886 that the controversy over Home Rule for Ireland had wrought a deep change in the allegiance of English political parties. Salisbury's Government depended upon the support of the Liberal Unionists, led by Hartington, though their most formidable figure, both in Parliament and in the country, was Joseph Chamberlain. They protested that they were still Liberals, and for ten years they continued to sit on the Liberal side of the House of Commons. This infuriated the followers of Gladstone, many of whom bitterly and publicly likened Chamberlain to Judas Iscariot. It was tacitly accepted, after the failure of a Round Table Conference between the leaders of the two sides, held at the beginning of 1887, that the gulf was too wide to be bridged. This decisive split produced strange bedfellows. Salisbury had to work with the man whom he had denounced as a mob-leader and a "Jack Cade" only a few months before. Chamberlain, now tied to the Conservative chariot, was impelled for his part to retract many of his former policies and opinions. On the Liberal side Gladstone, deprived of his Whig supporters, was forced to make concessions to the radical sections of his party, whose views were far in advance of his own.

Salisbury's Government was not much different from that of the previous year, except that Lord Randolph Churchill became Leader of the House and Chancellor of the Exchequer. His career had reached its pinnacle. In the course of six years his skill in debate and political tactics had carried him beyond all his rivals. His position in the Commons was unchallenged by any other member of his party, although many distrusted his methods and disliked his policies. Inside the Cabinet there was little harmony. Lord Randolph's ideas on Tory Democracy struck no spark in Salisbury's traditional Conservatism. The Prime Minister had no great faith in betterment by legislation. He believed that the primary business of government was to administer the existing order, and that the Conservatives owed their first duty to the classes who relied upon them to defend their interests. This clash was intensified by Lord Randolph's excursions into the field of foreign affairs. In October he had publicly attacked the policy of friendship for Turkey and declared himself in favour of independence for the Balkan peoples. The differences between the two men, both in character and policy, were fundamental. The final collision occurred over a comparatively trivial point: Lord Randolph's demand for a reduction in the army and navy estimates. He resigned on the eve of Christmas 1886 at the wrong time, on the wrong issue, and he made no attempt to rally support. He lived for another nine years, enduring much ill-health, but his career lay in ruins.

This dramatic fall came as the finale to a year of political sensations. Salisbury made George Goschen, a Liberal Unionist of impeccable Whig views, his Chancellor of the Exchequer, thus proclaiming that Tory Democracy was now deemed an unnecessary encumbrance. Thereafter his Government's record in lawmaking was meagre in the extreme. The main measure was the Local Government Act of 1888, which created county councils. Three years later school fees were abolished in elementary schools, and a Factory Act made some further attempt to regulate evils in the employment of women and children. It was not an impressive achievement. Even these minor measures were largely carried out as concessions to Chamberlain, who from outside the Government constantly preached a policy of active reform.

Salisbury's interest, however, and that of a large section of public opinion lay in the world overseas, where the Imperialist movement was reaching its climax of exploration, conquest, and settlement. Livingstone, Stanley, Speke, and other travellers had opened up the interior of darkest Africa. Their feats of exploration paved the way for the acquisition of colonies by the European powers. It was the most important achievement of the period that this partition of Africa was carried out peacefully. The credit is largely due to Salisbury, who in 1887 became Foreign Secretary as well as Prime Minister. The French, seeking consolation for their defeat at the hands of the Prussians in 1870, had been first in the field, with the Germans, in the early eighties, not far behind. Gladstone and Disraeli, had they wished, with the naval and economic power at their disposal, could have annexed much of the continent which their countrymen had mapped and explored.

STANLEY FINDS LIVINGSTONE

David Livingstone, Scots missionary and explorer, led an expedition to central Africa in 1866, reaching Lake Tanganyika in early 1869. Some of his team deserted, spreading the rumour that he had been killed by tribesmen. The New York Herald *sent a correspondent, Henry Stanley, to find him. He did so on November 10, 1871.*

We are but a mile from Ujiji now, and it is high time we should let them know a caravan is coming; so "Commence firing" is the word passed along the length of the column, and gladly do they begin. They have loaded their muskets half full, and they roar like the broadside of a line-of-battle ship. Down go the ramrods, sending huge charges home to the breech, and volley after volley is fired. The flags are fluttered; the banner of America is in front, waving joyfully; the guide is in the zenith of his glory. The former residents of Zanzita will know it directly and will wonder—as well they may—as to what it means. Never were the Stars and Stripes so beautiful to my mind—the breeze of the Tanganyika has such an effect on them. The guide blows his horn, and the shrill, wild clangour of it is far and near; and still the cannon muskets tell the noisy seconds. By this time the Arabs are fully alarmed; the natives of Ujiji, Waguha, Warundi, Wanguana, and I know not whom hurry up by the hundreds to ask what it all means—this fusillading, shouting, and blowing of horns and flag-flying. There are Yambos shouted out to me by the dozen, and delighted Arabs have run up breathlessly to shake my hand and ask anxiously where I come from. But I have no patience with them. The expedition goes far too slow. I should like to settle the vexed question by one personal view. Where is he? Has he fled?

Suddenly a man—a black man—at my elbow shouts in English, "How do you do, sir?"

"Hello, who the deuce are you?"

"I am the servant of Dr Livingstone," he says; and before I can ask any more questions he is running like a madman towards the town.

We have at last entered the town. There are hundreds of people around me—I might say thousands without exaggeration, it seems to me. It is a grand triumphal procession. As we move, they move. All eyes are drawn towards us. The expedition at last comes to a halt; the journey is ended for a time; but I alone have a few more steps to make.

There is a group of the most respectable Arabs, and as I come nearer I see the white face of an old man among them. He has a cap with a gold band around it, his dress is a short jacket of red blanket cloth, and his pants—well, I didn't observe. I am shaking hands with him. We raise our hats, and I say: "Dr Livingstone, I presume?"

And he says, "Yes."

Stanley wrote of this picture: "This engraving . . . represents my meeting with Dr Livingstone at Ujiji, Lake Tanganyika, and is as correct as if the scene had been photographed."

TRADE UNIONISM

BEFORE THE INDUSTRIAL REVOLUTION, craftsmen had often banded together to try to raise their wages or to control the conditions of their craft. The concept of formal trade unions, however, did not develop until the 1790s, when machine spinners' unions were created in industrial Lancashire. Although laws against such "combinations" were passed in 1799 and 1800, they did not in fact inhibit unionisation or prevent strikes.

In 1824 the "combination laws" were repealed after vigorous and well-organised agitation, the hope being that if there was no opposition to the unions then they would disappear. They did not. Indeed, during the early 1830s, a time of relative prosperity, attempts were made to form a "general union" of all trades. But as prosperity gave way to economic depression after 1836, labour's bargaining power inevitably decreased, and with it many workers' enthusiasm for unions.

By 1836, too, there had been trade union martyrs: six rural trade unionists from Tolpuddle in Dorset had been found guilty of administering unlawful oaths and transported to Australia. But neither this nor the depression completely suppressed trade union activity. In the middle years of the century it became organised, mainly on a skilled-craft basis, with well-drafted rules, and in 1868 a newly formed Trades Union Congress held its first conference. Three years later an Act of Parliament, followed by another in 1875, protected trade union rights and kept unions free from the interference of the law.

The legal powers of unions in general were successfully challenged in the courts in 1901, however, after unskilled workers' unions had also come into existence. Hoping to change the law, trade unionists threw their weight behind the new Labour Party. The movement grew and at the height of the unions' power, in 1970, there were eleven million members in four hundred and sixty-nine different unions.

THE SOCIAL STRUCTURE of Britain, with its layers of classes is satirised by George Cruikshank in this etching of 1867. The Beehive was the name of the Labour journal edited by George Potter, the militant leader of the London building trades and one of the thirty-four delegates to attend the first Trades Union Congress in Manchester, in 1868.

THE LABOUR PARTY arose out of the Labour Representation Committee of 1900, and from the start it depended on trade-union funds. At the general election of 1906 there were fifty-four Labour and Lib-Lab M.P.s. The Labour Party first came to power in 1924 but only secured an overall majority in 1945. The photograph below is of the 1924 Labour government.

FAIR WAGES AND HOURS *were the motive for the labourers' strike at the West India Dock, on August 13, 1889, after the London gas workers had demanded—and got—an eight-hour day. Ben Tillett, the strikers' spokesman, received immediate help from militant trade unionists and brought the Port of London to a standstill. The dockers' flamboyant marches through the City (above) were stage-managed by John Burns (below). They attracted much public attention, but without funds it seemed as if the dockers would be forced back to work. Then money began to pour in from sympathisers, including dockers in Australia, and they obtained a minimum wage of sixpence an hour (the "dockers' tanner").*

TRADE UNION MEMBERSHIP *certificates were issued as unions came into existence in the first half of the nineteenth century. There were also handsome trade-union banners. The emblem above is that of the Amalgamated Society of Engineers, Machinists, Millwrights, Smiths and Pattern Makers, formed in 1851. In 1868 there were already a quarter of a million members in the T.U.C.*

STRIKING FOR COMPENSATION *for industrial injuries and occupational hazards, and for equal pay for men and women, the Match Girls of Bryant and May (above) won their case in 1888. The harmful effects of working with phosphorus sometimes produced a condition known as "phossie-jaw". The strike was organised by Annie Besant, famous not only for her work as a trade unionist but as a pioneer of birth control for women.*

But neither man showed any enthusiasm for adventures in tropical Africa.

When Salisbury took office he himself promoted no great schemes of imperial expansion, but he was prepared to back up the men on the spot. The work of consolidation and political control was entrusted to three chartered companies. The Royal Niger Company operated in Nigeria, the British East Africa Company controlled what are now Kenya and Uganda, and Rhodes's British South Africa Company acquired the territory of the Rhodesias. All were launched between 1886 and 1889. Many border disputes with the other colonising powers arose, but Salisbury pursued a steady policy of settlement by negotiation, culminating in the signing of agreements with Germany, France, and Portugal in 1890. The German agreement, which was the most important of the three, defined the boundaries of the two countries' possessions in Central and South Africa. Germany had, since the Franco-Prussian war, become one of the most powerful nations in Europe, but Britain was still not fully awake to the Teutonic menace, and as part of the bargain Heligoland was ceded to Germany in compensation for the recognition of the British protectorate of Zanzibar. A future German naval base was traded for a spice island. Still, Salisbury's foreign policy was swayed by these colonial affairs, and by 1892 he had largely succeeded in his aims. The assertion of British control over the Nile Valley and the settlement of the boundaries of the West African colonies were the only outstanding problems.

The key to Salisbury's success lay in his skilful handling of the complications that arose between the powers in an age of intense national rivalries. He once said that "British policy is to drift lazily downstream, occasionally putting out a boat hook to avoid a collision". No British Foreign Secretary has wielded his diplomatic boat hook with greater dexterity.

However, the relentless question of a sullen and embittered Ireland still overshadowed politics. "What Ireland wants," Salisbury had asserted before the election campaign, "is government—government that does not flinch, that does not vary", and in his nephew, A. J. Balfour, who became Irish Secretary in 1887, he found a man capable of putting this into practice. The situation that Balfour faced was very difficult. Agricultural prices were steadily falling, but the Government had rejected Parnell's argument that the only way to prevent mass evictions was to reassess rents. The Irish peasants, organised by William O'Brien and John Dillon, had taken matters into their own hands by launching the "Plan of Campaign". The basis of the Plan was that, if the landlord refused a reduction, rents were to be withheld and the money paid into a campaign fund. The Plan was enforced with the terrorist methods which had now become an implacable feature of Irish disputes. The Government's answer was to make a few concessions, and pass a Crimes Act which gave to the executive arbitrary powers of the most sweeping kind.

Balfour stretched his authority to the limit and acted with a determination that fully matched the ruthlessness of his Irish opponents. In defending his actions in the House of Commons he displayed such skill and resource that he rose rapidly to the front rank of Parliamentarians.

Parnell stood aloof from these tumults. He now perceived that Home Rule could only be won by conciliating a broad section of English opinion. But his adherence to cautious and constitutional action was stricken by the publication in *The Times* on April 18, 1887, of a facsimile letter, purporting

The arrest of John Dillon, M.P., at Loughrea was illustrated in The Graphic *in December 1886. Dillon had been collecting tenants' rent for the "Plan of Campaign", and was arrested under the terms of the Crimes Act.*

to bear his signature, in which he was made to condone the Phoenix Park murders. Parnell, while denouncing the letter as a forgery, refused to bring an action in an English court. Such forbearance, and the public acceptance by men as eminent as Salisbury that this and other letters were authentic, convinced most Englishmen of his guilt. But in the following year the Government set up a commission of three judges to investigate the whole field of Irish crime. They had been sitting for six months when, in February 1889, they at last began to probe the letters. They discovered that they had been forged by a decrepit Irish journalist named Richard Piggott. The effect on the public was dramatic. Long execration of Parnell turned into sudden, strange, and short-lived popularity. A General Election was approaching, the Government was out of favour, and nothing, it seemed, could prevent a victory for Gladstone and Home Rule.

But the case was altered. On November 13, 1890, the suit of O'Shea *v.* O'Shea and Parnell opened in the Divorce Court. A decree *nisi* was granted to Captain O'Shea. Parnell, as co-respondent, offered no defence. He had been living with Mrs O'Shea for ten years. The Nonconformist conscience, powerful in the Liberal Party, reared its head. Gladstone, single-minded for Home Rule, refused to join in the moral censure, but he was convinced that the only way to stop the Conservatives from exploiting Parnell's adultery was for the Irish leader to retire, at any rate for a while. Tremendous pressure was put on Parnell. His friend and admirer Cecil Rhodes telegraphed, "Resign—marry—return." It was wise advice. But Parnell's pride revolted. He refused to bow to "English hypocrisy", whatever the cost to his country or his cause.

As a last measure Gladstone wrote to Parnell that he would cease to lead the Liberal Party unless the Irishman retired. Before the letter could be delivered the Irish Party confirmed Parnell in his leadership. Gladstone, in despair, sent his letter to the press. It was an irretrievable step, a public ultimatum. Next morning Gladstone wrote, "For every day, I may say, of these five years we have been engaged in laboriously rolling uphill the stone of Sisyphus. Mr Parnell's decision . . . means that the stone is to break away from us and roll down again to the bottom of the hill." The rest of the story is anticlimax. After Parnell had made a bitter attack upon Gladstone, the Catholic Church declared against him and he was disavowed by most of his party. In vain he made a series of wild and desperate efforts to regain power. Within a year he died.

Liberal prospects were now badly clouded and they were not improved by the adoption of the comprehensive "Newcastle Programme" of 1891 which in trying to meet the demands of every section of the party gave far more offence than satisfaction. When the election came in the summer of the following year the result was a Home Rule majority of only forty, dependent on the Irish Members. In the House there were two hundred and seventy-five Liberals and eighty-two Irish Nationalists, as against two hundred and sixty-nine Conservatives and forty-six Liberal Unionists. The majority was too thin for Gladstone's purposes, but he formed a Cabinet which included men as gifted as Harcourt, Rosebery, Morley, and Campbell-Bannerman. The brightest star of them all was H. H. Asquith, the most able Home Secretary of the century.

Gladstone was resolute. Work began immediately on a second Home Rule Bill, and in February 1893 he introduced it himself. At the age of

Kitty O'Shea had been Charles Stuart Parnell's mistress for several years before her husband, Captain W. H. O'Shea, filed for divorce, naming Parnell as co-respondent. In 1891 Parnell and Kitty O'Shea were finally married, but the publicity caused by the affair ended his political influence.

Lord Salisbury (1830–1903) was concerned more with foreign affairs than with domestic reform. One reform that was instituted, mainly through the influence of Chamberlain as shown in this cartoon, was the Workmen's Compensation Act which made employers directly responsible for industrial injuries.

eighty-three he piloted the Bill through eighty-two sittings against an Opposition led by debaters as formidable as Chamberlain and Balfour. There have been few more remarkable achievements in the whole history of Parliament. It was all in vain. Passing through the Commons by small majorities, the Bill was rejected on the second reading in the Lords by four hundred and nineteen votes to forty-one. Thus perished all hope of a united, self-governing Ireland, loyal to the British Crown.

The immediate reaction in England was one of indifference. Encouraged by their victory, the Lords hampered the Government incessantly. Only one major issue was successful, a new Local Government Act, which established urban, rural district, and parish councils. After the defeat of the Home Rule Bill, Gladstone fell increasingly out of sympathy with his colleagues. They refused to support his scheme for a dissolution and an attack on the Lords. He, for his part, hated their plans for heavier taxation and increased expenditure on armaments. "The plan is mad," he said of one proposal. "And who are they who propose it? Men who were not born when I had been in public life for years." He resigned on March 3, 1894, fifty-two and a half years after his swearing in as a Privy Counsellor. His parting with his ministers was emotional, and Harcourt made a tearful speech of farewell. Gladstone, who remained unmoved, afterwards referred to this meeting as "that blubbering Cabinet". He died in 1898. His career had been the most noteworthy of the century, leaving behind innumerable marks on the pages of history. He was the greatest popular leader of his age, and he has hardly been equalled in his power to move the people on great moral issues. Few of his conceptions were unworthy. Gladstone's achievements, like his failures, were on the grand scale.

Gladstone was succeeded as Prime Minister by Lord Rosebery. His was a bleak, precarious, wasting inheritance. Rosebery had the good luck to win the Derby twice during his sixteen months of office. Not much other fortune befell him. He had a far-ranging mind, above the shifts and compromises indispensable in political life. He had been most at ease as Foreign Secretary. He was the Queen's own choice as Prime Minister, but his Imperialist views made him unpopular with his own party. The Cabinet was rent by clashes of personality and the quarrels of Imperialists and "Little Englanders". Then the Chancellor of the Exchequer, Sir William Harcourt, included in his Budget proposals a scheme for the payment of substantial death duties. This caused violent feeling throughout the capitalist class affected. When the Government was defeated on a snap vote in June 1895 it resigned. The quarrels of the Liberal leaders were now no longer confined by the secrecy of the Cabinet, and the years that followed were dark ones for them. At the General Election the Conservative-Liberal Unionist alliance won a decisive victory. Its majority over the Opposition, including the Irish Nationalists, was one hundred and fifty-two.

Lord Salisbury thereupon formed a powerful administration. He once again combined the offices of Prime Minister and Foreign Secretary, and his position in his own party and in the country was unrivalled. His methods of dispatching business were by now unorthodox. It is said that he sometimes failed to recognise members of his Cabinet when he met them on rare social occasions. He loved to retire to the great Cecil house at Hatfield, whence he discharged his vast responsibilities by a stream of letters written in his own hand. His authority and prestige derived in part from the air of patrician assurance which marked his public speech and action. He cared little for popular acclaim, and such disinterestedness in a democratic age was accepted and even approved. His deputy and closest adviser was his nephew, Arthur Balfour, who became First Lord of the Treasury. But the man who in the public eye dominated the Government was the Liberal Unionist leader, Joseph Chamberlain, now at the height of his powers and anxious for the office which had been denied to him for so long by the events of 1886. By his own choice Chamberlain became Colonial Secretary. His instinct was a sure one. Interest in home affairs had languished. In its five years of office the Government passed only one substantial reforming measure, the Workmen's Compensation Act of 1897. The excitement of politics lay in the clash of Imperial forces in Africa and Asia, and it was there that Chamberlain resolved to make his mark.

King Pempeh 1 of the Ashanti submits to the British forces on a parade ground. Pempeh was then exiled to the Seychelles.

Chamberlain approached his task with the reforming enthusiasm of his radical days. A great change had taken place in him. The municipal Socialist and Republican of his Birmingham years was now the architect of Empire. "It is not enough," he declared, "to occupy certain great spaces of the world's surface unless you can make the best of them—unless you are willing to develop them." Chamberlain could not fulfil this promise in the way he would have wished, although some advances were made, especially in West Africa. From the moment he took office projects of reform were pushed into the background by the constant eruption of questions inseparable from a policy of expansion. The first was a small one, that of the Ashanti, who continued to terrorise much of the Gold Coast by their slave-raiding. An expedition was sent against them under Sir Francis Scott, and by January 1896 the Ashanti kingdom had been crushed. The situation in Nigeria was much more difficult, since another great power was involved. The French, by moving overland to the south of the Sahara Desert, were attempting to confine the British to the coastal areas by using their superior military strength. Chamberlain, who, as Salisbury said, hated to give anything away, retaliated by organising the West African Frontier Force, under Sir Henry Lugard. His measures were successful; skilful diplomacy backed resolute action, and the Anglo-French Convention of June 1898 drew boundary lines in West Africa which were entirely satisfactory to the British.

These were not the only external preoccupations of the Government. Throughout these years Germany was hard at work promoting her plans for the penetration of Asia Minor, and there was much talk of a Berlin-Baghdad railway. To this Salisbury raised no objection. He preferred to see the Germans rather than the Russians busy in Turkey. In the Far East the Russian threat to China, made possible by the building of the trans-Siberian railway, perpetually agitated the Foreign Office. The province of Manchuria, with the naval base of Port Arthur, was falling into the grasp of the Russians. Few foresaw at that time the startling defeats which Japanese arms would shortly inflict upon the Tsar. Chamberlain, who had a large say in foreign affairs, was provoked into making an ill-considered bid for an alliance with Germany. Salisbury held aloof, and restrained his ardent colleague, perceiving more perils in a European alliance than in a policy of isolation. His confidence in Britain's power to stand alone was now to be tested. For the great events on the world stage, and the diplomatic manoeuvres that attended them were, for the island, about to be eclipsed by colonial conflict in the continent of Africa.

Part Two: from James Morris's
Farewell the Trumpets

CHAPTER 1

THE GRAND ILLUSION

QUEEN VICTORIA OF ENGLAND WENT HOME happy on her Diamond Jubilee Day, June 22, 1897. The sun had shone all day—"Queen's weather" the English called it—and there was nothing artificial to the affection her people had shown during her hours of celebration. She had passed in procession through London intermittently weeping for pleasure, and studded her diary that evening with joyous adjectives: indescribable, marvellous, deeply touching.

It was more than a personal happiness, more even than a national rejoicing, for the British had chosen to commemorate the Diamond Jubilee as a festival of Empire. They were in possession that day of the largest Empire ever known to history, and since a large part of it had been acquired during the sixty years of Victoria's reign, it seemed proper to honour the one with the other. It would proclaim to the world, flamboyantly, that beneath the Queen's dominion lay a quarter of the earth's land surface, and nearly a quarter of its people—literally, as Christopher North the poet had long before declared it, an Empire on which the sun never set.

So the day had been a proud, gaudy, sentimental, glorious day. Through the venerable streets of the capital there had passed in parade Rajput

Queen Victoria's Diamond Jubilee was a day of great celebration, as can be seen in this photograph. The Queen's carriage, drawn by eight cream horses, is passing London Bridge station.

princes, Dyak headhunters, strapping troopers from Australia. Cypriots wore fezzes, Chinese wore conical straw hats. English gentlemen rode by, with virile moustaches and steel-blue eyes, and Indian lancers jangled past in resplendent crimson jerkins. Here was Lord Roberts of Kandahar, and Wolseley, hero of Tel-el-Kebir. Loyal slogans fluttered through the streets— "One Race, One Queen", "God Bless Her Gracious Majesty!" Patriotic songs resounded. Outside St Paul's Cathedral, where the Prince of Wales received the Queen in her barouche, a service of thanksgiving was held, with archbishops officiating and an Empire in attendance.

That morning the Queen had telegraphed a simple Jubilee message to all her subjects. "From my heart I thank my beloved people," she said. "May God bless them."

"My people". If to the Queen herself all the myriad peoples of the Empire really did seem one, to the outsider their unity seemed less than apparent. Part of the purpose of the Jubilee jamboree was to give the Empire a new sense of cohesion: but it was like wishing reason upon the ocean, so enormous was the span of that association, and so unimaginable its contrasts and contradictions. Some of its constituents were complete modern nations, the self-governing white colonies in Australia, Canada, New Zealand and South Africa. Some were Crown Colonies governed, in one degree or another, direct from London. Some were protectorates so isolated and naive that the very idea of Empire was inconceivable to most of their inhabitants. At one extreme was India, a civilisation in itself; at the other was Ascension, a mere speck in the South Atlantic. Every Faith was represented, every colour of skin, every philosophy. It was a gigantic jumble of origins, influences, attitudes and intentions.

If there was one characteristic diffused throughout this bewildering gallimaufry, it was an almost feverish enthusiasm. The British Empire was a heady outlet for the imagination of a people still in its prime. Through the gate of Empire, Britons could escape from their cramped and rainy islands into places of grander scale and more vivid excitement, and since the Queen's accession at least three million had gone. In India one thousand British civil servants, protected by seventy thousand British soldiers, ruled three hundred million people in a subcontinent the size of Europe. Other Britons in 1897 were commanding the private armies of the Sultan of Sarawak, accepting the pleas of runaway slaves in Muscat, charting the China Sea, commanding the Canadian Mounties' post on the Chinook Pass in the Yukon, governing the Zulus and the Wa, invading the Sudan, laying telegraph wires across the Australian outback, prospecting for gold in the valley of the Limpopo, and patrolling the Caribbean.

Essentially most of these possessions had been acquired for profit—for raw materials, for promising markets, for investment, or to deny commercial rivals undue advantages. The British were proud of the fact that when they acquired a new territory, its trade was open to all comers. Economics, though, must be sustained by strategy, and so the Empire generated its own extension. To protect ports, hinterlands must be acquired. One valley led to the next, each river to its headwaters, every sea to the other shore.

To these material, if often misty, impulses were added urges of a higher kind. At least since the start of the nineteenth century the British Empire had regarded itself as dedicated to the elevation of mankind. Through the agency of Empire the slave trade had been abolished, and on the vehicle of

This group photograph of colonial soldiers was taken at the time of Queen Victoria's Diamond Jubilee. It vividly illustrates the great diversity of troops in Britain's colonial army.

Victorian missionaries left Britain for distant parts of the Empire to teach the Christian message and to establish the Church. They took with them not only valuable medical and educational skills but also Victorian values and ideas. This formal photograph shows a native missionary and his family. One of his daughters cuddles a Victorian doll.

Empire many a Christian mission had journeyed to its labours. The desire to do good was a true energy of Empire, and with it went a genuine sense of duty—Christian duty, for though this was an Empire of multitudinous beliefs, its masters were overwhelmingly Church of England. In the middle of the nineteenth century, their duty was powerfully Old Testament in style, soldiers stormed about with Bibles in their hands, administrators sat like bearded prophets at their desks. By the 1890s it was more subdued, but still devoted to the principle that the British were some sort of Chosen People, touched on the shoulder by the Great Being, and commissioned to do His will in the world.

Technically they were as well fitted as any to govern a quarter of the world. Their own country had escaped the social convulsions that shook the rest of Europe, providing a model of liberal but traditional stability. Their original mastery of steam, and all that came from it, had given them a technological start over all other nations. The flexibility of their unwritten constitution was handy for an expansionist State. The semi-divine nature of their monarchy gave them a mystic instrument that was often useful. Being islanders, they knew more about the world than most of their neighbours: they possessed more ships than all other nations put together, and there were few British families who had not sent a man abroad, if not to settle, at least to sail a vessel or fight a foreign war. They were an immensely experienced people. Compact, patriotic, paradoxically bound together by an ancient class system, theirs had been an independent State for nearly a thousand years.

Over the years they had, too, created an imperial elite to whom Empire was a true vocation. Everybody knew its members. They were products of those curious institutions, the English public schools. These nurseries of Empire taught a man to be disciplined, tough, uncomplaining, reserved, good in a team and acclimatised to order. Their members stood to gain directly from the existence of Empire, in jobs, in dividends, or at least in adventurous opportunity.

In the beginning the mass of the British people had been far more remote from the imperial enterprise, except when they wished to emigrate or join the army. In the past twenty-four years, however, the new penny press, preaching to a newly literate and newly enfranchised audience, had swept the people into a highly enjoyable craze of Empire. What events there had been! Anybody over thirty, say, at the time of the Diamond Jubilee had experienced a period of British history unexampled for excitement. What theatre! Gordon martyred at Khartoum! "Dr Livingstone, I presume?" Never a year passed without some marvellous set piece, of triumph or of tragedy. In 1895, the Conservatives and their Liberal Unionist allies, the party of Empire, had won an overwhelming victory over the Liberals. The nation talked Empire, thought Empire, dreamt Empire. Two geniuses, Rudyard Kipling and Edward Elgar, were translating the emotions into art, and a thousand lesser practitioners were putting it into jingle, march or tableau. There was calculation to this climax, of course, the cunning of financiers, the opportunism of politicians, the ambitions of soldiers and merchants. The England of the Diamond Jubilee was essentially insular, for its people saw the whole wide Empire only as a response to themselves.

The British as a whole would have been shocked at any notion of wickedness to their imperialism, for theirs was a truly innocent bravado.

They really thought their Empire good, like their Queen, and they were proud of it for honest reasons: they meant no harm, except to evil enemies, and in principle they wished the poor benighted natives nothing but well.

Yet these were brittle times—times of change and sensationalism, of quick fortunes, outrageous fashions and revolutionary ideas. Socialism was an intellectual fad, the New Woman smoked her cigarettes ostentatiously in the Café Royal, and only a month before the Jubilee, Oscar Wilde had ended his sentence for homosexuality in Reading gaol. The grand Victorian synthesis of art, morals and invention was already fading, and with it would presently fade the certainty and the optimism. Many Britons in 1897, looking around them at the feverish high jinks of the capital, saw omens of disillusionment to come. The times were too gaudy to be safe.

Part of the triumph was bluff anyway. The people might think themselves citizens of the happiest, richest, strongest and kindest power: their leaders knew that Great Britain was no longer beyond challenge. The Germans and the Americans were fast overtaking her in technique, brute power and public education. She had few friends in the world, and no allies. And there was nothing sacrosanct to the British command of the seas—any power could defy it, if prepared to put enough money into a fleet. The very state of the world was increasingly precarious to the Empire: Germany, France and Russia were all potential enemies; the moribund Ottoman Empire was a perpetual problem; an unstable Austria-Hungary threatened instability to everyone else; a derelict China seemed an incitement to colonial rivalries.

To seers, then, there was a detectable element of disquiet to the celebrations of 1897, an unease not often declared, nor even perhaps realised. It was a thunderstorm feeling—a heaviness in the air, an unnatural brightness to the light. Queen's weather it might have been on Jubilee Day, but the outlook was changeable.

The safety bicycle was manufactured in c.1885 and, unlike its predecessors, had wheels of equal diameter and a chain-drive that linked the pedals with the rear wheel. This young lady is wearing the latest bicycling fashion of 1898.

CHAPTER 2

FASHODA

THE TUMULT AND THE SHOUTING SLIGHTLY DIED, as Jubilee year came to an end, but on the frontiers the British Empire tremendously proceeded—especially in Africa, the last undeveloped continent, where the imperial dynamic was providing a whole new pantheon of heroes and martyrs. Two of them in particular were in the public mind, for far away on the Upper Nile, General Sir Herbert Kitchener, the rising star of the British army, was avenging the death of "Charlie" Gordon, "the noblest man who ever lived".

Gordon's death had been one of the great romantic tragedies of the Victorian age. Ever since, the British had dreamt of recovering the Sudan, and avenging the memory of the martyr. The Mahdi, "The Leader", had died in 1885, but his successor, the Caliph, held similarly revolutionary views, and by the 1890s the reconquest was at hand. The obvious man to conduct it was Kitchener, whose hooded eye, huge figure and commanding bearing were imperial factors in themselves. Kitchener was made Sirdar, commander in chief, of the Egyptian army, which was in effect an imperial force, and for years he grimly planned the operation, designing his own

Raising the flags on the only remaining walls of Gordon's Palace in Khartoum. Kitchener (1850-1916) had avenged the murder of Gordon and won back the Sudan.

gunboats for the passage up the Nile, and commissioning his own railway to take his armies to Khartoum.

It was slow, but it was inexorable. By the end of 1896 Kitchener had an army of twenty-five thousand men, eight thousand of them British, the rest Egyptian and Sudanese, deep in the Sudan. His method of campaign was barbarically deliberate and symbolic. The soldiers went into action crying "Remember Gordon!". Gordon's nephew directed the shelling of the Mahdi's tomb at Omdurman, and Kitchener seriously thought of keeping The Leader's skull as a souvenir. It all went like very slow clockwork. By Jubilee Day Kitchener was preparing his advance upon Khartoum, and by the autumn of 1898 he had annihilated the Mahdist army in the battle of Omdurman, killing at least ten thousand Sudanese for the loss of twenty-eight Britons. On the morning of Sunday, September 4, 1898, he crossed the Nile into the ruined capital.

Beside the shattered remains of Gordon's Palace, the British sealed their victory with a requiem. Its altar was the Palace itself, upon whose surviving walls, their windows still barricaded with bricks and sandbags, the Union Jack was triumphantly hoisted, with a much smaller Egyptian flag. Elbowing his way to a better view of the ceremony, we may be sure, was the most bumptious subaltern of the army, Lieutenant Winston Churchill.

At the head of his men, ramrod still, one hand on the hilt of his curved scimitar, one booted foot raised upon a convenient boulder, Kitchener himself stood impassive and immaculate. A salute was fired by a gunboat at the quay. Three cheers for the Queen were called. As the solemn men's voices sang the old words of "Abide with Me", Gordon's favourite hymn, to the uncertain harmonies of a Sudanese band, a tear was seen to roll down the Sirdar's brown and flinchless cheek. "The sternness and harshness had dropped from him for the moment," wrote one of the war correspondents, all of whom he despised, "and he was gentle as a woman." The parade had to be dismissed by the chief of staff, so incapacitated was the victor by his emotions.

When he returned to his camp at Omdurman across the river, though, General Kitchener was recalled at once to harsher realities. He knew that sacramental revenge was not the true purpose of the army of the Nile. On the previous day Kitchener had opened sealed orders from London, to be read immediately after the capture of Khartoum. They required him to proceed at once still farther up-river, to forestall any French annexation of the Upper Nile.

Although the British were not the only Europeans expanding in Africa, they did possess the lion's share. They had had footholds in West and South Africa for generations. By the 1890s they were also established in Egypt, Kenya and Uganda, and in the vaguely defined territories between the Limpopo and the Zambezi.

At the end of the century the general direction of their expansion was north-south. Their most remarkable activist, the South African financier Cecil Rhodes, foresaw a British axis running from Cairo to the Cape, fed by access lines to the coast east and west, and giving the Empire effective domination of the whole continent. Though this scheme was blocked for the moment by the presence of the Germans in Tanganyika, still the proposed railway line was already north of the Limpopo River at one end, south of the Egyptian frontier at the other: the first of its feeder lines, from Mombasa to Lake Victoria, was nearly finished, and Kitchener had presciently built his Sudan railway to the South African gauge. Essential to the vision was British control of the whole Nile valley, and to secure this without war was the principal imperial purpose as declared by the Prime Minister, Lord Salisbury.

The French, who were the principal contenders for African mastery, thought transversely, east to west. Besides their large possessions in North Africa, they were strongly established on the Niger, in the west, and had an east-coast port at Djibouti, in Somaliland. They looked always across the continent, and they dreamt of uniting their eastern and their western footholds to establish their supremacy throughout Central Africa. This ambition clashed with the British, and took the two Empires on a collision course. The farther the British forces advanced along the Nile valley, the less the French chances of a corridor across Africa.

In 1893 a well-known French hydrologist, Victor Prompt, had suggested that the key to the control of the Nile valley might lie in the area some three hundred miles south of Khartoum, where the River Sobat joined the greater river. There was nothing much there except an isolated fort called Fashoda, used by the Mahdists as a penal colony, but Prompt suggested that a dam there might effectively control the flow of water into Egypt. Since Egypt depended entirely upon the flow of the White Nile, control of Fashoda could mean command of Egypt; a French presence there could give the French an almost unanswerable bargaining power in Africa.

So as the British strengthened their hold on Egypt, and majestically advanced southward through the Sudan, the French, fortified by a new alliance with Russia, resolved to make a race of it, and prepared an expedition to travel from their base at Brazzaville, on the Congo, clean across Africa to the Upper Nile. Accordingly, in the English Jubilee summer of 1897, Captain Jean-Baptiste Marchand of the French Marines set out to cross the continent and "establish French claims in the region of the Upper Nile". He took with him twelve Frenchmen and one hundred and fifty Senegalese; his destination was Fashoda.

The day after the Khartoum memorial service, while Kitchener was still considering his secret orders, British outposts on the river south of the city intercepted a small steamer flying the crescent flag of the Mahdists. Its crew, who were unaware that Khartoum had fallen to the British, were taken ashore for questioning, and said they had been far up the Nile foraging for the Caliph's armies. Near the mouth of the Sobat, they said, they found a strange flag flying over the old fort at Fashoda, and had been fired upon by white men. Several of their crew had been killed.

The British interrogators were startled by this tale. Colonel Reginald Wingate, Kitchener's brilliant intelligence chief, asked the Mahdist captain to draw in the sand the flag he had seen at Fashoda, and to describe its colours, and thus learnt that it was the French tricolour. So the French were there already! Five days later Kitchener sailed southward from Omdurman with five gunboats and a dozen barges, with one hundred Cameron Highlanders and two thousand five hundred Sudanese askari, with field guns and Maxim guns.

So one of history's famous meetings came about. Purposefully up the Nile went the imperial flotilla, its trim little steamers in line ahead. Lashed alongside or towed behind were barges carrying the troops.

In 1896 the British began building the railway between Mombasa and Lake Victoria, primarily to transport troops and supplies. During its construction, the railway became known as the "lunatic line" because the workers had to contend not only with the exceptionally difficult terrain but also with the threat of man-eating lions. This photograph, taken at the Great Rift Valley, shows a specially built lift used in the construction of what was to become a massive viaduct.

Horatio Herbert Kitchener was a fearless commander in the field and an able administrator, who gave selfless dedication to the army and expected the same from his officers. In Britain he became a popular hero and his portrait was used in the famous recruitment poster for the First World War, "Your Country Needs YOU".

It was a week's voyage from Omdurman to Fashoda, and the flotilla made good speed, the stern-wheels of its steamers frothing the muddy waters. Sometimes great storks and cranes flapped away from their passage. Sometimes hippopotami emerged muddy from the swamp. At villages along the way notables flocked to the water's edge to offer their submission, and intelligence officers went ashore to scribble them notes of pardon.

Kitchener was a Francophile. He would be reluctant to dislodge any French outpost by sheer force—there would be no primitive triumph at Fashoda, and Captain Marchand's skull ran no risk of immortality as a table ornament. But he did not know the strength of the French force, he had no idea how truculent it might be, and he decided to move cautiously. When they were about twelve miles from Fashoda two Sudanese orderlies were put ashore with a message addressed to the "*Chef de l'expédition Européenne à Fashoda*". It announced the news of Omdurman, thus implicitly declaring the British to be suzerains of the Upper Nile, and said that General Kitchener hoped to be in Fashoda the following day. Kitchener signed it not as a British general, but as Sirdar of the Egyptian army, and at Wingate's suggestion he ordered that only the Egyptian flag would be flown by the flotilla as they approached Fashoda, and that he and his officers would wear their Egyptian uniforms. The impact would be less pointed and the suggestion of a clash between two great empires less direct.

Next morning as the ships steamed slowly on, the lookouts saw approaching them a small rowing boat, flying at its stern a Tricolour, and carrying a black sergeant in French uniform. He brought a reply from Fashoda: "Mon général,

I have the honour to acknowledge the receipt of your letter dated 18 September 1898. I hear with the greatest pleasure of the occupation of Omdurman by the Anglo-Egyptian army. I shall be the very first to present the sincere good wishes of France to General Kitchener, whose name for so many years has epitomised the struggles of civilisation against the fanatical savagery of the Mahdists. . . . These compliments therefore I send with all respect both to you and to your valiant army.

This agreeable task completed, I must inform you that, under the orders of my government, I have occupied the Bahr-el-Ghazal as far as Mechra-er-Req and up to its confluence with the Bahr-el-Jebel also all the Shilluk country on the left bank of the Nile as far as Fashoda. . . . I signed a treaty on 3 September with Abd-ed-Fadil, their Reth, placing all the Shilluk country on the left bank of the White Nile under French protection. . . . I have forwarded this treaty to Europe . . . by Mechra-er-Req, where my steamer the *Faidherbe* is at the moment with orders to bring me such reinforcements as I judge necessary to defend Fashoda. . . .

Again, I give you my good wishes for a happy visit to the Upper Nile. I also note your intention to visit Fashoda, where I shall be happy to welcome you in the name of France.

Signed MARCHAND"

This engaging persiflage, full as it was of meaningless treaties, non-existent reinforcements and unenforceable claims, paved the way for a meeting between the two commanders. Later in the day the British sighted Fashoda. Forlornly above a rotted swamp, stretching away as far as the eye could see, the little fort stood half-derelict upon a peninsula, with a few conical huts of the Shilluk tribesmen outside its walls, a group of palms, and a soggy garden of vegetables. It looked hot, wet and verminous, but the Tricolour flew boldly above it, and at the water's edge, as the gunboats approached, an honour guard of Frenchmen and Senegalese stood bravely at the salute. The British were touched by this show of pride, and by the defiant isolation of the fort. "It was a puny little thing," one officer wrote in reminiscence. "Were we to be compelled to break it down?"

At midday, September 9, 1898, the commanders met on board Kitchener's gunboat. Kitchener wore his Sirdar's regalia with tarboosh. Marchand, a small bearded figure, wore no military insignia at all—wisely, perhaps, since he was only a captain. They sat with Wingate and Marchand's adjutant on the deck, watched intently from shore and ship by officers with binoculars. Peace and war hung in the balance, and their conversation was tense. Sometimes, the watchers thought, the talk seemed less than amicable, and Marchand was to be seen gesturing angrily at the Sirdar. Presently, though, a steward climbed up the ladder to the deck carrying a tray of glasses, "full of golden liquid", and a moment later Kitchener and Marchand, raising their glasses, were clinking them in agreement and good wishes—in relief too, no doubt, as they sat there, half in shade, half in sunlight, on the deck of the little ship.

The senior members of Marchand's mission at Fashoda are photographed here having been awarded the French Legion of Honour in recognition of their stand against the British.

It had been a close thing. Kitchener had declared flatly that the episode might lead to a European war—did Marchand, with such stakes at issue, really mean to prevent the representatives of Egypt from hoisting the Egyptian flag over an Egyptian possession? Marchand replied that obviously he was powerless to prevent it, since he was outnumbered ten to one, but that without contrary orders from France he could not retire from his position, and that all his men could do, if Kitchener insisted, was to die at their posts. Since he was undoubtedly ready to defend his awful fort to the end, the British elected to establish their own garrison at a discreet but practical distance—five hundred yards to the south, on his only line of retreat through the marshes. The British would formally take possession of the area, but in the name of the Khedive of Egypt, and only the Egyptian flag would fly above their own quarters. There the matter was left, in a compromise that seemed to protect everybody's face, and would allow the two imperial governments, far away, to achieve a solution.

It was a soldier's formula, and the soldiers liked each other. After the talks the British mounted a parade, and the Egyptian flag was hoisted by a Sudanese detachment, to a twenty-one-gun salute. Everybody saluted quiveringly and did their best to be tactful.

Later Kitchener was entertained in Marchand's mess. The two sides toasted each other in sweet champagne, and exchanged fairly ornate pleasantries. A Senegalese guard was then inspected in the blazing heat, and as the Sirdar left the soil of Fashoda—Fort St Louis to the French—he was presented with a huge basket of vegetables and flowers from the garden: French flora from French soil, it was tacitly suggested as the last salutes were exchanged and the boats rowed out to the waiting gunboats.

Almost at once the flotilla sailed, leaving only a regiment of Sudanese and some guns in a bivouac on their mudflats. Kitchener left behind him, nevertheless, a steely aftertaste, for before he embarked he handed Marchand a formal letter of protest at the presence of the French in the Nile valley, and a list of stern restrictions of their movements. Not even private letters were to be sent down the river without British approval: in

In 1894 Captain Alfred Dreyfus was convicted of treason for passing French secrets to the Germans. Throughout his trial Dreyfus protested his innocence, but it was not disclosed until 1898 that the evidence against him was false and that he had been used as a scapegoat. Dreyfus was finally acquitted in 1906, reinstated as a major and presented with the Legion of Honour.

effect the French were to be imprisoned in their fort with their flowers, flags and vegetables. This was the iron within the glove. No pretence was made now that Kitchener was acting purely in Egyptian interests. The protest was made in the name of Great Britain, and Marchand was left in no doubt that the British Empire itself had passed that way.

The British also sent the French, as a parting gift, a package of newspapers. It was a Parthian courtesy, for the papers contained the news of the Dreyfus affair, the cancer in French public life which festered around the imprisonment on Devil's Island, for alleged espionage, of the innocent Jewish captain, Alfred Dreyfus. "You have achieved something remarkable, very remarkable," Kitchener had told Marchand in his mess hut, but he had added enigmatically, "but you know the French Government will not back you up." This was why. The Dreyfus scandal, which divided French society from top to bottom, also hamstrung French foreign policy, while the Russians had chosen the moment to tell their allies that they wanted no part of the Nile dispute.

Sure enough, war never came. The negotiations between London and Paris were protracted, but the British held all the cards, if only because they really were ready to go to war over Fashoda. "We've only got arguments," said Theophile Delcassé, the French Foreign Minister, "they've got troops." George Wyndham, one of the most promising of the younger Conservative imperialists, put the British attitude in a nutshell: "We don't care whether the Nile is called English or Egyptian or what it is called, but we mean to have it and we don't mean the French to have it. . . ."

Lord Salisbury mischievously described poor Marchand as "an explorer in difficulties on the Upper Nile", and in fact the French presence at Fashoda, invested north and south by British power, did become more and more ridiculous. By the time Paris recognised realities, in November 1898, the six Frenchmen and seventy Senegalese left at Fashoda felt themselves cruelly betrayed and humiliated. They withdrew that December, and were played away by the strains of the "Marseillaise" from the Sudanese band of the British garrison—"sad yet proud," as one of them recorded, "with moist eyes yet with our heads held high."

"Now," wrote Churchill, "the British people may . . . tell some stonemason to . . . cut on the pedestal of Gordon's statue in Trafalgar Square the significant, the sinister, yet the not unsatisfactory word, 'Avenged'." In fact Gordon was doubly avenged, by the defeat of his murderers and by the final extension of British power to the headwaters of the Nile.

CHAPTER 3

THE IMPERIALISTS

THE BRITISH AT HOME WERE COCK-A-HOOP, glorying in Kitchener's successes. The bourgeoisie, in particular, revelled in their colonial wars, and a picture popular around the end of the century portrayed them doing it. It was called "Following the Flags". On the left sits Papa, wearing a frogged smoking-jacket and holding that morning's copy of *The Times*. On the right are grouped his family: mother in lace jabot and speckled muslin, daughter with ribboned hair over her striped blouse, son in Eton collar and kilt. On the table between them lies a map of the current campaign, wherever it happens to be, stuck about with Union Jacks—for all the world as if they are indulging in some favourite nursery game. The British were not merely interested in imperial affairs. At this climactic moment of the Empire's history the British were imperially brainwashed.

The Empire was as immemorial as the Palace of Westminster itself—which, though it had been built less than half a century before, was popularly assumed to be as old as anything. This was partly because the long reign of Queen Victoria had given the British a sense of organic permanence. Foreign countries had coups or revolutions, invaded one another, replaced kings with emperors. Britain progressed differently, quietly and steadily. The idea that Kitchener had not really gone to the Sudan to avenge Gordon, but rather to forestall foreign competition in Africa, would strike most people as sophistry, if not actually sacrilege.

Even the soldiers and the administrators in the field did not generally think of imperialism as power politics. The Empire was there, it was patently beneficial, they would do their best for it. The old idea of an imperial trusteeship had been transmuted by Kipling into the more readily comprehensible image of the White Man's Burden:

> Take up the White Man's Burden—
> In patience to abide, . . .
> By open speech and simple,
> An hundred times made plain,
> To seek another's profit,
> And work another's gain.

These two indomitable women were photographed at the beginning of a journey into the heart of West Africa. They are both clad in typical Victorian outfits which make no concession to the African climate, and they carry no greater protection than a parasol.

Most British imperialists, at the end of the nineteenth century, would probably have shared these sentiments, especially as the verse went on to be tinged with complaint—"the blame of those ye better, the hate of those ye guard". The Empire-builder often felt himself to be unappreciated. The ingratitude of subjects, the lack of material reward, the interference of politicians—all these figured often in letters home. It was seldom, however, a grumble about the life itself. For many imperialists theirs was a true calling, often transmitted through generations in the imperial service.

For on this, the professional level of Empire, the idea of service really was paramount. The imperial profession catered for every preference, and over the years the Empire had built up a vast body of knowledge, scientific, anthropological, strategic, economic. Each extension of Empire widened this expertise. Hardly were the imperial soldiers on the Upper Nile than the imperial hydrologists were following them: after the gun came the butterfly net.

Flora Annie Steel's *Complete Indian Housekeeper* (1892), dedicated to "Those English Girls to whom Fate may assign the task of being House-mothers in our Eastern Empire", told its readers how to build a camp-oven, how to make snipe pudding or mange ointment for dogs, how to treat cows with colic or husbands with prickly heat, the best means of keeping sparrows out of the house, the cost of hiring a bullock-drawn van in Ootacamund, the right underwear to take to the Punjab, the proper way to load a camel and the only correct recipe for boot-dubbin (fish oil, mutton suet and resin).

Languages especially were an imperial concern. The Englishman might be notorious for his inability to learn French or German, but the most unlikely members of the imperial services, dim infantry subalterns or district

The size of the British Empire at the end of the nineteenth century led to calls for greater consolidation and closer communication with the home country. The Imperial Congress of 1887 set out to strengthen Britain's ties with the Empire, especially with those colonies that had become self-governing. The Imperial and Colonial Magazine was started three years later to further the aims of the Congress.

officers reserved to the point of misanthropy, seemed able to master Burmese or Arabic, Nguni or Fijian. Many languages were first lexicographed by the British: some were first put into writing by them.

The mastery of technique was the key to authority, whether it was knowing more about soil composition, or understanding the historical origins of Honduran folklore, and most of the imperial administrators were diligent in their specialities. As "A Gentlemen of Experience" wrote in his *Guide to the Native Languages of Africa* (1890), "In the matter of language it is always better to go to a little more trouble and learn the exact equivalent if possible. 'I am an Englishman and require instant attention to the damage done to my solar topee' is far better than any equivocation that may be meant well but will gain little respect."

Behind this decency and conscientiousness, though, beyond the naive ardour of the general public, very different energies directed the affairs of Empire. Of the few dozen men who really ran the British Empire in the dangerous years after the Diamond Jubilee, scarcely any were English gentlemen as the world knew the breed.

Lord Salisbury, the Prime Minister, was an aristocratic eccentric. Joseph Chamberlain, the Colonial Secretary, was a Birmingham screw manufacturer, a Unitarian by creed, a dandy by pose. Lord Cromer, the ruler of Egypt, was the great-grandson of a Hamburg merchant. Lord Milner, the High Commissioner in South Africa, was a German-trained lawyer of authoritarian principles. Lord Curzon, the Viceroy of India, was an intellectual landowner of almost preposterous grandeur, with a faint Midlands accent and an insatiable ambition. Lord Kitchener had spent so long abroad that he knew almost nothing of English life. Cecil Rhodes was a half-crazed visionary who wanted the whole world British—"the moon too, I often think of that."

Most of them looked cynically upon the gaudy patriotism of the day—some indeed chose to work in the Empire because they so detested life in late Victorian England. Yet they were heroes to the masses. Country doctors and suburban solicitors nodded their heads in agreement when they read Mr Chamberlain's latest speech in the *Morning Post*. Crowds flocked to quay or platform when the great Kitchener came home from the wars. The British saw in their leaders the best of themselves, the truest: they did not often know, and would not willingly believe, what excesses were sometimes committed in their name.

Take the young Mahdist commander Emir Mahmoud, captured by Kitchener at Berber in 1897. Would the proud father of "Following the Flags" like his children to know what happened to him? Chains were riveted round his ankles, an iron halter was put round his neck, his hands were bound behind him, and he was paraded in ignominy through the town. Kitchener rode in front, magnificently on a white charger: Mahmoud came behind, sometimes dragged, sometimes running. Whenever he fell, Sudanese soldiers drove him on with whips. The crowd hooted and pelted him as he passed. Every Empire rests on force, and though the British were not habitually cruel, they were certainly ruthless on their frontiers. By any standards but their own they might be considered bullies—almost the worst category of villain in the vocabulary of Victorianism. "Severity always," was an old imperial maxim, "justice when possible". "Butcher and bolt" is how they described that familiar imperial exercise, the punitive expedition.

For by now an assumption of superiority was ingrained in most Britons abroad. When ennobled, the British imperialist often formalised the status by including some foreign fief or battleground in his title: Kitchener became Kitchener of Khartoum and Vaal in the colony of Transvaal, Roberts was Roberts of Kandahar, Wolseley was Wolseley of Tel-el-Kebir—for all the world as though they really were hereditary squires of those recondite properties. The Englishman expected to be treated, by a quarter of the world's people, with a proper respect, even with the gratitude due from a tenant to a benevolent landlord. Men of the middle classes acquired patrician pretensions, while the ancient social orders of the subject nations were all too often ignored or mocked.

Yet if there was something loathsome to this arrogance, there was often something impressive too, and even Britain's enemies begrudgingly conceded it. The implacably hostile Boers, to whom the whole British arrangement of life was inexplicable, if not actually deranged, were nevertheless moved to admiration by the certainty of it all.

Joseph Chamberlain, the Colonial Secretary, hoped to channel this intangible power into efficiency. The white self-governing colonies, who now liked to be called dominions, were gradually coalescing; Canada had been a single federation since 1867, the six Australian colonies were about to become a federal commonwealth. Chamberlain wished to see these "overseas Britains" supplemented by the black, brown and yellow colonies in one self-supporting, self-sufficient political unit—a new kind of superpower, embracing supply and demand, raw materials and manufacturing ability, malleable labour and constructive capital.

"There is no article of your food," he told the British, "there is no raw material of your trade, there is no necessity of your lives, no luxury of your existence which cannot be produced somewhere or other in the British Empire . . . nothing of the kind has ever been known before." Empire should be an economic system, a political solution, a modern career, and he campaigned assiduously to place this idea at the centre of British politics. It was, however, too late. The Empire had gone too far, was too odd, too heterogeneous, for centralist reforms. Its separate units were more competitive than complementary, and the only real unifying bond was the authority of London. The white colonials, far from wanting closer ties with the motherland, only wanted more independence for themselves: the subject peoples, when if ever they achieved equality, were bound to demand control of their own resources. The Empire was essentially irrational, not to be transformed into a smooth-running joint stock company, and its truest energies were highly individualist.

Chamberlain was a utilitarian. He never did see that the poetry, the absurdity of Empire was not merely half its point, but actually its chief support: as the bumblebee aerodynamically could not fly, so forty million northern islanders patently could not rule three hundred and seventy million subject peoples in the face of the world's jealousy. Yet as the bee flew, so the Empire stood. Bluff, pageantry, faith, habit, tradition, even sleight-of-hand—all these were to prove, in the end, more resilient than Chamberlain's common sense criteria of advantage.

Before the end of the century, however, many of the fallacies of Empire were to be exposed, and its high style irrevocably chastened by a catastrophe of the imperial story, the war against the Boers.

CHAPTER 4

THE BOER WAR

Winston Churchill (1874–1965) had served as a subaltern under Kitchener at Omdurman in the Sudan. Having resigned his commission, he was offered an appointment as principal war correspondent of the Morning Post *with, as he wrote in his early autobiography, "two hundred and fifty pounds a month, all expenses paid, entire discretion as to movements and opinions. . . ." Following his capture and escape from the Boers, he was commissioned into the South African Light Horse, and this photograph shows him wearing the uniform of the regiment.*

THE OSTENSIBLE CAUSE OF THE BOER WAR was the presence within the Transvaal of a large foreign population, much of it British. These were the men who worked the gold mines, and they actually formed a majority in the republic. They paid eighty per cent of the taxes, they mined the gold, but they were allowed no rights of citizenship, being treated by President Kruger of the Transvaal with a disagreeable mixture of contempt and suspicion. In 1897, just before the Jubilee, Cecil Rhodes had connived in a conspiracy to overthrow Kruger by a *coup d'état*, along with a filibustering invasion from British territory. The "Jameson Raid", as it was called, ended in fiasco and ignominy, but war had to come.

The Boers actually started the war, by a preventive invasion of British territory. On October 11, 1899, after presenting an impossible ultimatum, they crossed the frontiers of Natal and Cape Colony to invest the railway towns of Ladysmith, Mafeking and Kimberley. Within the week General Sir Redvers Buller, VC, one of the boldest generals of the British army, was on the high seas with three divisions of his army corps, twice the size of Wellington's army at Waterloo, in eager expectancy of greater fame and further glory. With them, now a journalist for the *Morning Post*, was the ubiquitous Winston Churchill, soon to be captured and then escape with great publicity from a Boer prison.

The Boers had only thirty-five thousand men at their disposal, out of a total population of one hundred thousand. General Buller had eighty-five thousand, and the British Empire had a population of three hundred and seventy million. On the face of it the odds against the Boers were farcical, which is why they had pinned their hopes upon a sudden attack. Yet the British army was essentially an imperial force, accustomed to colonial wars against primitive opponents. Within its specialised limits it had been very successful, but since the Crimean War the only European enemies it had faced had been the Boers themselves, who had effortlessly trounced it at Majuba Hill. It had no general staff, and only two intelligence officers to keep in touch with military affairs throughout the Empire. Its rigid conceptions of class made for discipline and unshakeable camaraderie, but reduced the private soldier to a willing cipher. His was just to do or die. It was an army instinctively drawn to the battle-square and the close-order advance, those glorious specialities of British arms since the days of the great Marlborough. Though it was now armed with machine-guns and repeater rifles, it tended to use them like cannon and muskets. It went into action with bands and pipers and had only recently abandoned the redcoat as standard battledress.

The Boer army, on the other hand, was hardly an army at all—the Boer manhood mustered in local mounted units called commandos, owning its own horses, electing its own officers, wearing its own casual interpretations of uniform, and relying heavily upon the enterprise of its individual soldiers. Its discipline, like its morale, was variable. The Boers had armed themselves, though, with the most modern equipment from European arsenals, they kept open minds on military matters if on no others, and above all they were born to the terrain. All in all they were born irregulars, perhaps the best guerrilla soldiers in the world.

These were opponents, then, different in kind. They had much in common nevertheless, and in particular they shared an emotional sense of brotherhood and purpose. When, at the start of the war, the Transvaal commandos assembled in Pretoria to collect their arms and orders, the occasion was likened to the gathering of a huge family.

From every part of the republic they came, riding their tough and shaggy ponies with a shambling ease, their saddlebags bulging with biltong, their slouch hats hard over their heads, greeting friends and relatives everywhere as they rode into the little capital, and saluting President Kruger himself, as they passed his modest frame house on Church Street, as they might greet a family patriarch on the farm.

On the other side the fellowship was just as strong. Here is the coded message by which an approaching British column declared itself to the besieged British garrison at Mafeking: *Our numbers are the Naval and Military Club multiplied by ten; our guns, the number of sons in the Ward family; our supplies, the O/C 9th Lancers.* No Boer alive could crack this impenetrable cipher, but almost any British officer in Mafeking could interpret it. Everyone knew the Naval and Military, the "In and Out", was No. 94, Piccadilly; most people knew the Earl of Dudley, Bill Ward, had five brothers; and anybody in a decent regiment was aware that the colonel commanding the 9th was that very nice fellow Malcolm Little.

First the Boers, investing the three railway towns, pushed deep into Cape Colony, hoping that the Boers living there under British rule, the "Cape Dutch", would join their cause in rebellion. The British, when they had assembled their expeditionary force, responded with two main counter-attacks: the first out of Natal to relieve Ladysmith, the second through the Orange Free State to relieve Kimberley, where Rhodes was shut up in his own diamond fields, and on to Mafeking. Both these thrusts disastrously failed. After a succession of defeats which became known as Black Week, 1899, Buller was replaced as commander in chief by the aged and adored Lord Roberts of Kandahar. With him as chief of staff there arrived inevitably, fresh from his governor-generalship of the Sudan, Lord Kitchener of Khartoum, by now the most imperial of all the imperial soldiers.

In the New Year Roberts opened the second phase of the war with a massive and skilful offensive directly up the railway line to Pretoria. Bloemfontein, Johannesburg and Pretoria were all captured, the three besieged towns were relieved, the two republics were officially annexed to the British Empire and Kruger fled to Europe. The war seemed to be over; but instead the Boers transformed it into a protracted guerrilla campaign, in which the huge British armies, repeatedly reinforced, were harassed by roaming self-supporting commandos, while raiding columns struck deep into Cape Colony.

Let us peer through our field glasses at three of the most significant Boer War battlegrounds—each offering its own dramatic unity, each to be immortalised in legend.

Look first at Spion Kop. There it stands in our lenses now, a bulky flat-topped hill above the Tugela river, in northern Natal: grander and more imposing than its neighbours along the ridge, bare, silent, and looking much

DON'T BITE OFF MORE THAN YOU CAN CHEW, JOHN.
From the *Tribune* (Minneapolis)

This caricature appeared in the Tribune, *in Minneapolis, in January 1900, and shows an American view of British expansion in Africa.*

Boers manning the trenches outside Mafeking. The Boer fighters were men of all ages, from youths to grandfathers, and often different generations of the same family would fight together. Boer units, or commandos as they were known, fought mainly on horseback, using guerrilla tactics, and often outmanoeuvred the conventionally trained British army.

higher than its fifteen hundred feet. Doves coo among the shrubby trees; bees hum among the mimosa. There is a scent of flowers and dry grass.

General Buller, leading his southern army to the relief of Ladysmith, was persuaded that this hill was the key to the beleaguered town, twenty miles beyond. Handing over executive command to his subordinates, he set up his headquarters on the south side of the river, and ordered an assault. British maps of the area were rudimentary—five miles to the inch—and nobody really knew what shape the mountain was, or what lay immediately beyond it. Nevertheless on the night of January 23 an assault column climbed a steep spur to the summit, overwhelmed the small Boer picket there and dug itself in as best it could on the plateau.

A heavy mist hung around, but so far as they could tell, the British were masters of the mountain. When the sun came up, though, and the mist cleared, they found to their horror that Spion Kop was not as they supposed. The small green triangle they occupied, perhaps an acre of gently sloping grass, was overlooked by two outlying knolls, and from these positions a terrible point-blank rifle fire was opened upon the crouching soldiers. Boer artillery soon found the range, too, and fired high-explosive shells almost without pause into the exposed British positions.

Buller's entire army, massed in the valley below, could see the smoke and the shell-bursts far above, and through binoculars could even make out the figures of soldiers, crouched or stumbling through the shell fumes. But Buller wavered; orders were muddled, mislaid, misinterpreted; at one time three different commanders all believed themselves to be in command on the hill; when an enterprising cavalry brigadier mounted a diversionary attack along the ridge, he was testily recalled and reprimanded. Twice reinforcements were ordered up the mountain, and throughout the day a straggle of individual officers, war correspondents and stretcher-bearers clambered like pilgrims up the track. But nothing essentially happened. Pinned to their ground, the British on Spion Kop simply sweated and died throughout the long day, holding an objective that had no meaning.

Boers and Britons were only a few yards apart up there, and the battle sometimes degenerated into roughhouse, the men falling upon each other with rifle butts, bayonets, boulders and even fists. Half the force was killed and wounded. When darkness fell, and the Boer fire ended, the senior surviving officer on the summit declared that he and his men would fight no more: and so, trudging down again with his long line of wounded, exhausted and appalled soldiers, on his own initiative he ended this squalid and futile engagement.

A British failure. For a famous British success, let us inspect the besieged railway town of Mafeking, away to the north. It was really hardly more than a village, and the Boers did not invest it very resolutely, but it was defended so jauntily by its dapper commanding officer, Colonel Robert Baden-Powell, that its very name became synonymous with British pride and spirit. Some twelve hundred Britons were shut up there, with about as many black Africans, and though they did not really suffer very greatly (except the Africans, who nearly starved), they did defend the place with true panache.

It was a tiny place, a square, a church, a station, a couple of hotels, a grid of half a dozen streets, clustered in greenery around a muddy river in the heart of the high veld, and throughout the siege it retained some of the English village spirit. Baden-Powell was the undoubted squire of Mafeking, around whose cheerful conceited figure everything revolved. The centre of activity was Dixon's Hotel in Market Square and from there every kind of enterprise was mounted. It might be a foray into the enemy lines. It might be a jolly ruse to deceive the Boer sentries. It might be a fancy-dress ball for Sunday evening, or a comic couplet for the *Mafeking Mail*.

"B-P" dominated it all, and gave to the defence a perky humour that caught the fancy of the world. He disseminated it carefully, in a flow of vivacious and not always strictly accurate messages home. If he made things in Mafeking seem more desperate than they were, that did not detract from the tonic effect it all had upon the spirits of the people at home, or its propaganda value elsewhere. B-P's cocky dispatches recalled the heroic eccentricity of Gordon at Khartoum. The presence of women and children recalled the tearjerkers of the Indian Mutiny, and the attendance of numerous swells was an assurance that British imperialism still had *class*. It was wonderfully true to the Mafeking myth that when, after eight months, the first men of the relieving force clattered into the outskirts of the town, they got a distinctly laconic greeting from the first man they met. "Ah yes," was all he said, "we heard you were knocking about."

For the saddest Boer humiliation of the war we must make our way along dusty veld tracks, through low hills prickly with thorn, to the infinitesimal hamlet of Paardeberg, on the Modder River in the Orange Free State. There, at the climax of Lord Roberts's campaign, the main Boer army, with all its waggons, animals, women and children, was surrounded in the riverbed. It was February 1900, the height of the South African summer. The weather was hot and heavy, with thunderstorms now and then, and black clouds piled often over the southern horizon. Within their *laager*, ramparted by waggons and earthworks, General Piet Cronje's army was tensely concentrated. On the crest of the riverbanks the commando marksmen were entrenched. Behind them in the shaley gorge all the paraphernalia of the army was jammed this way and that—waggons tilted on the shingle, piles of ammunition boxes in the muddy lee of the banks, field kitchens, hospital tents, horses tethered restless among the trees. Rough shelters had been scooped out in the bluffs, and there the women and children sheltered behind awnings of old canvas. The men lived in their

A newsboy's poster gives the news of the relief of Mafeking on May 17, 1900. The siege lasted for two hundred and seventeen days and a thousand British troops held eight thousand Boers at bay. The news led to national rejoicing and restored British confidence.

waggons, or in bivouacs at the river's edge. Their *laager* was two miles long, like a trench-grave in the veld, the epitome of the last-ditch stand.

For ten days the Royal Artillery tried to blast the Boers out of this place. The riverbed was thick with cordite fumes, rubble, wrecked waggons, the smoke of burning wood, the stink of dead horseflesh, and sometimes the Boers could see, in the patch of sky between the trees, the round shape of an observation balloon, like death's scrutiny. Several times the British attacked frontally across the veld, to be beaten back with fearful losses. All hope of relief was lost, but Cronje, a huge, tragic, shambling figure of a man, declined offers of safe conduct for his noncombatants and refused all calls to surrender. Instead day by day the Boers fought back.

This spirit broke at last on February 27, Majuba Day, the proudest day in the Boer calendar, usually the day for celebrating their earlier great victory over the British. When Cronje, in his wide hat and shabby green frock coat, climbed out of the ravine to surrender to Lord Roberts, he did not reply to the victor's courteous greeting—"You have made a gallant defence, sir." And when his four thousand ragged and half-starved burghers filed into captivity with their wives and children, carrying blankets and bundles of possessions, some with umbrellas, they looked less like an army than a band of dispossessed peasants. Cronje himself rode stormy-faced and erect in an open cart, Mrs Cronje implacable at his side.

An American observer, watching a British battalion prepare yet another frontal assault upon yet another impregnable hill, is said to have inquired, "Say, Colonel, isn't there a way *round?*" The story of the Boer War is full of such sudden pungencies. It was not war on the gargantuan twentieth-century scale, huge conscript armies pursuing inconceivable objectives. It was war recognisably between *people*, fighting for targets all could see, commanded by generals everyone knew, animated by public emotions. "It is our country you want!" Kruger once cried to a visiting Englishman, tears falling down his cheeks. "I thank God," General Sir George White told his soldiers, when Ladysmith was relieved at last, "I thank God we have kept the flag flying."

Time and again we read of chivalries in the field—a wounded enemy given free passage, a parched patrol allowed to water its horses, the exchange of wounded. Sober in victory as in defeat, the Boer soldiers never crowed over their enemies, and were frank in their admiration of British qualities. The British regulars came deeply to respect the best of the Boers, and cherished the very name "commando" to use one day for themselves.

The heroic spirit faltered, however. Kitchener, assuming the command from Roberts, beat the Boers in the end only by ruthless and laborious methods of attrition, burning their farms, herding their women and children into the first detention camps, and crisscrossing the entire countryside with eight thousand interconnecting blockhouses. The struggle degenerated into a messy and generally inglorious manhunt. Mile after mile the countryside was left scorched and desolate. Between the blockhouses, thousands of fortified posts divided the country into enormous stockades, into which the commandos were laboriously penned. In one of Kitchener's drives nine thousand soldiers, twelve yards apart, formed a beaters' line fifty-four miles long, moving twenty miles a day. The Boers thought the British were resorting to genocide. The British accused the Boers of treachery, fighting as they did, unconventionally in civilian clothes.

By the Autumn of 1900 the British army had virtually defeated the Boers, but the war still dragged on for another two ignominious years.

When at last the Boers surrendered, in May 1902, twenty thousand commandos were still in the field, but both sides were exhausted and embittered. The British had suffered terribly from heat and disease: of their twenty-two thousand deaths, two-thirds were from cholera and enteric fever. The Boer guerrillas ended the war half-starved and virtually destitute, and their families were decimated by the appalling conditions of Kitchener's concentration camps: twenty-four thousand Boers died in the war, twenty thousand of them women and children.

The Peace of Vereeniging was concluded in May 1902. In London the treaty was greeted far less boisterously than the relief of Mafeking two years before. The Queen had died, Rhodes had died, Salisbury retired as soon as the war ended, Kitchener's bludgeon methods had taken the fun out of following the flag.

The peace settlement was widely greeted as generous, especially by the British. It handsomely compensated the Boers for devastation of their country, and it eventually gave them full equality of law, as of language, within a self-governing African union of all four European colonies. It seemed a peace of reconciliation. In this as in much else, though, the Boer War was deceptive. The treaty *was* magnanimous, but by its terms the British hoped to establish a secure, British-dominated South Africa, to establish a lasting hold over the gold of the Rand, and to ensure some measure of fair play for the black peoples of the land. Lord Milner, the High Commissioner, now brilliantly restored the ravaged countryside to normal life, resettling the landless families, building new schools and farms, evolving constitutions for the new Boer colonies and founding municipalities in the Boer townships. He really did lay the foundations of a union, in which eventually the Boers would enjoy constitutional equality with the British. But it aimed at giving Britain permanent British control in South Africa. When Milner built new schools for Boers, he intended that the instruction should be in English. When he founded experimental farms, he hoped that British farmers would come and settle there.

The Boer leaders, however, had no intention of allowing the British to swamp or pervert the *Volk*, and they were no less calculating, even in defeat. They reasoned that within a constitutional union they might one day achieve mastery not only of their own former republics, but of all South Africa, with the freedom to treat their native subjects just as the Old Testament suggested.

They were right. Jehovah survived the Queen-Empress, and the Boers were to win in the end.

Meanwhile, the world watched thoughtfully. "My dear, you know I am not proud," wrote the Tsar Nicholas II to his sister during the Boer War, "but I *do like knowing that it lies solely with me* in the last resort to change the course of the war in Africa. The means is very simple—telegraph an order for the whole Turkestan army to mobilise and march to the Indian frontier. That's all."

He was exaggerating in fact, for until his central Asian railway system was complete he had no way of getting the Turkestan army to the Indian frontier, but he was only expressing the instinct of the nations. The Boer War had cracked the British mirror; the Jubilee was over; the Empire had grown too big for itself. It had seemed to most of its citizens invulnerable. It was clear to everybody that a single colonial war, against an enemy with

The high death rate in the South African War was mainly due to the spread of disease. This is a photograph of the officers' hospital at Wynberg, Cape Province.

a population half that of Birmingham, had tried the Empire to its limits.

The British still had their supporters, from the Anglophiles of the eastern United States, who hardly felt themselves to be foreigners at all, to Greek and Italian liberals who still saw in Britain the old champion of their freedoms. But they had far more enemies. The German Kaiser Wilhelm II, Queen Victoria's own grandson, had been openly pro-Boer ever since the Jameson Raid. The Boers had been armed mostly with German weapons, and their artillery had been actually officered by Germans. Most of the other European states had declared their sympathies too, if only unofficially. Editorialists had damned the British, cartoonists had lampooned them, public opinion everywhere had been at once shocked by Britain's policies, and entertained by her discomfitures. From many parts of the world young men had volunteered to fight with the Boers: Germans, Frenchmen, Americans, and a ferocious and treasonable corps of Irishmen, Blake's Brigade. "Fashoda is revenged!" a Frenchman cried as he climbed to the roof of a captured British fort outside Mafeking, carrying a bottle of brandy. They had been inspired partly by idealism, partly by a taste for adventure, but largely by the resentment with which, beneath the unwilling respect, the world had long regarded the British Empire. It was a resentment often envious and often hypocritical, but nonetheless profound.

The white colonies had staunchly supported the mother country in the struggle. Some seventeen thousand Australians, eight thousand five hundred Canadians, eight thousand New Zealanders had fought in South Africa, and there were white volunteers too from India, the Malay States, Burma, Ceylon and most of the scattered island possessions. Black and brown volunteers, however, had not been invited and among the coloured subject peoples loyalty was not so absolute. The Boer War had given some encouragement to those few visionary leaders who saw that the British Empire would not last forever. But it took vision indeed to see this, from the wrong side of the colour-line. Across the globe the British presence still lay apparently immovable, and so immeasurably superior was the white race in all the techniques of command, so cowed were the coloured peoples

THE FIRST RADIO SIGNAL ACROSS THE ATLANTIC

G.M. Marconi describes how, on December 12, 1901, in a hut on the cliffs at St John's, Newfoundland, he received the first transatlantic signals from Poldhu, Cornwall.

Shortly before midday I placed the single earphone to my ear and started listening. The receiver on the table before me was very crude—a few coils and condensers and a coherer—no valves, no amplifiers, not even a crystal. But I was at last on the point of putting the correctness of all my beliefs to test. The answer came at 12.30 when I heard, faintly but distinctly, *pip-pip-pip*. I handed the phone to Kemp: "Can you hear anything?" I asked. "Yes," he said, "the letter S"— he could hear it. I knew then that all my anticipations had been justified. The electric waves sent out into space from Poldhu had traversed the Atlantic—the distance, enormous as it seemed then, of 1,700 miles— unimpeded by the curvature of the earth. The result meant much more to me than the mere successful realisation of an experiment. As Sir Oliver Lodge has stated, it was an epoch in history. I now felt for the first time absolutely certain that the day would come when mankind would be able to send messages without wires not only across the Atlantic but between the farthermost ends of the earth.

G.M. Marconi at the controls of his early radio transmitter.

by European technology and assurance, that the Empire really did have an eternal look. Governors and commissioners moved freely about without bodyguards, and the viceroy of India sometimes went walking all by himself through the Calcutta slums; for the Englishman was to his subject peoples, Gandhi thought, as the elephant was to the ants.

But in the years after the Boer War the ants began to stir. In Ireland, where patriotism had survived eight hundred years of British occupation, the old undercurrent still ran, secret societies drilled and plotted, and the Irish people only needed another in their long line of heroes to inspire them into rebellion. In Burma the Young Men's Buddhist Association, built upon its Christian model, advanced from healthy sports and social work into nationalist discussion. In West Africa the Sokoto people rebelled, in South Africa the Zulus, in East Africa the black tribes of Kenya.

Indian nationalism had already found a voice as the Indian National Congress, originally dedicated to cooperation with the Raj, developed more militant postures. And it had an inspiring spokesman in the Hindu visionary Bal Gangadhar Tilak, who had already been imprisoned for subversion, but was irrepressible. No country, though, was less likely to coalesce in rebellion than India—fragmented into a thousand parts by race, religion, history and geography, held so long in fee to the British that the habit of obedience was deeply ingrained in the people.

Mohandas Karamchand Gandhi, (1869–1948) is shown here in c.1887 during his law student days in England. In 1893 he went to South Africa and became a successful lawyer and a leader of the Asian community. He returned to his native India in 1914, where he led the Home Rule movement.

In 1905 the British decreed the partition of Bengal, the most intractable province of British India, whose population was rather larger than England's. They proposed to divide it into two lesser provinces, one predominantly Hindu, one predominantly Muslim, and their intention was self-evident: divide and rule. At first the Indian leaders of Congress objected in constitutional terms. The British were unimpressed, being for the most part thoroughly contemptuous of Congress and all it represented, but as the day of partition approached they found themselves faced by a very different kind of protest. There were none of the habitual Indian riots, which were a nuisance, but easily suppressed. Instead, at Tilak's inspiration, thousands of Bengalis protested passively, with a silent boycott of everything British. Shoppers would not buy British goods. Students would not do their examinations on British paper. Washerwomen would not wash British clothes. Lancashire textiles were ceremonially burnt in the streets.

Although this passive resistance was unsuccessful in changing the fate of Bengal, the British soon recognised it as the first stirring and chief weapon of a decisive revolutionary process.

Even more significantly, at this time, the world observed a first hesitation of British morale at home. The seeds of a deep and subtle disillusionment had been sown. The conduct of the war had hinted at fundamental flaws in the imperial assumptions. "Before 1900," wrote the polemicist Arnold White in his *Efficiency and Empire,* the "accepted creed of average Englishmen" had included the following clauses:

The British Empire is the greatest the world has ever seen, and being free from militarism is safe against decay.

The British army, though small, can do anything and go anywhere.

One Englishman can beat two foreigners.

We are the most enlightened people on the face of the earth.

By the end of the war, as White commented, every one of those propositions was disputable, and some were obvious falsehoods.

EDWARDIAN PEOPLE

LONG BEFORE QUEEN VICTORIA DIED, many of the tenets, customs and behaviour which made up Victorianism began to lose ground. Even among those people who stood fast by its values there were fears that it could not last.

Edward VII came to the throne in 1901, when he was fifty-nine years old, and for many years his lifestyle as Prince of Wales had been utterly at odds with that of his mother. His men friends were rich—such as Thomas Lipton, who had made his fortune out of grocery, and the financier Ernest Cassel—and he liked to have attractive women about him, some of whom were his mistresses. His critics might attack plutocracy or moral laxity, but Edward, popular with the press, did not care. He cut an important figure in Europe, too, particularly in France.

This was a glittering age for the rich, what the French called *la belle époque*, the age of the country house party, the great shoot, the long weekend, a time when actresses married peers and London was lavish with entertainment in theatres, clubs and hotels. Income tax was low.

But there were shadows as well as sunshine. Real wages fell, unemployment was high in bad years, and statisticians demonstrated the existence of substantial poverty countrywide, not only in London but in old provincial cities like York and Lincoln.

There was political excitement too. The Liberals, under the premiership first of Sir Henry Campbell Bannerman, and then of Herbert Asquith, were in power from 1906 until 1916, and faced strong minority protests from suffragettes fighting for women's rights, trade unionists "in strife" (as the novelist and playwright John Galsworthy put it) with employers, and even disgruntled peers, who did not like Lloyd George's Budget of 1909.

Finally, and familiarly, there was trouble once more with Ireland, where the Unionists pledged their full support for the Protestant Ulstermen.

THE KING SET THE STYLE *for high living. Edward VII was sixty before being crowned but, as Prince of Wales, had been a leading light in London and European society for years. His love of horse racing, gambling and women had become legendary, but he was also a keen sportsman, a patron of science and the arts and, when he became King, a gifted diplomat who helped to achieve the "entente cordiale" with France. The photograph above shows him seated in a Daimler driven by Lord Montagu of Beaulieu.*

THE RICH DINED LAVISHLY, *as suggested in this 1902 cartoon above. Some Edwardian writers, however, recognised the limitations of the social round. An extract from Harold Nicolson's* Small Talk, *(1937) recalls a country weekend. "Dinner was at half-past eight. The women would retire an hour before to change their tea-gowns. The men also would change into clothes even more galling and restrictive than those they had worn all day. Dinner would be ptarmigan and champagne. Champagne and ptarmigan. At nine forty-five women swept, with backward glances, from the room. The host would take his glass of port and move to the seat vacated by his wife . . . . And next Saturday it would all begin again."*

THE SEASIDE HOLIDAY, *already popular with the Victorians, increased in popularity in Edwardian days. Cameras were now available to rec*

DAVID LLOYD GEORGE (1863–1945), the son of a Welsh schoolmaster, was one of the founders of the welfare state. He was elected a Liberal M.P. in 1890 and, as Chancellor of the Exchequer (1908–15), he introduced old-age pensions which gave people aged over seventy years old 5s. per week. The National Insurance Act of 1911, modelled on the German social insurance scheme, earned the nickname of "Ninepence for Fourpence". Each worker contributed 4d. weekly to the fund, while his employer paid 3d. and the State 2d.

THE PLIGHT OF THE POOR is well illustrated in this photograph of a downcast father with his wife and five ragged children (above). In 1901, following his study of poverty in York, Seebohm Rowntree calculated that a family could exist on £1 1s. 8d. per week but without meat, bus fares, newspapers, postage stamps, or church collection monies. The children could not have toys or pocket money, the father must neither drink nor smoke and the mother must never buy any clothes. The wage earner must never be absent from his work.

...rd the fun of the beach in family snapshots. This shot, of the beach and pier at Skegness before the First World War, demonstrates the greater freedom which prevailed with the relaxation of some of the more moralistic and repressive Victorian attitudes.

THOSE MAGNIFICENT MEN in their flying machines were the new heroes of the Edwardian era. The American inventors, Wilbur and Orville Wright, pioneered the first powered flight in 1903. Louis Blériot flew across the English Channel in 1909. By 1913, aircraft enthusiasts could flock to the Hendon Air Display as advertised on this London Underground poster (above). The outbreak of war in 1914 stimulated research into aerodynamics.

CHAPTER 5

CURZON AND INDIA

This photograph of Lord Curzon of Kedleston was taken in 1903 when he was Viceroy of India. Curzon believed that the relationship between the governors of empire and their subjects was akin to that between good landlords and their tenants and that their power should be absolute but paternal.

MANY ASPECTS OF VICTORIANISM died with Victoria and many aspects of imperialism too. All of a sudden, it seemed, the giants were leaving. Gladstone had already gone. The Boer War had brought to fame a politician of an altogether new kind, David Lloyd George, the cobbler's ward from Llanystumdwy in North Wales—a man not simply of the people, but somebody totally alien to the English traditions of hierarchy and dominion, a man who did not even believe English to be necessarily best, but surrounded himself with Welsh aides and secretaries, spoke Welsh most of the time, and paid no attention to British conventions of reticence and decorum.

The new King, Edward VII, was not very interested in his Empire, and the Edwardian age never did recapture the flair, conviction or vulgarity of the great enterprise. In the first years of the new century, nevertheless, some remarkable Britons found in the imperial métier a satisfaction almost, if not entirely, worthy of their gifts. First among them was Lord Curzon, Viceroy of India, the chief Edwardian grandee of Empire.

To understand the posture of Curzon in India, we must first visit Kedleston, his country home. The Curzons had lived at Kedleston in Derbyshire for eight hundred years, providing not only its squires, but often its vicars too. They were not a particularly distinguished family, but they were evidently tenacious. *Let Curzon Holde*, ran the family motto, *What Curzon Helde*.

Kedleston Hall was a famous house, designed by James Paine and Robert Adam in the eighteenth century. With its wide parkland, its sweep of colonnade and rose garden, its tremendous Great Hall with columns of pink alabaster, it was also overpoweringly English. It was like a country seat in a novelette (though Dr Johnson, who thought it all much overdone, said it would do "excellently well for a town hall"). In the parish church, like a family chapel, Curzons of every reign lay beneath their honorifics.

Out of such a background came George Nathaniel Curzon. He was the eldest boy in a family of two sons and nine daughters, and among the most precocious of his contemporaries at Eton and at Balliol, Oxford, where he was cruelly immortalised in the famous verse:

> My name is George Nathaniel Curzon,
> I am a most superior person.
> My cheek is pink, my hair is sleek,
> I dine at Blenheim once a week.

At an early age Curzon decided that only two ambitions in life were worthy of his pursuit: to be Viceroy of India, to be Prime Minister of England. The first of these he achieved at the almost unexampled age of thirty-nine when, with his graceful American wife (the first of two), he landed on the blazing quayside at Bombay on December 30, 1898 for the first of two viceregal terms—seven years in all.

Curzon was an imperialist out of his period. Not many of the landed gentry were much enthralled by the imperial mission, and it was at Kedleston

THE AGE OF THE MACHINE

Machinery made possible an unprecedented increase in national wealth. It led to the creation of new classes, the posing of new problems, and the waging of new wars. It also inevitably produced reaction against the machine itself.

"LA MITRAILLEUSE" BY CHRISTOPHER NEVINSON,
TATE GALLERY, LONDON

"DOVE AND ROSE", (above) a textile design by William Morris, hangs in the Victoria and Albert Museum, London. In an age of mass production, Morris championed craftsmanship. His ideals foundered, but his designs live on.

"OPHELIA", (above right) by John Millais, may be seen in the Tate Gallery, London. The picture illustrates the passionate concern of the Pre-Raphaelite painters with minute detail and literary allusion.

"SIDONIA VON BORKE", (above) from the Tate Gallery, London, was painted by Edward Burne-Jones, the most fashionable artist of the Pre-Raphaelite Brotherhood, whose popularity was founded on a style that deliberately evoked images of a medieval Golden Age. In contrast, "WORK", (detail, right) by Ford Madox Brown, in the Manchester City Art Gallery, sets out to glorify the gospel of hard work. It is one of the most intensely symbolic of Victorian narrative pictures.

SCHOOL OF ART, GLASGOW, STRATH-CLYDE, *was built between 1897 and 1909, to the designs of Charles Rennie Mackintosh. The north façade (left) is notable for its huge functional windows and decorative ironwork. The beautifully proportioned boardroom (above) provides the setting for Mackintosh's high-backed chairs. The doors of Glasgow's* WILLOW TEA ROOMS *(right) contain his most elaborate designs in metalwork and stained glass. Mackintosh and his followers provided a vital link between Victorian and twentieth-century design.*

FIRST WORLD WAR POSTERS, (right) of which there is a collection in the Imperial War Museum, London, enlisted for the first time the skills of the new art of advertising design to the propaganda and promotion of war. This was a war that would require civilian commitment as never before, demanding first the raising of a volunteer army, then extra money through Liberty Bonds, and the active participation of women behind the lines. The Germans ran similar campaigns. Both sides had to justify to their people the appalling casualty lists and acute shortages of food at home. Meanwhile, the reality of life at the front was to inspire poetry and paintings that stood in stark contrast to the propaganda posters.

"TRAVOYS ARRIVING WITH WOUNDED AT A DRESSING STATION", (above) by Stanley Spencer, and "TROOPS RESTING", (left) by Paul Levinson, are also from the Imperial War Museum, London. All Spencer's work was imbued with a compassionate religious mysticism, and he was to distil his experience of war in an extraordinary set of murals in the Sandham Memorial Chapel at Burghclere, Hampshire. Paul Levinson's view of the futility of war, perfectly captured here in "Troops Resting", and so at odds with the heroic image projected by the government's propaganda, often fell foul of the censor.

"THE MULE TRACK", (above) by Paul Nash, and "A BATTERY SHELLED", (right) by Percy Wyndham Lewis, both hang in the Imperial War Museum, London. Nash fought in the trenches, was a friend of the poet Siegfried Sassoon, and shared his detestation of the war. "I am no longer an artist interested and curious," he wrote. "I am a messenger who will bring back word from the men who are fighting to those who want the war to go on for ever." Wyndham Lewis was a founder member of the Vorticist artistic movement, aiming to build up a "visual language as abstract as music." He used the bleakness of the war landscape, covered with cogs, wheels and abandoned inhuman machinery, to create an impression of mechanical violence.

MONARCHS OF THE OCEAN AND THE
ROAD: *the 1939 Mark V Bentley
(above), and the P. & O.'s liner,
SS Stratheden (right), were, in their
own fields, outstanding examples of
British engineering at a time when
Britain had lost its lead in mass
production, but still retained its
reputation for de luxe transport. In
the Second World War, many of the
P. & O.'s liners would play major
roles, and the car industry provided
much of the engineering expertise
for armaments and transport.*

*"THE SNACK BAR", (above) by Edward
Burra, was painted in 1930, and
now hangs in the Tate Gallery, London. Burra was then famous for his
satirical paintings of the cheap and
squalid side of British life.*

BATTERSEA POWER STATION, LONDON,
*(right) was built in 1929. Shaped
like a table upside down, this much-
loved feature of the London landscape, no longer needed in the
nuclear age, remains a listed monument to the romance of early twentieth-century power. The interior is
to become a leisure complex.*

"TOTES MEER", (above) from the Tate Gallery, London, was painted by Paul Nash in 1941. This leading painter from the First World War was appointed an Official War Artist in 1940, and created many unforgettable images of destruction.

"WOMEN WORKING AS BRICK DRESSERS", (left) an early colour photograph, portrays the spirit of a war that depended heavily on the resolution of the civilians.

"WATERLOO", (below) by Helen McKie, from the National Railway Museum, York, shows Waterloo Station crowded as usual — but with wartime crowds totally different in appearance from the days of peace. Not only are there marching soldiers. There are landgirls, Highlanders, Indian and American soldiers, women in the WRNS and ATS. In the Second World War, almost everyone was in uniform.

"TAKE OFF", *now in the Imperial War Museum, London, is one of a number of important paintings of the Second World War by Dame Laura Knight. She had made her name before the war with her paintings of the circus and the Russian ballet, and was the first woman elected an Associate of the Royal Academy for over one hundred and fifty years.*

indeed that a perceptive young Indian maharajah, viewing the idyllic scene around him, wondered why on earth Englishmen went to India at all, when they could stay at home in such a place, "playing the flute and watching the rabbits". Curzon was one of the few. Having a taste for lordliness, having travelled in his youth extensively in Persia and Central Asia, being by nature an autocrat, a connoisseur, a humorist, he responded readily to the magnificence of Empire, and believed in its usefulness. He thought it, "under Providence, the greatest instrument for good that the world has seen . . . there has never been anything so great in the world's history."

At home Curzon moved in the quickest and most elegant of English circles. In India he found himself among a very different kind of Briton. The men of the Indian Civil Service were, as a whole, diligent, incorruptible, highly educated, but less than scintillating. Since the Mutiny half a century before they had become increasingly institutionalised, growing ever more convinced that in India especially there could be nothing new under the sun. Their methods had been tested down the generations, and were by now embodied in a thousand precedents and corollaries, docketed in a million cubbyholes and wrapped up in red tape from Dacca to Karachi.

Curzon was much depressed by these colleagues, and by the style of bureaucratic life in India. The pace of it he found unbearably ponderous— "Like the diurnal revolution of the earth," he wrote, "went the files, steady, solemn, sure and slow"—and every initiative he made seemed to be muffled, diverted or referred back. He made few friends in India, and he was sadly homesick. "The echo of the great world," he wrote to a friend, "hums like the voice of a seashell in one's ears."

So he withdrew ever more haughtily into the powers of his own autocracy: and since the idea of India, India in the abstract, India as a supreme field of British enterprise and imagination, still moved him greatly, in a curious fashion this most devotedly English of politicians became the most nearly Indian of viceroys. We see him riding to the manner born, in the howdahs of elephants, or passing with benevolent inclinations of his head beneath arches proclaiming him the Benefactor of India.

Though he much admired efficiency, and spoke proudly of his own "middle-class methods", still he acted in the spirit of earlier times, as though there were no obstructive bureaucrats to hamper him, or daily directives from Whitehall. He was excited rather than daunted by the magnitude of the task, and by the daring of the British presence there—"a speck of foam," he called it once, "upon a dark and unfathomable ocean." In his ideas if not his methods he was like one of the tremendous enthusiasts who, with gun and Bible and unshakeable assurance, had established British rule in the Punjab sixty years before. Like them, he believed that no aspect of life should be beneath the notice of a great ruler. Land revenues, railway systems, universities, the growth of industry, the control of commerce, irrigation, corruption in the police, provincial administration, border con- trol—in matters petty or incalculable, Lord Curzon laid down a policy, instituted an inquiry, or at least made his opinions known.

He was constantly chafing against the interference of London in Indian affairs. He considered India a power in its own right, with the authority to extend its discipline over lesser neighbours. He sent an aggressive expedition into Tibet, the most private of all countries, and made a viceregal visitation to the sheikhdoms and emirates of the Persian Gulf, impressing upon those fractious and frequently murderous princelings the power of India and the Empire—the Great Government, as the Arabs gratifyingly learnt to call it.

Curzon was easily moved, to tears and to laughter, and if he distinctly lacked the common touch, he responded to style and sensitivity in men of all races—racial pride, he thought, was a lower-class attribute. Certainly he was less at home with the British bourgeoisie than he was with a delicate maharajah, an entertaining Kurd or the wild frontier chieftains of the northwest—"gigantic," as he approvingly described them, "bearded, instinct with loyalty, often stained with crime."

Curzon grew to relish India's tangled history. Surveying the disturbances and fomentations of the 1900s he wrote: "I have observed the growing temper of the native. The new wine is beginning to ferment in him, and he is awaking to a consciousness of equality and freedom." The movement was inevitable, he believed, and if it was not to end in violent rebellion the arrogance of the British must be held in check. He considered that arrogance vulgar, the prejudice of the uneducated man, and in trying to control it he made many enemies among Anglo-Indians. Once again he was consciously enacting a lofty imperial role, the role of trustee, and never more consciously than in his famous quarrel with the 9th Queen's Royal Lancers.

The 9th were a fashionable cavalry regiment, rich in titles as they were in battle honours, and intensely snobbish towards inferior regiments. In 1902 some of their troopers, it was alleged, brutally attacked an Indian, leaving him dying outside their camp. Who the culprits were, nobody knew. Several courts of inquiry failed to discover, and though the regiment itself offered a reward for information, nobody came forward.

Curzon was much distressed by the affair. During the previous twenty years there had been eighty-four recorded cases in which Europeans had killed Indians, yet since 1857 only two Europeans had been hanged. "You can hardly credit," he wrote, "the sympathy with wrong-doing that there is here—even among the highest—provided that the malefactor is an Englishman." He was convinced that the 9th Lancers had deliberately withheld evidence, and he ordered that, since no individual could be punished, the whole regiment must be instead. All leave was cancelled for nine months, and throughout that period a sentry from another regiment was placed outside each of the regimental barrack blocks.

The regiment was infuriated by this despotism, and was angrily supported by most Anglo-Indians. The case became a *cause célèbre*. The Indian newspapers were full of it, society at home gossiped about it. Even the King protested at Curzon's action. Six months later, at the Delhi Durbar for his coronation, the 9th were detailed to provide the escort for the Duke of Connaught, who was representing the Royal family. A proud escort they formed, the horses sleek and powerful, the soldiers wearing the medals of the South African campaign, with the pennants flying from their lance heads and their spiked helmets gleaming white. When this splendid equipage rode by the saluting base, where Lord Curzon was taking the review, Anglo-India made its feeling known: a loud and pointed cheer went up from the assembled Europeans, unmistakable in its meaning and apparently unanimous—even the Viceroy's personal guests, so Curzon noted wryly, could not forbear to cheer.

Curzon was upset by the demonstration, implying as it did that the vast majority even of educated Europeans in India regarded the Indians as less than fully human, but was intensely conscious too of his own patrician response. "As I sat alone and unmoved on my horse, conscious of the implication of the cheers . . . I felt a certain gloomy pride in having dared to do the right."

He dared, too, to approach the civilisation of India with a respect rare among the pig-stickers and the box-wallahs, and tried to convince the Indians themselves that they should not simply wish to be brown Britons. At the Durbar—"the Curzonation"—he insisted that every detail of the decorations should be Indian so that the whole huge camp became a display of woodworks, enamels, carpets, potteries and lovely silks. He devoted himself to Indian archaeology. He it was who restored the Taj Mahal to its original perfection, and by reviving the moribund Department of Antiquities, gave to the British Raj in India a scholarly distinction that would remain among the more honourable imperial legacies.

Yet he was out of his time—in some ways too soon, in others too late. It was Kitchener, now commander in chief in India, who baulked Curzon of his Indian mission. In an historic quarrel, they clashed over the degree to which the civil government should control the Indian army. Kitchener won, obliging Curzon to resign in 1905, and never afterwards did a viceroy of such difficult originality grace the administration of India.

He left behind mixed feelings: gratitude for much of what he had done, contumely for his eventual partitioning of Bengal, widespread resentment at his high-handedness. He had mixed feelings himself. On the one hand he was a frank imperialist, working always "to rivet the British rule more firmly onto India and to postpone the longed-for day of emancipation". On the other he was a man of civilised sympathies, and hoped that he had helped India towards "the position which is bound one day to be hers— namely that of the greatest partner in the Empire."

Though he later became Foreign Secretary, he never did get to 10 Downing Street, and he looked back on his years in India, for the rest of his life, with a nostalgic pride. Out of it all he distilled as memorable a philosophy of Empire as was ever expressed: "Let it be your ideal," he told his countrymen in India, "to remember that the Almighty has placed your hand on the greatest of his ploughs, in whose furrow the nations of the future are germinating and taking shape, to drive the blade a little forward in

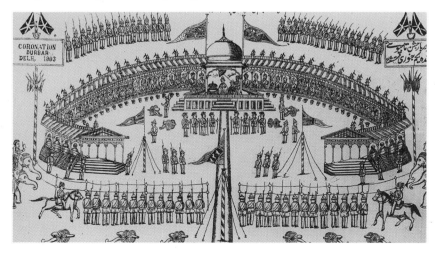

This is an Indian view of the Durbar in 1903, which was held in honour of the coronation of Edward VII, King of Great Britain and Ireland and Emperor of India. The Durbar was designed to be a magnificent display of British military strength and Indian splendour.

your time, and to feel that somewhere among these millions you have left a little justice or happiness or prosperity, a sense of manliness or moral dignity, a spring of patriotism, a dawn of intellectual enlightenment, or a stirring of duty where it did not exist before—that is enough. That is the Englishman's justification in India."

CHAPTER 6

THE FIRST WORLD WAR

WITH THE ADVENT OF A LIBERAL GOVERNMENT in 1905 came the end of Jingo—what Henry Campbell-Bannerman had once called "the vulgar and bastard imperialism of irritation and provocation and aggression . . . of grabbing everything even if we have no use for it ourselves." However, there was war in the air, not now the running colonial war in which the British had been engaged for a century or more, but a greater international conflict which their own dominant power had so long prevented. All the symptoms were brewing; economic rivalries, patriotic frustrations, the ambitions of leaders, dynastic squabbles, the general sense that an epoch was disintegrating and could only be cleared away by violence.

The British could not escape this gathering maelstrom, however pacific their new mood. They were traditionally the regulating power of the world. Their navy made them militarily significant beyond their size, their command of raw materials gave them unique economic leverage, their

YEAR OF DISASTER
British prestige suffered two blows in 1912 with the failure in March of Captain Scott's expedition to reach the South Pole, followed shortly afterwards by the sinking of the Titanic on April 15, after she struck an iceberg whilst on her maiden voyage. The last pages of Captain Scott's journal record the death of his gallant companion, Captain "Titus" Oates. The account of the Titanic disaster which follows is given by the Wireless Operator.

The Death of Captain Oates
Friday, March 16 or Saturday 17—Lost track of dates, but think the last correct. Tragedy all along the line. At lunch, the day before yesterday, poor Titus Oates said he couldn't go on; he proposed we should leave him in his sleeping-bag. That we could not do, and we induced him to come on, on the afternoon march. In spite of its awful nature for him he struggled on and we made a few miles. At night he was worse and we knew the end had come.

Should this be found I want these facts recorded. Oates's last thoughts were of his Mother, but immediately before he took pride in thinking that his regiment would be pleased with the bold way in which he met his death. We can testify to his bravery. He has borne intense suffering for weeks without complaint, and to the very last was able and willing to discuss outside subjects. He did not—would not—give up hope till the very end. He was a brave soul. This was the end. He slept through the night before last, hoping not

This photograph taken at the South Pole on January 18, 1912 shows (from left to right) Capt. L.E.G. Oates, Lt. H.R. Bowers, Capt. R.F. Scott, E.A. Wilson (zoologist) and Petty Officer E. Evans. Bowers holds the shutter string.

to wake; but he woke in the morning—yesterday. It was blowing a blizzard. He said, "I am just going outside and may be some time." He went out into the blizzard and we have not seen him since.

The *Titanic*. The Wireless Operator's Story
From aft came the tunes of the band. It was a ragtime tune. I don't know what. Then there was "Autumn" . . . I went to the place I had seen the collapsible boat on the boat deck, and to my surprise I saw the boat, and men still

possessions everywhere gave them a universal stake, while the immense accumulated wealth of the City of London was a factor even in the banks and chanceries of Europe. The British really had kept the peace of the world for three generations. Now, for the first time since the end of the Napoleonic wars, the task seemed beyond them.

So we see the British, so recently all confident, apprehensively looking for allies. The newly federated German empire, under Wilhelm II, was emerging as the potential enemy; almost anybody would do as a friend. Nation by nation the British patched up their relationships in agreements, concessions or full-blown alliances: with Japan, with France, by 1907 even with Russia, when the Great Game was ended at last in an Anglo-Russian convention. Within the Empire, too, they repaired their friendships. Lord Kitchener toured the dominions to enlist their military potential. Churchill, by now a Liberal politician, and already in the Cabinet, even devised a scheme for an Imperial Squadron of warships from all the major colonies, to be based upon Gibraltar and sent wherever it was needed.

If there was a slight air of desperation to these preparations, it was because time was running short. The Edwardian age, that mellow epilogue of Victorianism, died with its eponymous patron in 1910, and the world became more urgent. There were repeated naval scares, when tales of the vast new German battle-fleet cast a chill over England. Louis Blériot flew the English Channel, making the islanders feel a little less insular, and the liner *Titanic* sank on her maiden voyage, making them feel rather less titanesque. The trade deficit grew bigger every year: by 1910 the profits Britain made from invisible exports, insurance, banking, services of many

---

trying to push it off. I guess there wasn't a sailor in the crowd. They couldn't do it. I . . . was just lending a hand when a large wave came awash of the deck. The big wave carried the boat off. I had hold of an oarlock and I went with it. The next I knew I was in the boat . . . and the boat was upside-down, and I was under it. And I remember realising I was wet through and that whatever happened I must not breathe, for I was under water. I knew I had to fight for it, and I did. How I got out from under the boat I do not know but I felt a breath of air at last. There were men all around me. . . . The sea was dotted with them, all depending on their lifebelts. I felt I simply had to get away from the ship. She was a beautiful sight then. Smoke and sparks were rushing out of her funnel. There must have been an explosion, but we heard none. We only saw the big stream of sparks. The ship was turning gradually on her nose—just like a duck that goes for a dive. I had only one thing on my mind—to get away from the suction. The band was still playing. I guess all of them went down. They were playing "Autumn" then. I swam with all my might. I suppose I was 150 feet away when the *Titanic* . . . began to settle—slowly.

I was very cold. I saw a boat of some kind near me, and put all my strength into an effort to swim to it. It was hard work. I was all done when a hand reached out from the boat and pulled me aboard. It was our same collapsible. The same crowd was on it. There was just room for me to roll on the edge. I lay there not caring what happened.

Others came near. Nobody gave them a hand. The bottom-up boat already had more men than it would hold, and it was sinking. . . . I kept straining my eyes for a ship's light, and somebody said, "Don't the rest of you think we ought to pray?" The man who made the suggestion asked what the religion of the others was. Each man called out his religion. One was a Catholic, one a Methodist, one a Presbyterian. It was decided the most appropriate prayer for all was the Lord's Prayer. We spoke it over in chorus. Some splendid people saved us. They had a right-side-up boat and it was full to capacity. Yet they came to us and loaded us all into it. I saw some lights off in the distance and knew a steamship was coming to our aid.

An artist's impression of the sinking of the Titanic *after it struck an iceberg in the Atlantic.*

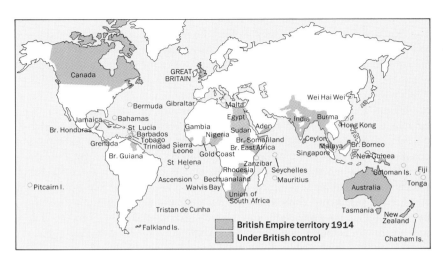

British Empire territory 1914

Under British control

It was boasted that the sun never set on the British Empire, since it circled the globe. The wide distribution of territories gave Britain immense wealth and power. The Empire provided men, resources, strategic bases and overseas markets for its rulers. Rivalry between the European nations over trade, colonies and naval and military power was to be one of the chief causes of the First World War.

kinds, no longer covered it, so that for the first time the British could not pay their way in the world by their own skills, but depended upon investment income from abroad.

In this shifting world only the Empire itself seemed to stand firm, still maintaining in its bases across the continents a posture of unassailable power: and this magnificent façade exerted a profound psychological effect upon its enemies, as well as upon itself. Just as the British economy now depended upon investments made by a previous generation, so the British reputation rested upon the constructions of earlier imperialists.

But in many ways the Empire made the British weaker rather than stronger—it presented, John Morley, the Liberal, had said in 1906, "more vulnerable surface than any empire the world ever saw". Now the British reluctantly attended to their defences. A succession of reformers worked to implement in the British army the lesson of Spion Kop: its structure was altered top to bottom, its tactics and weaponry were drastically revised, and at last the hidebound traditions of the parade ground were jettisoned in favour of fieldcraft and initiative. By 1914 it was to be no longer an imperial army in the old sense, trained specifically for the imperial purposes. Its core was a highly professional expeditionary force ready for service anywhere, but particularly against European enemies.

At the same time Admiral Fisher, the volcanic and visionary First Sea Lord, prepared the Royal Navy, ruthlessly cutting away the dead wood of the fleet, most of it the rot of the Empire: ships that were good only for showing the flag, drills that were performed only for exhibitionism, unnecessary stations, irrelevant exercises. Oil power was introduced, and the British Government acquired a controlling interest in the oilfields of southern Persia, specifically for the fuelling of the new warships. The focus of the fleet was shifted from the blue waters and the far horizons to greyer waters nearer home. The commander of the home fleet, Fisher used to say, was the only man who could lose a war in an afternoon. By the summer of 1914 almost all the great ships were home, ready to face a European enemy in northern waters.

They were just in time. In 1897 the Kaiser, already in possession of Europe's most powerful army, had ordered the construction of a German High Seas Fleet. He had seen it from the start as a deliberate challenge to

Kaiser Wilhelm II with General von Moltke, German Chief of Staff (in effect the Commander in Chief) and officers of the General Staff inspecting the front in 1914. Kaiser Wilhelm, the son of Queen Victoria's eldest daughter, the Princess Royal, was a cousin of George V.

Britain's command of the seas. One day, he told his admirals and construc-
tors, it would be God's instrument of justice—"until then, silence and
work". By 1914 the work was done, the silence broken, and as Europe burst
like an abscess into war, the Empire found itself, for the first time, challenged
by equal force of arms.

That August, it went to war with Germany and her allies, all four
hundred and fifty million subjects of the Crown being bound by a single
declaration from the King-Emperor, George V. The imperial mobilisation
was presided over by the most famous of all the imperial fighting men,
Lord Kitchener, who was immediately appointed war minister, and the
Empire's response surprised even the British themselves. "Our duty is quite
clear," announced the Prime Minister of Australia, "to gird up our loins
and remember that we are Britons." Within ten days New Zealand had
dispatched an expeditionary force of eight thousand men. Within two
months thirty-one thousand Canadians had been recruited, drilled and sent
to Europe. The South Africans, led by the conciliatory Boers, General Smuts
and Louis Botha, not only sent soldiers to Europe, but also took on the
task of evicting the Germans from their colonies in southwest Africa, while
from every last island, promontory or protectorate came volunteers, offers
of money or at least flowery messages of support.

There were dissenters. In Ireland old enemies of the Empire obeyed an
old Irish dictum—"England's trouble is Ireland's chance." In India and in
black Africa a few premature nationalists chose this moment of crisis to
rebel. Generally, though, the Empire attained a unity in conflict which it
had never achieved in peace.

The poetic J. D. Burns of Melbourne wrote:

> The bugles of England are blowing o'er the sea,
> Calling out across the years, calling now to me.
> They woke me from dreaming in the dawning of the day,
> The bugles of England: and how could I stay?

To a volunteer in Winnipeg or Alice Springs, to the Sikh rifleman from
Amritsar or the illiterate Gold Coast askari, the bugles must have sounded
distant indeed. Why were they going? What were they fighting for? The
epicentre of the war was western Europe, its issue was essentially the
balance of power in Europe. The first Gurkha detachments for Europe
approaching Calcutta for embarkation, sharpened their kukris as the train
drew into the city, supposing that they were nearing the battlefront.

The imperial soldiers found themselves transported, all too often, direct
from their own sunlit spaces to the mud and drizzle of Flanders and France,
where they were gassed or mined or mutilated, shivered in the unaccustomed
cold or miserably ate their alien rations, year after year, trench after trench,
sadness after sadness to the end. But the war reached out to the imperial
territories, too. German ships were hunted down in atolls of the Pacific or
in African creeks, campaigns were fought to capture the German colonies
of Africa and the Pacific, and at the back of British strategic thinking there
often lay an imperial aim or instinct. The more imaginative of the British
strategists cast their eyes beyond the confined butchery of western Europe
towards the greater landscapes and grander chances of their imperial
tradition. They looked in particular towards an old arena of imperial
intrigue and aspirations, the Ottoman Empire

Traditionally Britain had supported the Turks, but in October 1914 they

The Eastern Front was the boundary of the Ottoman Empire. In 1914 the Middle East was already a tinderbox. The British feared that when the Ottoman Empire entered the war on the German side, supplies of oil from the Persian Gulf would be cut off, and the Royal Navy would be out of commission.

entered the war on the German side. Theoretically they were suzerains of almost all the Arab world: the Sultan of Turkey, in his capacity as Caliph of the Faithful, commanded the spiritual allegiance of some seventy million Indian Muslims, and was not lightly to be antagonised by the temporal rulers of India. The British already possessed, though, a shadow-empire of their own in the countries that lay between India and the Mediterranean. They ruled Egypt and Aden, they controlled the Persian Gulf, and, as the greatest Muslim power, they felt themselves to have special interests in Arabia, the Holy Land of Islam.

The emergence of the Turks now as enemies conveniently clarified the British position in the Middle East. By April 1915, an official committee was discussing what ought to be done with the Ottoman Empire after the war. Whatever happened, the committee agreed, British interests must first be safeguarded: and the best way to safeguard interests, as everyone knew, was to control the place yourself, whether you did it frankly or covertly. The war against Turkey *was* an imperial war. The Turks, whose military reputation was dim but whose armies were powerfully stiffened by German generals, officers and men, made unsuccessful attacks upon Aden and the Suez Canal. The British responded in kind, and embarked upon three offensives against the Turks. One, the Mesopotamian campaign, was a miserable kind of victory. One, the campaign in Syria, was a success. One, at Gallipoli, was a great defeat, and gave to the imperial annals the most poignant of all their tragedies.

The Turkish province called Mesopotamia, now Iraq, had been a subject of British anxiety for years. Recently the Germans had been active there, building their Berlin to Baghdad railway, and the imperial strategists had long been agitated by the thought of an enemy moving down the line of the Tigris and Euphrates to the Persian Gulf. By 1914 they were concerned too for the security of the Persian oilfields and the refinery on the island of Abadan, at the head of the Gulf, which lay directly across a narrow channel from the Mesopotamian port of Basra. Once Turkey came into the war, the British assumed, it might only be a matter of hours before the oil was cut off, and half the Royal Navy immobilised.

The invasion of Mesopotamia—"Mespot" to the British army—began then, in November 1914, as an operation to seal off the Persian Gulf and protect Abadan by seizing Basra. The Gulf had always been supervised from India rather than Britain, so it was an Indian army expedition which successfully disembarked in the port of Basra. The local Turkish forces did not long resist. In London the War Cabinet felt that, with Abadan safe, the expedition's task was done; but the activists of the Indian Empire had their eyes on greater prizes, on Baghdad, everyone's epitome of an oriental city, and on Mesopotamia itself. The British general in Basra, Sir John Nixon, was ordered to prepare plans for an advance and, at the end of May 1915, the imperial forces set off for their first objective, Amara.

Southern Mesopotamia, however, was more beguiling in history than in fact. Here were Babylon and Nineveh, here indeed, some said, had been the Garden of Eden. But it was a fearful country now, much of it empty desert, inhabited by lawless predatory Arabs who loathed nearly everyone, the rest a wide and fetid fen. There were no paved roads, no railways. Such towns as existed were hardly more than excretions of mud, like piles of rubbish in the wasteland, relieved only by the minarets of shabby mosques, or the lugubrious walls of forts. In the dry season everything was baked like leather, in the wet season ten thousand square miles were flooded, the waters gradually oozing away to leave malodorous wastes of marsh. Fleas, sandflies and mosquitoes tormented the place.

The British field commander was Major General Charles Townshend, of the 6th (Poona) Division. As a promising captain, he had stood at Kitchener's side in the ruins of Gordon's Residency. Now fifty-four, he was a soldier of mercurial gifts, who studied Napoleon assiduously, and perhaps thought himself a successor. He was much liked by his British soldiers, but not by his Indians, and this was perhaps because he had no high regard for Africans and Asians in general, having beaten them in battle from Chitral to Omdurman, and was proposing to do so again now.

The country south of Amara was flooded, and the main Turkish defence position was a series of islands in the flats, protected by mines. To attack it Townshend put one of his brigades upon the water. His infantry paddled out in five hundred commandeered Tigris boats, called bellums. His machine-guns were on rafts, his field guns in tugs and barges, and there were launches to sweep the minefields, with three sloops of the Indian Marine to give supporting fire. When they came to a Turkish position, their every gun was turned upon it until, the frightful mess of mud and explosives having subsided, the infantry waded ashore with fixed bayonets to capture it. By nightfall on the day of this unnerving attack the Turks could be seen scurrying away in boats, the whole Turkish force in retreat, helter-skelter up the Tigris to Amara.

First thing in the morning, Townshend was off, personally, in pursuit. His brigade was embarked upon paddle steamers, but the general himself, with his staff and a few soldiers, boarded the sloop *Espiègle* and with her two sister ships, *Clio* and *Odin*, and four steam launches, charged up the river at full speed after the retreating enemy. This was "Townshend's Regatta", "the Mespot Navy", and it was one of the most exuberant little actions of the First World War.

Far ahead of them raced the Turks—two steamers towing bargeloads of troops, and railed by a fleet of dhows. In the evening when the British spotted their distant sails and opened fire, the Turkish steamers hastily slipped their tows and left the soldiers to their fate; but Townshend, detailing the *Odin* to take them prisoner, pressed on excitedly for Amara.

Next day they caught the two steamers, one abandoned, one flying a white flag, and it was time for the sloops to turn back. The water was only a few feet deep now. Townshend, though, had the bit between his teeth. With a handful of soldiers he transferred to one of the launches, and with the other three, each towing a barge with a 4.7-inch gun on it, sailed impulsively on. By now his brigade was far behind, but as his boats raced up the river, white ensigns fluttering, white flags appeared in one astonished riverside village after another.

Early the next afternoon, June 3, 1915, they saw Amara, a big brown sprawl beside the river. It was swarming with Turkish troops, but when the first of the launches approached its quay hundreds of them walked down to the bank with their hands above their heads. Townshend's brigade was one hundred miles behind him. His total force on the spot comprised one brigadier-general, one naval captain, one hundred soldiers and the crews of the launches. Townshend sent ashore a corporal and twelve men,

The Western Front stretched from Northern France to Switzerland. The initial German advance of September 1914 was successful, but soon both sides dug themselves into an elaborate trench system. Trenches were easy to defend, but difficult to attack. There was virtual deadlock until March 1918, when the Germans made a determined attempt to reach Paris. They were so weakened by their efforts, however, that an Allied counterattack managed to break through their defences in the autumn of 1918 and secured the Armistice on November 11.

and to them the Turkish commander surrendered the town and its garrison of two thousand men.

"How much I enjoyed the whole thing," Charles Townshend wrote to his French wife. "I told you, darling, that I only wanted my chance! I have only known the 6th Division for six months, and they'd storm the gates of hell if I told them to. . . ."

Elated though Townshend was by the success of his Regatta, after so long in Mesopotamia his army was tired, ill-equipped and under strength. It was debilitated by dysentery and paratyphoid. It was known that thirty thousand Turkish reinforcements were on their way. Though London was lukewarm about further advances, and Townshend himself was cautious about taking inadequate forces too deep into enemy territory, back in Basra General Nixon still had his eyes upon Baghdad. So, by the beginning of September 1915, the 6th Division was ready to move north again.

At first all went as brilliantly as before. Townshend captured the next river town, Kut-el-Amara, in a *tour de force* of surprise and deception, and seemed both to his own men and to the Turks one of those generals who cannot lose. General Nixon reported to London that he felt strong enough for an immediate attack on Baghdad itself, and since the Cabinet was obsessed with the greater war elsewhere, and desperate for victories anywhere, the advance was sanctioned.

Townshend prepared the new advance with misgivings. He thought Kut was as far as they could go—his forces were inadequate, his lines of communication were insecure. Sure enough at Ctesiphon, eighteen miles

WAR ON THE WESTERN FRONT

Life in the trenches was marked by terror, drudgery and discomfort, occasionally lightened by flashes of humanity. In the first passage below, Robert Graves, the author and poet, describes a courageous deed amid the desolation of war. In the second passage, Wilfred Ewart, soldier author of Scots Guard, *recalls the extraordinary Christmas armistice of 1915.*

Bravery on the Western Front

From the morning of September 24 to the night of October 3, 1915, I had in all eight hours of sleep. I kept myself awake and alive by drinking about a bottle of whisky a day. I had never drunk it before, and have seldom drunk it since; it certainly helped me then. We had no blankets, greatcoats, or waterproof sheets, nor any time or material to build new shelters. The rain poured down. Every night we went out to fetch in the dead of the other battalions. The Germans continued indulgent and we had few casualties. After the first day or two the corpses swelled and stank. I vomited more than once while superintending the carrying.

On the morning of the 27th a cry arose from No Man's Land. A wounded soldier of the Middlesex had recovered consciousness after two days. He lay close to the German wire. Our men heard it and looked at each other. We had a tender-hearted lance-corporal named Baxter. He was the man to boil up a special dixie for the sentries of his section when they came off duty. As soon as he heard the wounded Middlesex man, he ran along the trench calling for a volunteer to help fetch him in. Of course, no one would go; it was death to put one's head over the parapet. When he came running to ask me I excused myself as being the only officer in the company. I would come out with him at dusk, I said—not now. So he went alone. He jumped quickly over the parapet, then strolled across No Man's Land, waving a handkerchief; the Germans fired to frighten him, but since he persisted they let him come up close. Baxter continued towards them and, when he got to the Middlesex man, stopped and pointed to show the Germans what he was at. Then he dressed the man's wounds, gave him a drink of rum and some biscuit that he had, and promised to be back again at nightfall. He did come back, with a stretcher party, and the man eventually recovered. I recommended Baxter for the Victoria Cross, being the only officer who had witnessed the action, but the authorities thought it worth no more than a Distinguished Conduct Medal.

Christmas Goodwill in the Trenches

So soon as it grows light . . . we start peeping at each other over the top of the parapet . . . calling across to each other. And presently, at about 7.50, a German stands up openly on the parapet and waves his arms. He is followed by two in field-grey overcoats and pill-box caps. Then they come out all down the line, stand up on the parapet, wave, shout, and finally swarm forth from their trenches on either side.

It spreads like contagion. Only we officers, the sentries, and a few non-commissioned officers remain in our trench. The men meet at the willow-lined stream in the middle of from the capital, there stood a Turkish army of very different calibre, powerfully reinforced by veterans from other fronts, skilfully positioned behind wire entanglements. Exhausted and thirsty in the terrible heat, encumbered by sick, wounded and thousands of prisoners, the 6th Division drove the Turks out, but could go no further themselves. Townshend decided to retreat with his army back into the walls of Kut-el-Amara. There, within a week, he was besieged. The Turks completely surrounded the town, and on December 8, 1915 a bombardment began.

Some thirteen thousand British and Indian soldiers, with thirty-nine guns, formed the garrison of Kut. They still had faith in their general, "Our Charlie", who had led them with such racy skill all the way north from Basra, and at first his communiqués to them were breezy and full of spirit. "Reinforcements are being sent at once from Basra to relieve us," he said. "The honour of our mother country and the Empire demands that we all work heart and soul in the defence of this place." It was a dreadful enough place to hold. Built within a loop of the Tigris, it was a muddle of baked mud buildings. Some six thousand Iraqis were immured there too. The sanitation was frightful and dysentery was endemic.

Down at Basra, where Nixon saw his ambitions in disarray, all was confusion. The port was a shambles of ill-organisation, so that when the Tigris relief force finally moved off, it moved so slowly, was led so badly, and faced such tough opposition, that it lost half its own men before it got within one hundred miles of Kut.

The siege itself was a squalid affair, the dingiest of the famous sieges

No Man's Land; they even cross it and mingle together in a haphazard throng. They talk and gesticulate, and shake hands over and over again. They pat each other on the shoulder and laugh like schoolboys, and leap across the little stream for fun. And when an Englishman falls in and a Boche helps him out there is a shout of laughter that echoes back to the trenches.

The Germans exchange cigars and pieces of sausage and sauerkraut and concentrated coffee for cigarettes and bully beef and ration biscuits and tobacco. They express mutual admiration by pointing and signs. It is our leather waistcoats and trenchcoats that attract their attention; it is their trenchoveralls, made of coarse canvas, that attract ours. We shout "Hullo, Fritz!" "Good morning, Fritz!" "Merry Christmas!" "Happy Christmas!" "How's your father?" "Come over and call!" "Come and have breakfast," and the like, amid roars of laughter. Even confidences are exchanged in broken English.

"When's the war going to end?"

"After the Spring offensive."

"What sort of trenches have you?"

"Rotten! Knee deep in mud and water. Not fit for pigs."

So for ten brief—all too brief—minutes there is peace and goodwill among the trenches on Christmas Day.

Then from the trenches of the Ninety-fifth Bavarian Reserve Infantry Regiment two officers in black accoutrements and shiny field-boots come out, wishing to take photographs of our Tommies, and offering them cigars. Their request is refused, and presently they say: "You will have five minutes to get back to your trenches before our artillery will open fire."

And it does. And two or three men are wounded almost at once. But for twenty-four hours not a shot is fired on either side. A common brotherhood of suffering—or is it an act of God, or just human curiosity? has united Englishmen and Bavarians in fraternity on the battlefield this grey Christmas morning which no one on either side who has taken part in this quaint scene will ever forget.

Trenches like the one shown above were "home" to thousands of troops in the First World War.

that brought drama and often despair to the story of the British Empire. Perhaps this is because for once there were no Englishwomen there, depriving the soldiers of the challenges to chivalry that ennobled or enlivened Lucknow and Ladysmith. The Turks sniped and shelled the town incessantly, and gradually it crumbled. The rations shrank, the sick-list grew, soon no more Arab looters were shot, as there was nothing left to loot.

Sometimes there were moments of heroism. Mostly, though, there was boredom. Morale began to sag. A few Indians tried to desert. By February 1916 the garrison was on half rations, and five or six men were dying every day from sickness and debilitation. By mid-March people were talking of surrender. Now General Khalil Bey, the Turkish commander, sent General Townshend a courteous but chill suggestion. "You have heroically fulfilled your military duty," it said. "From henceforth I see no likelihood that you will be relieved. . . . You are free to continue your resistance at Kut or to surrender to my forces, which are growing larger and larger."

By mid-April life at Kut had reached its limit, so Townshend reported to Basra. On the night of April 24 a Royal Navy gunboat was sent off to break through to the town with two hundred and fifty tons of supplies. But she set out on her desperate voyage in bright moonlight with no hope of surprise, and as she sailed upstream she was greeted by continuous fire from both banks. On she went nevertheless, until only a few miles from Kut, she ran aground. The Kut garrison had heard all the noise with gathering hope, but when dawn came and they looked eagerly downstream, they could see the silent shape of the gunboat stranded on the bank.

"Whatever has happened, my comrades," said Townshend in his last communiqué, "you can only be proud of yourselves. We have done our duty to King and Empire: the whole world knows that we have done our duty." The surrender, on April 29, 1916, was formal and full of ceremony. Khalil, who was thirty-five and very sure of himself, shook hands with the British officers, as each surrendered his sword; when it was Townshend's turn, the Turk made a short flowery speech, and handed back his sword with the phrase, "It is as much yours by right as it has ever been."

But it was all a charade. Townshend indeed was taken away to a comfortable exile in Constantinople, where he spent the rest of the war in a pleasant island villa. His men were not so lucky. They entered upon two years of appalling captivity. More than half of them died, and of those that survived, many were never healthy again.

London took over, Nixon was removed, the army was reorganised and by the end of 1916 they were ready to try again, and in a campaign of cautious thoroughness, backed by overwhelmingly superior forces, a British army once more pushed up the two rivers, and on March 10, 1917, captured Baghdad at last. But later that year, on the western flank of the Turkish Empire, a very different offensive was launched. The style of the invasion of Palestine was set by a commander of forcible decision, Sir Edmund Allenby, "The Bull".

The Syrian war had begun in January, 1915, with a Turkish offensive against the Suez Canal. It was easily beaten off, but when in the following year the British counterattacked across Sinai, laying a railway and a water pipeline as they went, they were held at Gaza, on the southern edge of the fertile Palestine plain, and severely repulsed. It was a shoddy performance— "Nobody could have saved the Turks from complete collapse," said Lloyd

The Empire answered the call to arms. This photograph from The Illustrated War News *of February 1915 shows Indian soldiers with rifles and a Maxim gun on the Suez Canal, helping to defend Egypt against the Turks.*

George, "but our General Staff"—and in June 1917 Allenby was sent from France to redeem it.

By now Lloyd George was Prime Minister, heading a Coalition Government that included such imperialist stalwarts as Curzon, Balfour, Churchill and Milner. More even than the march upon Baghdad, the invasion of Palestine was to be an imperial campaign, for in London prescient minds saw the control of Syria as the key to the command of the Middle East. To General Allenby fell the task of staking out a new imperial province.

Allenby was descended from Oliver Cromwell. Commissioned into the cavalry, he was a very big man, big-featured and heavily-boned, and he struck strangers often as terse and austere: but he had a gentle private side to him, thoughtful and imaginative. Blissfully married for twenty-five years (he had lost his only son in France), he loved children, birds and books, and was a competent classicist. He had a terrible temper, and sometimes lost it unforgivably, but those who liked him loved him, and thought him truly a great man. There was an English strength and fairness to him which made men trust him—and when a man knows he is trusted, as Allenby said himself, "he can do things".

In Syria he seldom put a foot wrong. He surrounded himself with staff officers of high intelligence, sometimes of scholarly learning, and moved his headquarters from Cairo into the Sinai. There he studied every aspect of Syria, its history, its geography, its flora and fauna, its diseases and its resources. He even pored over the Old Testament. Around him he assembled an army of astonishing complexity, like a crusade. It included soldiers from Britain, Australia, New Zealand, India, South Africa, Egypt, Singapore, Hong Kong and the West Indies, besides three battalions of Jews enlisted in the Royal Fusiliers. In the Arabian peninsula, to the south, he had British agents encouraging Arab tribal leaders to launch their own rebellion against Turkish suzerainty, and raiding posses of Arab camel-men, often led by British officers, were active in blowing up Turkish railway lines and harassing isolated Turkish garrisons.

Allenby launched his main offensive in October, with the help of a famous ruse. One day that month Captain Richard Meinertzhagen, a clever young intelligence officer, rode into the desert no-man's-land that separated the British and Turkish lines some thirty miles southeast of Gaza. He was spotted and chased by a Turkish cavalry patrol. As he galloped away towards the British line, he suddenly lurched sideways, as though he had been hit. The Turks saw that he had dropped his bloodstained haversack.

When the Turks returned to camp and handed the haversack to their intelligence officers, it was found to contain orders for an attack on Gaza and a telegram reporting preparations for a reconnaissance around Beersheba. The Turks, and their German commanders, took the captured information seriously, standing ready for a reconnaissance at Beersheba, a major assault on Gaza. Allenby did precisely the reverse, capturing Beersheba first, thus outflanking the Turkish positions, and then switching his main thrust back to the coast again. So the pace and tone of the campaign was set from the start. Within two weeks Allenby's divisions had broken through the Gaza line and were streaming up the Palestine coast to Jaffa.

Allenby's invasion was the last great cavalry campaign in history, and he fought it as a cavalryman, making sweeping use of his twelve thousand horsemen. He experimented with every permutation of bluff, feint and innovation—aircraft, armoured cars, launches on the Dead Sea, offshore torpedo boats, Arab raiders, propaganda leaflets, even a few tanks, the first to be used outside Europe.

In December 1917 the first imperial troops, advancing into Judea, reached the heights of Nebi Samuel, traditionally the home of the prophet Samuel. The Crusaders had called this place Mons Gaudii, Mountain of Joy, because from here they caught their first sight of Jerusalem: now the British too saw the Holy City golden-domed below them. This was the capital of capitals, last entered by a Christian army seven hundred years before.

It had been agreed between the combatants that there would be no fighting in Jerusalem, almost as holy to Muslims as it was to Christians. The Turks resisted strongly in its outskirts, the Welsh Division having to fight hard for the Mount of Olives, but on December 8 they withdrew to the north and left the city undefended. When General Allenby officially took possession of the city, he entered it simply and quietly, on foot.

He went through the Jaffa Gate, "the Gate of Friends" in Arabic, which was traditionally the entrance of the foreigner and the travelling merchant. The last foreign visitor of such eminence had been the Kaiser, who arrived there in 1898 in a ceremonial entry of preposterous pomp. Allenby's entry was staged in deliberate contrast. He went more as a pilgrim than as a conqueror. The troops who lined the dusty road to the walls were dressed in their battle-frayed khaki, and so was the general himself. The citizens of Jerusalem jostled all about, as though it were not a moment of war at all. No guns were fired, no flags were flown. Only the bells of Jerusalem rang.

Behind Allenby walked the American, French and Italian military attachés serving with his armies, and a group of British staff officers, some looking elated, some looking reverent, as though they were going to church. To most people there the general undoubtedly represented not so much Christianity, or even the allied cause, as the British Empire. He walked briskly and expressionlessly, without a sword or stick, his boots dusty, his braided cap slightly tilted. Up the sunny incline he marched, in silence, and into the deep shadow cast by the gate, his footsteps echoing as he walked beneath its arch: and then, emerging into the bright sunshine on the other side, Cromwell's descendant, at the head of the armies of the Empire, entered the Holy City. He is said to have remembered the moment always as the climax of his life.

On the steps of the Citadel—St David's Tower, where some scholars believed Pilate passed his judgment on Jesus—Allenby read a proclamation, declaring Jerusalem to be under the jurisdiction of the British Empire. Already a British military administration, settling into the seat of Pilate, was reorganising the affairs of the city upon imperial lines.

The entire Syrian offensive, moreover, took only a further ten months, and its climax was the devastating victory of Megiddo in September 1918. There on the Plain of Esdraelon, in one of the most absolute victories of the entire imperial record, the British destroyed the Turkish armies in Syria, effectively putting an end to the Ottoman Empire, and leaving the Middle East vacant for new suzerains.

But of the three imperial campaigns the one most truly instinct with the grandeur and the hollowness of Empire was back in 1915, the one that ended in defeat. The British would presently forget they ever captured Baghdad or Jerusalem; but long after the Empire had ended altogether, Britons would remember the names of Gallipoli and the Dardanelles.

Linking the wine-dark waters of the Grecian world with the Sea of Marmara, the straits called the Dardanelles had always been close to the British imperial consciousness. Only through this single channel, a mile wide at its narrowest point, could Russian ships gain access from the Black Sea to the Mediterranean, and beyond lay Constantinople, the very cross-roads of international power, where Asia and Europe faced each other.

In January 1915 the British evolved a plan to force these famous straits, and send a fleet through the Sea of Marmara to Constantinople. Ostensibly its purpose was to give help to the Russian armies fighting the Germans in the east, and thus reduce pressure on the western front; but it was really to be a coup in the old style. Winston Churchill, at forty a dashing First Lord of the Admiralty, was its chief begetter, and he was a man brought up to the éclat of imperial enterprise. He believed that if the Royal Navy got through the Dardanelles fortifications, Constantinople would fall before its sheer presence. Then Germany would be threatened from the rear, at a bold stroke the whole war might be ended, and the British would hold in their hands the destinies of the nearer East.

The navy itself had doubts about its mission. For all its prestige, it was no longer the close-hauled force of Nelson's day, addicted to risk, blind eye and heart-on-sleeve. Ship pitted against fort was bad enough at any time: ships committed at such a moment to a sideshow, far from the war's centre, verged upon the irresponsible.

Admiral Fisher, who had already done so much to modernise the navy, was recalled at seventy-four to be First Sea Lord again. He had misgivings. He had inspected the Dardanelles in 1900, and he knew how strong were the forts, castles and emplacements, some modern, some medieval, which were embedded on each side of the Dardanelles from one end to the other. So it was mostly older battleships that he agreed, almost against his better judgment, to commit to the operation, reinforced for the sake of the alliance by a squadron of equally elderly French battleships. Fired though by Churchill's enthusiasm, for the two men loved each other, Fisher agreed to add two modern capital ships: the battlecruiser *Inflexible*, fresh from victory over the Germans in the battle of the Falkland Islands, and the *Queen Elizabeth*, the latest, fastest and most powerful battleship in the Royal Navy, so new that she would actually do her gunnery trials in action.

On December 8, 1917, General Allenby entered Jerusalem. Here a translation of his proclamation is read in Arabic, announcing that the Holy City is under British jurisdiction.

When the Turkish gunners, on the morning of March 18, 1915, looked down the strait, to the open sea between Cape Helles and Kum Kale, they saw approaching them out of the south the towering grey forms of sixteen capital ships. In the van was the splendid *Queen Elizabeth*, the largest warship ever to enter the Mediterranean, her unprecedented fifteen-inch guns cleared for action.

The battle lasted all day, but the ships never penetrated the Narrows, the strip of water between Kilid Bahr and Chanak which was the neck of the Dardanelles. All day long they bombarded the forts, trying to batter their way through. The noise of the guns echoed and re-echoed up and down the narrow waterway; the shores flashed with the fire of the Turkish guns. The sun shone all day, but it was obscured for hours at a time by the smoke, the dust and the spray of the battle.

The Turks showed no sign of surrender: it was the British who faltered. In the afternoon the minesweepers were sent into the Narrows. They were trawlers manned by civilian crews, and caught there in a storm of fire from both banks, they lost their nerve and turned tail.

In that moment the battle was lost. When the French battleship *Bouvet* suddenly exploded and disappeared before everyone's eyes in a couple of minutes, when the *Inflexible* hit a mine and withdrew, listing heavily, when the *Irresistible* was mined too and abandoned, and when the *Ocean*'s steering gear was hit and she began steaming in helpless circles before the

INNOVATIONS

Tanks and aeroplanes were developed under the impetus of war. The following accounts are by Bert Chaney, who witnessed the attempts of the American Holt tanks to break through on the Somme in September 1916, and by Major Tempest of the Royal Flying Corps, whose courage on the night of October 1916 won him the DSO.

The First Tanks in Action

We heard strange throbbing noises, and lumbering slowly towards us came three huge mechanical monsters such as we had never seen before. My first impression was that they looked ready to topple on their noses, but their tails and the two little wheels at the back held them down and kept them level. Big metal things they were, with two sets of caterpillar wheels that went right round the body. There was a bulge on each side with a door in the bulging part, and machine guns on swivels poked out from either side. The engine, a petrol engine of massive proportions, occupied practically all the inside space. Mounted behind each door was a motor-cycle type of saddle seat and there was just about enough room left for the belts of ammunition and the drivers. . . .

Instead of going on to the German lines the three tanks assigned to us straddled our front line, stopped and then opened up a murderous machine-gun fire, enfilading us left and right. There they sat, squat monstrous things, noses stuck up in the air, crushing the sides of our trench with their machine guns swivelling around and firing like mad.

Everyone dived for cover, except the colonel. He jumped on top of the parapet, shouting at the top of his voice,

"Runner, runner, go tell those tanks to stop firing at once. At once, I say."

By now the enemy fire had risen to a crescendo but, giving no thought to his own personal safety as he saw the tanks firing on his own men, he ran forward furiously and rained blows with his cane on the side of one of the tanks in an endeavour to attract their attention.

Although, what with the sounds of the engines and the firing in such an enclosed space, no one in the tank could hear him, they finally realised they were firing on the wrong trench and moved on, frightening the Jerries out of their wits and making them scuttle like frightened rabbits.

This early newspaper photograph is captioned, "Our monster tanks break down the belts of barbed wire and completely surprise the Hun at Cambrai."

Turkish guns, the other great ships, turning heavily in the narrow waters of the straits, abandoned the assault and disappeared to sea.

Of the one hundred and seventy-six guns that defended the Dardanelles, only four had been put out of action; of the three hundred and ninety-two mines, not one had been cleared; but the fleet had lost seven hundred lives and three great ships. The Turks fearfully awaited a renewal of the attack next day, but it never came. An age was over, and a myth was shattered. The Royal Navy was not omnipotent, and gunboat diplomacy, here carried to its ultimate expression, was no longer sufficient to discipline the natives.

Fisher resigned—"Damn the Dardanelles! They will be our grave!" Churchill wanted to try again, but he was overruled, and instead the commanders on the spot determined to land an army on the peninsula of Gallipoli, forming the western shore of the Dardanelles, and so open the way to Constantinople.

Everything about Gallipoli conspired to haunt men. The peninsula itself was an arid, empty place, like a blank slate awaiting a message. Its hills, from whose summits one could see the straits on one side, the Aegean on the other, were covered with scented scrub, and it lay there sparse and aromatic, a long pile of land above the sea, ribbed everywhere, like an old skin, with gullies and ravines. In summer it could be beautiful; in winter terrible: bitterly cold, eerie. Nothing had ever happened on the Gallipoli ridge, and the hills with their severe Turkish names, Anafarta, Keretch

Death of a Zeppelin

The airship must have been about fifteen miles away, flying at a height of between 15,000 and 16,000 feet, and regardless of the focused searchlights she began to make straight for London, diving steadily as she flew. I at once began to fly towards her at a mile and a half a minute. The next moment the anti-aircraft guns below opened fire

When I had reached a point about five miles from her, I was flying at a height well above her own, which must by now have been considerably below 10,000 feet. I had also come within range of our own guns, and shells were bursting all round me.

As I drew closer to the ship and came within the beams of the searchlights, I must have been seen, for she suddenly turned about and began to climb. On I flew in pursuit and, finding she could not shake me off, she suddenly shed all her bombs, which helped her to climb even quicker. I heard them hit the ground with a confused series of detonations.

At this moment my petrol pressure pump failed. If I was to maintain height, I would have to keep the supply going. There was nothing for it but to use the hand-pump.

I was now so close to the ship that I could see her propellers revolving. Realising that if I delayed my attack an instant longer she might climb out of my reach, I made a dive straight at her and, passing under her enormous envelope, which seemed to overshadow me, I put in a burst of fire from my Lewis gun. My ammunition was Pomeroy, Buckingham tracer and ordinary machine-gun bullets. Pomeroy penetrated and exploded, but Buckingham tracer, beside showing trajectory of the bullet, was incendiary.

My first round was without effect. Turning about, I flew under her in the same direction as she was going and let her have a further burst. Then, banking, I sat under her tail safely sheltered from the danger of attack from her own guns which were firing tracer shells in all directions.

I had almost begun to despair of bringing her down, when suddenly, after letting her have another burst, I saw her begin to go red inside like an immense Chinese lantern. Flames burst from her glowing envelope and licked her bows, and then she began to fall.

Only by putting my machine into a spin did I manage to corkscrew out of the way as the blazing mass roared past me, but I managed to right my machine.

This photo sketch from the First World War shows the dramatic collapse of a Zeppelin ignited by incendiary bullets.

General Sir Ian Hamilton (1853–1947), commander of the Mediterranean Expeditionary Force at Gallipoli. This portrait by John Singer Sargent can be seen in the National Portrait Gallery of Scotland.

An Anzac soldier carries a wounded comrade to safety at Gallipoli. The bravery of the Australian and New Zealand Army Corps in what was an appallingly badly handled campaign has now become legendary.

Tepe, Sari Bair, stood there loveless in the sunshine, sinister in the shade.

To this place, in the spring of 1915, there came an imperial army. Its soldiers bore themselves, so the poet John Masefield thought, "like kings in a pageant", and its commander was a courteous and cultivated Scottish gentleman. Ian Hamilton had seen more action than any other senior officer in Britain, probably in the whole of Europe. Yet he was not at all a belligerent figure, and he approached the military art sensitively, less like a general than an artist. Brave, imaginative, sixty-three years old, he went to Gallipoli in a spirit of grateful dedication, assured by Kitchener that if he won he might be winning not simply a campaign, but a war. As he sailed to his battle station the Aegean seemed to him "like a carpet of blue velvet outspread for Aphrodite", and he observed the subsequent campaign with the same lyric response, compassionately, without ferocity.

It was before he embarked for Gallipoli that Rupert Brooke wrote his elegiac poem "The Soldier":

> If I should die, think only this of me:
>   That there's some corner of a foreign field
> That is for ever England. There shall be
>   In that rich earth a richer dust concealed;
> A dust whom England bore, shaped, made aware,
>   Gave, once, her flowers to love, her ways to roam,
> A body of England's, breathing English air,
>   Washed by the rivers, blest by suns of home.

Englishry there was, cut to the finest bone, at Gallipoli. The 29th Division was one of the best formations of the regular army, and around its core of professionals, in staff appointments and elegant ancillaries, some of England's brightest spirits eagerly awaited the battle. There were young poets and writers—Masefield, A.P. Herbert, and Compton Mackenzie. There were sons of famous families, an Asquith here, a Herbert or a Napier there. Then there were the imperial contingents, including Sikhs, Punjabis, Gurkhas, the Ceylon Planters' Rifles, and the Assyrian Jewish Refugee Mule Corps. Above all they included the Anzacs, the Australian and New Zealand Army Corps. Nobody had seen such soldiers before. Tall, lean, powerful, cocky, their beauty was not merely physical, but sprang from their air of easy freedom. Their discipline was lax by British standards; they made terrible fun of British officers, but they brought to Hamilton's army a loose-limbed authority all their own.

Curiously thrown together under the command of upper-class Britons, in the spring of 1915 this imperial army, with a French division attached, was assembled in scores of transports in the waters around Mudros, guarded by the warships of the fleet. Never, perhaps, has an army been so exalted by the prospect of action. "Oh God!" wrote Brooke, "I've never been so happy in my life."

It was to be the most ambitious amphibious operation in the annals of war, but it sailed to the peninsula unprepared. Its intelligence was out of date, its maps were inaccurate, it had insufficient shells and mosquito nets. Two hospital ships were considered adequate for the campaign, and the army made its own grenades out of old tins. Nobody had any idea how many Turks were defending the peninsula. Security was appalling: every stevedore in Alexandria knew that the army was going to Gallipoli.

Hamilton's plan, nevertheless, was bold. He would assault Gallipoli bullishly from the south and west, and fight his way up it to command the Dardanelles from end to end—"take a good run at the peninsula and jump on, both feet together". The first objectives would be the commanding heights of the peninsula, Achi Baba in the south, Sari Bair in the centre, and the main striking force would be the 29th Division, which would be landed on five separate beaches around Cape Helles, the southern tip of the peninsula. At the same time the Anzacs would land some thirteen miles up the coast, to strike inland for Sari Bair. The fleet, with its terrific gun-power, would provide artillery support; the French would make a diversion on the Asiatic shore. Hamilton hoped that within three days the lower half of the peninsula would be captured, the Narrows would be cleared of their mines, and the navy could pass through the Dardanelles into the Sea of Marmara. Handing over tactical command to his subordinates, Hamilton set the assault in motion and transferred himself to the *Queen Elizabeth*, and in that magnificent vessel, surrounded by the transports of the army, the battleships, cruisers and destroyers, two hundred ships in all, he set sail for Gallipoli on the night of April 24, 1915.

There would be, General Hunter-Weston assured the men of his 29th Division, "heavy losses by bullets, by shells, by mines and by drowning". Still, the army landed on Gallipoli confident and excited, a tremendous naval bombardment having preceded it. Though the Anzacs were landed in the wrong place, and found their maps quite useless, they got ashore with few losses, and struck inland with such gusto that by dawn that morning a few soldiers had actually reached the central ridge of the peninsula. On three of the British beaches too, around the tip of the peninsula, there was little opposition. At Y beach there were no Turks at all; at S and X beaches there were only a few, and officers keyed up for blood and fire found themselves helped off their landing crafty by solicitous sailors, in case they got their feet wet.

At two beaches only was the assault as bloody as Hunter-Weston had feared. At W beach the Lancashire Fusiliers ran into such violent resistance from Turks hidden in trenches in the commanding bluffs, that in a matter of minutes, before the British could dig themselves in, one hundred and ninety men were killed and two hundred and seventy-nine wounded.

At V beach, the southernmost beach and the most crucial, the landing was to be made on Cape Helles, below the village of Sedd-el-Bahr, where a medieval castle stood at the water's edge like a memorial to more ancient battles. A collier, the *River Clyde*, was to be beached to act as a large landing craft and from its hull, it was hoped, two thousand men of the Munster Fusiliers and the Hampshire Regiment would move across lighters to the shore and so up the bluffs that rose, steep but not high, immediately behind. The assault went in silently at 6.20 a.m. The naval bombardment had ended, only a cloud of smoke and dust hung over the Cape, and there was no sign of life at Sedd-el-Bahr. The sea was calm, the morning sunny. Gently and quietly, the *River Clyde* ran herself ashore beside the castle, towing her lighters, and at the same time a flotilla of boats approached the beach with a battalion of the Royal Dublin Fusiliers. Everything was silent. The place seemed deserted, or stunned by the awful bombardment.

However, the moment the boats grounded a vicious fusillade of machine-gun and rifle fire fell upon them, from hidden positions in the escarpment. The beach was an almost symmetrical crescent, like an amphitheatre, and

The object of the Gallipoli campaign was to clear the Dardanelles, held by Turkey, so that reinforcements could be sent to Russia through the Black Sea ports. Unfortunately, the rules of strict security were not observed, and the area was well-defended when British, French, Australian and New Zealand troops landed in April 1915. They withdrew nine months later.

the Irishmen scrambling ashore were as unprotected as actors on a stage. Boat after boat was riddled with fire, the soldiers slumping over the gunwales, screaming, or leaping terrified into the water. Boats full of dead men drifted away from the beach, or lay slowly tilting in the water, and a slow crimson stain of blood spread out to sea. Out of an entire battalion only thirty or forty survivors, scrambling up the beach, reached the cover of a ridge of sand.

Meanwhile the captain of the *River Clyde*, finding nothing to moor the lighters to, had leapt into the water with an able seaman and was holding the bridge of boats in position by his own muscle, crouching in the water with only his head and shoulders showing. A few moments later, when the sally-ports of the collier were flung open, and the Munsters and Hampshires sprang out, they were met with a blast of fire like the smack of heat on a tropical day. They died almost as fast as they appeared, blocking the doors and gangplanks, falling into the sea; only a handful foundered ashore and took shelter with the Dubliners in the lee of the escarpment. The whole beach now was littered with corpses—"like a shoal of fish," said the

THE YEAR OF THE STALEMATE

Two immense battles were fought in 1916, but although both were proclaimed official British victories, neither was decisive. One of the witnesses of the first encounter between the rival battle cruisers at the Battle of Jutland on May 31, 1916, was the Navigating Officer of HMS New Zealand. His account of the action is followed by a German officer's description of a courageous British attack during the Battle of the Somme. The battle began on July 1, 1916, and petered out in the middle of November with the loss of 400,000 British soldiers and nearly 200,000 French.

The Battle of Jutland

At about 3.50 the action was commenced by both sides opening fire almost simultaneously. We had only been in action a few minutes, when the Admiral's Secretary came across to where the Torpedo Officer was stationed in the conning tower and drew his attention to the *Indefatigable*. He crossed at once to the starboard side and laid his glasses on her. She had been hit aft, apparently by the mainmast, and a good deal of smoke was coming from her superstructure aft, but there were no flames visible. He thought it

was only her boom boats burning. We were altering course to port at the time, and apparently her steering gear was damaged, as she did not follow round in our wake, but held on until she was about five hundred yards on our starboard quarter, in full view from the conning tower.

Whilst he was still looking at her through his glasses she was hit by two shells, one on the fo'c'sle and on the fore turret. Both shells appeared to explode on impact. Then there was an interval of about thirty seconds, during which there was absolutely no sign of fire or flame or smoke, except the little actually formed by the burst of the two shells. At the end of the thirty seconds the ship completely blew up, commencing apparently from for'ard. The main explosion started with sheets of flame, followed immediately afterwards by a dense, dark smoke, which obscured the ship from view. All sorts of stuff was blown high into the air, a fifty-foot steam picket boat, for example, being blown up about two hundred feet, apparently intact though upside down.

The loss of our next astern happened so suddenly that, almost before we realised she had gone, our attention was entirely absorbed in the very fierce battle that was now

The German fleet was proceeding towards Sunderland before unexpectedly encountering Beatty's battle squadron at Jutland.

Turkish commander—and through the noise of the battle one could hear always the cries of the wounded men. When General Napier, the brigade commander, approached in a cutter to take command, the men on the *River Clyde* shouted at him through the din to go back—"Go back! You can't land!" "I'll have a damn good try!" the general shouted back, and almost at once he and his officers were slaughtered like the rest.

The hours dragged on in stalemate. At midday the vast form of the *Queen Elizabeth* loomed inshore, and poured salvoes into the bluffs above the beach. The little village was a ruin, the escarpment was pockmarked and crumbled with shell-holes, but still the Turks raked the beach with their fire. It was not until night fell that the men trapped in the *River Clyde* could clamber ashore.

The imperial armies had landed at Gallipoli, but the experience of V beach was to be the true index of their enterprise. Almost as the campaign began, news reached the armies that Rupert Brooke, their exemplar and their laureate, had not even reached the peninsula, but had died of blood-poisoning at sea, on St George's Day, and had been buried on the island

progressing. All seemed to be going well with us, when suddenly I saw a salvo hit *Queen Mary* on her port side. A small cloud of what looked like coal dust came out from where she was hit, but nothing more until several moments later, when a terrific yellow flame with a heavy and very dense mass of black smoke showed ahead, and the *Queen Mary* herself was no longer visible.

This second disaster was rather stunning, but the only sign from the flagship was a signal, "Battle cruisers alter course two points to port"—i.e. towards the enemy.

The Battle of the Somme

Red rockets sped up into the blue sky as a signal to the artillery, and immediately afterwards a mass of shells from the German batteries in rear tore through the air and burst among the advancing lines. Whole sections seemed to fall, and the rear formations, moving in closer order, quickly scattered. The advance rapidly crumbled under this hail of shells and bullets. Men could be seen throwing their arms into the air and collapsing, never to move again. Badly wounded rolled about in their agony, and others less severely injured crawled to the nearest shell-hole for shelter.

The British soldier, however, has no lack of courage, and once his hand is set to the plough he is not easily turned from his purpose. The extended lines, though badly shaken and with many gaps, now came on all the faster. Instead of a leisurely walk, they covered the ground in short rushes at the double. Within a few minutes the leading troops had reached within a stone's-throw of our front trench, and while some of us continued to fire at point-blank range, others threw hand grenades among them. The British bombers answered back, while the infantry rushed forward with fixed bayonets. The noise of battle became indescribable. The shouting of orders and the shrill British cheers as they charged forward could be heard above the violent and intense fusillade of machine guns and rifles and the bursting bombs, and above the deep thunderings of the artillery and the shell explosions. With all this were mingled the moans and groans of the wounded, the cries for help and the last screams of death. Again and again the extended lines of British infantry broke against the German defences like waves against a cliff, only to be beaten back. It was an amazing spectacle of unexampled gallantry, courage, and bulldog determination on both sides.

British troops go "over the top" at the Battle of the Somme. This is a frame from one of the first official war films.

of Skyros. Hamilton was greatly moved. "Death grins at my elbow," he wrote. "I cannot get him out of my thoughts. He is fed up with the old and sick—only the flower of the flock will serve him now . . . ."

The Gallipoli campaign lasted two hundred and fifty-nine days, April 1915 to January 1916. In all half a million men were landed on the peninsula. Far from capturing their objectives by the third day, the British never captured them at all, but were confined first to last to footholds on the shore. Within forty-eight hours of the landings the two allotted hospital ships were on their way to Egypt, full of wounded; even the Anzacs had been driven off the crest of the hills, and their commander was recommending evacuation at once.

Four months after the first assault a second invasion was launched, the landing this time being at Suvla Bay in the north, so that at the climax of the campaign there were three separate bridgeheads, with British forces north and south, Anzacs in the centre. But the three never joined up, and what began as a campaign in the imperial kind, a war of sweep and movement, degenerated into trench warfare, just as static and dispiriting as the fighting in France. Only the setting was different, for behind the Gallipoli soldiers there lay always the sea. At night the lights of the warships suggested a great floating city, friendly and reassuring, and officers were sometimes taken out there, direct from their squalid dugouts to the armchairs and starched linens of battleship wardrooms. The sea was always there, and at the back of the soldiers' minds, no doubt, was the thought that if the worst came to the worst in their long fight for the peninsula, the navy could always snatch them off.

On May 25, though, the beloved and familiar battleship *Triumph* was torpedoed by a German submarine. In full view of the soldiers she capsized with a deep metallic rumble, floated upside down for half an hour, and sank. Within hours all the big ships were withdrawn to Imbros, and the soldiers, looking forlornly out to sea, saw them retreating fast into the evening. There was a momentary hush over the peninsula, as every man, British or Turk, watched them go. By nightfall they were out of sight. The

Men of the Royal Naval Division leave their trenches to attack the enemy at Gallipoli. The campaign was to end as a total failure for the allied forces.

British felt a chill sense of abandonment, even betrayal, as darkness fell upon Gallipoli that night.

In hideous attack and counterattack, interspersed with exhausted lulls, they passed the rest of 1915. Reinforcements arrived. British and Australian submarines, in feats of prodigious daring, passed through the Narrows and roamed the Sea of Marmara, sinking Turkish ships and sometimes bombarding roads—the submarine E2 actually reached Constantinople, torpedoed a freighter berthed beside the arsenal, and started a panic in the capital. But on the peninsula nothing was gained. The spring gave way to the ferocious summer, and then to a wet raw winter. The men grew dirtier, thinner, more unkempt, plagued by dysentery, septic sores, frostbite. "The beautiful battalions of April twenty-fifth," Hamilton wrote, "are wasted skeletons." Of the five hundred thousand men who landed on the peninsula, rather more than half were killed or wounded. Corpses lay everywhere, unburied between the lines or lost in inaccessible ravines, and their smell was inescapable; off the beaches the navy tried to sink the floating bodies of horses and mules by churning them up with their propellers.

This German war poster states, "The U-Boats Are Out!" By April 1917 German U-boats were sinking one in four of Britain's ships, and food supplies were scarce. To combat the U-boat threat the convoy system was started, whereby naval vessels escorted large groups of merchantmen to their destination. As a result, British losses fell by two thirds.

General Hamilton lacked one quality of generalship: fury. He was not a man to fall upon his enemies with a criminal hail of fire, steel and explosive, and it was his tragedy that the Gallipoli campaign needed just such a man of blood. Risky at the best, Gallipoli was an action that could succeed only by outrage and audacity. A few more old ships sunk, and the Royal Navy might have burst through the Narrows. An instant advance from Suvla Bay, rammed home despite all dangers, and the whole peninsula might have been captured in a day. They were terrible chances to take, involving thousands of human lives. Hamilton, an Edwardian gentleman, lacked the cruelty to take them. He also flatly refused, despite pressure from London, to use poison gas. He failed by the narrowest of margins, for by the end of 1915 the Turks were almost at breaking-point: but in the conduct of great affairs, nothing fails like failure.

Gallipoli was the greatest reverse to British arms since the American Revolution, and if it was launched in a resurgence of the imperial bravado, it was lost in the deadweight of the imperial tradition. Its senior commanders had all been nurtured in the colonial wars, a debilitating legacy, and the soldiers, though they fought on bitterly to the end, lost faith in their leadership. "Are we downhearted?" shouted a shipload of new arrivals, approaching the peninsula that summer. "You bloody soon will be," came the mordant reply from a departing hospital ship.

By the autumn of 1915 the British War Cabinet, looking bleakly out at the tragedy across the deathfields of France, had lost hope for the venture. Churchill was no longer at the Admiralty, and when Lord Kitchener came out to Gallipoli to see for himself, he recommended withdrawal. Although game to the last and ready for another offensive, Hamilton was replaced by a very different general, the bluff and practical Sir Charles Monro. By Christmas, silently and secretly, most of the army had been withdrawn from the peninsula. To Monro, Churchill bitterly attributed the apophthegm: "I came, I saw, I capitulated."

The British public, however, was encouraged to think of the withdrawal from Gallipoli as a compensating triumph—the stealthy withdrawal from the forward trenches, the skilful assembly of guns, stores, horses, the transport ships stealing away. "In that marvellous evacuation," wrote the

THE GREAT WAR

W HEN WAR BROKE OUT in August 1914, many people expected that it would be over within a few months. In fact it was to last more than four years, and by the time it was over 850,000 British servicemen would have been killed, and more than a million wounded.

This first large-scale European war since the defeat of Napoleon was a relentless, utterly unromantic struggle, the outcome of which was always uncertain. There were six thousand miles of trenches in France, through blasted, treeless wastes, and conditions in them were appalling. "No glimmer of God's hand is seen anywhere," wrote the painter Paul Nash. The great battles of the Somme and Ypres took a terrible toll in dead and wounded. At Passchendaele in 1917, over 240,000 British troops were killed. Five miles of muddy battlefield were gained.

The war effort called for a vast mobilisation of human and material resources, and there were inevitable strains and crises, economic and political. At the end of April 1917, for example, after the Germans had intensified their U-boat campaign against British and other allied shipping, the country was left with only six weeks' stores of food. Rationing was adopted just in time to avert disaster. And although in that same year the United States of America were brought into the war, revolution took the Russians out of it.

By the Armistice in 1918, Britain's national debt was four times the 1914 figure and fifteen per cent of the country's foreign assets had been lost for ever.

The scale of the horror had been such that people felt nothing so bad could ever happen again, that it had indeed been a war to end wars. They were terribly wrong. In the end, perhaps the worst consequence of the war was that faith in civilisation itself was lost. A comfortable reliance on so-called "civilised behaviour" was seen to be no longer an intelligent option for securing the future.

THE GERMAN SUBMARINE FLOTILLA (above assembled at Wilhelmshaven in 1912 wa an indication of things to come. The creatio of powerful European alliances was boun to lead to conflict, particularly whe the Great Powers had built up such massiv armaments. In the early years of th century Britain and Germany becam involved in an arms race, and the Britis construction of the battleship HM Dreadnought in 1906 temporarily made a others obsolete. Ironically, the rival fleets me only once, at Jutland in May 1916 The Germans claimed more ships but faile to break the British control of the sea and thereafter remained in harbour. I 1917, however, Britain was almost brough to her knees by German submarines, an only the adoption of a convoy system b which fifty ships sailed together protected by six destroyers, enable supplies to get through.

BRITONS

"WANTS" YOU

JOIN YOUR COUNTRY'S ARMY!
GOD SAVE THE KING

VOLUNTEERS FLOCKED TO ENLIST, inspired by the call of King and country in posters such as the one above featuring Lord Kitchener. But many of the recruits did not know why the war was being fought and it soon proved necessary to introduce conscription, which was highly controversial. Although the murder of Archduke Ferdinand of Austria provided the pretext for Germany's invasion of Belgium, the underlying cause of the war was the growth of economic and colonial rivalry among the European powers.

FIGHTING ON THE WESTERN FRONT *wiped out huge numbers of young men. By 1915 there was a continuous line of trenches, sandbags and barbed wire stretching from the North Sea to Switzerland, which moved backwards and forwards over little more than forty miles for the greater part of the war. Machine guns and heavy artillery were an ever-present menace. Tanks, a potentially decisive innovation, were little used. Poison gas used by both sides in 1915 was later abandoned, for if the wind changed direction it slaughtered those who had released it. The war artist John Singer Sargent depicts a line of soldiers blinded by gas (below); the poet Wilfred Owen (left) described the unendurable conditions suffered by the ordinary British soldier with uncompromising honesty and compassion.*

THE AIRCRAFT *as a fighting machine was one of the permanent legacies of the Great War. Until the war, British industry had not been able to maintain adequately the mere sixty-six aircraft which made up the infant Royal Flying Corps. But by the time the Armistice was signed the RFC had become the Royal Air Force, with twenty-two thousand aircraft, the largest air force in the world.*

WOMEN UNDERTOOK THE JOBS OF MEN *who were away at the Front. They worked on the land, ran businesses, made munitions, drove buses and nursed the wounded. Here they are seen delivering bread, which became rationed in 1917. Food shortages threatened Britain, France and Germany, but it was in Germany that the greatest hardship was felt.*

official naval historian, "we see the national genius for amphibious warfare raised to its highest manifestation." The Turks awoke on the morning of January 9, 1916 to find that not a British soldier was left in the crannies and hidden valleys of the peninsula.

"I hope *they* don't hear us go," one Australian is supposed to have murmured, as his battalion stole through the graves of their comrades down the cliff-tracks to the boats.

Many imperial instincts had found their epitome, or their disillusionment, in these several campaigns, so far from the crux of the world conflict. For, although Gallipoli ended in total failure, the Middle Eastern campaigns, sweeping up to the very frontiers of Turkey, ended in absolute success. So that, when the war ended and the Turks sued for peace, the British controlled the whole of the former Turkish Empire, except only the Arabian interior, and upon this achievement they would erect the last of their great imperial structures, an empire among the Arabs.

In a wider spectrum too, the war at first seemed only to have strengthened the Empire. After all, if it had not been an imperial war, it had certainly been an imperial victory, for Britain's fundamental weapon had remained that oldest instrument of Empire, the Royal Navy. The navy might have failed to intimidate the Turks, but it had succeeded in inhibiting its greater opponent, the German High Seas Fleet, and won the war in the end simply by existing—the profoundest use of sea power. The Germans gave at least as good as they got in the great naval battle of Jutland, distinctly a Trafalgar manqué for the British, but for most of the war their magnificent surface ships stayed uselessly in harbour, blockaded by an idea.

The surrender of the German fleet took place on November 21, 1918, stage-managed in the classic Spithead style, and pictured like a sombre regatta in magazines and newsreels across the world. Everyone knew its meaning. Fourteen capital ships, fifty-six cruisers and destroyers were led into the Firth of Forth by a single British cruiser. It was a victory of Order over Anarchy, of the Real Thing over Upstarts, of permanent, organic values over petty ambitions and impertinences.

"The British flag," Lord Curzon told the House of Lords after the Armistice in November 1918, "has never flown over a more powerful and united Empire." For a time it had seemed that Joseph Chamberlain's vision of imperial federation might after all be realised. The victory celebrations in London were almost like the Diamond Jubilee again, as soldiers from the four corners of the King's dominions marched through the adulating crowds. The Empire seemed more than ever a band of brothers. "Never while men speak our tongue," wrote *The Times*, "can the blood spent by the Canadians at Ypres and by the Australians and New Zealanders at Anzac [Cove] be forgotten. That rich tribute of love and loyalty to the highest ideals of our race has not been wasted. . . ."

It was true, and it was false. The Empire really had gone to war united, and it fought together to the end. Even India provided an army of one and a half million men. As for the twenty-five million people of the "white" Empire, they had sent eight hundred and fifty-seven thousand of their men overseas, and one hundred and forty-one thousand of them were killed. A sense of common sacrifice and accomplishment really did give to the Empire's scattered peoples a new and triumphant brotherhood—"What remains to us?" cried William Morris Hughes, the spectacular Welsh-born

Prime Minister of Australia. "We are like so many Alexanders. What other worlds have we to conquer?" The Empire was more powerful than ever, possessing at the end of the war not only the greatest fleet, but also the greatest air force in the world, and from the conflict it was to win great prizes: new territories in Africa and the Pacific, a whole new paramountcy in the Middle East.

Yet it was false, for behind the triumph, the illusion was spent. After so many miseries in its name, glory was discredited in the hearts of the people, and war, which had given the British such vicarious satisfaction in the past,

ARMISTICE DAY, 1918

In his book, The World Crisis, *Winston Churchill recalls his vivid memories of the celebrations in Trafalgar Square on that historic day.*

It was a few minutes before the eleventh hour of the eleventh day of the eleventh month. I stood at the window of my room looking up Northumberland Avenue towards Trafalgar Square, waiting for Big Ben to tell that the War was over. My mind strayed back across the scarring years to the scene and emotions of the night at the Admiralty when I listened for these same chimes in order to give the signal of war against Germany to our fleets and squadrons across the world. And now all was over! The unarmed and untrained island nation, who with no defence but its navy had faced unquestioningly the strongest manifestation of military power in human record, had completed its task.

And then suddenly the first stroke of the chime. I looked again at the broad street beneath me. It was deserted. From the portals of one of the large hotels absorbed by Government Departments darted the slight figure of a girl clerk, distractedly gesticulating while another stroke resounded. Then from all sides men and women came scurrying into the street. Streams of people poured out of all the buildings. The bells of London began to clash. Northumberland Avenue was now crowded with people in hundreds, nay, thousands, rushing hither and thither in a frantic manner, shouting and screaming with joy. I could see that Trafalgar Square was already swarming. Around me in our very headquarters, in the Hotel Metropole, disorder had broken out. Doors banged. Feet clattered down corridors. Everyone rose from the desk and cast aside pen and paper. All bounds were broken. . . . The street was now a seething mass of humanity. Flags appeared as if by magic. Streams of men and women flowed from the Embankment. They mingled with torrents pouring down the Strand on their way to acclaim the King. Almost before the last stroke of the clock had died away, the strict, war-straitened, regulated streets of London had become a triumphant pandemonium.

Jubilant, cheering crowds gather outside Buckingham Palace during the celebrations on Armistice Day, November 11, 1918.

was recognised now in its true obscenity. They found among the papers of Wilfred Owen, killed in France in the last week of conflict, an unfinished poem called "An Imperial Elegy". This is all it said:

> Not one corner of a foreign field
> But a span as wide as Europe,
> Deep as (   ).
> I looked and saw.
> An appearance of a titan's grave,
> And the length thereof a thousand miles.
> It crossed all Europe like a mystic road,
> Or as the Spirits' Pathway lieth on the night.
> And I heard a voice crying,
> This is the Path of Glory.

The Empire stood wiser but more cynical for the experience of holocaust. Kipling, having lost his only son in the fighting, never again wrote a lay of Empire. Kitchener had shrunk in stature as the conflict extended, until, shipped off on a mission to Russia in 1916, he died far from his imperial exploits, drowned in the cold North Sea.

"I hope *they* can't hear us," said the Australian soldier retreating from Gallipoli, and one hopes the dead could not: for all too often the sacrifices of the Great War, as its contemporaries called it, were given to a cause that was already receding into history, like those discredited grey battleships, their smoke-pall filling the sky, hull-down on the Aegean horizon.

CHAPTER 7

SELF-DETERMINATION

So THE BRITISH EMPIRE moved out of the old order, which it had dominated and to some degree moulded, into a new and unfamiliar world. Convinced imperialists had been influential in the conduct of the war, and had their say in the shaping of the peace. They had to work subtly, however. The straightforward annexation of colonies was unacceptable now, as distasteful to the mass of the British people as it was to the world at large, and the prevailing orthodoxy was American: President Wilson's concept of "self-determination"—the right of every people to decide its own future. "Peoples may now be dominated or governed," Wilson optimistically told Congress in February 1918, "only by their own consent." His Fourteen Points, the basis of the peace settlement, did theoretically end the imperialist age. They specified that the interests of the subject peoples should have equal weight with those of the imperial powers.

In practice, however, the British Empire took shrewd advantage of the peace terms to extend its power and safeguard its security. Under American inspiration the victorious countries devised the system of mandates, trusteeships over former enemy territories awarded by the hopeful League of Nations to liberally-minded powers—generally, as it happened, those that had overrun the territories in war. This concept served the Empire usefully. In theory the League of Nations retained supervisory rights over the territories: in effect the British ruled their mandated acquisitions like any other Crown Colony.

This cartoon, which appeared in the Citizen, *Brooklyn, USA, was captioned, "An Expected Arrival. Will the stork make good as to this infant?" The League of Nations was born out of the Treaty of Versailles in 1919. It was created to preserve the peace and to settle future disputes through arbitration.*

In Africa the Empire gained control not only of Southwest Africa, satisfactorily rounding off imperial South Africa, but also of Tanganyika, at last fulfilling the vision of a Cape-to-Cairo corridor. In the Middle East, Iraq, Transjordan and Palestine became British mandates, and Persia was virtually a protectorate under British supervision, so that India was linked with Egypt and the Mediterranean by a continuous slab of British-controlled territory, and one could travel overland from Cape Town to Rangoon without once leaving the shelter of British authority.

The Empire seemed, on the face of it, safe and solid as never before.

In the sadness of the war, however, Britain had lost the *brio* of success, and she had no grand idea to offer, no message of hope or change to answer the challenges of Communism from revolutionary Russia, Wilsonian liberalism from America. In the Hall of Mirrors at Versailles, where the peace treaty with Germany was signed and the future of the world decided, the British did not play the decisive role. On the one hand they failed to curb the vindictive intentions of the French: on the other, though their chief representative was the inspired and fascinating Lloyd George, they were upstaged by the presence of the Americans. The British Empire represented tradition and continuity, but the USA represented a fresh beginning, and the idealism of the new world seemed marvellously hopeful and exciting, set against the plumed and fatal loyalties of the old.

For though self-determination was a clumsy word, it was full of lucid suggestion. It spoke not merely of national freedoms, but of all those inalienable personal liberties that the Americans had won for themselves, and now seemed to be claiming on behalf of everyone else. The very notion of self-determination was incompatible with the Empire's survival; the whole concept of a world order embodied in the League of Nations ran directly counter to British imperial positions. At least, however, the British Empire delegates at Versailles narrowly prevented the inclusion of a clause in the League Covenant actually declaring all races to be inherently equal, a close shave indeed for the imperial comfort.

The peace treaty was signed not only by Great Britain, but by delegates from Canada, Australia, South Africa, New Zealand and India, giving the Empire six separate votes. This seemed at first a majestic demonstration of imperial brotherhood. But it was really less a declaration of imperial solidarity than of dominion independence. In 1917, when the imperial prime ministers assembled in London in conference, they had unanimously voted that after the war the dominions should have an "adequate voice in foreign policy and in foreign relations". Smuts of South Africa, indeed, described them frankly as "autonomous nations", and thought they should not consider themselves an Empire any more, but a British Commonwealth of Nations. The victory had strengthened these impulses.

The white colonials who had gone to war trustingly, innocently almost, had seen the structure of British society forlornly exposed once more, and the myth of omniscience, to which they had been educated, proved a fraud. The British private soldier, so passive, so uncomplaining, they looked upon with a fraternal sympathy, often offering him cigarettes from their own more plentiful supplies, or giving him a pair of their superior boots. The British senior officer they grew to despise. Their impertinence to the brass, which began as a cheerful lark, grew into an expression of resentment, as they saw all their high purposes, their journeys across half the world, the

The four leaders in the negotiations for the Treaty of Versailles were known as the Big Four. From left to right: Britain's David Lloyd George, Italy's Vittorio Emanuelle Orlando, France's Georges Clemenceau and Woodrow Wilson of the United States. Defeated Germany played no part in the Versailles Conference, and German dissatisfaction with the peace terms was an important factor in the later rise of the Nazi movement.

lives of their comrades, so often wasted by the incompetence of the British high command.

Their leaders too, loyally though they supported the war to the end, chafed against the leading-strings of Westminster. From the start the Canadians had demanded complete control of their own armies, and among Australians the story of Gallipoli, which began as heroic legend, degenerated into an object lesson—never again would Australians be committed to war under absolute British command.

In September 1922 the British found themselves looking apprehensively once more towards the Dardanelles. Under the peace treaty Turkey had been dismembered. The Greeks occupied parts of Asia Minor, the British maintained garrisons along the Dardanelles. In 1920, however, a virile new Turkish state was formed, under the leadership of the visionary Mustafa Kemal, a general who had played a brilliant part in the defeat of the British at Gallipoli. Kemal repudiated the peace agreements, and resolved to rid his country of foreign troops. First he drove the Greeks out, then he turned his attention to the British. The main British outpost on the Asian side of the Dardanelles was Chanak.

In itself Chanak was not much: a shabby little Muslim town at the water's edge with a fortress still badly knocked about by the guns of the Royal Navy. For Kemal to threaten it, though, was an astonishing challenge. He was the representative of a defeated lesser power: the British not only represented the victorious nations, but were, in their imperial capacities, now the towering suzerains of the Middle East. To the British Government under Lloyd George the situation was charged with emotional nuance.

The colonial secretary was Winston Churchill, who had first sent the

WIMBLEDON'S LEGENDARY QUEEN

Suzanne Lenglen, a twenty-year-old French girl, was the star of the first postwar Wimbledon, in 1919. This account of the tennis player's trailblazing performance comes from Memory's Parade *by A.W. Myers.*

Mlle Lenglen won her first championship at Wimbledon after a dramatic final at which the King and Queen and the Princess Royal were watching from the committee-box as excited as any member of the packed crowd. Suzanne was to win the title six times in all, eluding defeat in any singles match. More significant than her record was the vogue she created and the barriers of tradition which she broke down. . . . She lifted lawn tennis from the level of a pastime for women, whose movements were restricted by a convention of dress and decorum, and raised it to an acrobatic art, claiming the freedom of limbs, and converting the stylist into a spectacular artist.

The champion's dress, even more than her strokes or perhaps because of them . . . received the favour of imitation and, of course, of the camera, so that when Miss Helen Wills first appeared in England in 1924, offering an eye-shade instead of a bandeau at the altar of fashion, the visor of a feudal challenge was suggested. Later, as women's play began to focus as much attention as men's, the question round the stands was not "How will she play?" but "What will she wear?"

Suzanne Lenglen's performance on the tennis court was not only athletic, but balletic and stylish.

imperial fleets and armies to the Dardanelles, and it was he who addressed an "inquiry" to all the dominion governments, asking if they would send troops to the straits if fighting broke out. At the same time he told the press what he had done. This was a terrible gaffe. The dominions had been left altogether in the dark about British policy towards Turkey and all their leaders were infuriated by what seemed to be Churchill's assumption of their support.

Only New Zealand and Newfoundland, the most thoroughly British of all the dominions, unequivocally agreed to send troops if needed. The Australians agreed under protest. The South Africans did not answer. But the Canadians' reply was the conclusive one. Mackenzie King, the prickly Canadian Prime Minister, cabled that he was not competent to commit troops to the Dardanelles upon a British request—such an action required the consent of the Canadian parliament. Only eight years after George V's unilateral declaration of war on behalf of his entire Empire, this was a portentous rebuff, and Mackenzie King well realised its meaning. "If membership in the British Empire", he wrote in his diary, "means participation by the dominions in any and every war in which Great Britain becomes involved, without consultation, conference or agreement of any kind in advance, I can see no hope for an enduring relationship." The Chanak crisis itself came to nothing, for the British presently concluded an agreement with Kemal and the town was never attacked after all. But the episode presented a very different imperial image from those brave assemblies of loyal statesmen which had expressed the unanimity of Empire in the flush of victory. As Kipling had written earlier in a famous poem on Canada:

> A Nation spoke to a Nation,
> A Throne sent word to a Throne:
> Daughter am I in my mother's house,
> But mistress in my own.

Though the Empire was to expand still further, from now on its story would be one of decline. The British vision would contract, and the abilities of the nation would chiefly be applied, not to projects of aggrandisement, but to social reform at home. Economics rather than diplomacy would be the first preoccupation of British statesmen. Nothing revealed this more frankly to the world than the surrender by the British Empire, four years after that triumph at the Firth of Forth, of the maritime supremacy which had been its inalienable prerogative, and its surest protection, since the Battle of Trafalgar. This surrender was called the Washington Treaty.

In the heyday of Empire it had been a maxim of British policy that the Royal Navy should be equal in power to any two navies that might combine to oppose it. Wasted by the war, Britain could no longer afford to maintain such overwhelming odds. Besides, two of her allies, Japan and the United States, were now great maritime powers themselves. In 1922, symbolically in Washington DC, a new ratio of sea power was devised by international agreement. In future, it was agreed, the navies of Great Britain, the United States and Japan would be limited to the ratio 5:5:3, with those of France and Italy at 1.75. The Royal Navy would no longer be able to design its ships to its own requirements, for there was agreement too on what type and size of ships each fleet might have. Even Britain's imperial fortresses were no longer hers to use as she pleased: under the Washington Treaty she specifically undertook not to develop Hong Kong as a base.

As a result of this treaty the British scrapped six hundred and fifty-seven ships: they included twenty-six battleships and battlecruisers. As the world declined into economic depression hard times were coming for the British people; and only sailors, imperialists and shipyard men much resented, or perhaps even noticed, the end of Rule Britannia.

For another twenty-five years, though, Empire would not let the British be. The Afghans were troublesome again; the Indians were restive; the Egyptians also. Above all the British were plagued by the anxieties of the closest, oldest and most reproachful of all their possessions, Ireland: for it was in Ireland, even before the Great War ended, that the prototype of imperial revolution was launched.

The English had been in Ireland now for nearly eight hundred years, keeping their hold upon it from the fortress-palace of their viceroys, Dublin Castle. Anglo-Irish gentry, the Protestant Ascendancy, owned most of the land and governed the destinies of the country. The Irish, for their part, consistently resented this occupation. Overwhelmingly Catholic in a predominantly Anglican Empire, proud of traditions as ancient as the English, they were never reconciled to government from London. Time and again the Catholic Irish had risen, always to be subdued. Ireland was the running sore of English politics. To most Englishmen it was a domestic problem, concerning a constituent part of the United Kingdom, but to the Irish, and their sympathisers abroad, it was a matter of Empire, and the Irish patriots claimed to represent all the subject peoples in their struggle for liberty.

The Liberal solution for the problem had been Home Rule—limited self-government for Ireland—but Gladstone's two Home Rule Bills had failed to get Parliamentary assent. In 1911 the Liberals introduced a third Home Rule Bill. The veto of the peers was now limited to a delaying power of two years, so its passage seemed almost certain. All being well, Ireland would be self-governing within five years. The Irish Nationalist Party, Ireland's constitutional representatives at Westminster, accepted the promise and worked to implement it.

Not everyone, though, viewed the prospect sanguinely. The Conservatives remained immovably hostile—and there was always the chance that they might come to power before Home Rule became established. The more extreme of the Irish Catholic patriots would accept nothing but absolute independence. And most fiercely of all, Home Rule was opposed by the Protestants of Ulster in the north. Descended from Scottish settlers, implacably anti-Catholic, they wanted nothing of a self-governing Ireland.

The peculiar situation of Ireland was to prove harbinger to the disintegration of Empire itself, and it was brought to a head by the arrival on the coast of Antrim, one spring night in 1914, of a small and undistinguished steamship. She was a collier, the *Clydevalley*, four hundred and sixty tons, twenty-eight years old. On April 25, 1914, this unlovely vessel, its hull red with rust and blackened with decades of coal-grime, sailed quietly into the small packet-port of Larne, eighteen miles north of Belfast, with a cargo of twenty-five thousand German rifles and two and a half million rounds of ammunition. They were to be used, if need be, to prevent by force the creation of a united self-governing Ireland.

All Protestant Ireland looked metaphorically towards Larne that night, for "Home Rule", they had been told by their leaders, "is Rome Rule", and they were prepared to resist it even at the price of rebellion against the

British Government at Westminster—of treason, in fact, against the Crown. All classes were united in this resolve, from the industrialists of Belfast who foresaw economic catastrophe in a self-governing Catholic-dominated Ireland, to the labourers' wives of the Londonderry slums, who simply hated Catholics. A Provisional Ulster Government was already in being, a shadow-regime for the north, and the public resolve was passionate, sometimes fanatic. Only guns were needed, to give it teeth.

It was a resistance movement of the oddest kind: the Ulster Protestants were intensely loyal to the Crown and to the Empire, they felt that the Liberal Government's policies were treacherously mistaken. Far from wishing to leave the Empire, they wished only to remain forever part of the United Kingdom itself. Though the movement was potentially revolutionary, half the British Establishment sided with it. The British army was almost unanimously with these rebels, and so were all the imperial activists.

Edward Carson (1854–1935) was a brilliant Irish lawyer who had become prominent during his cross-examination of Oscar Wilde in the Queensberry libel case of 1895. Fiercely opposed to Home Rule, which would lead to the Catholic south's domination of Protestant Ulster, he used brilliant rhetoric to attack the movement at public meetings.

Its political chief was the formidable King's Counsel, Sir Edward Carson, leader of the Irish Unionist Party in the House of Commons. Carson was not an Empire man; he was an Irishman, born in Dublin, a lawyer, and his concern was habitually concentrated, in the lawyer's way, on small intense issues. He was a heavyweight with a narrow imagination, whose harsh and resonant brogue could be terrifying, and comforting, and even inspiring, but never poetic. Carson's particular kind of rhetoric, ominously flamboyant, exactly suited the passions of the Ulster Protestants, whose dour manners masked such impetuous beliefs. They called him "King Carson".

Beneath Carson's aegis, an army of resistance awaited the outcome of the third Home Rule Bill, laboriously passing through its successive Parliamentary stages. The Ulster Volunteer Force was no raggle-taggle army of idealists. It was as professional and thorough as Carson himself. Its organisers were mostly men of the Ulster gentry, retired soldiers very often, who believed passionately in the unity of the British Empire. Its financiers were the businessmen of Belfast. Its patrons included great Ulster grandees. It had no uniforms and was armed—at that time—with no better weapons than sporting rifles, shotguns or even dummy rifles (supplied on demand, 1s 8d in pitch pine, 1s 6d in spruce): but its organisation was sophisticated, its activities ubiquitous. Every village in Ulster had its members, and the police knew all about it from the start, loopholes in the law making it theoretically legal. When Sir Edward Carson visited Portadown in 1912, he was escorted through the streets in an open carriage by cavalrymen with bamboo lances, field guns made of wood, infantry with wooden rifles and pipers in neo-military dress.

By 1914 some fifty thousand men, aged seventeen to sixty-five, had enlisted in this force. They were organised conventionally in divisions, regiments, platoons, and all military services were represented. There was an astute intelligence unit. There were supply and medical branches, artillery, signallers and dispatch riders, three squadrons of cavalry. Half the car owners of Ulster had pledged their vehicles to the transport branch. The force had a pension scheme for the wounded. It had a headquarters (the Old Town Hall, Belfast), a slogan ("For God and Ulster"), a flag (the Red Hand of Ulster). Above all it had a Manifesto. Back in September 1912 Carson had presented to the people of Ulster a declaration of intent, in the form of a pledge to "use all means which may be found necessary to defeat the present conspiracy to set up a Home Rule Parliament in Ireland". It

Members of the Ulster Volunteer Reserve in west Belfast in radiotelephone contact with head-quarters. The Reserve was made up of mainly Protestant Ulster gentry, who were deeply committed to remaining part of the Empire.

was called the Ulster Covenant, and nearly half a million Ulster men and women put their signatures to it, some of them in their own blood.

Across the water, too, many men of Empire pledged their support. Bonar Law, the Canadian-born leader of the Conservative opposition, and an implacable opponent of Home Rule, assured the Ulster Unionists that they were holding the pass not just for Ulster, but for the British Empire—"You will save the Empire by your example". The King himself had doubts about coercing Ulster by force of arms—"Will it be wise," he asked, "will it be fair to the Sovereign as head of the army, to subject the discipline and indeed the loyalty of his troops to such a strain?"

When in March 1914 officers of the Curragh, the British military base outside Dublin, were asked for an assurance that they would be ready to deal with Ulstermen by force, fifty-eight of them, including their commanding general, threatened to resign. The proposed operations were cancelled.

This was the inflammatory situation, then, into which the *Clydevalley* sailed that April night. At Larne all was ready for her. Every member of the Motor Car Corps had received a warning instruction: "Sir, in accordance with your kind agreement to place a motor-car at the disposal of the Provisional Government in a case of necessity, it is absolutely necessary that your car should arrive at Larne on the night of Friday/Saturday 24th/25th instant . . . for a very secret and important duty." Larne was virtually commandeered. A regiment of volunteers was assembled in the demesne of the Dowager Lady Smiley; another formed a cordon on the hills above, blocking every road into the town. Telephone lines were cut. Down at the docks the arrangements were supervised by the chairman of the harbour company, and the local volunteers stood by to unload the ship.

As night fell the first of the cars and lorries approached Larne. All the lights in the harbour were switched on; at eleven o'clock the *Clydevalley* slipped into harbour and made fast. The arrangements went perfectly, and the Catholic citizens of Larne, like the police, tactfully kept to their beds.

By 2.30 a.m. the last of the cars with its load of guns was away. The army of Ulster had weapons, and Home Rule could never be imposed upon the Irish Protestants without a civil war.

In the south few Irish Catholics were actively anti-British. It was generally assumed that Home Rule was on the way. The Crown's chief representatives in Dublin were anything but bullies, and Augustine Birrell in particular, the chief secretary, seemed to personify the very spirit of conciliation. A charming fellow of literary tastes, the son of a Methodist minister, he loved the company of Irishmen, and was a popular guest at the homes of the Dublin intelligentsia.

The defiance of Ulster came as a shock to moderate Catholics, and foreseeing that Protestant resistance might prevent Home Rule and wreck the cherished unity of Ireland, thousands of Irishmen joined their own private armies. Much the largest organisation was the Irish Volunteer Force, formed in 1913, in direct emulation of the Ulster Volunteers. Its ten thousand men wore grey uniforms with peaked caps, and drilled openly enough in parks and squares across Ireland. It too had its agents and sympathisers everywhere, in every police station, in every government office, and especially in every post office, giving it an excellent intelligence system. It was, though, quite unlike the tightlipped and splendidly organised militia of the north. There were no traditions of Empire to sustain it, few great demesnes to offer it parade grounds, munition stores or refuges. It was a ramshackle, amateurish, thoroughly Irish affair. Its commander was a lecturer in Gaelic literature, and it numbered in its ranks many teachers, not a few poets, eccentrics and folk-enthusiasts of all kinds, together with a mass of simple Irishmen who joined it out of guileless patriotism. They had many friends abroad, powerful bodies of Irish exiles in America and Australia, enemies of Britain everywhere. But though there was always money available, weapons there were not.

Their situation was to be changed by two remarkable members of the old Protestant Ascendancy, in particular. The first was Sir Roger Casement, one of the saddest figures of the whole imperial story. Like many another patriot of Catholic Ireland, he was a Protestant. The son of a British army officer, he was an instinctive and often muddled supporter of underdogs, wherever they were. He was a very sensual man, tall, distinguished, rather quixotic, melancholy, whose life seemed to lead him unerringly down dark and terrible paths.

Casement had become well-known as a member of the British consular service in West Africa. A report he made about conditions on the rubber estates of the Belgian Congo horrified the British public with its revelations of cruelty, and later he repeated the performance after a visit to the rubber estates of Peru. His reputation stood high in England. He was knighted in 1911, retired in 1913, and went home to Ireland apparently full of honour, achievement and duty satisfied. There in his late forties he became possessed by the enchantment of the island—"bewitched", so a contemporary wrote, "by the beauty of his own country"—and devoted himself to its causes as to a late love affair. He became one of the most extreme of Irish patriots, and reached the conclusion that in the coming world war, which he thought inevitable, it might be better for the Irish to side with Germany, and so achieve freedom by treason. When, in April 1914 the news of the *Clydevalley* coup reached him, Casement decided that his duty lay in enlisting German sympathisers for the Catholic Irish cause. As the last months of peace passed, and Europe mobilised for war, he prepared secretly to go to Germany, via New York, to conclude an alliance with the King's enemies.

The other conspirator was Erskine Childers, a popular Dublin writer and a man-about-town. A Protestant like Casement, he was the son of an eminent Anglo-Irish oriental scholar and had been a clerk at the House of Commons at Westminster. He had fought in the Boer War, and had made himself famous with an imaginary account of a German plot to attack Britain, *The Riddle of the Sands*.

A Liberal since the Boer War, the passing years made him an Irish patriot and gradually a revolutionary. When the *Clydevalley* brought her guns into Larne, he volunteered to match the feat for the patriot forces of the south. So there enters our story a second fateful vessel, the forty-nine-foot gaff ketch *Asgard*.

She had been given to the Childers as a wedding present. Built at Larvik in Norway, she was modelled upon Nansen's Arctic exploration vessel the *Fram*, and was very strong and exceptionally seaworthy. Childers loved her dearly. Though his wife was a cripple, the two of them sailed the *Asgard* on long oceanic voyages, frequently to the Baltic, and their seamanship was expert. In late April 1914 they took her to Hamburg, where Irish emissaries had already bought a consignment of arms. With them went a crew of four

(Robert) Erskine Childers (1870–1922) was an Irish author and politician, active in the fight for Home Rule for Ireland. In 1921 he became a Sinn Fein deputy in the Irish Assembly, and in the civil war that followed the creation of the Irish Free State he was arrested for carrying arms, court-martialled and shot as a traitor.

men and the Honourable Mary Spring-Rice, another fervent Anglo-Irish patriot. The voyage home was complex. The boat had no engine and no radio, they had to evade frequent Royal Navy patrols, they ran into a terrible storm in the Irish Sea. Off Devonport Childers brazenly sailed his yacht clean through the vessels of the British Home Fleet. But all went well, and on July 4, 1914, early in the morning, the *Asgard* sailed into Howth Harbour, five miles north of Dublin itself.

The coastguards took no notice, and within an hour a detachment of Irish volunteers marched onto the quay to collect the guns. With more enthusiasm than organisation they unloaded the crates of weapons and ammunition, some into handcarts, some into taxis.

It has all gone into legend, and was to be described over and over again, with growing embellishments and disagreements, and a deepening sense of veneration, as the years passed. But it was only a small episode really. There were no more than one thousand rifles, and within an hour they were all off. The volunteers set off for Dublin with their weapons on their shoulders or in their carts.

When the volunteers approached Clontarf, around the curve of Dublin Bay, they found a force of Scottish soldiers and policemen blocking their way. There was a fierce little engagement. Shots were fired, bayonets fixed, the police made a baton charge. Three civilians were killed and thirty-two wounded. When the victims were buried, vast crowds of Dubliners attended the funeral in a gesture as much of anger as of mourning.

But most of the guns had got through anyway, and were hidden away in clandestine armouries in Dublin. Now the Catholics of the south, like the Protestants of the north, could fight if the need arose.

Few expected to use their guns to seize their independence. They were satisfied with the promise of Home Rule, and they needed weapons, they thought, only to prevent the Ulster Protestants from wrecking it. When war came, John Redmond, the leader of the Irish Nationalist Party at Westminster, at once declared his party's support for it. Half a million southern Irishmen fought with the British army. Childers himself went off to the Royal Navy, and was decorated for his services. The Ulster volunteers had mostly joined the army too, seeming to suspend the threat from the north, and though Home Rule was postponed again, this time for the duration of the war, most Irishmen accepted the delay as reasonable.

But the fiercest of the patriots were not mollified. Among these one now emerged to prominence who saw in the preoccupations of wartime England the perfect realisation of his dreams. Patrick Pearse, a member of the Supreme Council of the Republican Brotherhood, still so secret that most people in Ireland had never even heard of it, was half Irish, half English, a poet and a kind of patriotic voluptuary. He really did believe that the cause of Irish liberty was more sacred than life or human love. "From the graves of patriot men and women," he wrote, "spring living nations."

By now Roger Casement was in Germany, where he was trying to enlist German support for an Irish revolution, and to recruit volunteers for an Irish Brigade among the prisoners of war taken in France. He did not have much success in his recruitment, most of the Irish prisoners being old sweats of the British army and impervious to subversion, but by 1915 he had persuaded the Germans to back a full-scale Irish rebellion. He arranged that he himself should be taken by U-boat to the west coast of Ireland, and

Although an Ulster Protestant, Sir Roger Casement (1864–1916) became an ardent Irish nationalist. Convicted of treason for his part in the 1916 Easter Rising, he was hanged in Pentonville prison. In 1965 his remains were exhumed and sent to a final resting place in Dublin.

that a shipload of weapons would run the British blockade. The rising would take place at Easter 1916, throughout Ireland, and it was hoped that the Germans would help by diversionary Zeppelin raids on London, by submarine attacks on shipping in Dublin Bay, and by providing German officers to stiffen the revolt. Dublin Castle would be seized, and an Irish Republic would be declared with Patrick Pearse as its first president.

It was a desperate plot. Admiralty intelligence in London had been privy to it almost from the start. Trawlers, sloops, destroyers and a light cruiser were deployed to intercept the arms ship: inevitably she was caught and scuttled herself with all her arms. Casement himself tried to cancel the rising, but he was too late, and coming ashore from the U-20 at Banna Strand near Tralee, was picked up almost at once by the local constabulary and shipped away to England, where he was held in the Tower of London and presently tried and hanged for treason.

The Germans provided no officers and no diversions, and the grandiose plan for a revolution throughout Ireland fizzled out. Only about a thousand patriots rose to arms in Dublin and raised the green flag of an Irish Republic—not over the castle indeed, where the viceroy remained impregnable, but over the General Post Office.

The British in Ireland were unprepared for the rising, and for intricate reasons of security the Admiralty's intelligence had not been passed on to Dublin. Many senior officers and officials had gone to the Bank Holiday races at Fairyhouse, twelve miles away. The army commander had gone home to England for the weekend. Still, the British army surrounded Dublin in overwhelming force, and the ordinary Dubliner regarded the whole enterprise as treasonable madness. If there was one sure way of *preventing* Home Rule, most people thought, it was by stabbing the British in the back at their moment of greatest peril.

We will not trace the course of the Rising, so petty by the terrible standards of 1916—the seizure of key points across Dublin, the inexorable massing of British troops. It lasted only five days, and ended inevitably in the suppression of the rebels. Within the post office in Sackville Street, their leaders, the first true revolutionaries of the British Empire, were trapped and doomed. They had no chance. There was Pearse himself, radiant with the prospect of martyrdom. ("Any hope?" somebody once asked him. "None at all," he cheerfully replied.) There was the Marxist Jim Connolly, who was fighting from dual convictions, nationalist and ideological. There was Joseph Plunkett, an Anglo-Irish aristocrat, foppish with his ringed fingers and the sabre always at his side, twenty-four years old but dying already of tuberculosis. There was Sean MacDermott twisted by polio, and Michael Collins, "The Big Fellow", gigantic and relentless.

With them a small band of men and women fought back uncomplainingly as the cordon closed. It was blazing hot in the post office, the wounded lay all about, upstairs the women were always at work bandaging, typing orders or cooking food. Now and then foraging parties crept out, but almost from the start there had been a sense of entombment in the building, as the guns from the Royal Navy's auxiliary patrol boat *Helga* boomed from the river, as the massed British troops waited behind their barricades.

By the evening of April 28 much of central Dublin was in ruins, and the toppling walls of offices and stores, the barbed wire and empty streets, the piles of rubble, the looted shops, the patrolling soldiers, made it look like

The Battle of Dublin

SOLDIERS OPENING FIRE ON THE SINN FEINERS, WHO ARE SNIPING FROM HOUSES 200 YARDS AWAY

This photograph of "The Battle of Dublin" appeared in The Graphic *on May 6, 1916. It shows British soldiers pinned down by snipers.*

British soldiers in the ruins of the General Post Office, over which the green flag of the Irish Republic had fluttered briefly during the Easter Rising.

a city enduring some much greater war. When, on April 29, Pearse and his dazed survivors emerged from the scarred post office to surrender, they were greeted with contempt by the British, with hostility by their fellow-countrymen. Stones and vegetables were thrown at them as they were marched away and angry Dubliners jostled them with obscenities.

But over the next fortnight fourteen leaders of the rising, among them Pearse, Connolly, Plunkett and MacDermott, blindfolded against a court-yard wall in Kilmainham Prison, were shot in ones and twos by the British army. It was done in the utmost secrecy, the city being under martial law, after macabre rituals of justice. The patriots were court-martialled within the prison, and only in later years did the details of the proceedings become known. The dying Plunkett was given permission to marry before his execution. The ceremony took place at midnight, in the prison chapel, and the condemned man and his bride had about fifteen minutes together before his execution at dawn. Connolly, who had been severely wounded in the fighting, was court-martialled in his bed and taken to his death in a chair.

Thousands of other patriots were arrested, and two thousand five hundred were sent to prison camps in England and Wales. The retribution of the English was swift and terrible, and when the Irish realised what was happening, the Easter Rising acquired a new meaning. Trust in the British was shattered once more, and the very citizens who had thrown rotten tomatoes at the patriots a few weeks before now mourned their memory in horrified remorse. The promise of Home Rule, which might have been a reconciliation, now became a mockery, and many a loyal Dubliner wondered for the first time if the English had really intended it at all.

"We seem to have lost," Pearse had told his court-martial. "We have not lost. . . . You cannot conquer Ireland, you cannot extinguish the Irish passion for freedom. If our deed has not been sufficient to win freedom, then our children will win it with a better deed." This was a true prophecy.

The Easter Rebellion was soon overshadowed by the vaster events of the Great War—a few weeks later the Battle of the Somme began and twenty thousand British soldiers died on its first day. Ireland relapsed into a sullen resentment. After the Armistice, when British governments turned their attention to Ireland once again, Ulster—rewarded for its loyalty, or its contumacy—was excepted from the long drawn out Irish independence arrangements, and became a self-governing province of the United Kingdom.

The Catholic Irish, on the other hand, became ever less loyal to the Crown as the years went by. Ireland itself fell into chaos, until out of the turmoil of rebellion and civil war, recrimination and revenge, there emerged in 1923, the Irish Free State—still subject to the Imperial Crown, shorn of the six counties of the Protestant North, but at least a nation of its own, with its own government and its own parliament.

So the Irish won in a way: but they lost too, for they never made friends with themselves. The old enmity of sect and loyalty was to simmer on, sometimes latent, sometimes murderous, until the British across the water no longer much cared what happened to Ireland.

The events there, however, were to play a seminal role in the slow retreat of the British Empire. The militancy of the Ulstermen was copied by white settlers in Kenya and Rhodesia, when they felt the imperial government to be neglecting their interest; the example of the southerners was watched with admiration by nationalists everywhere.

CHAPTER 8

THE ANGLO-ARABS

ELSEWHERE THE EMPIRE, LIKE AN OLD FATHER of young sons, had been finding a temporary new lease of life, for the conquered possessions of the Ottoman Empire offered fresh fields of enterprise. Before the war the British dealt warily with the Arabs of the Arabian peninsula, theoretically subjects of Turkey, but in practice largely autonomous. The sheikhs of the Persian Gulf they made more or less their vassals, the chieftains of the interior they generally left well alone. Still, even then, they kept in touch with the redoubtable Ibn Saud from their bases on the Persian Gulf, and at the same time, on the other side of the peninsula, they cautiously contacted the Grand Sharif Hussein of Mecca, head of the Hashemite clan, descended directly from the Prophet Mohammed, who held the hereditary guardianship of the Holy Places.

They liked the desert Arabs. The Bedouin struck a responsive chord in them. With his patrician style and his picturesque appearance, his great flocks of goats and camels, his blend of arrogance and hospitality, his love of pedigree, his fighting ability and what would later be called his *machismo*, the Bedouin was every Englishman's idea of Nature's gentleman.

The Hashemites, the most high-flown of the Bedouin clans, had pretensions to some kind of primacy, religious and temporal, over all the Arabs. Hussein was an ambitious figure, coveting the position of Caliph, spiritual leader of all the Muslims, which was held *ex officio* by the Sultan of Turkey. He had no love for the Turks, having spent some years as a political prisoner in Constantinople, and after the outbreak of war he conspired with the British to rise against the Ottoman Empire, in return for British arms, money and expertise, and promises of favours to come.

The Empire's compact with the Hashemites was deliberately vague and

The Middle East acquired major importance in the postwar years because of the growing dependence on oil within the economies of the developed nations. This photograph shows Arabs drilling for oil in the early days of the Persian oilfield development, in 1909.

opportunist. It was wartime, and the British were concerned first to win the war. The Arab Revolution, to be led by Hussein and his sons, was thus seen differently by its several participants. The Hashemites represented it as a national movement, to unite all the Arabs in an independent united kingdom. Their rivals in the peninsula, notably Ibn Saud, saw it as an unprincipled attempt by one Arab clan to impose its authority on the others. And the British saw it as tool of their own intent.

The conspiracy with Hussein was hatched from Cairo and Khartoum, and fostered by an intelligence agency called the Arab Bureau, working under the British high commissioner in Egypt, Sir Henry McMahon. The men in Cairo did not really know much about the desert Arabs. McMahon himself was a cautious freemason who spoke neither Arabic nor French, and was ignorant of Arabian matters. Everything about the liaison was vague: McMahon's promises to Hussein were deliberately vague; Hussein's claims to universal Arab leadership were necessarily vague; and, since nobody had really defined, for example, the limits of Syria or the extent of Palestine, the geographical terms employed were unavoidably vague. All was veiled in a courteous opacity, and the messages which McMahon exchanged with Hussein, encouraging him to rebellion, were to become, as "The McMahon Letters", synonymous with diplomatic ambivalence. The British couched their letters to Hussein in sickly honorifics, addressing him as "The excellent and well-born Sayid, the descendant of Sharifs, the Crown of the Proud, Scion of Mohammed's Tree and Branch of the Koreishite Trunk, him of the Exalted Presence and the Lofty Rank . . . ."

In fact they did not take him very seriously, or perhaps the Arabs either. They generally regarded him as a tiresome and faintly comic old rogue, and the idea of a true Arab State, taking its place in the comity of the nations, probably seemed so remote to them that their assurances of Arab independence were given lightly and heedlessly.

Far from frivolous, however, were the assurances they gave elsewhere about the future of the Middle East, for in fact the British were working to contradictory plans. With the Grand Sharif they had apparently agreed that, if he rebelled against the Turks, the Hashemites should rule over the whole of Syria, Transjordan and Palestine, the northern provinces of Iraq, and most of the Arabian peninsula. With their French allies they had concluded a quite separate pact, "greatly confusing", as Winston Churchill observed, "the issue of principles." Under this, the Sykes-Picot agreement, Syria, Lebanon, Transjordan and Iraq would be divided into British and French spheres of influence or exploitation, with Palestine under some kind of international control, and the Arabs only truly independent within the Arabian peninsula. Finally, because Jewish money, talent and sympathy were very important to a Britain at war, they made a fateful pledge to the leaders of the Zionist movement, that they would encourage the development of a Jewish national home in Palestine—a country whose population in 1916, was ninety-three per cent Arab.

The man who set the tone of what was to prove a febrile relationship with the Arabs was T. E. Lawrence, archaeologist, scholar of Jesus College, Oxford, the confused and enigmatic exhibitionist who was to be known to the world as Lawrence of Arabia.

He entered the arena modestly enough. He had worked as an archaeologist in Syria, spoke Arabic, and had taken part in a clandestine intelligence survey in Sinai. When the war came, he was recruited into the Geographical Section of the General Staff and posted to Cairo; and from there he was sent to the Hejaz as one of the British officers lent to Hussein to stiffen his revolt. His was a strange genius. Confused in his own spirit by doubts of the profoundest kind, he exerted an astonishing power over the most unlikely subjects—statesmen, common soldiers, society women, Arab tribesmen, even regular soldiers of the British army. He was a very good man, kind, generous, and perhaps this, the deepest trait of his nature, was apparent to people beneath all the flummery and the deceit (for he was a gifted and enthusiastic liar). Nobody remotely like Lawrence had ever played a part in the extension of the British Empire.

He proved himself an inspired guerrilla leader, and soon became the effective commander of Hussein's revolt. He himself led its first foray out of the Peninsula, into the country at the head of the Red Sea, and he presently came to see himself as a kingmaker, escorting the Hashemite family to the thrones of the Arabs. He became not simply a colleague of the Arab leaders, but actually a friend, so restoring to imperial affairs a relationship between imperialist and client that had scarcely existed since eighteenth-century India. It might have come to nothing, though, and the Hashemites might have faded from the imperial scene, if Lawrence had not persuaded General Allenby, then organising his invasion of Syria, of the potential importance of the Arab revolt.

When Allenby launched his campaign through Syria, his right flank consisted of the Hashemite army, commanded by the Emir Feisal, third son of the Grand Sharif, and directed by Lawrence; and when Damascus fell, Arabs and British rode into the city together, something new in imperial victories. Feisal set up an Arab administration in Syria; Abdullah, his brother, was promised by his father the throne of Iraq. Everywhere the flag of the Hashemites flew, and the wide kingdom of the Arabs seemed to be at hand. Lawrence had given McMahon's promises meaning, it seemed, and Allenby had sealed them.

From Cairo and London, though, the prospects looked different, for the British were already preparing—with the Great War now over—to divide the Arab lands with their European allies. At the peace conference the United Arab Kingdom collapsed in disillusionment, and Feisal was presently ejected by the French from his throne in Damascus. And when the final arrangements for the Middle East were agreed, the Hashemites were not represented. This is what was decreed. In the Arabian peninsula the *status quo* would be maintained, with King Hussein confirmed in his sovereignty of the Hejaz. France was given a mandate over Syria and Lebanon. The Zionists got their national home. The rest would be British, embodied in mandatory government in Palestine (including Transjordan) and Iraq.

Among many British Arabists a profound sense of shame set in, to dog their attitudes until the end of the Empire. They felt they had betrayed their friends and believed the imperial policies to have been dishonourable. The Arabs were no less bitter in their disillusionment. Feisal retired sadly to the Hejaz; the Iraqis burst into rebellion against their British overlords; Transjordan subsided into squabbling groups of tribes and petty states, precariously held in check by a handful of Englishmen.

Among those most deeply affected by this denouement was Lawrence, whose private mortifications were thus sublimated into a public emotion.

T.E. Lawrence (1888–1935), romantically known as "Lawrence of Arabia", was sent in 1916 to help organise Arab rebellion in the Turkish empire. His guerrilla actions, employing small bands of Arabs, managed to tie down the Turkish army. Although he became a legendary figure, Lawrence rejected fame by joining the RAF as an aircraftsman and changing his name, first to Ross and later to T. E. Shaw. He died in May 1935 in a motorcycle accident.

Shame was to be the leitmotiv of his epic memoir, *Seven Pillars of Wisdom*, and he was outspoken in his view that Britain had ill-treated the Hashemites. Fortunately Winston Churchill presently came back to office, one of those public men improbably held in thrall by the Lawrentian enigma. Setting up a Middle East Department at the Colonial Office, and appointing Lawrence as his particular adviser, he set out to straighten accounts, if not with the Arabs in general, at least with the Hashemites. In 1921 he summoned a conference at Cairo to interpret in imperial terms the decisions of the Peace of Versailles. "Practically all the experts and authorities on the Middle East," he later wrote, "were summoned . . ." which meant in the context of the times that of the thirty-eight participants, thirty-six were British and two Arab. There is a famous photograph of this conference taken at the Mena House Hotel in which we may see, frozen forever in their official poses, the true progenitors of the Anglo-Arab Empire. The chubby-faced, balding man in the centre is of course Churchill himself, twenty years older than he was at Spion Kop, and by now an experienced imperialist. The young man in the three-piece suit, papers untidily protruding from his jacket pocket, is T. E. Lawrence. The only woman in the group, wearing a wide flowered hat and a fox fur, is Gertrude Bell, writer, orientalist, explorer, and forceful protagonist of the British presence in Iraq.

It was scarcely a conference really. Churchill and Lawrence had already made its decisions. Churchill's solution was to create two new kingdoms in the Arab world, the Kingdom of Iraq, and the Emirate of Transjordan. Both would have Hashemite monarchs, Feisal in Baghdad, Abdullah in Amman, but both would be unmistakably protégés of the British.

So the new Empire was established. By the middle 1920s Britain was overwhelmingly paramount in the Middle East, and her control of the Arab world was absolute, if not in principle, at least in fact. The routes to India were safe as never before, the oil wells of Iraq and the Persian Gulf, the Abadan refinery, all were securely in British possession. "I must put on record my conviction," Lawrence wrote after surveying this consummation,

This famous photograph was taken at the Cairo conference in 1921 to which, wrote Churchill, "practically all the experts and authorities on the Middle East were summoned".

"that England is out of the Arab affair with clean hands. . . ." Or if not with clean hands, he might have added, at least with full pockets.

None of the new territories became colonies, and Aden was to be, first to last, the only true British possession among the Arabs. Elsewhere the new suzerainty was veiled in euphemism. Egypt was proclaimed independent in 1922, but remained a British fief just the same. The Persian Gulf emirates were officially Protected States, but did what they were told. Iraq and Transjordan had their own monarchs and governments, but were effectively run by British advisers, and policed by British forces. Palestine was a Mandated Territory, but was governed by the familiar Colonial Office hierarchy. The vassal dynasty of the Hashemites, the front of British control among the Arabs, adopted under the tutelage of the Empire all the trappings of western kingship, and there were Baghdadi tailors By Appointment to the Royal House.

Among and around the Hashemites a group of Anglo-Arab satraps rose to power. Some were Arabs themselves; many more were Britons, discovering for themselves opportunities for adventure and advance. Most of these Britons were men of the rural gentry, and they felt at ease with Arab gentlemen, and affectionately paternal towards the Arab rank and file. They were probably the happiest of all the imperialists. More than any colonial servants since the great days of British India, they felt themselves fulfilled; they believed the British presence to be good for the Arabs and for the world in general.

For three decades it worked. The British were able to safeguard their oil supplies and their strategic interests at minimum cost to themselves, and more than any other of their suzerainties, more even perhaps than their Empire in India, it was their position in the Middle East that kept them among the ranks of the Great Powers into the middle years of the century.

But it was to go sour in the end. The younger Arabs, especially the urban intellectuals, proved to be nationalists of a sophistication and intensity unknown to the imperialists elsewhere. For they believed the whole imperial structure in their midst, disguised as it was in mandate, protectorate or formal independence, to be false.

So it was. Iraq and Transjordan, the bulwarks of the British position, were only semi-nations. Their kings were creatures; their diplomatic missions were mere sops to their self-esteem; their trade, commerce and industry were ancillary to imperial needs; their armies were trained, equipped and often commanded by Britons. The British Empire was a true ally of reaction in the Middle East, depending as it did upon the alliance of sheikhs and princes, distrustful of urban values and intellectual tastes. The progressives were bound to rebel against its presence sooner or later, and their antipathies were given an extra focus by the problem of Palestine, where the Zionists were busily building their national home under British auspices— an imperialist bridgehead, as every Arab agreed, upon the shore of Islam.

The Arab Awakening, as it came to be called, was sporadic and scattered—an assassination in Egypt, a mutiny in Iraq, a riot in Palestine—but it was never altogether quiescent. As the decades passed the British stance among the Arabs became more and more defensive, and the high commissioners, the residents, the advisers, the general officers commanding, the conservators of the forests, fortified themselves with their sheikhly partners against the assaults of change.

CHAPTER 9

GANDHI AND INDIA

IN THE MEANTIME, WHILE THIS FRAIL new empire came into being, a terrible event occurred in the greatest of the old possessions, India. It was the massacre at Amritsar, which was recognised even then as the worst of all stains upon the imperial record. It happened in a public enclosure, something between a square, a rubbish dump and a garden, called the Jallianwalla Bagh, in the very heart of Amritsar. This was a venerable city of the Punjab, and it contained the Golden Temple, the holiest shrine of the Sikhs, where the splendid major-domos of the Faith, sashed and staved, all day long marshalled the pilgrims towards their holy places beside the pool. The city was a brown maze of narrow streets, mud-paved, always crowded, with open-fronted bazaar shops, toppling merchants' houses, and fetid lanes with open drains. It was a volatile place, and in April 1919 it was in a state of uproar. A wave of nationalist protest had been sweeping India, and in Amritsar there had been riots and demonstrations, culminating in the deaths of five Englishmen and an assault upon an English woman missionary, riding her bicycle through the town.

Nobody doubted that the British would retaliate, but by now the city was too inflamed to count the risk. Though public assemblies had been forbidden, on April 13 many hundreds of people defiantly crowded into the Jallianwalla Bagh for a political meeting. It was an ominous scene. The Bagh, surrounded by high walls, was sunk below the level of the surrounding streets, and overlooked on all sides by towering houses. There were only three entrances: two gates at the southern end, and a narrow passage, hardly wide enough for two men to pass, at the northwest corner.

Near this passage a patriotic orator, clambering onto a pile of rubble, began to read to the crowd a passionate poem of liberty. With every word the tension rose. The people swayed, stirred, sighed, and sometimes shouted responses—and the heat was so great, the place so jammed, the emotion of the occasion so high, that one could almost feel the heart of the crowd thumping there, and hear its excited breathing.

Suddenly there was a rumble of engines outside the walls, and people near the entrance passage could see, gleaming in the street outside, the brown steel shape of an armoured car. In a moment the corridor was full of armed men, pushing their way fiercely into the garden and onto the higher ground behind the speaker: Gurkha riflemen, taut, purposeful little mercenaries like tamed wild beasts, with rifles in their hands and kukris at their belts. In a matter of moments they were briskly deployed along the top of the garden, and were kneeling with loaded rifles facing the crowd.

When the orator looked over his shoulder and saw them, he shouted to the crowd not to be alarmed. Hardly had he spoken than a command rang out, and the impassive Gurkhas began to shoot at point-blank range into the crowd. The panic was frightful. People fought each other to get to the gates. They scrabbled at high walls, they trampled one another down, they rushed this way and that, they tried to hide, to take shelter behind each other, to lie flat on the ground. The Gurkhas were unmoved. Loading in

The Golden Temple at Amritsar, capital of the Punjab, is the holiest shrine of the Sikhs. The massacre there of three hundred and seventy-nine people on April 13, 1919, by British troops, was described by Winston Churchill as an episode "Without precedent . . . in the modern history of the British Empire."

their own time, they aimed especially at the two exits at the bottom of the garden, until the gates were jammed with dead and wounded Indians, and nobody else could escape.

The shooting went on for about six minutes. When the soldiers withdrew, three hundred and seventy-nine people had been killed, and another fifteen hundred wounded.

This was the tragedy of Amritsar, when Brigadier General Reginald Dyer, CB, felt it his duty to make an object lesson of the demonstrators in the Jallianwalla Bagh. He was obliged to resign his commission, but he had many supporters, for he believed he had been forestalling another Indian Mutiny. His superior officers condoned his action; the guardians of the Golden Temple enrolled him into the Brotherhood of Sikhs; the House of Lords passed a motion in his support; the readers of the *Morning Post* subscribed a £25,000 testimonial; in his attitude he was only reflecting the innate sense of inadequacy that would presently debilitate the British in India. Still, as Winston Churchill said, it was an episode "without precedent . . . in the modern history of the British Empire . . . an event which stands in singular sinister isolation."

This was true: the British had seldom behaved murderously towards their subjects, except in battle. But then the situation in India in the years after the Great War was itself without precedent. India was not like any other British possession. So long as anyone remembered, Britons had been coming and going between the two countries. Maharajahs were common figures in London society. Indian cricketers and polo players were popular performers. In an illogical way India was, to the British and to many Indians too, a part of England, a distant part that only a minority knew, but so interwoven with English destinies that the association seemed indivisible.

There was profit in it, even now. India was one of the most valuable fields of British investment—in 1914 some £800 million of capital was invested there. Rubber, coffee, indigo, tea, coal, jute, railways—all these Indian industries were very profitable to British financiers: jute mills in the 1920s were said to be making an annual profit of ninety per cent. Prestige and authority accrued from the mastery of this vast possession in the east, and generations of Englishmen had benefited directly from the Indian link.

Yet the truth was dawning on the British that their dominion was foreseeably coming to an end.

The Indians were becoming restive. A million had served the British during the Great War, and concessions of independence were expected in return. The moderates wanted dominion status, like the white-settler colonies; the extremists wanted to be quit of the Empire altogether. They were angry and disappointed when all the British conceded was the system called "diarchy" (joint rule), which certainly gave Indians a far greater share in government, but was a long way from liberty.

"The people are restless," reported a percipient deputy commissioner to his superiors back in 1918, "and discontented and ripe for the revolution": and Mahatma Gandhi was that revolution's prophet.

The son of a palace official in the minuscule Gujarati princedom of Porbandar, on the shore of the Arabian Sea, Gandhi had been trained as a lawyer in London, and had briefly anglicised himself, dressing in high white collar and dark suit, cultivating the art of small talk, even learning the violin, before gravitating to South Africa as legal adviser to an Indian firm

A game of polo being played at a hill station in southern India in about 1910. The origins of polo are not clear: some historians believe it originated in Persia, whilst others think it may have been started by British army officers in India in about 1862. Having watched a display of Manipur tribesmen's horsemanship, the British officers are said to have imitated their feat of hitting a ball whilst at full gallop, and adapted various rules from the game of soccer.

Gandhi with his associates, when he was practising law in Durban. As a leader of the Asian community in South Africa, he advocated non-violent resistance to unjust laws, particularly those that discriminated against Indians.

in Durban. There he had taken to politics, by way of the grievances of the Indian community, and had become well-known as a champion of Indian rights and self-respect. He was a stretcher bearer at Spion Kop, and was decorated by the British for his courage in the war. Returning to India in 1914, he plunged at once into the furious world of nationalism, and reverted to his Indian origins. Now he dressed altogether Indian-style, professed a frugal vegetarianism, and year by year prepared himself for the vital role he was to play in the struggle for Indian liberty.

Gandhi of the round disarming spectacles and the toothless smile shared with T. E. Lawrence the quality of enigma, so that he seemed to one man a saint, to another a hypocrite. A very small man, five feet four inches, and slight to the point of emaciation, he had vivid black eyes, spoke very pure English with a vestigial South African accent, and enthralled nearly everyone with his suggestion of almost unearthly wisdom. "The saint has left our shores," General Smuts wrote when Gandhi left South Africa for the last time, "I sincerely hope forever." He was truly innocent in some ways, calculating and self-conscious in others. Like Lawrence again, he well understood the value of publicity. Like many another Indian guru, he veiled his shrewdness in platitudes and truisms, and sometimes cheapened it with opportunism. His repeated political fasts to the death never *were* to the death, as the British wryly noted.

He was an Anglophile. "Hardly ever have I known anybody", he wrote of himself in his youth, "to cherish such loyalty as I did to the British Constitution." For years he continued to declare his devotion to the British: "The Emperorship must go, but I should love to be an equal partner with Britain, sharing her joys and sorrows."

Over the years his ideas of national independence became fused with thoughts about human dignity, raising the struggle for Indian emancipation to a level beyond the vision of the Easter Rising heroes. He was lucky, however, that the British in India were, by and large, tolerant rulers, so that he was able to work out his moralities on a political stage, without being shot on the spot.

Gandhi's revolutionary formula was a conglomeration of political ambition, social theory, religious precept, personal intuition. He rationalised it all into a single metaphysic, and called it *satyagraha*—truth-force. If imperialism was essentially a glorification of force, satyagraha was just the opposite—it postulated, Gandhi said, "the conquest of an adversary by suffering in one's own person". Satyagraha was the means: the end was *swaraj*, independence, which was as much a personal as a national condition.

To the Indian masses Gandhi became semi-divine. They believed him capable of miraculous feats. The people did not understand him, though, and he did not always understand them. He was repeatedly warned, by friends as by enemies, that satyagraha, hazily grasped by a vast illiterate populace, would inevitably lead to violence. Nevertheless when the Rowlatt Acts were announced in 1918, giving almost unlimited power against subversion, he launched a nationwide protest against them. The result was savagery all over India. The mob came out in Gandhi's name, breaking windows in Calcutta, destroying offices in Bombay, molesting the woman missionary in Amritsar.

The British responded with massive troop movements, arrests, curfews and prohibitions. "I have made a Himalayan miscalculation," Gandhi said, surveying the bloodshed and misery that swept across the country: and in Amritsar General Dyer gave the order to fire.

Gandhi recognised that force as such could not expel the Raj. British firepower was still overwhelming in India, and there were many more Dyers ready to obey their inherited instincts of command. Other revolutionary methods were needed. "He was like a powerful current of fresh air that made us stretch ourselves and take deep breaths," wrote his disciple Jawaharlal Nehru. Until Gandhi, Nehru said, fear kept things as they were, and allowed the British to retain control. Gandhi changed all that. He deliberately made use of India's disadvantages, her poverty and backwardness, to reinforce his own methods, and so very soon became master of the Indian political scene. The Indian National Congress closed its ranks behind him, and the constitutionalists who wished to progress more sedately towards more limited goals were left discredited.

Though his own misjudgment had caused it, Amritsar convinced Gandhi that compromise with the British was now impossible—sinful he said at the time. So horrified was the world by the massacre, so shaken and even remorseful were the British themselves, so infuriated were the Indians, that *swaraj* immediately assumed a new force, and from that moment until the end of the Empire, the true initiative was always with the Indians.

It was to prove a muddled progress. Sometimes the impetus seemed to wane. Sometimes non-violence failed and the Indian masses burst into riot again. They were convulsive times—the Indians riding the tide of history, but weakened by their own feuds and rivalries, the British gradually losing the will to rule.

Once Gandhi was arrested, charged with subversion, and the puzzled sensitivity of the presiding magistrate, Robert Broomfield, exactly reflects the bewilderment of the time. The case was heard on March 18, 1922, in the Circuit House at Ahmedabad, in Gandhi's own province of Gujarat. This was not a courtroom, but a house used by visiting judges and officials, and was chosen because it stood on the outskirts of the city, away from the mob and close to the British cantonment. There was no dock or witness-box, and the atmosphere was informal. Most of the spectators wore the white homespun of the patriotic movement, and when Gandhi entered the room, wearing only a loincloth himself, they stood in his honour.

Gandhi was charged with sedition, because of articles he had written in his political journal *Young India*, and he admitted his guilt at once—indeed he urged it. He had come to the conclusion, he said that the British connection with India was fatal to the welfare of the country, so that it had been a privilege to write articles demanding its end. "To preach disaffection towards the existing system of government has become almost a passion with me . . . . I am here therefore to invite and submit to the highest penalty that can be inflicted upon me, for what in law is a deliberate crime, and what appears to me to be the highest duty of a citizen."

These were confusing submissions to a conventionally educated official of the Indian Civil Service. Broomfield had been in India for fourteen years, but nothing in his training and experience could have prepared him for the peculiar accused who now stood before him surrounded by his friends and supporters, looking spindly, saintly and almost demure. Gandhi made a very long statement to the court, and in the course of it suggested, not very seriously perhaps, that only two courses were open to the judge—to resign

Jawaharlal Nehru (1889-1964), also known as Pandit Nehru, was educated in England, at Harrow and Cambridge, and was admitted to the English Bar. He was a supporter of independence for India and a colleague of Gandhi.

his post on the grounds that the law was bad, or to hand down the severest possible sentence. Gandhi spoke gently, and everyone was impressed. Robert Broomfield himself was clearly touched by the occasion, and he produced a judgment that would be quoted always, when the manners and values of the British Raj were later to be debated.

"Mr Gandhi," he said, "you have made my task easy in one way by pleading guilty to the charge. Nevertheless what remains, namely the determination of a just sentence, is perhaps as difficult a proposition as a judge in this country could have to face. The law is no respecter of persons. Nevertheless it will be impossible to ignore the fact that you are in a different category from any person I have ever tried or am likely to have to try. It would be impossible to ignore the fact that, in the eyes of millions of your countrymen, you are a great patriot and a great leader. Even those who differ from you in politics look upon you as a man of high ideals and noble and even saintly life."

There were few people in India, said the judge (optimistically perhaps if he counted the British) who would not sincerely regret that Gandhi could not be left at liberty. But it was so. He was going to sentence the Mahatma, said Judge Broomfield, to six years' imprisonment, as a balance between what was due to the prisoner and what seemed to be needed in the public interest: "And I should like to say in doing so that if the course of events in India should make it possible for the government to reduce the period and release you, no one will be better pleased than I."

The course of events did, for Gandhi spent less than two years in his prison at Poona.

Meanwhile, the British in India were groping. Nobody really knew what best to do, because few really believed in their hearts that Indians were capable of governing themselves. "To me it is perfectly inconceivable," said Lord Birkenhead, Secretary of State for India in 1925, "that India will ever be fit for dominion self-government," while it was Ramsay MacDonald, the Socialist, who once observed that parliamentary democracy could no more be transferred to India than ice in an Englishman's luggage.

Successive governments wavered in their policies, offering a nibble of freedom one year, apparently discouraging all progress the next. The Coalition Government of 1918 had given India diarchy, the Conservative Government of 1927 set up an Indian Commission of Inquiry which included no Indians at all. The Prime Minister of the Labour Government of 1929 was Ramsay MacDonald, who promptly ate his words about parliamentary democracy for India, and announced that within months rather than years there was likely to be an Indian dominion modelled as far as possible on Westminster.

It was not enough for Gandhi, who had long lost his faith in the imperial system, and was committed now to absolute independence. A new revolutionary campaign was necessary, he said, and to launch it he declared an Independence Day. On January 26, 1930, at meetings all over India, citizens were invited to make a pledge of independence—"Mahatma expects everyone to do his duty", said the lead headline in the *Bombay Chronicle*—and soon afterwards Gandhi set off upon an allegorical mission of defiance, to mark the moment when the British Raj no longer had meaning for Indian patriots. He wanted to do something that would be instantly understood by the Indian masses. He decided to challenge an official ruling known to

Ramsay MacDonald (1866-1937) was instrumental in the establishment of the Labour Party and in 1924 became Britain's first Labour Prime Minister. In 1931, in his second term of office, MacDonald met Gandhi to discuss plans for Indian independence, but they were able to achieve very little.

everyone: the government monopoly on the production and sale of salt.

The salt monopoly was an old staple of Anglo-Indian affairs. It affected the life of each citizen, and it affected the state of government—half the retail price of salt went in taxes. Gandhi conceived the idea of publicly producing a quantity of salt himself, out of seawater, and inviting the Indian people to do the same. It was a masterly application of satyagraha. It was easy, it was harmless, it had moral content, it would appeal to everyone. On March 12, 1930, Gandhi set off from his headquarters in Ahmedabad on his Salt March to Dandi on the Arabian Sea two hundred and fifty miles away, and he turned the march into a triumphant pilgrimage.

Farmers knelt beside the road when he passed; women came out of their houses to offer him food, rest or comfort, as though he were on his way not simply to a political demonstration, but to his own Calvary. When they came to a village they stopped and Gandhi, accepting with a princely calm the obeisance of the elders, climbed to a platform or a mound and addressed the people; when he moved on the elders generally went with him.

The Government stayed prudently aloof, and on April 5 the great company of patriots approached the fishing village of Dandi. There were scenes of wild excitement as he entered the village, dancing, music, prayers beneath the great banyan tree, and he was taken along the single street to a villa, the property of rich Muslim sympathisers, which was to be his lodging. An expanse of tidal marsh lay between Dandi and the sea reef where the village fishing boats were drawn up on the sand, and here each day the tide left patches of salt for the picking. The plan was that early next morning Gandhi would go to a spot immediately below the villa, and pluck a lump of salt from the ground in frank and exuberant contempt of the law.

The world watched Dandi that day. Scores of reporters and cameramen had arrived to record the occasion. The little village was crammed with sightseers, and there were crowds camping on the hard salty ground around it. In the morning, when Gandhi's aides went to the appointed spot to make things ready, the tide having ebbed, they found that unfortunately there was no salt there—police agents, it was suggested, had brushed it into the

Gandhi and his followers on the famous Salt March of 1930, protesting against the government's salt tax. As a result of the march and subsequent protests, Gandhi and nearly one hundred thousand other Indian patriots were arrested and imprisoned.

mud during the night. It did not matter, though. They found some elsewhere, and by the time Gandhi emerged from the villa after his morning prayers, surrounded by his disciples and followed by photographers, all was ready.

The crowd burst into song, and in a matter of hours newspapers across the world carried photographs of the Mahatma stooping like a bony seabird to pick up his illicit mineral from the mud.

Some nights later, when Gandhi and his followers were camping beside a river in a village five miles away, a police posse arrived. His Majesty's magistrate had come with a warrant for Gandhi's arrest, in the small hours of the morning to avoid a riot. The Mahatma was to be held under a law of 1827, allowing Authority to detain a suspect without trial indefinitely: and when he had said his prayers, they took him away to prison once more.

Again he was not there long, for the events that had started with the Salt March rolled on all around him and made his imprisonment a dangerous embarrassment for the British. He had launched a gigantic new wave of patriotic protest. Suddenly salt was everywhere. People ostentatiously made it, or gave it away to crowds, or dug it out of the earth, or auctioned it (Gandhi's original spoonful was sold for 1,600 rupees). People rioted over salt, newspapers were banned because of it, soldiers mutinied, professors led their entire classes to collect it from the seashore. In Wadila the government salt depot was raided. The British responded fiercely, with violent police action and mass arrests. Most of the Congress leaders were gaoled and by the end of May 1931 nearly one hundred thousand Indian patriots were in prison.

Conciliation fell to the King's viceroy. Lord Irwin was tall, grave and imposing. His presence was given a medieval piquancy by an atrophied and handless left arm, as though he had been maimed by some stroke of sorcery, but in many ways he was an imperial modernist. The son of a great Yorkshire landowner, a devout High Anglican and a Fellow of All Souls, he was by no means a reactionary. He was above all a man of God and of peace, uneasy with the arrests, baton charges, declaration of martial law, by which the British responded to the Salt March rising, and in fact felt a strong fellow-feeling for Gandhi as a colleague in metaphysics. He had met the Mahatma several times, and felt he understood him. After all, he said, when people remarked upon Gandhi's infuriating ways, "Some people found Our Lord very tiresome."

In January 1931, accordingly, Irwin decided to release Gandhi from his imprisonment, and invited him to come to Delhi to negotiate a settlement of India's problems. This was drastic action indeed, and the consequent meetings between the viceroy and the revolutionary were to become legendary. It happened that in 1929 Lord Irwin had moved into the immense new palace that had been completed for the viceroys at New Delhi—a stone epitome of British authority in India. Here it was, in the most magnificent of all the imperial palaces, that the two men met, the viceroy aristocratically at ease in that stateliest of homes, the Mahatma, fresh out of prison, barefoot, with his staff and simple white robe. The spectacle enthralled the world. Foreign correspondents rushed to Delhi, and wondering crowds watched through the wrought-iron gates on the afternoon of February 17, 1931, as the Mahatma, huddled in a shawl against the winter chill, clambered up the monumental steps of the palace and disappeared inside.

They met eight times, and innumerable anecdotes of their relationship went the Delhi rounds. They laughed a good deal, it seemed. Gandhi was quite ready to be amused at himself, and when they toasted and Gandhi chose water, lemon and a pinch of salt, Irwin wryly regretted that it must be *excise* salt.

The agreement they reached meant little. For the moment it ended the disturbances, but it displeased Indians by its moderation, and British conservatives by its concessions. Nevertheless, the meeting represented something altogether new in the old dialogue between Britons and Indians. From the Indian point of view it was a significant advance, and Gandhi and Irwin appeared together in innumerable cartoons and posters, and even gave their names jointly to a match factory. To old-school imperialists it was a surrender. Winston Churchill was revolted, he said, in a famous parliamentary anathema, by "the nauseating and humiliating spectacle of this one-time Inner Temple lawyer, now turned seditious fakir, striding half-naked up the steps of the viceroy's palace . . . to negotiate and parley on equal terms with the representative of the King-Emperor." By his own lights he was right to be sickened, for he had truly seen in Irwin's hospitality the pattern of the imperial end.

Later in the year Gandhi went to England, to a round-table conference convened by Ramsay MacDonald's Labour Government. The conference did not achieve much, however, and the British went ahead with their own ponderous constitutional plans for India. The Mahatma, though, made a profound impression upon the kindly British public, who never forgot him. The publicity was enormous. One day he was toothlessly smiling as the women of a Lancashire textile factory gave him three cheers in their flowered pinafores. Next day he was bartering quips with London street-urchins—"Hey, Gandhi, where's your trousers?"

He had tea with King George V and Queen Mary at Buckingham Palace. The King took the occasion to "warn" the Mahatma that civil disobedience was a "hopeless and stupid policy", and Gandhi must put a stop to it. "Remember, Mr Gandhi, I can't have any attacks upon my Indian Empire." It probably did not occur to the King that if he was the monarch of an island kingdom off the coast of Europe, Gandhi was the almost deified prophet of a subcontinent.

The irony did not escape the Mahatma, though. When he left the palace reporters asked him if he had felt properly dressed for the occasion, in his

Gandhi travelled to the Round Table Conference in London as a deck passenger. He took with him his own goat to provide milk, and in London he chose to stay at a settlement house in the slums. He won the hearts of the British people by his simplicity and friendliness. Everywhere he went people flocked to catch a glimpse of him, as when he arrived in Canning Town to meet film star, Charlie Chaplin, as shown here.

No man in recent times has so captured and embodied the spirit of a country as Mahatma Gandhi, as he came to be known. With his loin-cloth, sandals and round spectacles, Gandhi became a familiar figure throughout the world. The epithet "Mahatma" means "great soul" and is used to describe a person of deep knowledge and love of humanity.

loincloth and sandals. "It was quite all right," he replied. "The King had enough on for both of us."

By now Gandhi was a great world figure. Letters reached him from everywhere, sometimes addressed "Gandhi, India", or even simply with his picture pasted to the envelope. Cartoonists had merely to sketch a loin-cloth and spectacles, and every reader would understand.

Gandhi's opponents, imperialism's rearguard, were men of a different calibre and carriage—decent British gentlemen, bravely grappling with the bickering, sectarian rivalries and snaky intrigues of Indian politics, but lacking now the magic and mystery of success. Obsessed as they were with the day-to-day conduct of affairs, they did not often seem to grasp the grandeur of the historical processes in which they were playing a part—only Churchill sensed the scale of it all, and George V could see nothing more to the Gandhi-Irwin meetings than a social ordeal.

More profoundly, the British, whatever their public views or political convictions, instinctively hated the idea of leaving India. Well into the 1930s they argued and conferred, seeking always, if they did not always recognise it, a few more years of grandeur. Eventually, under the pressure of all the separate interests, they got as far as a new Indian Constitution, giving the Indian people for the first time a substantial share in the running of their country. This was the Government of India Act, 1935, the longest single act of legislation ever passed by the British Parliament, its purpose being to unite within a federalist India not only the Muslims and the Hindus, but also all the hundreds of princely states, each one bound by a separate treaty to the Empire. Churchill called it, with his preference for the bold and simple, "a gigantic quilt of jumbled crochet work". It was certainly elaborate, but it was a true step towards Indian self-government. If the federal government was to be essentially British still, the provincial governments would be autonomous, and Indians would be getting their first experience of parliamentary responsibility. The British applied it diligently. Elections were held, provincial governments came to office, some of the forms of democracy were for the first time introduced to the Indian people.

But it was not a solution, only a starting point. The British were generally thinking in terms of generations before India became a dominion: the Congress leaders were counting the years before she became a republic. Nehru indeed had already appointed a kind of shadow government at the centre, appointing its own ministers to the new provincial governments.

By 1935 only some five hundred Britons were left in the Indian Civil Service, and it was becoming more difficult each year to attract recruits from home. The outline of an Indian state was already becoming visible. Gandhi took a year off from politics, devoting himself to meditation and social work; Lord Irwin became Lord Halifax, and went home to be Foreign Secretary in Neville Chamberlain's Conservative Government of 1938. General Dyer, paralysed by a stroke at his home near Bristol, died uncomforted by the expressions of support he still received. "I don't want to get better," he told his daughter-in-law. "I only want to die, and to know from my Maker whether I did right or wrong."

As for Winston Churchill, when Lord Irwin urged him to bring his views on India up to date by talking to some Indians, he remained immovable. "I am quite satisfied with my views on India," he said, "and I don't want them disturbed by any bloody Indians."

CHAPTER 10

THE COLONIAL ADMINISTRATORS

THE BRITISH HAD LOST THEIR TASTE for the far-flung. Emigration declined so rapidly after the war that soon more migrants were entering the British Isles than were leaving them. The ruling establishment, however, even when government was in the hands of the Labour Party, had by no means abandoned the imperial purpose. Its members knew that the world influence of Great Britain, its wealth, its self-esteem perhaps, depended upon the possession of the Empire. Repeated attempts were made therefore to boost the imperial image.

The most lavish exercise in indoctrination was the British Empire Exhibition at Wembley in 1924. The biggest fair Britain had ever known, this was a vast advertisement, inspiring to some, laughable to others, innocently entertaining to the vast majority, for the principles, practice and above all continuation of Empire.

Wembley in those days was a suburb on the edge of the countryside, at the end of the London underground railway. The exhibition made it famous, for to its two hundred and twenty acres of pavilion and display ground there came, during its one hundred and fifty days' opening, twenty-seven million people. It was mounted with the maximum publicity throughout the Empire—the very first broadcast in Johannesburg was an organ recital to raise funds for it. Everything that was imperial was packed into its fifteen miles of streets. There was a great stadium, to signify sportingness. There was a Palace of Engineering, the largest concrete building in the world, to illustrate invention. There was a statue of the Prince of Wales made of Canadian butter. There was a reproduction of Niagara Falls, which, being on the Canadian-American frontier, were at least half-imperial, and a reconstruction of the tomb of Tutankhamun, who, since he had been

This photograph shows the extent of the magnificent British Empire Exhibition at Wembley in 1924. The sports stadium, which is still standing, can be seen on the skyline.

YES.WE HAVE NO BANANAS

NO TINNED
SALMON
NO CURRANTS
NO APPLES
NO LIME JUICE
NO HONEY
NO TOBACCO
NO SUGAR
NO TEA —

BUT WE HAVE
MORE TAXATION TO-DAY
STOP TAXING FOOD
VOTE
LABOUR

This electoral poster for the Labour Party is a satirical adaptation of a popular song and shows Stanley Baldwin, the Conservative leader, as a grocer.

disinterred by Lord Carnarvon, was at least posthumously British. The whole arena was fluttered over by a perpetual cloud of Union Jacks, and at night it was "floodlit", as a recent Americanism had it; while round and round the entire exhibition, night and day, there trundled on elevated tracks, like a figure of the imperial momentum, its private railroad line, the Never-Stop Railway.

The show was opened imperially, too, by the King himself, his speech being "broadcasted" into a million homes by the transmitters of the British Broadcasting Company, and turned into a gramophone record that same afternoon by His Master's Voice. Many of the surviving imperialists helped. Kipling named the exhibition streets—Drake's Way, Dominion Way, and running grandly down a slight hill through the centre of the great display, Empire Way itself, with the Empire Stadium standing Romanly at the end of it. Edward Elgar, Master of the King's Musick, conducted the massed choirs at the opening ceremony on St George's Day, and they sang his great hymn, almost an alternative national anthem, "Land of Hope and Glory". Edwin Lutyens, the architect of the viceroy's palace at New Delhi, designed the Queen's Doll's House, which was probably the most popular exhibit in the entire show. The exhibition cost four million pounds, but much of the cash was provided by commerce and industry (and it lost one and a half million pounds in the end).

There can hardly have been a soul in the kingdom who did not know about the British Empire Exhibition, and the lion rampant which was its symbol became part of the nation's visual currency. Even so, many people saw something flaccid, even ludicrous, to this self-conscious projection of the imperial theme. The intellectuals of Hampstead, by now almost unanimously anti-imperialist, disapproved of it on principle, and some of them formed a society called WGTW—the Won't-Go-To-Wembleys.

The millions who did go often went for the wrong reasons, paying altogether too little attention to the New Zealand dairy products, and altogether too much to the amusement park, the dance hall and Joe Lyons' gigantic grill room. "I've brought you here to see the wonders of the Empire," says Father in Noel Coward's *This Happy Breed*, "and all you want to do is go to the Dodgems."

The middle-aged and the governing classes might care about the British Empire: the young and the working people did not. There were other sources of excitement. There was Hollywood, for instance. Hollywood easily out-dazzled the fading splendours of the pro-consuls and the Empire-builders, and through its illusory window people glimpsed new worlds more compelling, more voluptuous than ever the Raj had been.

Thick and fast came rival historical movements, too, which seemed to make the existence of Empire more than ever peripheral to English life. The rise of the Labour Movement had nothing to do with Empire. Empire did not save the British people from the Great Depression or the General Strike. Empire contributed nothing to the new functional architecture, the new abstract art, the social experiments that were gradually changing the form of English society.

Opposition to Empire was not yet a political platform, not even among the Socialists, but it was a temper of thought growing ever more fashionable among the British middle classes, and was allied with pacifism, internationalism and a woolly sort of Marxism. Among students it was the contemporary orthodoxy—"This House", as the Oxford Union blandly voted in 1933, "will on no account fight for King and Country." Kipling found himself reviled by the trendier critics; "Land of Hope and Glory" no longer seemed to sing the majesty and beneficence of Empire, only its vainglory.

There was a reaction then against all things Victorian, and this inevitably rebounded against that ultimate Victorianism, the British Empire. The social structure of the nation was slowly changing, the landed classes were giving ground to the up-and-coming bourgeoisie, and so the hold of Empire weakened too, for it took loyalty, consistency, discipline to rule a quarter of the world.

Most damagingly of all, the imperialness of Great Britain was now more often treated frivolously. It became rather funny.

In the field, some of the imperialists, too, especially the younger men, shared the new national attitudes. To some of them it was now apparent that the British Empire was not eternal after all, that parts of it indeed might not outlast themselves.

One senses consequently a new modesty in their approach, a new frankness with their literate subjects. Public education had never been a forte of the British Empire, which had frequently left the task to missionaries and private enterprise, but even so an educated subject class had emerged in several parts of the Empire. In India the western-style universities, established in the previous century, had by now produced thousands of men with western manners and ideas, and Indians vastly outnumbered Britons in all but the highest ranks of the administration. In Africa there was a sizeable class of educated blacks, mostly mission-trained, and many young men were now going for further education in England. In the new provinces of the Middle East there existed already an urbane and sophisticated intelligentsia, rooted in the Islamic culture, and as the years went by many more young men there, too, absorbed western ways and values, until the anglicised subject of Empire, with his upper-class English accent, his freedom with English literary quotations, his acquaintance with the Wars of the Roses, became almost a generic figure, whatever his own language, origin or religion, from Sierra Leone to Calcutta.

All this meant a modification of the aloofness of the imperialists. India was lost, anyway, and the imperialists were more concerned with the Crown Colonies, once poor relations of Empire.

The colonial administrative service offered more coveted careers than India. Some colonies chose men by competitive examination, but most recruits were selected by patronage. Officially the patron was the Colonial Secretary: unofficially, throughout the 1920s, it was one of his private secretaries, Major Ralph Furse, and it was Furse more than any other who set the tone of the imperial services in the postwar years.

The son of a crippled agnostic—"he taught me to ride a horse, to tell the truth, to love my country and to honour soldiers"—Furse was a member of Pop, the ruling society of Eton, and he remained a very responsible schoolboy all his life. Though he had an unexpected passion for ballet, he stood for manly values; during his service on the western front he took a cold bath every morning, often in the open air. Furse was not a brilliant man, but he had many of the traditional qualities of the Englishman: courage, patience, fitness, sympathy, good humour.

For thirty-eight years this man chose the rulers of the colonial Empire.

THE GENERAL STRIKE

Britain's only general strike lasted for just nine days, between May 3 and May 12, 1926. It was not planned in advance, and in fact many people not directly concerned with its outcome treated it as a kind of unusual holiday.

The origins of the strike lay with a coal industry troubled by steadily falling markets and the subject of public inquiries since 1919. A subsidy to coal miners was withdrawn on April 30, together with a temporary wage agreement. Refusing to accept this, the miners persuaded other trade unionists to support them in a strike.

The situation worsened when printers' chapels at the *Daily Mail* refused to handle an editorial which they believed was an invitation to strike-breaking. But even then it was only after the Prime Minister, Stanley Baldwin, had refused to discuss the matter with leaders of the Trades Union Congress that the Labour movement was drawn into a sympathetic general strike which few of them really wanted.

There was little violence during the strike. Enthusiastic middle-class volunteers, backed by Churchill, maintained essential services. Emergency plans worked. Even so, more than three million trade unionists stayed out until their leaders called off the strike on May 12. Only the miners persisted in their strike action.

Disillusioned and angry, they continued their conflict, suffering increasing hardship for another six months. The T.U.C. had secured no pledges as to their future, and there was much talk of betrayal, particularly from the secretary of the Miners' Federation, the effervescent A.J. Cook.

In the end, Baldwin proved conciliatory, but the scars of the strike were to linger, and in 1927 the Trade Disputes and Trade Union Act was passed making all sympathetic strikes illegal and restricting the political use of trade-union funds.

ESSENTIAL SERVICES *were maintained by the armed forces. The photograph above shows a convoy of food lorries being escorted by an armoured car through London's East End. Although the strikers had always guaranteed the free passage of foodstuffs, this promise was hard to fulfil when the docks and railways were not working, and when there was no electricity supplied to people's homes. Sailors (below) manned Neasden power station. Many services were run by volunteers, most of whom were badly informed about the very real grievances underlying the strike. The miners and the T.U.C. had few means of publicising their case, and they were badly organised for the strike when it came.*

VOLUNTEERS *flocked to take the place of those who had gone on strike. The middle classes left their businesses to register for work while hundreds of undergraduates ran the London buses (above), sometimes with the driver's cabin encased in wire netting.*

ECONOMIC BOOM, THEN SLUMP *and unemployment, followed the Great War. At first business prospered, but people could not afford to buy all that was being produced. Old industries faced slackened demand and were unable fully to modernise, while Britain's return to the gold standard in 1925 added to the burdens placed on exporters. The dramatic climax came not in London but in New York where the Wall Street crash of prices on the New York Stock Exchange, on October 23, 1929, had effects which were felt throughout the* world. *In the photograph above crowds of stockbrokers can be seen thronging the London Stock Exchange after hearing the news. A collapse of trade and industry followed the crash, with unemployment rising sharply, and while there was some recovery in the later 1930s, unemployment remained high. Some of the unemployed took part in hunger marches to the capital. The photograph below shows the Jarrow Marchers passing through the village of Lavendon, near Bedford, on their way to London in October 1936.*

THE MINERS' LEADER, A. J. Cook, *(above) addresses a meeting in Trafalgar Square during the strike. His slogan, "Not a penny off the pay, not a minute on the day", arose from the colliery owners' decision to reduce wages and lengthen working hours.*

He worked like a mole, he said, burrowing, tunnelling, establishing private contacts with headmasters and university tutors, so that likely men were sometimes unwittingly shunted, by one means or another, along the corridors of the establishment to his office in Westminster. A new genre of imperial service had come into being during the past half-century, since the acquisition of Britain's vast African empire. Those ragbag black territories, it was thought, strewn across a continent without culture, without history, did not require intellectuals, but all-round men of practical skills. The men they needed, said Frederick Lugard, Governor of Nigeria, were plain English gentlemen, "with an almost passionate conception of fair play, of protection of the weak, and of playing the game."

Furse had got a third at Oxford, and it was the game man with the third-class degree that he favoured for the Empire. He recruited thousands, most of them ex-servicemen, most of them public-school boys. For the most part the new recruits had no lofty sense of mission. They generally took the job because it offered them honourable responsibilities, excused them the drab British grindstone, sounded fun and promised a pension. They were very decent men. "Never since the heroic days of Greece has the world had such a sweet, just, boyish master," wrote the American philosopher George Santayana, in one of the most widely quoted of imperial compliments.

Furse's men were, without doubt, the *nicest* rulers the Empire ever sent abroad, but they were not the strongest. They saw the other side too generously, and if it ever came to My Empire Right or Wrong, one did not need to be a medicine man to prophesy their resignation.

The imperialists were undismayed. George V combined imperial duty with kingly pleasure by going several times to *Rose Marie*, Rudolf Friml's smash musical about the Royal Canadian Mounted Police, and by planting an Empire Plantation of trees in Windsor Great Park, each tree representing one of his colonies.

A steady stream of imperial propaganda still emerged from the London publishers: books decorated with the crests of dominions and colonies, with chapter headings like "The Thread That Binds our Race", and with maps to illustrate the variety of minerals within the British Commonwealth. Schoolchildren from Eton to Hackney Primary got a half-holiday on Empire Day. Boy Scouts still wore wide-brimmed hats derived from the Boer War, crouched round campfires murmuring incantations from Kipling, and shared a motto, "Be Prepared", with the South African police. At Oxford the Rhodes Scholarships, financed by Cecil Rhodes's will, supposedly indoctrinated a constant stream of young colonials in proper modes and values.

There survived, too, many institutions from the turn of the century: the British Empire League and the Victoria League, and the Patriotic League of Britons Overseas. Most insistently of all, there was the Conservative popular press, which had built its original fortunes upon jingoism, and remained shrilly faithful to the theme. The *Daily Express* in particular, owned by the Canadian Presbyterian Lord Beaverbrook, born Max Aitken of New Brunswick, made an Empire Crusade the basis of its editorial policies. Beaverbrook's panacea was fiscal. He wanted to turn the British Empire into a self-contained Free Trade area, surrounding it with tariff walls against the world outside, but allowing absolute freedom of commerce among its constituent parts. The British were, with progressively less conviction, still wedded to the idea of universal free trade which had made

Robert Baden-Powell founded the Boy Scouts in 1908 after the publication of his booklet, Scouting for Boys, *which described the advantages of being a Scout. The Scout movement had no class or religious barriers and each boy was given an equal opportunity to develop his own skills, sporting prowess and character, following the Scout motto "Be Prepared".*

them a rich country a century before: even in 1930, eighty-three per cent of imports paid no duty at all. Beaverbrook's plan, which after all honoured *half* the old dogma, was accordingly very persuasive. It would not only restore the prosperity of the British, it was argued, it would give the Empire new meaning, and perhaps make of it at last the economic super-power Joe Chamberlain had imagined. Immensely vigorous, with powerful friends and heaps of money, Beaverbrook founded his own political party, the United Empire Party, and plugged his theme until the phrase Empire Free Trade, if not its meaning, was familiar in every British household, and the impish face of the millionaire became the face of contemporary imperialism.

It never happened. Economically the Empire did help to cushion Britain's decline, and trade with the dominions and colonies increased in the postwar decades. Seventy per cent of New Zealand's exports, more than half Australia's and South Africa's, came to Britain. The dominions welcomed the idea of limited trade preferences—in particular they wanted Britain to put higher duties on foreign food and raw materials, lower ones on Empire produce, and in 1932 this came about. Anything so grandiose as Beaverbrook's ideal, though, which really went far beyond economics, smacked to them of imperial centralism, relegating them to perpetually second-class status—how could their own infant industries, they reasoned, compete with Britain's long-established factories?

Still the Empire proceeded, by the force of old momentum. Most Britons still considered it, all in all, a force for good in the world, and only a minority could conceive of its actually coming to an end. The fleets and armies were still disposed around the world. There were still colonial wars—against Arabs and Jews in Palestine, against Yemenis in Arabia, against Afghans, against Iraqis, against the Mad Mullah of Somaliland, and a Burmese monk who claimed to be able to fly.

The system of treaties by which the British pacified the refractory chieftains of the Hadramaut in Southern Arabia was perhaps the last true expression of High Empire. It imposed universal peace upon a part of the world where incessant warfare between neighbours had been for centuries part of everyday life. The truce was conceived and concluded by a single British political officer and his wife.

Posted by the Colonial Office to Arabia in 1934, when they were in the field Harold Ingrams and his wife Doreen lived as the Arabs lived. They wore Arab clothes, they ate Arab food, they laughed at Arab jokes, they responded to Arab poverty. No conduct could be more excruciating to your conventional Empire-builder, but the Ingrams really meant it, and by these means, in 1937, they brought peace to the Hadramaut.

Some one thousand three hundred leaders signed the truce, from the rulers of powerful tribes to the brawl-leaders of village factions, and life in the Hadramaut was transformed by it. "Shut up," children were alleged to tell each other, "or I'll tell Ingrams." And so impressed were the chiefs by the potency of the peacemaker that several of them pressed their daughters upon him in marriage. ("He doesn't want your dirty daughters", was the official interpreter's habitual frank response.)

The origins of Ingram's Peace were soon to be forgotten, but still this was, in the afternoon of Empire, an achievement worthy of its noonday—worthier, perhaps, for it was done without bluster, with only a minimum of punitive bombardment, by a single servant of Empire and his wife.

Lord Beaverbrook (1879-1964) was a millionaire financier by the age of twenty-six, and used his wealth to become a press baron. He bought the Daily Express *and founded the* Sunday Express *in 1918, and used his newspapers to express his views on strong imperial ties and free trade within the Empire. In the Second World War he played a significant role as Churchill's Minister of Aircraft Production. This portrait, by W.R. Sickert, is in the National Portrait Gallery.*

CHAPTER 11

BRITISH INVENTION

THE GREAT GOVERNMENT MIGHT STILL be great in the fastness of South
Arabia; elsewhere its command of events was less than absolute, and within the white Empire its position was now distinctly
equivocal, nobody quite understanding how it worked. Britishness itself
had become a debatable condition. In Victoria's day it had been embodied
above all in the monarchy, the distant, unfailing source of power and
justice. The Crown was the one abstraction that could unite the loyalties
of disrespectful Australians, half-American Canadians and distinctly un-
English South Africans.

Now all had changed. The monarchy was still immensely popular in
most parts of the Empire, even in India, even in Ireland, but its mystique
had faded. Britishness needed more than a George V to keep it whole, and
by now even the most British of the overseas Britons were acquiring
identities of their own. The Britishness was wearing off. Even their languages
were diverging fast. The Canadians now sounded much more American than
English. The Australian language had acquired a truly noble robustness, its
original Cockney long since matured into something altogether antipodean.
If it sounded harsh in women's voices, it could sound glorious in men's.

It was the Australians, indeed, who convinced the world that colonials
were no longer so many English alter egos. The Australian relationship
with England had been sweet-sour from the start. Born out of convict
transportation, at once envious and resentful of England, sentimental about
blood-ties, self-consciously egalitarian, Australia by the 1920s had evolved
a national character more pungent and aggressive than that of many much
older states. The Australians were a belligerent people, intensely proud of
their record in the Great War, and perhaps expansionist too—in 1933 they
claimed a third of Antarctica as Australian territory. At the same time they
were profoundly anti-heroic. Suffering as they did from an ancient sense of
inferiority, they coped with their own self-doubts partly by virile postures,
but partly by a wonderfully dry and self-deprecatory philosophy of life.

So the dominions diverged, and there was no pretending either that the
scattered peoples of the British stock were always in harmony. British
governments at home were at best bored, at worst infuriated by the average
dominion leaders, and often treated them disgracefully, ignoring them in
their economic and strategic calculations, imperiously demanding their
compliance when needed, and sometimes being downright rude. The only
colonial leaders they really welcomed to their homes and councils were the
cultivated statesmen of Afrikanerdom, and as the legends of Anzac and the
Great War faded so the dominions became ever mistier, ever less interesting
in the public mind.

The colonials themselves still viewed the British with an astonishing
ambivalence. On the one hand they possessed a profound sentimental
loyalty to the *idea* of England, constituting even in the 1920s a powerful
political energy. The colonials were stirred by England, responding almost
despite themselves to its age, its grandeur, its continuity, even its damp and

misty climate. At the same time they were by and large more realistic about the state of the Empire than were the policy-makers of the mother country. Even the New Zealanders, the most conformist of the colonials, complied with British wishes chiefly because they were, economically, hardly more than an agricultural annexe of the United Kingdom. The Australians were often at loggerheads with British governments, while the Canadians doggedly pursued, year after year, their object of absolute independence within the Empire, formal and actual.

Their interests differed widely. On race, for instance, while the British fitfully honoured the criterion of equal rights for all civilized men, the Australians and New Zealanders were concerned to keep all Asiatics out of their territories, the Canadians had allowed no Asian immigrants since the turn of the century, and the South Africans denied their vast black majority any rights of citizenship whatever. On defence, while the British were now concentrating their strength in the Middle East, the Australians and New Zealanders saw Singapore as the most important imperial base, while the Canadians looked most anxiously to the Pacific. On economics the British were eager to balance their own industries with the raw materials of the Empire; the dominions were only anxious to industrialise themselves.

The Imperial Conferences which met in London, and once in Ottawa, regularly during the postwar years, though they were commemorated always in dutiful group portraits, wing-collared and pinstriped, were in fact full of acrimony and exasperation, some of their participants very much disliking one another.

No wonder King George V was often perturbed about his Empire. He had visited all its major territories, the first British monarch to travel widely in his dominions, and he doubtless looked back nostalgically to the heyday of Empire—to his Indian visit of 1906, perhaps, when fourteen thousand people with six thousand elephants escorted him on *shikari*, when a road fifty miles long was built to connect his two hunting camps, and when in a single day he and his party shot thirty-nine tigers, eighteen lions and five Himalayan bears.

He was concerned to restore some of that old splendour, and to preserve the strength of the Crown Imperial. A proposal that his four princely sons should become governors-general of Canada, Australia, New Zealand and South Africa, came to nothing; but instead the heir to his throne, Edward, Prince of Wales, went on a series of imperial tours. One of these took him to India, where he was boycotted by Gandhi and frequently booed by disloyal demonstrators. The most successful visits were to the white dominions; and the flavour of these tours, the picture they offered of the young prince, freed from the restraints of Windsor and Balmoral, almost becoming a colonial himself, is preserved in many books and thousands of photographs, piquantly reflecting the spirit of the colonial Empire during the years of transience.

This is hardly a king-to-be visiting his future dominions, this is a young man seeing a new world. Gone is the stately progress of the viceroys, calm beneath their panoplies, or the grave composure of George V himself, when he sat with his wife as in marble on the coronation dais at Delhi. The Prince of Wales, heir to all this, wore his shirt without a tie, his trousers short, his cap a'tilt, his heart on his sleeve. It is true that he sailed in the battle cruisers *Repulse* and *Renown*, at thirty-two thousand tons among

King George V, visiting the workers of a Scottish steel company in 1917. It was during the First World War that George V changed the name of the royal house from the Germanic "Hanover" to the quintessentially English "Windsor".

Edward, Prince of Wales, young, dashing and debonair, at the Calcutta races in 1922. The unconventional Prince toured his Empire with a new, refreshingly informal style.

the great warships of the world. It is true, of course, that he was greeted with pomp and eulogy, was fawned upon everywhere, flattered at garden parties, blessed by manly bishops in surplices and war ribbons, saluted by old soldiers with crutches and eye-patches. When Edward's battle cruiser passed through the Suez Canal, biplanes of the Royal Air Force escorted her to the Red Sea, and Indian troops of the Canal Zone base cheered her on her way. When she put in at Aden a huge banner greeted her beneath massed Union Jacks: "Tell Daddy we are happy under British rule". The Maharajah of Bharatpur came to meet him in an open landau which was drawn by eight elephants. The King of Nepal gave him a rhinoceros, a baby elephant, two bears, a leopard, a black panther, an iguana, a python, several partridges and two Tibetan mastiffs.

All visiting royalty met these people, unveiled these monuments, accepted these gifts. The Prince of Wales's tours were different, though, for he represented in his own person an almost reckless break with tradition. He seemed to be visiting his future subjects not in a spirit of authority, but almost with fellow-feeling, and so took to life on the Canadian prairies, for example, that he bought himself a ranch in Alberta. The white colonials loved him, and many of the coloured subjects too, for he seemed a foretaste of emancipation, a young, fresh embodiment of an ancient legend.

His father was less impressed. Like the Wembley Exhibition, the royal tours seemed to please people for quite the wrong reasons, and the King was much disturbed by the newspaper cuttings which reached him from his far dominions. Riding bucking broncos indeed! Foxtrotting in the small hours! This was not the spirit that made the British Empire—or rather, His Majesty perhaps corrected himself, for in point of fact it was exactly that, it was not the spirit that would keep the Empire British!

New realities must be recognised. The white Empire was not exactly an Empire any more, but rather a group of independent powers of more or less common origin and generally compatible policies. In 1930, therefore, the assembled prime ministers approved a new device of the pragmatic

British political imagination, a Commonwealth of Nations. Though the name was old, the idea was said to have been perfected by Arthur Balfour, and it was full of sophistry. Britain and her white dominions, it was decreed, were "autonomous communities within the British Empire, equal in status, in no way subordinate to each other in any aspect of their domestic or foreign affairs, though united by a common allegiance to the Crown, and freely associated as members of the British Commonwealth of Nations."

This proposition aroused long and intricate discussion. Was the Crown indivisible, or could one man be King of England and King of Canada? Could the King give his signature to opposing Acts from two different countries? Could he indeed be at war with himself? Since nobody was subordinate, could anybody be expelled? King George was much disturbed by it—"I cannot look into the future," he wrote, straining his grammar to the limit, "without feeling no little anxiety about the continued unity of the Empire." The people of New Zealand felt the same, and did not subscribe to the new Statute of Westminster until 1947.

In the future, according to the statute, the governors-general, the King's representatives in each dominion, would no longer be nominated by the British Government, in future they would be chosen by the dominions and would have no contact with the Government in London, only with the King. Now dominion parliaments could pass legislation in direct contradiction to Westminster. Even the grand machinery of the imperial law, all its multifarious courts culminating in the Judicial Committee of the Privy Council in London, was now shorn of its certainty: the dominions were free to withdraw from it when they wished. A man could still say he was a British citizen, but he could no longer look with certainty to those remote and impartial justices in Westminster: British citizen my foot, a judge might soon say in Bloemfontein or Montreal, and there would be an end to it.

The British had tried hard, since the death of Queen Victoria, to give substance to a mystery. Now they gave mystery to a substance. The British Commonwealth of Nations was cloudy from the start. At the time many people claimed to see the Statute of Westminster as a final charter of imperial development, and Balfour, once Prime Minister himself, described it as "the most novel and greatest experiment in Empire-building the world has ever seen." But it was really an admission of failure.

The Empire would never be a super-power now. Its Roman aspirations were abandoned. As the Empire's diverse parts matured into independent nations, first the dominions, then India, then inevitably the great African and Asian colonies, so the British Empire would cease to be among the prime movers of the world, and Britishness would hive off once and for all in separate and often conflicting patriotisms.

It soon began to happen. Within a couple of years the Irish Free State took advantage of the Statute of Westminster to abolish the oath of allegiance to the Crown. Within four years Catholic Ireland was proclaimed "a sovereign, independent and democratic State", and before long it was a republic and not a member of the Commonwealth at all. The British, though dismayed by so bold and contrary an interpretation of their vision, expected no better of the Irish, and had no choice but to acquiesce. But, reluctant to admit that even an Irishman could opt out of being British altogether, they decided to classify citizens of the new republic not as un-British exactly, but as "non-foreign".

On October 4, 1930, when the imperial prime ministers were about to assemble in London to conclude the Statute of Westminster, when Gandhi was about to celebrate his sixty-first birthday in prison at Poona, when the chiefs were still squabbling in the Hadramaut, there took off from its mooring mast at Cardington in Bedfordshire the airship R101, the largest, most expensive flying machine ever built in Britain. Ever since the end of the Great War the imperialists had been planning to link the components of the Empire by the thrilling new medium of the air. The idea that the King-Emperor might be in London one week, Canberra, Bombay or Vancouver the next, offered altogether new imperial prospects.

Fortunately there was to hand an invention awesome enough to match the grandeur of the conception. Few people thought the aeroplane could ever master the prodigious distances of the Empire, but the airship, the rigid dirigible, certainly could. The Germans had done marvellous things with their Zeppelins during the war, sending one as far as Khartoum in an attempt to supply the German forces in East Africa, while the British R34, modelled on the German pattern, had become in 1919 the first aircraft of any kind to make a double crossing of the Atlantic. The airship could be at once the means and the symbol of the imperial revival. In 1924 Ramsay MacDonald's Labour Government officially adopted an Imperial Airship scheme, meant to provide a regular passenger and mail service along the principal routes of the Empire.

The R101, which was built by the Government itself, was to inaugurate the service with a return flight to Karachi, in India, via Egypt. Its construction had been one of the great national efforts of the postwar years. The airship sheds at Cardington, the Royal Airship Works, were the biggest buildings in the British Empire, and the design team, it was said, had "lived and worked like a religious community intent upon their single purpose". So proud of the project was Brigadier General C. B. Thomson, Secretary of State for Air, that when he was elevated to the peerage in 1924 he took the name of the airship works for his title, and became Lord Thomson of Cardington. The airship took six years to build, and was full of new all-British ideas—diesel engines instead of the usual petrol, steel framework instead of aluminium, new kinds of valves, harnesses for the gasbags, fabric dope. She was propelled by five engines and was designed to carry one hundred passengers at speeds of up to seventy miles an hour.

"She", because everything about her was consciously shiplike, as though the Empire Airships were in direct line of succession to the P & O. Passengers bunked two to a cabin, with portholes to heighten the nautical effect, and the crew wore neo-naval uniforms (though most of them were in the RAF). There was a promenade deck with deckchairs. The passengers' lounge, embellished with gilded pillars and potted palms in the Cunard style, was pictured in artists' impressions at the height of a tea dance, with young bloods and flappers waltzing among the wicker chairs, and distinguished seniors watching benignly from the sofa. The wireless transmitters were as powerful as any ocean liner's, with a range of over two hundred miles. The R101 was, so the publicity men said, one of the supreme examples of British inventiveness.

On the ground the arrangements for the airship scheme were just as elaborate. Immensely expensive mooring masts were erected at Ismailia, halfway to India, and Karachi, where another gigantic hangar was also

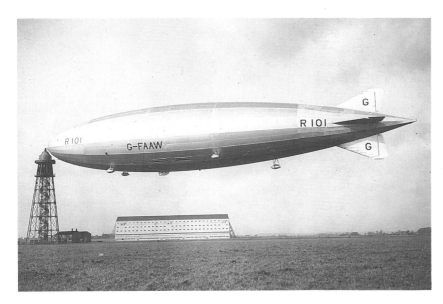

The R101 majestically swings from her mooring mast at Cardington before her ill-starred maiden voyage on October 4, 1930. The R101 was the largest commercial airship built in Britain. She was to be the prototype for a fleet that would carry passengers to every part of the British Empire in style and comfort.

built, and across the Empire other sites were prepared. Work started on a base at Montreal, terminals were surveyed at Durban and Perth, in Ceylon and on the island of St Helena in the South Atlantic.

It was Lord Thomson who conceived the Imperial Conference of October 1930 as a fitting moment for the launching of the project. How grand, thought Lord Thomson, if the biggest airship on earth could make its maiden voyage along the most imperial of all the imperial routes, to bring the Secretary of State for Air himself direct from the Empire's frontiers to the conference chamber in Westminster! So it was arranged. Lord Thomson would fly with the R101 to Karachi and back, his return to coincide with the start of the conference. On the way the airship would land beside the Suez Canal, the lifeline of Empire, for a celebratory banquet.

Everything was hastened to this end, and by October 4 the airship was ready for the flight. The publicity was terrific. The Prince of Wales drove up to Cardington to inspect progress, and the papers were full of the excitement of the project. "As I set out on this journey," said Lord Thomson at a farewell ceremony, "I am reminded of the great hopes that have been pinned on this magnificent ship of the air as a link with the furthest corners of that everlasting entity, the British Empire. . . ."

It was a grey cold night, but at Cardington the vast silver shape of the R101 was ablaze with light. Searchlights played upon it, and there were rows of bright lights from the passenger quarters and the control cabins, and green and red navigation lights on the fins. The headlights of hundreds of cars, too, illuminated the scene, so that from a distance the great hulks of the airship sheds, the resplendent silver of the airship at its tower, gave it an air of fantasy, or nightmare.

Fifty-four men boarded the R101 that evening—twelve passengers, all officials except Lord Thomson's valet, forty-two crew, from Flight Lieutenant Irwin, the captain, to J. Magginson, the nineteen-year-old cabin boy. By six thirty they were all aboard, and by six forty-five the airship's engines, spluttering one by one into life, were thundering at the mooring mast. Slowly the ship backed away, as the crowd sang "Land of Hope and Glory" below, and the cars around the airfield flashed their lights in farewell. Rain began to fall, and a gusty wind blew across Cardington as the R101 flew heavily away to the south.

By nine o'clock the R101 was crossing the coast near Hastings, and Irwin was preparing his route down the line of the Rhône. The passengers went to bed and the radio operator sent a reassuring message home. "After an excellent supper," it said, "our distinguished passengers smoked a final cigar, and having sighted the French coast, have gone to bed after the excitement of their leave-taking. The crew have settled down to watch-keeping routine."

The watch-keeping was not all routine, though. The weather worsened, strong winds blew up, the great airship rolled and pitched, and was sometimes blown sideways. From time to time the crew inspected the gasbags, clambering around the ropewalks that crisscrossed the interior of the airship's envelope. Everything in there creaked, groaned and hissed as they worked, the gasbags themselves creepily squelched themselves into new shapes as the pressure shifted inside them, and the metal chains that supported them clanked and chafed in the darkness. The night outside was very black. Only occasionally did a dim light show from the ground below, through the drifting cloud and rain.

Soon after two in the morning the radio operator exchanged messages with the airport at Le Bourget, and confirmed that the R101 was approaching Beauvais, a market city some eighty miles north of Paris. She was flying very slowly now. Soon afterwards an engineer in one of the nacelles, slung beneath the body of the airship, looked through his window in the darkness and saw an astonishing thing. Protruding grotesquely out of the rainy mist, only a few yards from the airship, was the roof of a building, a massive grey object stuck about with pinnacles and queer gargoyles. For a few seconds he saw it there, and then it was lost again in the rain and the dark. It was the roof of Beauvais Cathedral.

The engineer scarcely had time to tell his companion when the airship gave an abrupt lurch, dropped, recovered, dropped again, and with a colossal judder was suddenly still. There was a pause; then suddenly a tremendous breaking roar, like the lighting of a million bonfires, a frenzied ringing of bells, a clatter of feet along the companionways, and the shout of an officer somewhere—"We're down, lads! We're down!" In a moment the R101 was a mass of flames. She had covered some three hundred miles of the three thousand six hundred and fifty-two-mile route to India.

The R101 had hit a low hill on the outskirts of Beauvais, and was destroyed in a matter of minutes. All but six of her complement died. Lord Thomson, Flight Lieutenant Irwin, Sir Sefton Brancker, the Director of Civil Aviation, the representatives of the Indian and Australian governments, all died. So absolute was the catastrophe that the Empire Airship Scheme was abandoned at once, and the Empire never did see the grand spectacle of the dirigibles dipping their ensigns in the empyrean. It was an immense blow to British pride. Worse still, it was a revelation of British failure in that most basic of imperial elements, technique.

The story of the R101 was seen by the contemporary public as a heroic tragedy. Behind the tragedy, though, there lay a record of ineptitude. The building of the R101 had looked an imperial enterprise in the great tradition; in fact it possessed little of the daring confidence and commonsense that

Officials investigating the twisted wreckage of the R101, which crashed in a forest at Beauvais, near Paris. The debris was scattered over several acres. Forty-eight people lost their lives.

had characterised British technology in the nineteenth century. Compromise, amateurism, plagued the work from the start. The airship's engines were too heavy and too weak, the new valves were found to be more ingenious than practical, even the galley with its electric stove proved inadequate—a party of MPs lunched on board the airship at Cardington once, but the meal they had was surreptitiously prepared by RAF cooks on the ground.

As one fault after another was hastily mended, the inexorable light of publicity continued to shine upon the airship. "They're rushing us," Irwin had told visitors to Cardington in the week before the flight. "We're not ready, we're just not ready. . . ."

When the designers discovered that the airship's payload would be no more than thirty-five tons, instead of the seventy-seven tons predicted, they simply cut the airship in half, inserted an extra gasbag, and joined it together again. It was only two days after the completion of this major surgery that the R101 set off on her maiden voyage. She had made only eight flights, all in good weather, and she had flown only once since the insertion of the new gasbag which had increased her length by a quarter. Her engines had never been tested at high speeds.

The Royal Commission of Inquiry did its best to minimise the disaster, but the crash of the R101 was an indicator of the British condition. Technique had been the truest foundation of British power: Britain had been the workshop of the world, and the British Empire had eagerly seized upon each new product of technology—even the tiny colony of Mauritius had got its first electric street-lights in 1893.

Since the Great War, though, the nation seemed to have lost its touch. The world was moving out of the age of steam, and the British, who had been masters of the greased piston and the mighty boiler, did not adapt easily to the age of the automobile and the aircraft. Some people, in a superstitious way, traced the British technical decline to the loss of the *Titanic* in 1912. Economists argued that the nation had over-extended itself once and for all in the war, by becoming at the same time a naval, an industrial and a continental military power, and it was true that since 1918 British industry had consistently lost ground against its foreign competitors.

The British were paying for their old success. The overwhelming superiority of their Victorian technique had made them complacent. Even now, Britain was still geared to a rural hierarchy, in which country landowners were pre-eminent. Industry was hardly for English gentlemen. Not many of the country's best brains graduated from Oxford and Cambridge into industry, and there were no equivalents in England to the great technical universities of Germany and Switzerland. British industry stuck, by and large, to what it knew best: and what it knew best was the technology of the preceding century, when "Made in England" had been the universal hallmark of quality.

It was not that invention had failed. British scientists remained remarkably resourceful, and there was no shortage of striking prototypes: in the 1930s Britain held the world speed-records on land, on sea and in the air. But the nation seemed to lack the flair, the will or perhaps the incentive to translate ideas into solid achievement.

By and large, the imperial specialities of Victoria's day were the specialities of George V's. The great age of railroad building was over, but still here and there in the Empire the railway engineers were at work, and the lines they laid, the trains they dispatched, could still be spectacular. The most dashing of all trains were surely "The Silks", the nonstop expresses by which the Canadian Pacific Railway hurled the Chinese silk consignments from Hong Kong across Canada to the Atlantic ports and so to the London markets. The stateliest was unquestionably the white official train of the viceroy of India, twelve carriages for one man, with its quarters for aides and secretaries and servants and bodyguards, and its great crested locomotive. And the most romantic of railways, at least in conception, would have certainly been the Cape-to-Cairo line by which Cecil Rhodes had hoped to establish his British axis north and south through Africa. By the 1920s this had actually become possible. South Africa—Rhodesia—Tanganyika—Kenya—Uganda—Sudan—Egypt. Rhodes might have done it had he lived, under the Union Jack all the way. It never happened in fact, but it had its own great memorial anyway, for the centrepiece of the enterprise, the work which meant most to Rhodes himself, was the bridge by which the railway crossed the Zambezi River, on the northern frontier of Rhodesia. It had a symbolic quality about it that everyone felt. The river was one of Africa's greatest, and here, heralded across the bush by its perpetual rainbow, there fell into the great chasm the waterfall which Dr Livingstone himself had named for the Queen Empress long before. It was at Victoria Falls that Rhodes had decreed his railway should cross the Zambezi. "I should like," he observed, with his odd mixture of the banal and the poetic, "to have the spray of the water over the carriages."

The bridge was built after Rhodes's death, and it would have been much easier to cross the river a few miles upstream, where it was narrower, but his wishes were honoured, and the railway crossed the Zambezi within range of the spray. Nobody lived there then. The Africans would not go near the falls, and all round was dense bush, swamp and forest. In this place, where almost nobody could see it, one of the great imperial artifacts was erected. The gorge was three hundred and fifty feet deep, and Ralph Freeman, the chief designer, bridged it in a single steel span, at once a *tour de force* of engineering and a gesture of grand romance.

Ralph Freeman was also the designer of the greatest bridge of the 1920s,

Sydney Harbour Bridge, photographed shortly after its opening. It was designed by Ralph Freeman in the 1920s. The deep channel meant that the arch had to be built out from each side as two cantilevers. Today, views of the Sydney Harbour Bridge are enhanced by the nearby Sydney Opera House, one of the marvels of modern architecture.

the Sydney Harbour Bridge. For more than a century people had talked about bridging Sydney Harbour, to connect the original nucleus of the city with its growing suburbs on the northern shore, but the plan took time to crystallise. Not until 1921 did the well-known British firm of Dorman Long, after submitting seven alternative schemes, win a contract to build it. The bridge was a single-span steep arch structure. It was built to withstand gales of two hundred and fifty knots, and carried six lanes of roadway, four railway lines and two footpaths across a main span of one thousand six hundred and fifty feet. It was then the longest single-span bridge in the world, and the biggest arch ever made.

It was hailed, especially in Britain, as a triumph of imperial technology. It took seven years to build, and when it was finished in 1932 it really did present a striking image of Australian strength, its silhouette becoming a national symbol familiar everywhere on earth. Yet in the somewhat lumpish structure of the bridge itself, with its great white towers monumental at each end, later generations might see signs of the imperial ageing. It was a very big bridge, but it did not soar. Its function was disguised, as far as possible, in a tentative traditionalism. Its street lights were mock-lanterns. Its pylons were vaguely Egyptian in style, like something from the Wembley Exhibition, or war memorials, but they served no technical purpose, being there simply for effect. The Sydney Harbour Bridge was a true product of the imperial thirties, when the British Empire was larger than it had ever been before, but rather less tremendous.

Dams were another old British speciality, and the expertise of imperial hydrologists had been translated from British India, where thirteen per cent of all the cultivated land had been irrigated by the British, to the dependencies along the River Nile. By the 1920s hundreds of miles of canals had been cut or restored, new barrages had been built, and vast new areas opened to irrigation.

The greatest of all their works was the Aswan Dam, which was to be, after successive enlargements, the bulkiest of all the British Empire's artefacts. It stood at the head of the entire Egyptian irrigation system, for behind the dam a great reservoir extended upstream to Wadi Halfa, and out of this reserve the engineers could release water in dry periods to provide perennial irrigation all over Egypt. Imperial publicists called it the Eighth Wonder of the World, and with its immense line of dressed masonry, its massive buttresses and frothing line of sluices, set stupendously in the dun desert around the first cataract of the Nile, it did have a truly classical grandeur.

Trains, bridges and dams, then, were the traditional concerns of Empire. When it came to the internal combustion engine, and all that went with it, the approach was less sure. Most of the first cars in the Empire were foreign, French, German and American manufacturers having gained an early lead over the British. American cars dominated the Australian and Canadian markets from the start, and even in India the first car of all was French— the Maharaja of Patiala's De Dion Bouton, whose licence-plate number was O. The British built cars for the small easy roads of their own islands, and until the end of the Empire never did master the tougher imperial markets. When in the 1920s Morris Motors introduced a new model actually called the Empire they sold *four*.

THE DISCOVERY OF PENICILLIN

Alexander Fleming's historic chance observation of the behaviour of the fungus Penicillium notatum *was made in 1928, and research in Oxford by Howard Florey and Ernst Chain led to the development of the antibiotic, penicillin. This description of an early treatment in 1941 is taken from* Rise Up To Life, *Lennard Bickel's biography of Howard Florey, who shared the Nobel Prize in Physiology and Medicine in 1945 with Fleming and Chain.*

Alexander had been a burly forty-three-year-old officer in the County Constabulary before bacteria entered his system through a scratch at the side of his mouth, caused by a rose thorn. Now Alexander was fighting for his life. He was host to a primary infection by the murderous *Staphylococcus aureus*, and to a secondary infection by *Streptococcus pyogenes*—both of which were strains Florey had used in his successful mice tests.

By mid-January the bacteria had run riot. The attack was so bad that surgeons took away his right eye and then lanced the swollen mess of his left eye to relieve the pain. The infection was attacking his bones and fresh abscesses broke out. He was near to death when they took penicillin to him on February 12, 1941, four months after his admission to hospital.

The first injections of penicillin were intravenous and were repeated every few hours. Florey afterwards described the case as "forlorn", but he organised his team into a relay service so that every scrap of penicillin could be brought to the man's aid.

Each time Alexander passed urine into an attached bottle, it was unclipped and the member of the team in attendance at the bedside would cycle with it through the streets of Oxford, back to the laboratory where penicillin would be extracted for re-injection.

Inevitably with each injection they lost a part of their precious stock, as the penicillin in Alexander's urine would be little more than half the amount injected; and by the end of the third day the team had become entirely dependent on the penicillin they could extract from his urine. By the fourth day, however, the change in Alexander was remarkable. The suppurations from his head and from his eyes were drying up, and his fever was gone. With his temperature normal he had a return of appetite, and these improvements continued into the fifth day. Then his case notes show a grim entry.

"Penicillin supply exhausted. Total administered: 4·4 grammes in five days."

These words were the patient's death warrant. Though he fought to hold his ground for ten more days, he then deteriorated in condition. His lungs became suffused with fresh infection and he died on March 15, 1941.

Even so, Constable Albert Alexander did make a contribution to medical advance. He was the team's first case of recognised specific treatment against severe sepsis and he died not because penicillin had failed but because they could not supply enough.

Alexander Fleming, Professor of Bacteriology at St Mary's Hospital, London, examines bacteria through a microscope.

As to the air, the British never did establish the supremacy aloft which was so long theirs at sea. As one might expect, they were adventurous pioneers of flying. Englishmen were the first to fly an aircraft across the Atlantic, the first to fly to Australia, the first to fly over the Himalayas, the first to fly mail, and they established speed records in all directions. After the war they realised the uses of air power in imperial government, too—as early as 1931 two battalions of troops were airlifted from Egypt to a trouble spot in Iraq. But there was something laborious, even reluctant, in the application of all this initiative to the everyday business of air transport—a subconscious desire, perhaps, not to hasten the air age. Imperial Airways, the airline which did in the end launch an Empire Air Service, was born in 1924, and even then it seemed faintly anachronistic. If the splendour of steam could have been transferred to the air age, Imperial Airways would have done it; as it was, its plodding biplanes and flying-boats, nearly always slower, nearly always better upholstered than their rivals, sailed the skies with a distinctly maritime dignity, their captains talking of ports and moorings, coming aboard and going ashore, just as though they were in fact navigating the steamships of the imperial prime.

The airline was heavily subsidised, and as a carrier of the Royal Mail enjoyed semi-official privileges, punctiliously maintained by the management. If an Imperial Airways aircraft made a forced landing in imperial territory, its captain was authorised to stop any passing train and oblige it to take on the mailbags. When the airline began scheduled services to Iraq, the Iraqis were induced to dig a furrow right the way across the Iraqi desert, to guide its navigators more conveniently into Baghdad.

It was not very efficient. Its pomposity was a joke among competitors, and even the British themselves often found it too formal and officious. The imperial air routes, which looked so impressive on the maps, turned out to be, if you actually tried to fly them, less than handy. Flights were unpunctual, staging-posts were uncomfortable. A traveller to South Africa in the early 1930s had to change six times, flying in five different types of aircraft.

In 1934, the airline ordered, direct from the drawing-board, twenty-eight new flying-boats, called of course the Empire Class, and destined to set once and for all, in memory as in imagination, the tone of the imperial air services. They were still not very fast or reliable aeroplanes.

Like the R101, they tried hard to be ships. They had sleeping bunks, inhabited in the advertisements by elegant husbands in spotted silk dressing-gowns, bobbed wives in crepe de Chine. They had a smoking cabin, and a promenade deck, the chef in his galley wore a chef's hat, and the captain and his first officer, high in their cockpit above the mooring compartment, were splendid in blue, gold rings and medal ribbons. When the Empire flying-boats alighted on the Nile at Cairo or the Hooghly at Calcutta, flags proudly burst from the cockpit roof—the Blue Ensign of the Royal Mail, the crested emblem of Imperial Airways. For all the publicity, however, the British public were much more excited by the launching in 1934 of the greatest of all their Atlantic liners, the *Queen Mary*.

One innovation which did fire the British imagination was something more mysterious, something almost spiritual it seemed: wireless. It was, of course, a transforming agency for the Empire, and at one time the British had hoped to make it as much their own as undersea cable had been in the previous century. Before the Great War, Admiral Fisher had wanted to

The Queen Mary, *seen here at Southampton docks in 1936, was one of the finest liners of her generation. She won the Atlantic Blue Riband for crossing the ocean in three days, twenty hours. The Cunard Line, which owned her, sold the* Queen Mary *in 1976 and she is now anchored off Long Beach, California where she is used as a place of entertainment.*

WOMEN'S RIGHTS

DURING THE MID-VICTORIAN YEARS, as in preceding centuries, women were treated as subordinate to men. There was a double standard of morality for men and women, and there were separate spheres of work deemed appropriate for each. Large numbers of women were employed in the textile industries and far larger numbers still in domestic service, but there were many occupations from which they were completely cut off.

Single women were expected to make a life within their family circle. Married women had no rights to property, whether acquired before or after marriage, until the passing of the Married Women's Property Acts in 1870 and 1882.

Changes of attitude towards the role of women in society started when the size of families began to fall from the 1870s onwards. This trend was accentuated in the twentieth century by the increased use of birth control. Further changes were brought about by improved education, which in itself provided better work opportunities for women.

Women were still handicapped, however, as to their political rights, and there was a dramatic struggle in Edwardian Britain, much publicised in the press, to win the vote for women. The means employed in the struggle by the suffragettes were controversial, and the vote was not in fact won until after women had played an essential part in the First World War. Even then it came in two stages: for the over-thirties in 1918, and for the under-thirties, "the flappers", in 1928.

During the Second World War there were almost 500,000 women in the Armed Forces, another 200,000 in the Women's Land Army and over 300,000 in the Civil Service. Yet the fight for equal pay and promotion for women at work is still going on.

Britain has had several women on the throne but very few M.P.s and no woman Prime Minister until Margaret Thatcher was elected in 1979.

THE WOMEN'S SOCIAL AND POLITICAL UNION was formed in 1903 by Mrs Emmeline Pankhurst. She and her two gifted daughters, Christabel and Sylvia, regarded it as "unendurable to think of another generation of women wasting their lives." Their movement quickly gained support from women of all classes who were prepared to fight, with violence if necessary, for women to gain the vote. After a time, the movement divided between those called suffragists, who were non-militant, and those called suffragettes who were prepared to heckle politicians, chain themselves to railings, and cause civil disturbances. The photograph above shows the WSPU staff at the London Headquarters in 1908. Mrs Pankhurst and Christabel are in the centre, standing behind the placard.

MARTYR TO A CAUSE. *The accidental death of Emily Davison, who threw herself under the hooves of the King's horse at the Derby of 1913 (above), provoked intense emotion in Britain. Her funeral procession, when her coffin was carried to King's Cross to be taken by rail to her family home in Northumberland, attracted huge crowds. Women in purple or white carried purple irises or branches of laurel. Purple signified justice, while white represented purity and green was for hope. These were the colours that the suffragettes had made famous during the Edwardian era.*

DEMONSTRATIONS AND PROTEST *meetings in support of women's suffrage marked the decade before the First World War. In the photograph above, a suffragette is arrested by two policemen for demonstrating outside Buckingham Palace in May 1914.*

THE "CAT AND MOUSE" ACT, *passed by the Liberals in 1913, allowed women hunger-strikers to be released from prison when they became dangerously ill, and rearrested after they had recovered. Wishing to avoid the accusation of murder, the government tried' to force-feed those who refused to eat, but the brutality of their methods aroused much indignation and sympathy for suffragette prisoners. The anti-government poster (above) is an advertisement for the magazine, The Suffragette, edited by Christabel Pankhurst.*

THE FIRST WOMAN M.P. *was Viscountess Nancy Astor (1879–1964). Born in the United States of America, she married Waldorf Astor whose great-great-grandfather, John Jacob Astor, had been M.P. for Plymouth. When her husband succeeded to the peerage in 1919, Nancy Astor (above) was elected to John Astor's old seat, which she held for the Tories until 1945. The photograph (left) records a scene during the election of December 1918, the first in which women over thirty were allowed to vote. A mother proudly places her ballot paper in the box in a polling station.*

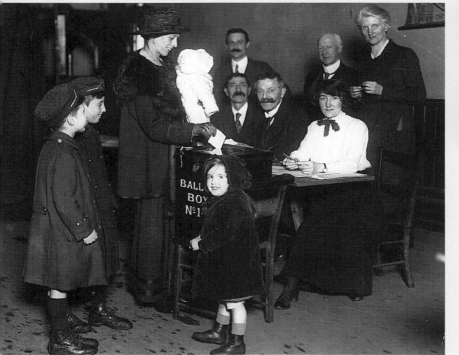

make it a worldwide government monopoly, to be shared only with the Americans—"It's *vital* for war! You *can't cut* the air! You *can* cut a telegraph wire!" He pressed the idea upon the Imperial Conference of 1911, and the assembled prime ministers did plan a series of wireless relay stations throughout the Empire which would effectively have dominated the world's communications systems.

The war prevented it, but wireless came to mean much to the British Empire. Kipling even wrote a short story about it. The British Broadcasting Company, founded in 1922, began regular Empire broadcasts ten years later, intended to "keep unshaken the faith the British nation has in its Empire", and the King himself said that wireless could "work the miracle of communication between me and my people in far-off places."

For most imperial citizens of the 1930s indeed, the wireless evoked above all the image of the King Emperor himself, presenting his annual Christmas broadcast. This was the one occasion in the year when Empire and modernity truly coincided, but even so it was technique not in the cause of power or development, but for old times' sake. How Queen Victoria would have loved it! The chimes of Westminster relayed so magically round the Empire, the faint crackle on the loudspeakers, as though Buckingham Palace were even then being plugged into the system, the plummy accents of the "announcer" (wearing, as everybody knew, evening dress for the occasion), the theatrical moment of absolute silence, and then, heard at that very instant in home and office, ship and barrack, kraal, hill-station, rubber estate and trading post across the British Empire, the thick bearded voice of His Majesty, speaking very carefully, as if to make allowances for the younger members of the family. "Another year has passed. . . ."

In 1935 T. E. Lawrence, having withdrawn into pseudo-anonymity as an aircraftsman in the Royal Air Force, riding his motorcycle fast through Dorset, crashed and killed himself. A rumour ran through the country then, that he was not killed at all, but that, spirited away by the Authority to secret duties, he would reappear when the moment came, when Drake's

Passengers on a railway journey, whiling away the time by listening to a wireless broadcast. The wireless was to become an important feature of daily life for many people in the 1920s.

Drum beat perhaps, to lead the British once more against their enemies. It was as though the British sensed that ahead of them lay one last great adventure of another kind, unwanted, unprofitable but magnificent, in which they would sacrifice not simply their lives, but their greatness too.

For if the spirit of Empire flickered dimly among the British now, the sense of destiny lay there still. This was a people bred to great things, after all, feeling itself a great nation still, equipped socially and historically for high enterprise. They were still convinced that on the whole their ways were superior to foreign ways, and still, as a rule of thumb, dedicated to Fair Play as the British approximation of the Sermon on the Mount.

If it was their weakness diplomatically, it was their truest moral strength: and so it led them in the end into the noblest of all their adventures, the most Pyrrhic of their victories, the Last War of the British Empire.

CHAPTER 12

THE SECOND WORLD WAR

HITLER WENT TO WAR, wrote King George VI of England in his diary in September 1939, "with the knowledge that the whole might of the British Empire would be against him." Fair Play was at stake, besides much else. As the good and simple monarch added, the British people were "resolved to fight until Liberty and Justice are once again safe in the World." Political theorists would argue that the Second World War had economic causes, or sprang from the inequities of the Treaty of Versailles. To most Britons, though, as to their King, it was started by an evil man in pursuance of wicked ends, and the rightness of the cause was never in doubt.

So the Last War assumed, for the British, a heroic quality. They alone fought the three great enemies—Germany, Japan and Italy—first to last. They alone held the breach in the dangerous months after the fall of France in 1940. Once again, and for the last time, their fleets and armies fought across the world, and the imperial strongholds from Bermuda to Hong Kong stood to their arms. The Empire did not always fight well. There were sorry defeats, timid failures, constant muddles and recriminations. Still on the whole it was a grand performance in a noble purpose, a swan song of some splendour, and a worthy last display of the imperial scale and brotherhood. "Alone at last!" ran the caption in a 1940 cartoon by David Low, and went on to answer itself, for there behind the resolute Tommy, steel-helmeted on the Dover cliffs, extended in endless line of march the soldiers of the overseas Empire. A cherished cable from the Caribbean was received in Whitehall that same summer. "Carry on Britain!" it said. "Barbados is behind you!"

This time it was unmistakably an imperial war. Hitler himself professed to have no quarrel with the British Empire, and would certainly have preferred the British as allies rather than as enemies. Like so many foreigners, he was seduced by history. He thought of the Empire as it had been, as history and legend made it still. He conceived of it as aristocratic, ubiquitous, imperturbable, immensely experienced. He admired the supposed consistency of British policy and the latent brutality and toughness that was, he

On September 1, 1939, German troops marched into Poland. Two days later Britain and France officially declared war on Germany, followed by all the members of the British Commonwealth and Empire except Eire.

said, common both to the national leaders of England and to the mass of its peoples. "I do not wish the crown of the British Empire to lose any of its pearls, for that would be a catastrophe to mankind." Commonsense, he said, suggested a free hand for Germany in Europe, for Britain elsewhere. Otherwise a great Empire would be utterly destroyed, "an Empire which it was never my intention to harm".

But the British Empire, when once the die was cast, would have none of him. Mackenzie King, the Prime Minister of Canada, warned him if he ever turned against England "there would be great numbers of Canadians anxious to swim the Atlantic", and so it proved. "In that dark, terrific, and also glorious hour," wrote Winston Churchill in retrospect of 1940, "we received from all parts of His Majesty's dominions, from the greatest to the smallest . . . the assurance that we would all go down or come through together." This was, however, by no means a foregone conclusion, for by 1939 the Empire was far more diffuse than it had been in 1914. Now

THE EVACUATION OF CHILDREN FROM LONDON

When the Second World War was imminent, plans were put into effect to evacuate children from the cities to the safer countryside. This is a journalist's account of children leaving London.

It was not until Friday morning, September 1, that I really took the sharp, agonised breath of war. That day it began, in a slum in London.

The office had told me to cover the evacuation of some of London's schoolchildren. There had been great preparations for the scheme—preparations that raised strong criticism. Evacuation would split the British home, divide child and parent. . . .

I went to a block of working-class flats at the back of Gray's Inn Road and in the early morning saw a tiny, frail, Cockney child walking across to school. The child had a big, brown-paper parcel in her hand and was dragging it along. But as she turned I saw a brown box banging against her thin legs. It bumped up and down at every step, slung by a thin string over her shoulder.

It was Florence Morecambe, an English schoolchild, with a gas mask instead of a satchel over her shoulder.

I went along with Florence to her school. . . . The classrooms were filled with children, parcels, gas masks. . . . The children were excited and happy because their parents had told them they were going away to the country. Many of them, like my little Florence, had never seen green fields.

I watched the schoolteachers calling out their names and tying luggage labels in their coats, checking their parcels to see there were warm and clean clothes. On the gates of the school were two fat policemen. They were letting the children through but gently asking the parents not to come farther. . . . So mothers and fathers were saying goodbye, straightening the girls' hair, getting the boys to blow their noses, and lightly and quickly kissing them. The parents stood outside while the children went to be registered in

Children wearing luggage labels queue for transport out of the nation's capital, accompanied by their teachers.

their classrooms. There was quite a long wait before this small army got its orders to move off. In the meantime I watched these thin, wiry little Cockneys playing their rough-and-push games on the faded netball pitch. It was disturbing, for through the high grille their mothers pressed their faces, trying to see the one child that resembled them. Every now and then a policeman would call out a child's name and a mother who had forgotten a bar of chocolate or a toothbrush had a last chance to tell a child to be good, to write and to straighten her hat.

Labelled and lined up, the children began to move out of the school. I followed Florence, her live tiny face bobbing about, white among so many navy-blue school caps. She was chattering away to an older schoolgirl.

On one side of the Gray's Inn Road this ragged crocodile moved towards the tube station. On the other, were mothers who were waving and running along to see the last of their children. The police had asked them not to follow, but they could not resist.

The children scrambled down into the tube.

there was no formal alliance among the King's separate dominions, no constitutional obligation to go to war at all. Ireland indeed never did, and was represented in Germany throughout the war by an ambassador accredited in the name of King George. The Australians and New Zealanders declared war at once, soon sending almost all their trained soldiers to the other side of the world, but the South Africans decided only after bitter parliamentary debates which side they wanted to be on, while the Canadians declared war on Germany after Great Britain, on Japan before Great Britain, and never declared war on Bulgaria at all. As for the four hundred million people of India, they were committed to war by the sole word of their viceroy, a Scottish nobleman, who consulted no Indians on the matter.

The British had no expansionist war aims this time. They hoped the Empire and Commonwealth would survive the struggle intact, but no more. Their purposes were as altruistic as political purposes ever are. Yet that old yearning for excitement came into its own once again, and helped the people through the ordeals of blitz, battle and separation. The aggressive instinct resurfaced, legitimised by war. Racy characters of the imperial legend reappeared from clubs or offices, to rediscover themselves in commando raids, parachute drops or weird prodigies of intelligence. The nation came to life again.

This time the very existence of the Empire was at stake. Germany might have no designs upon it, but Japan and Italy certainly did. The Japanese envisaged a Greater East Asia Co-Prosperity Sphere embracing all the British eastern territories, India to Hong Kong, and perhaps Australia and New Zealand too. The Italians let it be known that they wanted Malta and Cyprus as Italian possessions, Egypt, Iraq and the Sudan as Italian protectorates, and Gibraltar as an international port.

At the same time Britain's chief foreign allies in the struggle were hardly less dedicated to the redistribution of the Empire. The United States had actually come into being in reaction to Empire, and still earnestly supported the principle of self-determination for all peoples, while the Soviet Union equated imperialism with capitalism as surely as the muscular Christians of the previous century had associated cleanliness with God.

It was plain that when the war against Hitler's Axis was over, these ambiguous associates would see to it that the British imperial era was ended. Even the staunch dominions subtly shifted their attitudes and allegiances as the war progressed.

But the British put it all out of their minds and fought on. Theatrical arts had always been essential to their imperial methods, and in this their last exhibition they excelled themselves. Their initial defeat, their expulsion from the European mainland in 1940, they presented as the triumph of Dunkirk. Their initial success, the Battle of Britain later that year, they shamelessly exploited and exaggerated. Hitler thought their war propaganda "wonderful", and by their skill in it, by the magic of their historical reputations, they convinced half the world that they were uniquely brave in adversity, most unanimous in patriotism. The BBC was much the most trusted of the wartime broadcasting services, and persistently it was as an Empire that the British presented themselves.

In fact, the possession of the Empire vastly increased their burdens and anxieties, but they integrated it as a mighty asset, so that it never occurred to their own people, whatever their enemies sometimes thought, that on

Adolf Hitler (1889-1945), founder of the Nazi Party and German dictator, is shown here after the fall of Holland in 1940. Behind his left shoulder is the Gestapo chief, Heinrich Himmler, who was also Commandant of the concentration and extermination camps. To his left stands his deputy, Reinhard Heydrich, who became known as "the Hangman of Europe".

balance they might be safer without it. On the face of it, of course, it was indeed an enormous reservoir of manpower and materials. More than five million fighting troops were raised by the British Empire, and there was hardly a campaign in which imperial troops did not play a part. Canadians, for instance, provided half the frontline defence of England in 1940, a quarter of the pilots of the RAF, and a sizeable proportion of the invasion force that went back to the European continent in 1943.

At their head, from the summer of 1940, stood Winston Churchill. If Britain fell, he said, he would continue the war from Canada, and thither the fleets and armies of the Crown would sail with him—"I have not

---

BLOOD, TOIL, TEARS AND SWEAT

On May 10, 1940, Winston Churchill became Prime Minister and began what he himself termed his "walk with destiny". His inspiring speeches in those early months of the war gave courage to the whole nation.

House of Commons, May 13

I would say to the House [of Commons], as I said to those who have joined this government: "I have nothing to offer but blood, toil, tears and sweat."

We have before us an ordeal of the most grievous kind. We have before us many, many long months of struggle and of suffering. You ask, what is our policy? I will say: it is to wage war by sea, land and air, with all our might and with all the strength that God can give us: to wage war against a monstrous tyranny, never surpassed in the dark, lamentable catalogue of human crime. That is our policy. You ask, what is our aim? I can answer in one word: Victory—victory at all costs, victory in spite of terror, victory, however long and hard the road may be; for without victory, there is no survival.

House of Commons, June 4

We shall go on to the end, we shall fight in France, we shall fight on the seas and oceans, we shall fight with growing confidence and growing strength in the air, we shall defend our island, whatever the cost may be, we shall fight on the beaches, we shall fight on the landing grounds, we shall fight in the fields and in the streets, we shall fight in the hills; we shall never surrender, and even if, which I do not for a moment believe, this island or a large part of it were subjugated and starving, then our Empire beyond the seas, armed and guarded by the British Fleet, would carry on the struggle, until, in God's good time, the new world, with all its power and might, steps forth to the rescue and the liberation of the old.

BBC Home Service, June 18

I expect that the Battle of Britain is about to begin. Upon this battle depends the survival of Christian civilisation. Upon it depends our own British life, and the long continuity of our institutions and our Empire. The whole fury and might of the enemy must very soon be turned on us. Hitler knows that he will have to break us in this island or lose the war. If we can stand up to him, all Europe may be free and the life of the world may move forward into

The Prime Minister, Winston Churchill, strides purposefully out of Number 10, Downing Street.

broad, sunlit uplands. But if we fail, then the whole world, including the United States, including all that we have known and cared for, will sink into the abyss of a new Dark Age made more sinister, and perhaps more protracted, by the lights of perverted science. Let us therefore brace ourselves to our duties, and so bear ourselves that, if the British Empire and its Commonwealth last for a thousand years, men will still say, "This was their finest hour."

Harrow School, December 18

Hitler, in one of his recent discourses, declared that the fight was between those who have been through the Adolf Hitler Schools and those who have been at Eton.

Hitler has forgotten Harrow, and he has also overlooked the vast majority of the youth of this country who have never had the advantage of attending such schools, but who have by their skill and prowess won the admiration of the whole world.

When this war is won, as it surely will be, it must be one of our aims to work to establish a state of society where the advantages and privileges which hitherto have been enjoyed only by the few shall be far more widely shared by the many, and by the youth of the nation as a whole.

---

become the King's First Minister in order to preside over the liquidation of the British Empire!" When the apes of Gibraltar, traditionally the custodians of British rule, seemed likely to die out, Churchill personally saw to it that new stock was brought in from Morocco, and his speeches reverberated with the imperial idiom—"If the British Empire and its Commonwealth last for a thousand years, men will still say, 'This was their finest hour!'"

Churchill knew that powers, like people, are taken at their own valuation, and he behaved always as though Britain were a super-power, the leader of a great disciplined Empire destined to last a millenium. He approached President Roosevelt the American, Marshal Stalin the Russian, not simply as personal equals, but as political equals too. He gave to the British themselves, for the last time, the feeling that they were a special people, with honourable duties all their own.

Without her allies Britain could never have won the war, for she could no longer defend her Empire single-handed. In the first months of the war the Channel Islands, the oldest overseas possessions of the Crown, were surrendered to the Germans without resistance. Thereafter many an imperial property was attacked, and many lost. British Somaliland, Hong Kong, Burma, Malaya, Singapore, all the islands of the Pacific, were taken by the King's enemies. Egypt was invaded, Australia was bombed, Malta was almost obliterated, enemy submarines penetrated the harbours of Sydney, Muscat and St Lucia. Even the frontiers of India were crossed by enemy armies at last, fulfilling one of the Empire's oldest nightmares.

Just as, in 1915, the British sought to make a decisive assault by way of the Ottoman Empire, so a generation later they still saw the Middle East as the epicentre of their struggle. The Suez Canal was the fulcrum of their power in the world: their oil supplies, their links with India, their dominance of the Arab land mass—all seemed to depend upon their power in Egypt. Before the war their only standing expeditionary force was designed to go, not to France, but to Egypt: at the most crucial moment of the Battle of Britain, when an assault on England seemed imminent, they sent one hundred aircraft and an armoured brigade to the eastern Mediterranean. Whatever else might happen, Egypt, threatened first by the Italians, then by the Germans, must not fall.

Cairo in the 1940s was the last great assembly-point of the imperial power, the last place where, in a setting properly exotic, the imperial legions mingled in their staggering variety. Every kind of imperial uniform was to be spotted in Cairo, and although since 1936 Egypt had been nominally independent, and was officially neutral in the war, the whole capital was now in effect a British military base. From the British headquarters, conveniently close to the British Embassy, operations were directed all over the nearer East—the North African campaigns, the battles for Greece and Crete, the reconquest of British Somaliland, the capture of Ethiopia, the invasion of Syria, the reoccupation of Iraq, the occupation of southern Persia, guerrilla war in Yugoslavia. The Royal Navy's Mediterranean headquarters was up the road at Alexandria.

For some years of the war Cairo was the military capital of the British Empire. A British minister of state was in residence there. Dignitaries and celebrities were constantly passing through, from Noel Coward to the Duke of Northumberland; in 1943 Churchill, Roosevelt and the Chinese leader, Chiang Kai-shek, met there in conference. In Cairo life was still richly lived.

French wines and grouse in season were served, at the worst moments of the war polo was played most days, the brothels flourished, and military offices, like all others, closed from one till half past five each afternoon.

It was in this crowded and frenetic city, that the most traditionally imperialist gesture of the war was made. The British ambassador was Sir Miles Lampson, a gigantic man, six feet five inches tall and eighteen stone in weight, and an old-fashioned, robustly patriotic imperialist. Since his arrival in Egypt in 1934 he had become an inescapable figure of Cairo life, dancing, shooting, riding, gambling at the Mohammed Ali Club, learning to fly at Heliopolis airport, driving from appointment to appointment in the enormous embassy Rolls, the best-known car in Egypt.

Though Egypt was officially neutral, Lampson believed that any means were justified to keep it absolutely subjugated to the British Empire's war effort. Many Egyptians held different views, and prominent among them was the young king, Farouk, who was twenty-two years old. He had been

STANDING ALONE

In 1940, after the surrender of France, Britain stood alone against Nazi power. The nation's first challenge came when the Luftwaffe *attempted to destroy British airfields prior to an invasion. Having lost the Battle of Britain, the* Luftwaffe *turned its attention to the intensive bombing of the country's major towns and cities. In the first of the passages which follow, a Battle of Britain pilot, Richard Hillary, describes how he was shot down over the English Channel. The second passage, by Desmond Flower, a distinguished journalist, describes the aftermath of the bombing of London's Surrey Docks on September 1, 1940. This day is now remembered as the first day of the London Blitz.*

Dogfight over the Channel

September 3 dawned dark and overcast, with a slight breeze ruffling the waters of the Estuary. Hornchurch aerodrome, twelve miles east of London, wore its usual morning pallor of yellow fog, lending an added air of grimness to the dimly silhouetted Spitfires around the boundary. From time to time a balloon would poke its head grotesquely through the mist as though looking for possible victims before falling back like some tired monster.

We came out on to the tarmac at about eight o'clock. During the night our machines had been moved from the Dispersal Point over to the hangars. All the machine tools, oil, and general equipment had been left on the far side of the aerodrome. I was worried. We had been bombed a short time before, and my plane had been fitted out with a new cockpit hood. This hood unfortunately would not slide open along its groove; and with a depleted ground staff and no tools, I began to fear it never would. Unless it did open, I shouldn't be able to bale out in a hurry if I had to. Miraculously, "Uncle George" Denholm, our Squadron Leader, produced three men with a heavy file and lubricating oil, and the corporal fitter and I set upon the hood in a fury of haste. We took it turn by turn, filing and oiling, oiling and filing, until at last the hood began to move. But agonisingly slowly: by ten o'clock, when the mist had

The Spitfire, designed by R.J. Mitchell, was more than a match for its German counterpart, the Messerschmitt 109.

cleared and the Squadron strength was eight. We headed southeast, climbing all out on a steady course. At 12,000 feet we came up through the clouds: I looked down and saw them spread out below me like layers of whipped cream. The sun was brilliant and made it difficult to see even the next plane when turning. I was peering anxiously ahead, for the controller had given us warning of at least fifty enemy fighters approaching very high. When we did first sight them, nobody shouted, as I think we all saw them at the same moment. They must have been five hundred to a thousand feet above us and coming straight on like a swarm of locusts. I remember cursing and going automatically into line astern: the next moment we were in among them and it was each man for himself. As soon as they saw us they spread out and dived, and the next ten minutes was a blur of twisting machines and tracer bullets. One

educated, like other kings of Anglo-Araby, to be a puppet: schooled in England and tutored by an Eton master; kept always beneath the eye of the British Embassy, he held his throne on sufferance. He was, however, far from subservient. His entourage was chiefly Italian, at a time when the British were at war with Italy, and his devotion to the imperial cause was distinctly fragile.

Lampson, who habitually called him "the boy", treated him first with condescension, later with contempt, and the King responded predictably, by snubbing him, deliberately misunderstanding him, or keeping him waiting for appointments. The two men naturally detested each other, and when in 1942 King Farouk determined to appoint a new Egyptian Government more amenable to his own views, but less acceptable to the British, Lampson decided it could not be tolerated. Rommel seemed about to break through the British positions in the western desert and advance upon Cairo: at such a moment Lampson felt it within his authority to depose the King of Egypt.

Messerschmitt went down in a sheet of flame on my right, and a Spitfire hurtled past in a half-roll; I was weaving and turning in a desperate attempt to gain height, with the machine practically hanging on the air-screw. Then, just below me and to my left, I saw what I had been praying for—a Messerschmitt climbing and away from the sun. I closed in to two hundred yards, and from slightly to one side gave him a two-second burst: fabric ripped off the wing and black smoke poured from the engine, but he did not go down. Like a fool, I did not break away, but put in another three-second burst. Red flames shot upwards and he spiralled out of sight. At that moment, I felt a terrific explosion which knocked the control stick from my hand, and the whole machine quivered like a stricken animal. In a second, the cockpit was a mass of flames: instinctively, I reached up to open the hood. It would not move. I tore off my straps and managed to force it back; but this took time, and when I dropped back into the seat and reached for the stick in an effort to turn the plane on its back, the heat was so intense that I could feel myself going. I remember a second of sharp agony, remember thinking, "So this is it!" and putting both hands to my eyes. Then I passed out.

When I regained consciousness I was free of the machine and falling rapidly. I pulled the rip-cord of my parachute and checked my descent with a jerk. Looking down, I saw that my left trouser leg was burnt off, that I was going to fall into the sea, and that the English coast was deplorably far away. About twenty feet above the water, I attempted to undo my parachute, failed, and flopped into the sea with it billowing round me. I was told later that the machine went into a spin at about 25,000 feet and that at 10,000 feet I fell out—unconscious.

The Start of the Blitz

Suddenly we were gaping upwards. The brilliant sky was criss-crossed from horizon to horizon by innumerable vapour trails. The sight was a completely novel one. We watched, fascinated, and all work stopped. The little silver stars sparkling at the heads of the vapour trails turned east.

St Paul's Cathedral during the Blitz. Only one bomb scored a direct hit, and as it was at the entrance it did little damage.

This display looked so insubstantial and harmless; even beautiful. Then, with a dull roar which made the ground across London shake as one stood upon it, the first sticks of bombs hit the docks. Leisurely, enormous mushrooms of black and brown smoke shot with crimson climbed into the sunlit sky. There they hung and slowly expanded, for there was no wind, and the great fires below fed more smoke into them as the hours passed.

On Friday and Saturday morning the sky grew darker and darker as the oily smoke rose and spread in heavy, immobile columns, shutting out the sun. . . .

Now we were nearer to the docks. There were fire hoses along the side of the road, climbing over one another like a helping of macaroni, with those sad little fountains spraying out from the leaks, as they always seem to do from all fire hoses. Every two or three minutes we would pull into the gutter as a fire bell broke out stridently behind us and an engine in unfamiliar livery tore past at full tilt: chocolate or green or blue, with gold lettering—City of Birmingham Fire Brigade, or Sheffield, or Bournemouth. The feeling was something you had never experienced before—the excitement and dash of fire engines arriving to help from so far away, and the oily, evil smell of fire and destruction, with its lazy, insolent rhythm.

It so happened that among the British officials in Cairo, working in the propaganda department, was Walter Monckton, the lawyer who had, six years before, drafted the instrument of abdication for King Edward VIII. He was now instructed to draw up a similar document for Farouk.

The King was to be sent an ultimatum demanding the appointment of an administration more favourable to the British. He was given until 6 p.m. on the evening of February 2, 1942, to name the pro-British Mustapha el Nahas Pasha as Prime Minister, or else face the consequences.

Farouk replied only with a letter, received at the British Embassy a quarter of an hour after Lampson's deadline, protesting against such a blatant infringement of Egyptian sovereignty, and so there was set in motion one of the last acts of imperial swashbuckle. Shortly before nine o'clock that night, through the bright and noisy city, smelling as always of dirt, jasmine, food and inadequately refined petrol, a convoy of British tanks, armoured cars and military trucks rumbled across town to take up positions around the royal palace.

At nine o'clock precisely Lampson's Rolls arrived at the gates, and the ambassador, accompanied by the commander of the British troops in Egypt and followed by a specially picked posse of armed officers, entered the palace. True to his code even then, Farouk kept him waiting for five minutes in an anteroom, but once inside the royal chamber, with the general glowering at his back, Lampson allowed no nonsense. ("It doesn't often come one's way," he wrote in his diary next day, "to be pushing a Monarch off a Throne.")

First he read the King a statement, very loudly, "with full emphasis", as he later reported to the Foreign Office, "and increasing anger". It accused the King of assisting the enemy and thereby violating his commitments to Great Britain, and said he was "no longer fit to occupy the Throne". Lampson then handed Farouk Monckton's abdication instrument, and told him to sign it at once, "or I shall have something else and more unpleasant to confront you with". Even as he spoke, they could hear the growl and clatter of the tanks outside the palace gates.

The abdication instrument was typed on old British residence paper from which the letterhead had been removed, and Farouk's first response was to complain about its sloppiness. He was answered only by an overbearing silence, and after a moment or two of indecision, he picked up a pen to sign the abdication. But then he hesitated. Would Lampson give him one more chance? The ambassador agreed, provided that the King immediately complied with the ultimatum. Farouk thereupon submitted, "for his own honour and his country's good", and the ambassador and his cohorts stamped away down the corridors of the palace, into their cars and back to their great Embassy beside the Nile.

"So much," reported Lampson, "for the events of the evening, which I confess I could not have more enjoyed." They seemed to have been successful. Nahas Pasha, summoned to the palace next day, formed a government that remained loyal to the British connection for the rest of the war.

The Middle East never did fall—when the war ended the British military position there was stronger than it had ever been. Nor was the Mediterranean ever denied to those British fleets which had frequented it since the end of the Napoleonic wars: and this achievement was largely due to another peculiarly imperial episode of the war, the defence of Malta.

Sir Miles Lampson, the British ambassador to Egypt during the war, and Mustapha el Nahas Pasha, the British choice for Egyptian Prime Minister. Lampson was a true imperialist who thought it was well within his powers to depose King Farouk when the King's views differed from those of the British.

The peoples of the Empire were not so unanimous in their fidelity as they had been in the Great War. They were better informed now, and they had learnt to question the meaning of the war and the purpose of the imperial connection. Treason to the Crown, so rare in the First War, was not uncommon in the Second. The Mufti of Jerusalem, for instance, the leader of the Palestine Arabs, went to Germany and formed a Muslim Army of Liberation. Aung San, one of the most prominent Burmese nationalists, went to Japan and formed a Burma Defence Army. Subhas Chandra Bose, *quondam* president of the Indian National Congress, went first to Germany, where he formed an Indian Legion, then to Japan, where he formed an Indian National Army. One in six of Indian prisoners of war joined his forces (which included a Gandhi Brigade and were known to the British as "Jiffs"—Japanese Indian forces): Bose declared himself head of an Indian government-in-exile, and became in the end a national hero.

THE BATTLE OF THE ATLANTIC

The British convoy system, by which armed warships protected large numbers of merchant vessels, enabled supplies to get through to wartime Britain. In the end, improvements in radar meant that surface ships could detect German U-boats without themselves being detected. The following account comes from Life is a Four-Letter Word, *the autobiography of Nicholas Monsarrat. Famous for his novel,* The Cruel Sea, *Monsarrat was originally a pacifist and enlisted as a temporary member of the RNVR after answering an advertisement in* The Times *for "gentlemen with yachting experience".*

Since my father was a surgeon, and the captain, who came from Liverpool, knew this, I was also appointed the ship's Medical Officer within a few hours of reporting on board. This was the worst of all my jobs, the most moving, the most ugly, the most calculated to make me wish that I could revert to an innocent child again.

At first it meant nothing much; I landscaped a few ingrowing toe-nails, and bandaged a few scraped elbows. But then *Campanula* went to sea, and then to war, and then to violence and bloodshed; and after that my patients were all survivors from ships torpedoed in convoy, and the worst horror-film of my life began.

Survivors, climbing on board with gasping lungs, or hauled over the side like oil-soaked fish from the scrambling nets, or hoisted up with a rope to torture anew a shattered body, could be suffering from anything, no matter how terrible. They could have swallowed mouthfuls of that corrosive fuel oil, and be coughing up their guts until they died; they could be shuddering in the last bitter extremity of cold and exhaustion; they might have sustained gross wounds, and the shock that went with them; they could be screaming with the pain of deep, hopeless burns, and broken limbs, and bodies half-flayed by a rough ship's side as they slid down into the water.

But good or bad, bad or unspeakable, the survivors were all mine; and when they were brought below, or, too anguished to be moved, were propped up gently in the lee

Convoys brought food, equipment and civilian passengers to Britain during the German blockade in the Second World War.

of the depth-charge rails, I had to pick up my little black bag, and attend their sorrows.

I got used to it in the end. I grew hardened to the loathsome sights and sounds, and perhaps more skilful in rough-and-ready treatment, and less guilty when, in all compassion, I hurt a writhing man until the watching ring of his shipmates, and of mine, seemed likely to break their appalled silence at this butchery, and snatch the knife or the needle or the probe from my hand, and drive it into the back of my skull.

On the other hand the loyalty was often touching and was encapsulated best of all in Malta, which assumed not only a high strategic importance in the war, but a symbolic meaning too. When Italy entered the war Malta was made untenable as the main base of the Mediterranean fleet but it remained invaluable as a submarine base, from which to harass the enemy supply-routes to North Africa, and as a propaganda station. Through the long years of setback, Malta remained defiant in defence, furious in attack.

The five islands of Malta, with a total area of one hundred and twenty-five square miles, lay in so commanding a situation that Rommel himself saw them as the key to Mediterranean victory—in December 1941 three-quarters of his supplies were sunk by ships and aircraft from Malta, and one Italian convoy, comprising seven merchant ships and ten destroyers, was completely annihilated. Between June 1940, when Italy entered the war, and November 1942, when the British won the Battle of El Alamein in Egypt, Malta was under siege. Some sixteen thousand tons of bombs were dropped on the islands: during fifteen days of April 1942 there were one hundred and fifteen air raids.

There was never another imperial siege like this. Though the ships which supplied Malta, and the fighter aircraft which defended it, were all manned by Britons, the beleaguered population was notably un-British in everything but citizenship. Catholic, Latinate, speaking a language incomprehensible anywhere else, addled by political, religious and cultural rivalries, the Maltese were notoriously among the more difficult subjects of the Crown. Though since 1921 the colony had been ostensibly self-governing "in all matters of purely local concern", the constitution had been suspended in 1936 because of this continual rumpus. The British viewed the majority of the Maltese as less than absolutely pukka, and generally looked upon the

TURNING THE TIDE

After a series of reverses the British army achieved an inspiring success in Africa. One week after Montgomery's attack on El Alamein in October 1942, the Germans had only ninety tanks, the British, eight hundred. Yet Hitler forbade retreat. This account of the defeat of Rommel's Afrika Korps is given by the German General Bayerlein.

On the morning of November 4 the remnants of the German Afrika Korps, together with the 90th Light Division, held a thin front line on either side of the wide sand dune called Tel el Mampsra: though only some twelve feet high, this dune was a commanding feature. To the south was the equally weakened Italian armoured corps. Towards dawn I reported to General Ritter von Thoma, the commander of the Afrika Korps, that I was about to set off for the area south of El Daba, where I was to establish a rear command post. For the first time Thoma was wearing a proper uniform, with his general's insignia, orders and decorations, which hitherto in the desert he had never bothered to put on. He now said to me:

"Bayerlein, Hitler's order [not to withdraw] is a piece of unparalleled madness. I can't go along with this any longer. Go to the El Daba command post. I shall stay here and personally take charge of the defence of Tel el Mampsra."

I could see that Thoma was utterly disheartened and foresaw no good. His ADC, Lieutenant Hartdegen, remained with the General: he had a wireless transmitter. The General put on his greatcoat and picked up a small canvas bag. I wondered whether the General intended to die. Then I left Tel el Mampsra and drove to the rear.

It was eight o'clock before the British attacked, after approximately one hour's artillery preparation. Their main effort was directed against Tel el Mampsra. By committing all its forces the Afrika Korps was able to hold attacks by two hundred British tanks.

At eleven o'clock Lieutenant Hartdegen appeared at my command post and said, "General von Thoma has sent me back, with the radio transmitter. He doesn't need it any more. All our tanks, anti-tank guns and ack-ack have been destroyed on Tel el Mampsra. I don't know what has happened to the General."

I immediately climbed into a small armoured reconnaissance car and drove off eastwards. Suddenly a hail of armour-piercing shot was whistling all about me. In the noontime haze I could see countless black monsters far-away in front. They were Montgomery's tanks, the 10th Hussars. I jumped out of the armoured car and beneath the burning midday sun ran as fast as I could towards Tel el Mampsra. It was a place of death, of burning tanks and islands not as anybody's homeland exactly, but as a dockyard, a barracks and a sailors' tavern.

Yet the Maltese were to be the acknowledged heroes of the battle for Malta. Though Mussolini had long laid claim to the islands, and though Valletta, the capital, was less than half an hour's flying time from Italian air bases, the Maltese never wavered. Battered, half-starved, exhausted by noise and sleeplessness, they retained their morale from the very first trial blackout to the last fitful air raid from the retreating enemy.

Aesthetically it was a thrilling and romantic siege. The splendid architecture of the islands looked more splendid still, manned for war. The searchlights played ritually round the great cathedral of St John in Floriana; the tracer bullets flew in coloured streams from the castle ramparts; black submarines slid sharklike from their pens beneath the forts. At night warships at sea reported Malta like an explosion on the horizon. By day Valletta was often shrouded in a pall of golden dust from the rubble of its bombed buildings.

At the start of the battle three elderly biplanes represented Malta's entire air defence—*Faith, Hope* and *Charity*, whose lumbering sorties against colossal odds were publicised throughout the world. Later fighter reinforcements were flown in from carriers offshore, and this too was a spectacle full of excitement. Once, reinforcements arrived actually in the middle of an air raid, so that within minutes of their arrival on the island they were refuelled and in action. Once, there was a suicide Italian torpedo-boat attack upon Grand Harbour, when seventeen motorboats, hurling themselves against the nets, chains and buoys of the harbour defence, were caught in the searchlights and blasted out of the water by the rampart guns.

There was the spectacle too of a Mediterranean people behaving night

smashed flak guns, without a living soul. But then, about two hundred yards away from the sandhole in which I was lying, I saw a man standing erect beside a burning tank, apparently impervious to the intense fire which crisscrossed about him. It was General von Thoma. The British Shermans which were closing up on Tel el Mampsra had halted in a wide half-circle. What should I do? The General would probably regard it as cowardice on my part were I not to go forward and join him. But to run through the curtain of fire which lay between General von Thoma and myself would have been to court certain death. I thought for a moment or two. Then the British tanks began to move forward once again. There was now no fire being put down on Tel el Mampsra. Thoma stood there, rigid and motionless as a pillar of salt, with his canvas bag still in his hand. A Bren carrier was driving straight towards him, with two Shermans just behind. The British soldiers signalled to Thoma. At the same time one hundred and fifty fighting vehicles poured across Tel el Mampsra like a flood.

I ran off westward as fast as my legs could carry me. My car had vanished. After a while I met a staff car which took me to the command post at El Daba. There I found Rommel. I told him what I had seen. Huge dust clouds were now visible both southeast and south of the command post. The Italian tanks of the 20th Corps were fighting their last, desperate battle with some hundred heavy British tanks that had punched into the Italians' open right flank. After a brave resistance, the Italian corps was annihilated.

The Afrika Korps signals officer brought Rommel a decoded message, from the 10th Hussars to Montgomery, which our people had intercepted. It read: "We have just captured a General named Ritter von Thoma."

British Churchill tanks advance through the desert before final victory at the Battle of El Alamein.

after night with a truly imperial stoicism, spiced perhaps with a trace of Cockney bravado picked up from so many generations of contact with the navy. Labyrinths of chambers and galleries had been burrowed centuries before in the soft limestone of Valletta, and there the Maltese slept each night, while the city was pounded into ruin above them. Priests moved about them at night; great ladies of Malta, in the English manner, brought them food and comfort.

According to Churchill, the governor of the island, General Sir William Dobbie, was a Cromwellian figure. A member of the Plymouth Brethren, he believed implicitly in God's pro-British inclinations, and matched his Faith with his bearing, so that despite his Protestant views he appealed to the fervently Catholic Maltese, and even had a pub named after him—the "Everyone's Friend". "I call on all officers and other ranks humbly to seek God's help," said Dobbie's first Order of the Day, "and then in reliance in Him to do their duty unflinchingly." Almost every morning he repeated the message in a broadcast to the islanders: he had fought in the Boer War and the Great War, both victories in the end, and in his sixties regarded his call to the command of Malta as a summons directly from the Almighty.

Most thrilling of all were the days when, like wildfire round the battered streets, there ran a rumour that a supply convoy was approaching the islands. At the worst moments of the siege Malta very nearly starved, and very nearly ran out of fuel, water and ammunition too. In August 1942 only two weeks' supply of petrol remained, and the populace was rationed to half a bucket of water a week. Each convoy was a major Royal Navy operation. Even so, of the thirty merchant ships which set out for Malta in the first seven months of 1942, only seven survived to unload all their cargoes on the quay.

Single ships sometimes ran in and out of Malta—submarines, destroyers, or the forty-knot, three-funnelled minelayers, *Welshman*, *Manxman* and *Ariadne*, which maintained a desperate shuttle service from Gibraltar. In August 1942, however, no convoy had reached the islands since June, and even the indomitable Dobbie had reported that the battle was nearly lost.

The heavy bombardment of Malta by German and Italian bombers left the streets and houses in ruins, but the Maltese people remained resolute. In 1943 George VI awarded the island the George Cross "for heroism and devotion that will long be famous in history."

Surrender plans had already been drawn up. Accordingly, that month, Convoy S26, Operation Pedestal, sailed from the Clyde. It was the most powerful convoy of them all. The battleships *Nelson* and *Rodney* were accompanied by three carriers, seven cruisers and thirty-two destroyers, and this great fleet was escorting no more than fourteen fast merchantmen. Among them was the tanker *Ohio*, an American ship with a British crew, carrying eleven thousand tons of kerosene and diesel oil, without which air operations from Malta would almost immediately collapse.

The voyage of this convoy through the Mediterranean was one of the great naval exploits of the war. The freighters and their escort left Gibraltar on August 11, and from dawn the following day, all the way to Malta, they were under continual attack by aircraft, submarines and torpedo boats. The losses were terrible. First the carrier *Eagle* was sunk, then the carrier *Indomitable* crippled. Two cruisers and eight merchant ships were lost, two more cruisers, three merchant ships badly damaged. The *Ohio*, the one tanker in the convoy, was attacked more frequently and more heavily than any other ship, and on August 13, one hundred miles from Malta, her engines were put out of action. Twice her crew abandoned her, only to reboard her later. Once she was taken in tow by a destroyer, but she was holed so badly that she could not be pulled, and in the end, within sight of Malta, she was lashed to a destroyer and a minesweeper, one each side, and so carried rather than towed into the safety of Grand Harbour.

Only five merchant ships got through, but they saved Malta. As they sailed one by one into the harbour, huge cheering crowds waved them in, crossing themselves in thanksgiving, while the bands played "Rule Britannia", as in the old days. "The loss of Malta," Churchill had said, "would be a disaster of the first magnitude to the British Empire," and when the worst was over the Empire recognised Malta uniquely. King George VI awarded his colony the newly instituted decoration called the George Cross, "for heroism and devotion that will long be famous in history".

In 1943 he went to Malta in person to bestow it, and the medal, after being displayed like an icon in every Maltese village, was laid up like a battle honour in the governor's palace.

No such inspiriting epic sustained the imperial legend in the Far East. In India, Congress supporters boycotted the war effort in a campaign called "Quit India". There were riots and arrests, and to complete the suggestion of impending catastrophe, the worst famine for nearly a century. Hong Kong fell to the Japanese after a battle that lasted seventeen days, Malaya did not survive much longer, and in 1942 there occurred the most humiliating single disaster in British imperial history, the fall of Singapore.

The island colony of Singapore, two hundred and twenty-five miles square, was a British creation from scratch. Stamford Raffles had founded it one hundred and twenty years before, and it was specifically the alchemy of Empire which had made it, by the 1930s, the fourth port of the world. The island lay at the southern tip of the British Malay peninsula, linked to it by a causeway across the narrow Johore Strait. It was traditionally one of the main pivots of imperial power, intended to assure the security of the whole Empire east of Suez. It was designed to service and support battleships. The plan was that a battle fleet would be sent there as soon as war in the Far East impended. The Australians and New Zealanders looked to Singapore as the main guarantor of their security, and it had been frequently

THE WORLD AT WAR

THE SECOND WORLD WAR BEGAN in Europe when Nazi Germany's army invaded Poland in September 1939. By 1941 it had become a world war which would profoundly alter civilisation.

After a quiet, so-called "phony war" phase, the Second World War erupted violently in May 1940 with Hitler's invasion of Belgium, Holland and France. For a time after the British evacuation from Dunkirk and the fall of France, Britain stood alone. During the months that followed, and in face of the German assault from the air—the Battle of Britain—the nation showed that it could "take it". In the words of the new Prime Minister, Winston Churchill, this was the country's finest hour.

Thereafter the struggle was arduous and protracted as Britain was drawn into an alliance with the Soviet Union, following that country's invasion by Germany in the spring of 1941. Then in December of the same year the United States entered the war after the Japanese attack on Pearl Harbor.

It was a very different struggle from the Great War: it was an epic war spanning frontiers, deserts and oceans, a total war that involved whole civilian populations. Yet British casualties were far lower than between 1914 and 1918. The armed forces lost 300,000 killed, the merchant navy—a vital service—lost 35,000, and around 60,500 civilians were killed in air raids. There was one unprecedented horror: it is estimated that over six million Jews, and others, were killed in Nazi concentration camps.

Economic losses were enormous. Overseas assets were lost, debts were contracted and shipping was destroyed. Indeed, without American lend-lease, which was to end abruptly in 1945, the British war effort could never have been sustained. Nor could it have been sustained without high morale on the Home Front, and promises of a better world after the war.

RATIONING OF FOOD AND CLOTHES ensured that everyone had enough to eat and could keep warm. Extra milk and egg allowances were given to children and expectant mothers, and schools provided cheap, nourishing lunches.

ON HIS MAJESTY'S SERVICE

Your Ration Book

Issued to safeguard your food supply

HOLDER'S NAME AND REGISTERED ADDRESS

Surname *TAPPENDEN*

Other Names *J. Margaret*

Address *58. Beensfield Rd*

SE 3.

NAT. REG. NO. *AHAY 369 2*

Date of Issue *7 JUL 1941*   Serial Number of Book

If found, please return to

THE BLITZ, short for the German Blitzkrieg, or lightning war, was a term applied to war from the air as well as war on land. After the Germans had failed to invade Britain in 1940, they turned to large-scale air raids in an attempt to crack the morale of the British public. It did not crack. The photograph above records the devastation surrounding the Bank Underground station after a raid in January 1941. The "Dig for Victory" banner to be seen in the background was one of many urging people to grow more food. Information provided by the Ministry of Food helped to make the wartime generation healthier than earlier ones. It was necessary to produce more food at home so as to reduce the country's need for imports, and in the long run attacks on merchant shipping were an even greater threat to the population than was the Blitz. But the people responded magnificently to every kind of hardship. It was the retreat from Dunkirk which gave rise to the phrase "the Dunkirk spirit", so much in evidence during those years.

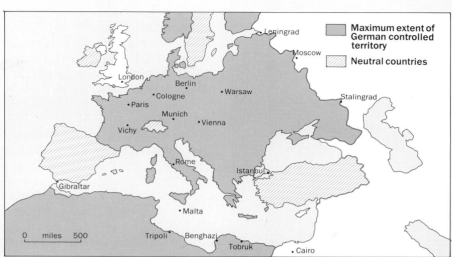

HITLER'S EARLY SUCCESSES were overwhelming. Norway and Denmark fell in April 1940, followed almost at once by the Low Countries and Luxembourg. On May 13, German forces outflanked the French defences on the Maginot Line. By June 4, the Royal Navy, assisted by hundreds of small craft, had rescued the British Expeditionary Force from Dunkirk. On June 17, France capitulated. Britain had only twenty ill-equipped divisions to confront Germany's two hundred divisions and to protect almost thirteen million square miles. Further German victories were inevitable in Europe and North Africa. The map (right) shows the extent of those successes. Above, Hitler in Paris in June 1940.

THE JAPANESE ATTACK on the American fleet in Pearl Harbor (below) on December 7, 1941, signalled that Japan wanted an end to American and British influence in the Far East. However, America's involvement in what was now a world war was to prove the decisive factor in ensuring an Allied victory in the Far East and Europe.

HITLER'S AMBITIONS cut short the life of the Soviet-German non-aggression pact of August 1939. On June 22, 1941, he felt confident enough to attack the Soviet Union, and by December his forces had overrun much of European Russia. The Russian winter halted their advance, and the Russians, led by Stalin, counter-attacked. Although they sustained losses of around twelve million, they drove the enemy from their land and went on to capture Berlin and occupy the whole of East Germany. The photograph above is of a Russian soldier celebrating his country's decisive victory at the Battle of Stalingrad in November 1942. By 1945 Churchill was afraid of Stalin's ambitions, and within a few years the war was followed by what was known as the "Cold War" of the 1950s and 1960s.

2 4 1

Native men, women and children being herded together by Japanese soldiers after the fall of Singapore. They were soon to discover that Asian imperialism was no better than that of the West.

represented to the world as impregnable. Some seven hundred miles of British territory lay to the north of it, while the sea-approaches to the island were commanded by batteries of guns. There was an air base too, and a garrison of some seven thousand men.

Singapore was a handsome city, with its white cathedral, its stately offices of law and government, the spruce bungalows of its British rulers and the haphazard quarters which housed the Chinese, the Malays, the Javanese, and all the other thousands who had flocked from half Asia to this profitable emporium. The British colony lived in Singapore complacently, enjoying the rewards of Empire without too many of its discomforts. It was inconceivable to them that British troops might actually be beaten by Asians, just as it was impossible to imagine an Englishman ordered about by Asians. It was not done, so it would not happen.

In this as in much else they were pitiably out of touch with developments at home. There, by 1940, the strategists had virtually dismissed the Far Eastern Empire, so overwhelming were the dangers nearer home. The Americans had already been warned that the defence of the region was beyond British capability. As for Singapore itself, a defence conference had secretly reported that, far from being impregnable, if Malaya were ever lost the island would be untenable—almost all its defences were on the seaward side, and there was almost nothing to stop an enemy crossing the Johore Strait from the north.

The Australians and New Zealanders, always afraid of Japanese intentions, pressed repeatedly for the reinforcement of Singapore, but British priorities were elsewhere. The fighter aircraft which should have flown in relays to the east were at home defending Britain. The battleships supposed to rush to the base were engaged in the Mediterranean. In the summer of 1941 the Far Eastern Fleet consisted of three old cruisers and five destroyers. There was not a single tank in the Malay Peninsula, and not a single modern fighter east of Egypt.

Churchill hoped in any case that the Japanese could be deterred from attacking the Empire by old-school imperial means—by a "show of force". In October 1941, when Tokyo's posture seemed particularly threatening, he ordered to Singapore two capital ships, the battleship *Prince of Wales* and the battle cruiser *Repulse*, the Prince of Wales's pleasure-ship twenty years before. They sailed there without air cover, their escorting carrier having been delayed by an accident in Jamaica, to intimidate by their presence a Japanese battle fleet eight times their size and with a formidable air arm. "Thus," said Churchill at a Lord Mayor's banquet in London, "we stretch out the long arm of brotherhood and motherhood to the Australian and New Zealand people. . . ."

Far away in Singapore the arrival of the great ships seemed no more than proper. The colony's sense of security remained absolute, and life went on exactly as before. It accordingly came as a terrible psychological shock when in December 1941 the Japanese, the most Asian of all Asians, who rode about on bicycles, who talked in absurd high-pitched voices and were always comically bowing to one another, fell with a hideous efficiency upon the British possessions in Asia. It was only to be expected perhaps that Hong Kong, isolated off the Chinese mainland, should soon be captured, though two battalions of Canadian infantry were rushed there when the attack began, arriving just in time to surrender. It was inevitable no doubt that the long line of island possessions, stretching away from the East Indies towards Australia, should be overrun. But it was an almost unimaginable blow when the two great capital ships, sailing from Singapore with four destroyers to prevent Japanese landings on the Malayan coast, were both sunk by Japanese bombers in the China Sea.

Even so, Singapore itself would surely stand. "I trust you'll chase the little men off," said the governor of the island, Sir Shenton Thomas, when the general in command told him that the Japanese had landed in Malaya. Even as the enemy divisions stormed southward through the Malay jungle, thirty miles a day towards the straits of Johore, life in Singapore proceeded placidly. They still had their Sunday singsongs at the Seaview Hotel. They still had a daily tea dance at the Raffles Club. Even when, on January 28, 1942, General Tomoyuki Yamashita arrived with his command post on the north bank of the Johore Strait and it was decided to make a strong point

CHILDHOOD MEMORIES

Here are two accounts of how young children experienced the Second World War. Firstly, Lionel King records his impressions, as an eight-year-old, of flying bombs in 1944. Then Agnes Newton Keith describes her son's birthday in April 1944 in Kuching prison camp, Borneo.

Flying Bombs: An Eight-Year-Old Remembers

On the night of June 12 the first of Hitler's V1s fell on London and the Southeast. News spread in from the Kent and Sussex coasts of aircraft with "jet nozzles", "fire exhausts" and odd engine sounds. Over Kent some of these craft had suddenly stopped and fallen with a devastating explosion to follow. Bombing of course was familiar to our family. We had moved from West Ham earlier in the war. I'd spent endless nights in the dugout in the garden unable to sleep because of Nanny's snoring. Now it was happening in the daytime too.

The first came over one afternoon. Our windows and doors were open in those fine June days and the drone of the approaching flying bomb was quite unmistakable. It gave us little warning. Ten seconds and the engine cut out directly overhead. There was an oddly resounding explosion about half a mile away.

Flying bombs looked exactly like miniature aircraft, as this specimen displayed at an exhibition after the war shows.

The Boy Foot, as my mother called him, cycled up there and reported back: "King Edward Road—there's debris everywhere. Fire brigade and wardens are there, still digging 'em out. I saw it coming. I was up on the roof."

I was envious of his roof. You could have seen anything from there.

Soon so many V1s were coming over that the authorities gave up air-raid warnings. They would have been sounding the siren all the time. When a bomb announced its approach, Doug and I dived for the shelter, not forgetting to grab our cat Jimmy if he was in sight. Sometimes Mum was out shopping and we went to the shelter alone. We were never worried or afraid. It was all over in ten seconds anyway.

Birthday In A Japanese Prison Camp

On April 5 George was four years old. It was his second birthday in prison camp. Harry [George's father] was in the guardhouse. George had no present from him.

At midday, Lilah and I got out the box of Red Cross food. We opened everything and divided each item into thirty-four sections. It required mathematical precision, but we did it. Every child then brought a bowl or plate to us, and watched with shining eyes.

We filled each plate with little mounds of salmon, sardine, butter, Spam, ham, jelly, meat, prunes, chocolate, cheese, and we had made a milk pudding with milk and rice, which we added. Then we called for cups, and distributed coffee with sugar. And all mothers were rewarded for being mothers, with cigarettes.

Each child took his plate, said "Thank you" politely, said "Happy Birthday" to George, and scurried home. Each face was pale with excitement. This was not fun or pleasure. This was tense, terrible, earnest participation in Paradise.

I had wondered beforehand if I was wrong in not saving the foodstuff for George, to feed to him over a period of time. But when I saw those faces I knew I was right.

George's melting gratification in having something to give, his pride in being a benefactor, made him swell all day long before my eyes, until by night-time he was twice-normal. How I loved him then!

on the Singapore golf course, the soldiers were told nothing could be done until the club committee had met.

There were more than one hundred thousand soldiers on the island. The Malayan garrison, what was left of it, had retreated across the causeway, ineffectually blowing it up behind them, and British, Australian and Indian reinforcements had arrived by sea. "The city of Singapore", Churchill cabled, "must be converted into a citadel and defended to the death. . . . Our whole fighting reputation is at stake and the honour of the British Empire. . . . There must be no question or thought of surrender."

But the muddle was terrible. Military clashed with civilian, commander with commander. The very word "siege" was banned, in case it weakened British prestige among the Asians. General Arthur Ernest Percival, the

D-DAY THROUGH GERMAN EYES

An anonymous German private describes his personal experience of the Allied invasion.

On that night of June 6 none of us expected the invasion anymore. There was a strong wind, thick cloud cover, and the enemy aircraft had not bothered us more that day than usual. But then—in the night—the air was full of innumerable planes. We thought, "What are they demolishing tonight?" But then it started. I was at the wireless set myself. One message followed the other. "Parachutists landed here—gliders reported there," and finally "Landing craft approaching." Some of our guns fired as best they could. In the morning a huge naval force was sighted—that was the last report our advanced observation posts could send us, before they were overwhelmed. And it was the last report we received about the situation.

It was no longer possible to get an idea of what was happening. Wireless communications were jammed, the cables cut and our officers had lost grasp of the situation. Infantrymen who were streaming back told us that their positions on the coast had been overrun or that our few "bunkers" had either been shot up or blown to pieces.

Right in the middle of all this turmoil I got orders to go with my car for a reconnaissance towards the coast. With a few infantrymen I reported to a lieutenant. His orders were to retake a village nearby. While he was still talking to me to explain the position, a British tank came rolling towards us from behind, from a direction in which we had not even suspected the presence of the enemy. The enemy tank immediately opened fire on us. Resistance was out of the question.

I saw how a group of Polish infantrymen went over to the enemy—carrying their machine guns and waving their arms. The officer and myself hid in the brush. When we tried to get through to our lines later in the evening British paratroops caught us.

At first I was rather depressed, of course. I, an old soldier, a prisoner of war after a few hours of invasion. But when I saw the material behind the enemy front, I could only say, "Old man, how lucky you have been!"

And when the sun rose the next morning, I saw the invasion fleet lying off the shore. Ship beside ship. And without a break, troops, weapons, tanks, munitions and vehicles were being unloaded in a steady stream.

The landing of British and American troops at Omaha Beach, Normandy, heralds the end of the war in Europe.

commanding general, was a brave but uninspiring man, and the morale of the British in Singapore, sustained for so long by myth and shibboleth, abruptly collapsed.

Presently the Japanese were shelling and bombing the port incessantly while queues of women and children waited at the dockside for passage on ships about to leave. On the night of February 8 the Japanese crossed the Johore Strait; on the twelfth a note from Yamashita was dropped by air, paying tribute to "the honour of British warriorship", and threatening "annihilating attacks" on Singapore unless the garrison surrendered; on the evening of Sunday, February 15, General Percival sued for peace. The convictions of two centuries were knocked topsy-turvy by this event, and Asians were never to look upon Englishmen in the same way again. The surrender was the worst reverse in the history of British arms. It was, however, the realistic and humane course of action, and if it hastened the demise of the Empire at least it saved thousands of human lives.

More than a hundred and twenty thousand soldiers and civilians were sent into captivity, and many ladies of the Seaview singsong were last seen, clutching a few bundles of their possessions, trudging along the coast road towards Changi Gaol, whose gates they entered, for three years of terrible imprisonment, singing a tawdry but beloved patriotic song of the day, "There'll Always Be an England".

The next edition of Whitaker's *Almanack* recorded Singapore as being "temporarily in hostile Japanese occupation", and though before long the whole of the eastern Empire was taken by the Japanese, and even India was seriously threatened, still the British thought of these as "temporary" setbacks. Throughout the war colonial officials interned in Stanley Prison, Hong Kong, maintained that the British government of Hong Kong was still in being, even if its writ ran no farther than the prison walls. A powerful stream of propaganda was directed towards the occupied colonies, assuring them that the British Empire would soon be returning; in most of them resistance movements were fostered or clandestine operations mounted, organised principally by the Special Operations Executive.

For example, Orde Wingate, with his Chindit guerrillas, penetrated behind the enemy lines in occupied Burma for months at a time until he was killed in an air crash in 1944. Other British forces in Burma, operating far beyond the Irrawaddy, got in touch with Aung San's traitorous Burma Defence Army and helped to turn it against its Japanese sponsors—Aung San himself being transformed from a "traitor rebel leader", as Churchill had called him, into a gallant ally. The imperial administrators of the Solomon Islands, when the Japanese landed there, took to the bush with their radio transmitters and stayed there for the rest of the war, protected by their former subjects, sending information to the American forces. In occupied Sarawak the anthropologist Tom Harrison, dropped by parachute with two companions, mustered the inland tribes into guerrilla units, and later turned himself into Officer Administering Interior, Borneo.

One by one, as the war progressed, the imperial territories were indeed repossessed. The British 14th Army, with seven hundred thousand Indians and two divisions of Africans, slogged its way back into Burma, finally defeating the Japanese in the greatest of all land battles against them—one of the fiercest hand-to-hand engagements being fought around the deputy commissioner's bungalow at Kohima in the Naga Hills. With a somewhat

The fall of Singapore in February 1942 saw the largest surrender in the history of the British army. About eighty-five thousand British and Commonwealth soldiers surrendered to a far smaller Japanese force and many were subsequently to lose their lives in Japanese prison camps, the most notorious of which was Changi. This photograph shows the British surrender party bearing both the Union Jack and the white flag of surrender.

obvious symbolism, when the British returned to Singapore, the Japanese had to await their conquerors outside the proud government buildings in Empress Place; the Union Jack was the very same flag beneath which General Percival had marched to his surrender; among the watching crowds were thousands of emaciated soldiers released from Japanese prison camps, and the imperial plenipotentiary accepting the submission of the Japanese command turned out to be no less than a royal admiral, Lord Louis Mountbatten, Supreme Allied Commander in Southeast Asia and a cousin of King George VI.

It was all too late, however. The return to the conquered territories might provide a transient satisfaction to the British, but it convinced nobody, least of all the subject inhabitants. The Empire could never be the same again. As the war proceeded the British had become progressively more dependent upon American supplies and equipment. We see Churchill still sitting as an equal with Roosevelt and Stalin at the Yalta Conference, deciding the future of the world; but it was more force of habit than political truth. There was pathos to Churchill's insistence, after the collapse of Germany in 1945, that the American fleets in the Pacific should be joined by a British battle fleet— so slow, so ill-equipped, so inexperienced in Pacific fighting that it was an embarrassment to its American commanders.

When it all ended, the British were unmistakably junior partners in the Grand Alliance. Yet as the world generously recognised, it had been, all in all, a fine conclusion to all the struggles, honourable and iniquitous, victorious or disastrous, by which the British Empire had established its presence across the world.

It had been a last glimpse of greatness for the British—through the muddle and the miseries, as Churchill said, "weary and worn, impoverished but undaunted, we had a moment that was sublime."

The full meaning of the Last War escaped the British at the time. They thought they were destroying a truly bestial enemy, but they were also

The historic meeting of the Grand Alliance, or "Big Three", at the Yalta Conference in February 1945: Churchill (left), Roosevelt (centre), and Stalin. After the Second World War, Britain's role as a major power was soon eclipsed by the Cold War confrontation between the Soviets and the Americans.

destroying themselves and their heritage. Even their leaders, it seemed, seldom perceived this truth, and read in the story of the war only its heroic texts. Harold Macmillan, a future prime minister of Great Britain, was present at the victory parade in Tunis which marked the end of the campaigns in North Africa—the first in which American arms participated. The omens he read into the occasion were inspiring, but altogether false. First in the parade came the French and their colonial troops, then the Americans. A long pause followed, and Macmillan began to wonder if there had been a hitch in the arrangements. But no: faint, strange and magnificent over the crest of the road came the skirl of bagpipes, and then in a slow and steady pace the massed pipes of the British armies swung tremendously past the reviewing stand, followed by fourteen thousand bronzed and cocky veterans of the desert war. "These men seemed on that day", Macmillan recorded, "masters of the world and heirs of the future."

In one sense they were. Even when the war ended, when Russian and American power was vastly greater than British, they controlled more territory than they ever had before. Not only was the whole of their Empire restored to them, not only did they share with their allies the governance of Germany, Austria and Italy, but to an unprecedented degree the Mediterranean was a British lake. It was an imperialist's dream. The whole of the North African littoral, the whole of the Levant was held by British arms, southern Persia was occupied and even Greece was more or less a British sphere of influence. With imperial armies deployed across the world, with a Royal Navy of three thousand five hundred fighting ships and a Royal Air Force of unparalleled prestige, in theory the British Empire was a power as never before, and the ageing Churchill, intoxicated by the honour of it all, was determined to keep it so. Things had worked out pretty well, he told an exuberant London audience. "The British Commonwealth and Empire stands more united and more effectively powerful than at any time in its long romantic history."

One of the survivors of Belsen. As the Allies pushed back the German army towards Berlin, they liberated the concentration camps in which more than six million Jews had died. It was only then that the full horror of the Holocaust was revealed to the world.

CHAPTER 13

THE AFTERMATH

IT DID NOT LAST LONG. The Churchills and the Macmillans might respond to glory, but still the mass of the British people were not interested in power or influence. A tremendous homesickness seized the exhausted armies, and a sense of duty completed lay upon the now shabby homeland. The people wanted only to live quietly and comfortably, and disillusioned as they had been by the torments of slump and unemployment in the 1930s, they saw in the aftermath of war the chance to make a fresh start—not in the distant fields of Empire, but in their own familiar island. They would not be gulled again by illusions of splendour.

Churchill was dismissed from office at the first chance, and went smouldering off to write his war memoirs and to complete his *History of the English-Speaking Peoples*. The Labour Government which took office under Clement Attlee in 1945 dedicated itself to social reform at home, internationalism abroad. The British Empire was held momentarily in abeyance while the new rulers of Great Britain decided what best to do with it.

Foreigners had firmer ideas, and the general opinion in the years after the Second World War was that it should now be abolished. The Americans viewed the British Empire confusedly. There was still a powerful class of Anglophiles in the United States, especially in the Protestant establishment of the east, and there was respect for the presence and the experience of the English, and for the common origins of the two nations. The Special Relationship, the Anglo-American axis forged during the war, survived into the peace, and made Britain, even in her straitened circumstances, more than a client state, but rather like a family adviser past the peak of his career. This understanding did not, however, extend to the British Empire.

In July 1941 Churchill had gone to Newfoundland to draw up with President Roosevelt the Atlantic Charter, a pietistic declaration of war aims.

HIROSHIMA, AUGUST 6, 1945

This account was given to the author, Marcel Junod, by a Japanese journalist who actually witnessed the cataclysm which has influenced international politics ever since.

On August 6 there wasn't a cloud in the sky above Hiroshima, and a mild, hardly perceptible wind blew from the south. Visibility was almost perfect for ten or twelve miles.

At nine minutes past seven in the morning an air-raid warning sounded and four American B-29 planes appeared. To the north of the town two of them turned and made off to the south and disappeared in the direction of the Shoho Sea. The other two, after having circled the neighbourhood of Shukai flew off at high speed southwards in the direction of the Bingo Sea.

At 7.31 the all-clear was given. Feeling themselves in safety people came out of their shelters and went about their affairs and the work of the day began.

Suddenly a glaring whitish pinkish light appeared in the sky accompanied by an unnatural tremor which was followed almost immediately by a wave of suffocating heat and a wind which swept away everything in its path.

Within a few seconds the thousands of people in the streets and the gardens in the centre of the town were scorched by a wave of searing heat. Many were killed instantly, others lay writhing on the ground screaming in agony from the intolerable pain of their burns. Everything standing upright in the way of the blast, walls, houses, factories and other buildings, was annihilated and the debris spun round in a whirlwind and was carried up into the air. Trams were picked up and tossed aside as though they had neither weight nor solidity. Trains were flung off the rails as though they were toys. Horses, dogs and cattle suffered the same fate as human beings. Every living thing was petrified in an attitude of indescribable suffering. Even the vegetation did not escape. Trees went up in flames, the rice plants lost their greenness, the grass burned on the ground like dry straw.

Beyond the zone of utter death in which nothing remained alive houses collapsed in a whirl of beams, bricks and girders. Up to about three miles from the centre of the explosion lightly built houses were flattened as though they had been built of cardboard. Those who were inside were

More than sixty per cent of the city of Hiroshima was destroyed when the atomic bomb fell. Eighty thousand lives were lost.

either killed or wounded. Those who managed to extricate themselves by some miracle found themselves surrounded by a ring of fire. And the few who succeeded in making their way to safety generally died twenty or thirty days later from the delayed effects of the deadly gamma rays.

Some of the reinforced concrete or stone buildings remained standing but their interiors were completely gutted by the blast.

About half an hour after the explosion whilst the sky all around Hiroshima was still cloudless a fine rain began to fall on the town and went on for about five minutes. It was caused by the sudden rise of over-heated air to a great height, where it condensed and fell back as rain. Then a violent wind rose and the fires extended with terrible rapidity, because most Japanese houses are built only of timber and straw.

By the evening the fire began to die down and then it went out. There was nothing left to burn. Hiroshima had ceased to exist.

Determined to do it in the imperial style, he sailed on board the battleship *Prince of Wales*, fresh from the battle in which the greatest of German warships, *Bismarck*, had been sunk in the north Atlantic, six months from her own end in the China Sea: and it was beneath her fourteen-inch gun turrets that the two leaders were photographed at the end of their talks, surrounded by all the ancient circumstances of the Royal Navy. The Charter, however, which the Prime Minister found himself obliged to sign was anything but an imperial document, for it referred specifically to "the right of all people to choose the form of government under which they live". Churchill tried vainly to write in a clause excluding the British Empire from this awkward philosophy, and explained, when he returned to London, that it was "primarily intended to apply to Europe". It was not, though. It was intended to apply to empires everywhere, not least Churchill's own.

Roosevelt himself was a vehement critic of the Empire—"the British would take land anywhere in the world," he once remarked, "even if it were only a rock or a sandbar." As early as 1942 he was suggesting to Churchill that India should be given immediate dominion status, with freedom to secede from the Empire altogether—but of course, he disingenuously added, "all you good people know far more about it than I do."

In the Far East the Americans were determined that Hong Kong, when it was liberated from the Japanese, should be handed over to their Chinese ally Chiang Kai-shek. When liberation came to Hong Kong in 1945 it was only the action of Franklin Gimson, the former Colonial Secretary, that kept it British—the moment he emerged from Stanley Prison, after three years of imprisonment, he ran up the Union Jack over Government House and resumed the colonial administration on his own initiative.

Nor were the American anti-imperialists much appeased by the disappearance of the diehard Churchill and the advent of a pacific and reformist Socialist Government in Britain. On the contrary, now they feared the development of a *socialist* Empire—tea, rubber, tin and cocoa, reported the *New York Times* gloomily in August 1945, would probably all be nationalised. For economically the Americans were determined that in the reformed postwar world they would be dominant. They had always resented the imperial tariff systems, and they saw now their chance to break into vast new imperial markets. By 1946 the dollar had succeeded the pound as the chief world currency, and the American industrial machine, far from being debilitated by the war, like the British, was buoyant and productive as never before. Britain had lost enormous overseas assets, a loss calculated as thirty-five times that of the United States. Great Britain, for so long the greatest exporter in the world, was now outclassed by the United States: American products of every kind, backed often by American loans, flooded the markets of the world, satisfying demands frustrated by years of war.

Wherever they went, the Americans presented an overwhelming image of opulence, vigour and generosity, more compelling by far than the dry modes of Empire. They cheerfully disregarded the old imperial taboos and superstitions, like the vital necessity of wearing topees in the tropic sun. They lacked the proper sahibs' aloofness, they laughed at the carefully devised orthodoxies of the imperial system, passed on so reverently from generation to generation. And they had quite patently inherited from the British the magnetism of power. "Australia looks to America," declared the Australian Prime Minister, John Curtin, "free of any pangs as to our

On August 14, 1945, little over a month after the Labour Party's landslide victory over the Conservatives in the general election, the Japanese surrendered. Clement Attlee (1883-1967), the Labour Prime Minister, is pictured here broadcasting the news from the Cabinet Room at Number 10, Downing Street.

EDUCATION FOR ALL

O F ALL THE REFORMS of the nineteenth century, W.E. Forster's Education Act in 1870 was the most far-reaching. The Act called for a system of schools "for all classes of the people, supported by the State and paid for by a rate on each district". The government's decision ten years later to make schooling compulsory—initially to the age of ten, later to twelve—was equally important.

The so-called "Board Schools" were not designed "for all classes of people", and many better-off families continued to send their children to private (in Britain, "public") schools. Yet the new schools provided efficient instruction—particularly in the three Rs of reading, writing and arithmetic—and training in social behaviour to children who, previously, would have received no education at all.

A further Education Act in 1902 transferred the powers of specially elected school boards to local authorities, and laid the foundations of a selective secondary education system in which the brightest children received the best facilities. And while further Education Acts were passed in 1918 and 1944 when the demands of war pointed to the need for an educated population, this concept remained dominant until the development of non-selective comprehensive schooling during the 1950s. By the middle of the 1970s, however, more than half of the secondary-school population were attending State-supported comprehensive schools. But the content of the education they provided remained, as ever, a matter for heated debate.

Since the 1960s increasing emphasis has been placed upon education as a lifelong process. The number of students in higher education increased rapidly as the old universities expanded and new universities and polytechnics came into existence. A belief that everyone should have a chance of higher education inspired the "Open University", which accepted its first part-time, home-based students in 1971.

COMPULSORY ELEMENTARY EDUCATION transformed many children's lives. Schools were purpose-built, like Leeds Kindergarten (above), and although discipline had to be strict in classes of about fifty, lessons could be fun. The objects on display and the pride shown by each child in holding a sample of work suggests that a variety of subjects was being taught in this school. With compulsory education came further laws to prevent truancy (1880), and to ensure the education of blind and deaf children (1893).

MEDICAL AND PASTORAL CARE in school initially meant that some children were washed by teachers before they entered class. Later, local education authorities were empowered to give medical treatment to school children. In the picture below, children's heads are examined for lice at a "cleansing station" in 1911. Free school meals and milk, inoculation against disease and dental, sight and hearing tests eventually helped to raise health standards and compensate for parental neglect.

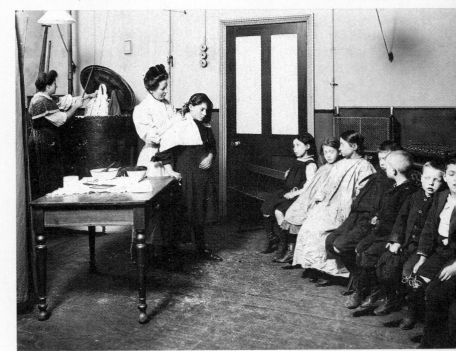

COMPREHENSIVE SCHOOLS *have now replaced most of the old grammar schools, technical schools and secondary moderns established by the 1944 Butler Education Act, which catered for three different types of intelligence. The authorities had claimed to be able to identify a child's aptitude by means of an examination taken at the age of eleven. The comprehensive system abolished the "11 plus" scholarship* examinations *and sought to provide a less rigid and divisive education which developed the whole of a child's potential. The photograph (above) shows some of the new aims of the comprehensive system in operation at the Garratt Green Comprehensive in Wandsworth. A small, informal class is held in a spacious hall designed for cultural, sporting and academic activities.*

EDUCATION FOR GIRLS *was pioneered by many dedicated single women such as Florence Nightingale, Frances Mary Buss and Dorothea Beale (above). Miss Beale had been head teacher in The Clergy Daughters' School, Casterton, Westmorland (the "Lowood" of Charlotte Brontë's* Jane Eyre) *before she became Principal of Cheltenham Ladies' College in 1857. She instituted the teaching of science and helped to found St Hilda's College for women teachers at Cheltenham (1885) and St Hilda's Hall at Oxford (1894). Public and grammar schools for girls were opened in many towns from 1880 onwards.*

ADULT EDUCATION *was made far more widely available in 1903 with the foundation of the Workers' Educational Association, which held regular classes and established summer schools with university extramural potential. These were the forerunners of the Open University which used old and new methods of learning, as shown in the photograph (left), in which a student prepares to watch a course module on television. Adult and community colleges now offer both academic and leisure-interest classes.*

Joseph Stalin (1879-1953). His family name was Dzhugashvili but he adopted the name Stalin, which means "man of steel". Stalin was in supreme command of the Russian war effort and attended the Allied conferences. Postwar Russia remained tightly under Stalin's control and his rule of terror and purges continued until his death in 1953. Stalin was buried in the Lenin Mausoleum, but in 1956 his rule was officially denounced in the Soviet Union. His body was removed from the Mausoleum in 1961.

traditional link or kinship with the United Kingdom," and young men throughout the Empire, of all races, turned to the American example.

An even more baleful view of the Empire prevailed in Moscow. This was only to be expected. Even in Tsarist days, Russia was considered the most insidious of the Empire's enemies, and the Bolshevik Revolution had done nothing to ease the mutual suspicion. Just the opposite, for while the Tsarist threat had been purely strategic, the massive pressure of one expanding empire upon another, the Communist threat was profoundly ideological. Marx had defined imperialism as the last stage of capitalism, and Ireland had always been the Marxist archetype of oppression: now the anathema was extended to the whole colonial empire.

Churchill's alliance with Soviet Russia, concluded in the desperation of war, was purely opportunist. He detested Communism, and had consistently opposed it. His fine words about Russian heroism and brotherhood, the propaganda adulation of the Red Army, the jewelled Sword of Stalingrad sent to Russia in tribute by the British people, the convoys taking supplies to Murmansk, meant nothing, beyond the immediate necessities of war.

It was "ridiculous" Stalin had once observed to Ribbentrop, Hitler's foreign minister, "that a few hundred Englishmen should dominate India." Also it did not fit the Communist dogma. The Marxist view of history meant that Empire was an instrument of capitalist profit. It was racialism, exploitation, capitalism, all mixed up, and was presently to become the favourite pejorative of the entire Marxist glossary.

For some years after the war the Russians let the Empire be. They were as exhausted as the British by the conflict, and they were inhibited perhaps by the fact that American nuclear power dictated the state of the world. Unlike the Americans, too, they seemed to miss the truth of the British decline, and far from depicting the Empire as a decaying and impotent tyrant, greatly overstressed its power. It was a decade before they achieved any obvious success in the imperial territories.

Economically they posed no threat. Their export industries were vestigial, their currency more or less private. But as the spectacle of America dimmed the allure of Empire, so in a subtler way the message of Communist Russia nagged away at the Empire's composure. The intelligent young of the subject peoples, denied real political expression, were attracted to an ideology which specifically declared itself to be raceless and classless, at once anti-imperialist and social-revolutionary.

Soon most of the infant nationalist movements of the Empire had their Marxist cadres, and their leaders found their way by one means or another to founts of Communist teaching, generally in London, sometimes in Moscow itself. In England, George Padmore, a West Indian Communist agent, instructed generations of young Africans, who had come to England to study medicine or the principles of Common Law, and went home politically indoctrinated from Moscow—among them the young Kenyan Jomo Kenyatta, and the Gold Coast leader Kwame Nkrumah. Most of the guerrilla leaders of Malaya and Burma were Communists, and having fought against the Japanese during the war, emerged to work against the British in the peace.

The British hardly knew what was happening. They still allowed almost no political activity in the subject colonies, and in many parts of the Empire the instinct of white supremacy had survived the war intact. The settlers of Kenya were as racialist as ever; in South Africa apartheid, the forcible separation of the races, was about to become the very basis of social life. The young activists of Afro-Asia (a convenient new geo-political concept) naturally turned to the force most unlike their rulers, and realised for the first time how false was their subjection. Communism was the party of universal brotherhood, sworn to rid the world of racialism and imperialism. Communism would cut the lordly British down to size.

However, the groundswell of discontent among the subject peoples was essentially patriotic. Though the British preferred to call it "nationalist", a word which had an obscurely disreputable ring to it, and its leaders were always said to be "agitators", it was really just love of country, of culture, of one's own people and one's own history. Social reform played little part in these early stirrings of rebellion. Independence was all.

In 1945 a Pan-African Congress was held in the town hall of Chorlton-on-Medlock, a suburb of Manchester dominated by the university. Delegates came from most African territories, and they passed a resolution demanding autonomy and independence for the whole of black Africa. The London newspapers took little notice. But the delegates at that meeting, the plans and the new resolves they took home with them to Africa, were presently to change the world.

Among the emergent patriots were some remarkable men. Some were familiar and comprehensible figures, like the brilliant Nehru, Harrow and Cambridge, who wrote an exquisite English prose, behaved like a gentleman, and spoke a language of politics that needed no interpreters. Others were much stranger. Nobody knew quite what to make, for instance, of Jomo Kenyatta, the Kenyan, the grandson of a Kikuyu magician whose education had been part Church of Scotland evangelicalism, part tribal ritualism, part London School of Economics. This powerful and clever man baffled the British first to last. He had been a Communist in his time, he had spent many years in England, he had written an anthropological study of his tribe, he had been an active Kenyan nationalist since the 1920s and returned to Nairobi in 1946 as president of the Kenya African Union. As his thick-set calculating figure rose from obscurity to fame, petty agitator to celebrated national leader, they never did master how many of his motives were urges towards power that Westerners could understand, and how many were mysteries of Africa, from another morality and another sensibility.

Another riddle was Gamal Abdul Nasser, the Egyptian revolutionary leader who was presently to oust both Farouk and the British themselves. The British had never heard of the fellow until he thrust himself to power, for he was a lifelong conspirator, full of charm and good sense, but recognising no accepted channel of dissent, publishing no manifestos, addressing no meetings, simply working quietly and anonymously until the moment of revolution came. Such men were baffling to the Empire. Fair play did not allow for them, and the rules did not apply. The Arab leaders who now set about destroying British suzerainty were men of a kind the British hardly knew—who had never played a hand of bezique with the ambassador up at the palace, nor even been invited. In Singapore the easygoing Malays were being supplanted by the formidable and secretive Chinese. In Cyprus a learned archbishop, Makarios III, theological graduate of Boston University, was allying himself with a murderous guerrilla, Georgios Grivas, in a campaign to achieve *enosis*.

It was not simply a new world, as it had been after the First World War. Now it was *several* new worlds, surrounding the perimeters of the British Empire, and erupting within. This great movement of change was more organic than deliberate. No universal conspiracy linked the scattered patriots. Some were Communists, some tribalists, some men of religion, some cultural nationalists. All, though, were encouraged by one common instinct: the British Empire was dying, and the heirs must prepare themselves.

The British themselves, however, continued to believe in the power of their prestige, a self-deception that prevented them from coming to terms with history, and accepting their reduced circumstances in the world.

Even now, at the end of the 1940s, most of them believed in their hearts that things British were necessarily things best. They believed that they, over all their allies, had won the war. They saw themselves still, like their grandfathers, as a senior and superior race. Foreigners were still inferior. Coloured peoples were still of a different class. Abroad was still comic. Not only within their Europe, but across half the world, they expected to be treated with deference. Nevertheless, it was not an *imperial* braggadocio. Except in matters of "prestige", the British cared little about their Empire, and knew still less. A poll in 1947 revealed that three-quarters of the population did not know the difference between a dominion and a colony, that half could not name a single British possession, and that three per cent thought the United States was still a British colony. Their pride was in themselves, not in their Empire, and in this if nothing else their instinct was right. If Britain was to be prosperous and influential in the future it must be as an island off the coast of Europe.

CHAPTER 14

THE INDEPENDENCE OF INDIA

ON MARCH 22, 1947, A NEW VICEROY arrived at New Delhi to take up office, and he and his wife were met by their predecessors on the steps of Lutyens's palace. Never was there such a contrast in styles between the old incumbents and the new. Down the steps came Lord and Lady Wavell, elderly and benevolent, he dressed in his field marshal's uniform, his face grey and haggard, his one eye heavy-lidded (he had lost the other in the Great War), she smiling in the background in a low-waisted dress of floral silk and looking for all the world like a bishop's wife welcoming a new curate.

Up the steps came Lord and Lady Mountbatten of Burma, in the prime of worldly life, dashing, good-looking, confident, he in the uniform of an admiral slashed with the medal ribbons of a triumphant wartime career, she svelte in green cotton, as though she might be going on later to cocktails in Knightsbridge. The field marshal was a cultivated, gentlemanly but not very demonstrative soldier, aged sixty-three, the admiral a pushing, rather conceited and brilliantly enterprising sailor, aged forty-six. One man bowed to the other, the younger woman curtseyed to the older, but later that day the viceroyalty passed from Wavell to Mountbatten, and the courtesies were reversed. Their meaning was ironic, for the admiral's sole purpose in assuming this, the greatest office the British Empire had to offer, was

The new Viceroy, Lord Mountbatten of Burma (1900-1979), in civilian dress, is flanked by the retiring Viceroy, Lord Wavell, and Lady Wavell. Lord Wavell is chatting to Lady Mountbatten. Mountbatten, the great-grandson of Queen Victoria, was the last British Viceroy. He presided over the transfer of power to the two separate states of India and Pakistan, and remained in India as Governor-General until 1948.

to end the Raj in India, and finally conclude the long line of the viceroys.

Since the constitution of 1935, India had muddled on, and she was no nearer independence ten years later. This was not for lack of trying. The nationalists had maintained their pressure throughout the war; the British, nagged by their allies, had gone so far in 1942 as to offer immediate dominion status after victory.

Most Englishmen, though, still doubted if Indians were ready for self-government; for one thing the populace was now apparently irrevocably divided on religious lines, for another there was the problem of the myriad princely states, not part of British India at all, but direct feudatories of the imperial Crown. Most Indians, for their part, still doubted if the British were sincere, suspected that the Muslim-Hindu rivalry was encouraged for imperial purposes, and had no patience with the pettifogging and sycophantic princes. The Hindus believed themselves to be the natural successors to the British as rulers of all India; the Muslims believed themselves to be natural rulers *per se*, never subject to Hindu rule and never likely to be; the Sikhs believed themselves to be superior to any other parties in the dispute. The British thought themselves, *au fond*, indispensable.

The war had sharpened these multiple antagonisms. The British were disillusioned by Indian behaviour during the war. Though Indian soldiers had fought on nearly every front, none of the chief Hindu leaders had helped in the war—they were all imprisoned for subversion in 1942—and the "Quit India" movement had brought the country to the brink of revolution at the most vicious moment of the conflict. The British were dismayed to find the defectors of the Indian army greeted as heroes by the populace, and their leader Subhas Chandra Bose hailed after his death as a martyr and a liberator.

Conversely, British prestige had been irrevocably eroded by the war. The viceroy's unilateral declaration of war had been bitterly resented. "There was something rotten," Nehru thought, "when one man, and a foreigner and representative of a hated system, could plunge four hundred million human beings into war without a slightest reference to them." The fall of Singapore fatally weakened the British military reputation, and as more and more Indians succeeded to senior jobs in the government at home, so the Raj itself lost its power of aloof command.

Anyway, ever since the Salt March, Indian leaders had felt themselves to be masters of their own destinies. It was only a matter of time. The Indians, Hindu and Muslim, were perfectly conscious of their power—all over the world public opinion, ignorant or informed, supported their cause, and it was inconceivable that the British would indefinitely defy it. Gandhi, now the guru of the Congress Party under Nehru's presidency, was already recognised by many of his correspondents as the *de facto* president of India, and the universality of his appeal, the implication that India represented, now as always, deeper spiritual values, gave to British actions a sadly parochial air. It seemed to the British only their duty to arrange matters with order and dignity; it seemed to the rest of the world only sophistry and procrastination.

Before Mountbatten, the British had aimed as usual at compromise. However, the Muslim League, under the inflexible M. A. Jinnah, now demanded a separate state for the country's ninety million Muslims—Pakistan, "Land of the Pure". Firm positions were taken over the many

The major Indian leaders met at the Indian Office in London in 1946, where vital talks on the future of their country were taking place. The photograph shows Jinnah on the extreme right, speaking into a microphone, with the shorter figure of Nehru second from the left. Jinnah was determined to safeguard Muslim interests in an independent India, and eventually Nehru and the Indian Congress reluctantly agreed to the creation of the state of Pakistan.

other disputes and anomalies and gradually, as the parties argued, riots and strikes swept the country. Illegal organisations proliferated. The Indian navy mutinied. There were rumours that the Afghans were about to invade the northwest frontier province, that the Sikhs were about to rebel in the Punjab. The spectre of communal war, Muslim versus Hindu, now stalked the country. In August 1946 the two religions clashed so violently in Calcutta that in a single day five thousand people were said to have died.

Still Wavell had laboured on, studying his interminable instructions from London, reasoning with Jinnah, debating with Nehru, hammering away at constitutional niceties. He blamed it mostly on Churchill's government. "What I want," he wrote, "is some definite policy, and not to go on making promises to India with no really sincere intention of trying to fulfil them." Once he had seemed almost to succeed, when the Indian leaders appeared ready to accept a constitutional settlement, but when that hope collapsed too, the exhausted, dispirited and now embittered viceroy gave up.

Presently he was sacked. Attlee, Prime Minister of the new Labour Government, had firm views about India. He had gone there on a parliamentary mission as long before as 1928, and had concerned himself with the subject ever since. He had long ago reached the conclusion that only the Indians themselves could solve their own problems, and even before the war he had argued that India should be given dominion status within a fixed period of years. By 1946 he was sure that the transfer of power must be made as soon as possible—with the rights of minorities protected if they could be, but above all quickly, and absolutely. The first necessity, he thought, was to be rid of poor Wavell, whom he considered ineffectual. It did not take him long to find a successor. "I thought very hard," he wrote, "and looked all around. And suddenly I had what I now think was an inspiration. I thought of Mountbatten."

Mountbatten! The perfect, the allegorical last viceroy! Royal himself, great-grandson of the original Queen-Empress, second cousin of George VI. He was a world figure in his own right, too, for as Supreme Commander in Southeast Asia he had been one of the four supremos who had disposed of the vast fleets and armies of the western alliance. Moreover he was a recognised progressive, sympathetic to the ideals of Labour.

"What is different about you from your predecessors?" Nehru asked Mountbatten soon after his arrival in India. "Can it be that you have been given plenipotentiary powers? In that case you will succeed where all others have failed." The viceroy had in fact *demanded* such absolute powers, enabling him to reach swift decisions on the spot. He had also committed Attlee to a date for the end of British rule in India. The Raj was to end not later than June, 1948.

This renunciation meant that Britain was genuinely disinterested at last, and was concerned only to see that India was left a workable state, preferably a member of the Commonwealth, at least friendly to Great Britain. She had nothing much to offer in return, nevertheless Mountbatten was marvellously, some thought overweeningly, self-confident.

The Mountbattens brought to the viceregal office an element of *brio* absent since the days of Curzon. They sustained the swagger of it all, with thousands of servants, the white viceregal train, the bodyguards, the curtseying and the royal emblems, but they made it contemporary. The only royal viceroy was the least grandiose of them all. At viceregal dinners

The Calcutta riots of 1946 highlighted the growing tension between the Muslim and Hindu communities as independence drew closer. This photograph shows Muslims trying to set fire to a Hindu temple. In the anarchy of the final days of the Empire, some two hundred thousand Indians died.

now half the guests were always Indian, and earlier incumbents might have been horrified to observe how frankly the Mountbattens talked to natives of all ranks. It was the very negation of imperial technique, but it was proper for the times and the purpose. "All this is yours," he said to Gandhi one day, when the Mahatma asked if he might walk round the viceregal gardens. "We are only trustees. We have come to make it over to you."

Mountbatten hoped to leave behind a federal united India. As second-best, he aimed at a peacefully divided one. He was adamant from the start that there would be no hidden clauses. During his first two months in India Mountbatten had one hundred and thirty-three recorded interviews with Indian political leaders, conducted always in an atmosphere of candid urgency—if the Indians wished to inherit a peaceful India, they must decide fast how to arrange it. He talked to scores of politicians, but the fate of the country was really decided by four men: the viceroy, Gandhi, Nehru and Mohammed Ali Jinnah.

Mountbatten recognised the force of these men. Day after day he received them, usually together, sometimes separately, in the sunny and fresh-painted study at his palace. His relations with the three greatly differed. Gandhi, past the peak of his career, he recognised as a kind of constitutional monarch, he was baffled by him, charmed by him, often, like all Englishmen, irritated by him. "Judge of my delight," he reported once, "when Gandhi arrived for a crucial meeting holding his finger to his lips—it was his day of silence!" Alone among the senior British officials of India, though, he became a friend of the Mahatma, who was attracted by the *soigné* youthfulness of the Mountbattens, their combination of the simple and the very urbane. Though Gandhi was never reconciled to the idea of a divided India, still by making his friendship publicly clear, by appearing often in happy companionship with the viceroy and his wife, he gave his imprimatur to the course of events.

Jinnah was a very different negotiator. He was dying of cancer, but nobody knew it; he was as decisive as Mountbatten himself, and as confident

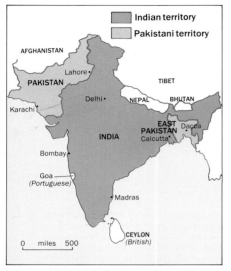

Indian territory	
Pakistani territory	

The partition of India was achieved in five months. Lord Mountbatten arrived in India on March 22, 1947, to become Viceroy, and on August 15 handed over the reins of power. The hastily drawn boundaries between India and Pakistan have been disputed ever since.

too. His lawyer's brain was sharper than the viceroy's, his purpose more dogmatic, and as the months passed towards independence day he became ever more adamant that the only solution was the partition of India and the establishment of Pakistan under the government of the Muslim League. A gaunt, wintry, rather alarming-looking man, with suits of irreproachable cut, Jinnah was very anglicised. He was, though, impervious to the Mountbatten charm. Mountbatten thought him the evil genius of the drama, the wrecker, and called him a haughty megalomaniac.

It was Nehru who became closest to the Mountbattens, and this was not surprising. Nehru was an agnostic intellectual, but of a sensual, emotional kind, a patrician like Mountbatten himself, a charmer and a lover of women. He was a Kashmiri Brahmin, and though he had spent his life fighting in the patriotic cause, he was highly susceptible to personal magnetisms. He needed a cause, a love, a leader. He was the devoted subject of Gandhi, and in a subtle, tacit way he was the passive collaborator of Mountbatten. The two men were of an age and of a taste: through all their tortuous talks an understanding ran.

Getting to know these three men, consulting many others, weighing the opinions of his administrators, Mountbatten quickly made up his mind about the fate of India—too quickly, his critics were to say, and there was something impetuous to his solution, something inherited perhaps from his experiences of war. But finding the parties irreconcilable, he decided that partition was inevitable. Two dominions would be created at once, with immediate independence, and the sooner the better. There would be no interim government of any kind, no gradual transfer of power. Punjab and Bengal, with almost equal numbers of Muslims and Hindus, would be bisected. The princely states would be urged to join one dominion or the other. Everything would be partitioned, the Indian army, the national debt, the railway system, down to the stocks of stationery at the New Delhi secretariat, and the staff cars of GHQ.

Mountbatten flew to London to get the Government's approval, and persuaded Churchill, in Opposition, not to delay the process. Then, in an enormous hurry to prevent the whole administration falling apart in communal violence, he set the plan in motion. Congress and the Muslim League both accepted the proposals, and together their leaders announced it to the nation on All-India Radio. Mountbatten himself gave a press conference to announce that the British could not wait until the following year after all—independence had to come before the end of 1947. Pressed by reporters to name a date, he decided there and then upon the anniversary of the surrender of the Japanese in 1945. They would withdraw from India by August 15, 1947. After two hundred and fifty years on Indian soil, the British had given themselves seventy-three days to retire.

This precipitate partitioning of India was hardly a dignified process, but at least it was decisive. It was, like Dunkirk, a failure dashingly achieved, with a touch of sleight of hand. The Indian princes, who had lost their own independence in return for the protection of the Crown, were to be betrayed. A subcontinent on the brink of civil war was to be subjected to an enormous social and governmental upheaval, millions of people were to assume new nationalities, ministries were to be shuffled here and there. Mountbatten himself called it "fantastic communal madness".

But it was final. In London the India Independence Bill ran through all its parliamentary stages in a single week, ending at a stroke all British claims to sovereignty in India, and abrogating all the hundreds of treaties concluded between the Crown and the princely states. Mountbatten kept a large calendar on his desk, to mark off the days, and with hectic resolution the British in India prepared the obsequies of their paramountcy. It had taken them centuries to pacify and survey the immense expanses of their Indian territories: now in a matter of weeks a boundary commission sliced the edifice into parts, laying new frontiers like string on a building site. The Indian army was bisected, regiments split by squadrons, companies that had served together for a century suddenly distributed among alien battalions. The white viceregal train chuffed away from Delhi for the last time, for it had been allotted to Pakistan.

As the British relentlessly cleared their office desks, India subsided into anarchy. Eleven million people abandoned their homes and moved in hordes across the countryside, hastening to the right side of the new communal frontiers. Violence erupted on a scale never known in British India before, even in the Mutiny. It was like a gigantic boil bursting, an enormous eruption of resentments suppressed for so long by the authority of Empire. Whole communities were massacred. Entire trainloads of refugees died on the tracks, to the last child in arms. In the Punjab, gangs of armed men roamed the countryside, slaughtering columns of refugees, and thousands of people died unremarked in the streets of Amritsar, where the death of four hundred had horrified the world twenty-five years before.

The viceroy was not deterred. Working day and night the last British officials of the Indian Civil Service established administrations for the two new dominions, one with its capital at New Delhi, the other at Karachi. A boundary force, commanded by a Welshman with Hindu and Muslim advisers, was hastily put together to try to keep the peace, and the British army was steadily and unostentatiously withdrawn.

The last days passed. The last of the wavering princely states opted for one dominion or the other, leaving only Kashmir, Hyderabad and Junagadh with their futures unresolved. The last of the British imperialists desperately worked against the clock, creating at least rudimentary governments to succeed themselves. As the bloodshed and the turmoil continued, as the migratory masses laboured this way and that across the Indian plains, in the midst of it all the British Empire came to an end in India. At 8.30 a.m. on the appointed day, August 15, 1947, the Union Jack was hauled down all over the subcontinent. In Karachi, Jinnah was sworn in as governor-general of the dominion of Pakistan. In Delhi, Lord Mountbatten gave up the viceroyalty, with its almost despotic power, and became the governor-general of the dominion of India, with no power at all.

Incalculable crowds celebrated the event in Delhi—the largest crowds anybody could remember seeing, in a country of multitudes. When, after the day's events, the Mountbattens returned in their state coach to the palace, thronged all about by hysterically happy crowds, Nehru sat on top of the hood "like a schoolboy" Mountbatten reported, and four Indian ladies with their children clambered up the sides, a Polish woman and an Indian newspaperman hung on behind. Thus loaded, and accompanied by several thousand running, cheering people, the last of the viceroys clattered up Kingsway to his great house, while fireworks sprayed the evening sky above him, and the thunder of a million people echoed across Delhi.

The mass migration of millions of people into either Hindu India or Muslim Pakistan caused a major refugee problem. Members of both Faiths banded together for protection. This photograph shows Muslim refugees from New Delhi seeking sanctuary in the city's old fort of Purana Quilla.

The end of the British Raj in India. Independence was granted to India on August 15, 1947, when the Viceroy, Lord Mountbatten, officially handed over power to Nehru, who became India's first Prime Minister. On the same day in Karachi, Jinnah was sworn in as Governor-General of Pakistan.

It was done. The flags of the new dominions, the Indian decorated with the Wheel of Ashoka, the Pakistani with Islam's star and crescent, flew all over the subcontinent and all the paraphernalia of authority was handed over to the successor States. King George VI, Emperor no longer, sent his somewhat stilted greetings. Mountbatten proclaimed it "a parting between friends, who have learnt to honour and respect one another, even in disagreement". Attlee said it was not the abdication, but the fulfilment of Britain's mission to India. The British public, casting a cursory eye over the reportage, thought that on the whole they were well out of it. Some two hundred thousand Indians had died.

The British left India euphorically touched by the goodwill they were shown, retaining most of their commercial advantages, and leaving behind at least cadres of government. Since both the new dominions chose to remain within the Commonwealth, they persuaded themselves that the Empire had been preserved anyway, and they persuaded the world that their withdrawal had not only been generous, but had been planned all along. Few of them felt bitter, many felt regret. Soon after the withdrawal Queen Mary, widow of George V, had a letter from her son the King. "The first time Bertie wrote me a letter with the 'I' for Emperor of India left out," she noted in her journal. "Very sad."

It was left to Gandhi to enact by sacrifice the bitter breaking of his own long dream. As the events of 1947 approached their climax, it had seemed to him that India's freedom was being gained without godliness. He had been unassailably opposed to partition, which was a surrender to religious prejudice, and withdrew from political life into prayer and fasting, emerging in public only to preach to the crowds that assembled wherever he appeared, or to calm by his very presence some communal disturbance.

Time and again he appealed for reconciliation between the fanatic religionists; twice he entered into protracted fasts to shame them into peace; he personally quelled riots in Delhi and Calcutta, so effectively that Mountbatten called him "a one-man boundary force". When independence came, and partition became a fact, Gandhi accepted it regretfully and fairly—too fairly, many of the Hindu extremists considered. They thought him altogether too conciliatory to the Pakistanis and his ideas on caste too liberal; and so the chief architect and ornament of Indian independence was killed by his own people for his opinions.

It was a crisp winter evening, January 30, 1948, and the usual throng of people had walked through the dusk to Birla House in New Delhi, where Gandhi held a weekly prayer meeting. It was the home of a rich sympathiser only half a mile from the viceroy's palace. The crowd was sitting on the big lawn behind the house. The Mahatma emerged from a side door, spindly as ever and bowed now over his staff, for he was in his seventy-ninth year, and made his way to his prayer platform at the far end of the garden. As he climbed the shallow steps, and turned to greet the people with his *namaste*, the joined hands and bow of Indian courtesy, a young man in khaki clothing stepped out of the crowd and fired three shots at him with a revolver. Gandhi died at once, and they took his body upstairs in Birla House, and placed it on a balcony for all to see, illuminated by a searchlight from the road below.

As soon as he heard the news Mountbatten hastened down to Birla House. A huge crowd was still milling about the place, and as the governor-general shouldered his tall way to the door a voice cried, "It was a Muslim who did it!" Mountbatten did not know who had done it, but he reacted instantly in the tradition of Empire. "You fool," he cried, so that the crowd could hear, "you fool! Don't you know it was a Hindu?"—and so the imperial instinct, for so long the keeper of the Indian peace, saved in the moment of its extinction a few last Indian lives.

Mahatma Gandhi was murdered on January 30, 1948, as a result of his commitment to reconciliation between Hindu and Muslim. The whole of India mourned his death, and this photograph shows his disciples praying beside his bier before his cremation.

CHAPTER 15

THE COMMONWEALTH

I<small>N 1953 QUEEN ELIZABETH II,</small> Victoria's great-granddaughter, was crowned on a drizzly day in June. The occasion was greeted optimistically as an omen of renewed greatness, a new Elizabethan age. The coronation ceremony was still recognisably imperial, and all the Commonwealth prime ministers were there: Nehru svelte in his silken jacket, bluff Robert Menzies from Australia ("British to my bootstraps"), even the dour Dr Malan of South Africa who was an outspoken republican. The imperial symbols were paraded as always, the flags and the bearskins, the battle-honours and the horse-drummers. On the night before the ceremony the Queen was given the news, rushed just in time by runner and diplomatic radio from the Himalayas, that Mount Everest, perhaps the last objective of imperial adventure, had been climbed by a British expedition.

But when, amid the splendours of Westminster Abbey, the Archbishop of Canterbury proclaimed Elizabeth Queen, he did so in evasive terms. She was "of the United Kingdom of Great Britain and Northern Ireland and of Her other Realms and Territories, Queen, Head of the Commonwealth, Defender of the Faith". The fanfares blared, the congregation stood, *Vivat! Vivat!* rang out across the fane: but there was no hiding the process of retreat that had given birth to this grey title. No longer could the Queen be an Empress of India, and in an association of nations in which Hindus and

The official coronation photograph of Queen Elizabeth II carrying the orb and sceptre and wearing the State Crown, taken by Cecil Beaton. The ceremony was broadcast on radio and television throughout the Commonwealth.

Muslims outnumbered Christians by three to one, she was only debatably a Defender of the Faith.

The end of the Raj in India had made the end of Empire certain. "As long as we rule India," Curzon had said, "we are the greatest power in the world. If we lose it we shall drop straight away to a third-rate power. . . ." And so it proved. Half the structure of Empire was mere scaffolding for the possession of India. Many a possession now lost its point, and the whole British attitude to the world, governed so long by the great possessions of the east, slowly and painfully shifted.

Almost at once Burma and Ceylon had fallen away from the Empire, without opposition from their imperial masters—"I only want to see Burma happy," said Governor Dorman-Smith, benignly surrendering his seals of office. Burma chose independence outside the Commonwealth, Ceylon became a dominion.

In 1918 the British Commonwealth consisted of some eighty-five territories, in every stage of development or esteem. More than half British exports went there, nearly half British imports came from there—eighty-two per cent of oil from the Middle East, eighty-one per cent of tea from India, fifty per cent of grain from Canada. It had fallen to Attlee's Government to decide its future: and like so many of its predecessors, that ministry decided that what the British Empire needed was logic. They rationalised the Commonwealth. The white members, whose combined population was about seventy-five million, were now joined by the brown, with a combined population of one hundred million, overwhelming the bonds of blood and common culture which had been the truest meaning of the association.

THE CONQUEST OF EVEREST

On May 29, 1953, just four days before Queen Elizabeth II's coronation, a British mountaineering team scaled the world's highest peak (29,028 ft). Edmund Hillary's account of how he and Sherpa Tenzing made the final assault is taken from his book, Nothing Venture, Nothing Win.

After an hour or so we came to a vertical rock step in the ridge. This appeared quite a problem. However the step was bounded on its right by a vertical snow cliff and I was able to work my way up this forty-foot crack and finally get over the top. I was rather surprised and pleased that I was capable of such effort at this height. I brought Tenzing up and noticed he was proving a little sluggish, but an excellent and safe companion for all that. I really felt now that we were going to get to the top and that nothing would stop us.

I continued on, cutting steadily and surmounting bump after bump and cornice after cornice looking eagerly for the summit. It seemed impossible to pick it and time was running out. Finally I cut round the back of an extra large hump and then on a tight rope from Tenzing I climbed up a gentle snow ridge to its top. Immediately it was obvious that we had reached our objective. It was 11.30 a.m. and we were on top of Everest!

Tenzing and I shook hands and then Tenzing threw his arms round my shoulders. It was a great moment! I took off my oxygen and for ten minutes I photographed Tenzing holding flags, the various ridges of Everest and the general view. I left a crucifix on top for John Hunt, the leader of the expedition, and Tenzing made a little hole in the snow and put in it some food offerings — lollies, biscuits and chocolate. We ate a Mint Cake and then put our oxygen back on. I was a little worried by the time factor so after fifteen minutes on top we turned back.

Edmund Hillary (standing) and Sherpa Tenzing plant the Union Jack on the summit of Mount Everest.

During the next decade the Commonwealth was then expanded beyond the reach of the Crown, as old imperial territories were promoted from subjection to nationhood, its members being of varying races, colour, religion and culture, linked mainly by the fact that the British had once ruled them. Now a man was a citizen of India, or Canada, or Ceylon, while the only British subjects were the islanders themselves and the residents of the colonies they still governed direct from Whitehall. Gone was the Roman aspiration of a common citizenship spanning the world. One by one the Commonwealth countries deserted even the imperial law—each year the Legal Committee of the Privy Council, the Empire's ultimate tribunal, heard fewer cases.

The word "British" disappeared from the title of the Commonwealth. The old Dominions and India Offices were merged into a Commonwealth Relations Office. Each member country was free to give the Queen its own title, so that "Defender of the Faith" soon dropped from the royal honorifics when local circumstance made it inappropriate. In short, logic was given to the association, but it was a logic shrouded more than ever in imprecision. The Commonwealth had no constitution. Its members were bound by no obligations. They could leave when they pleased, devise their own status, decide whether they would have a queen or not, adjust almost anything to suit themselves. It was a very obliging club.

The Indians had decided they wanted to be a republic, so they became one. The Pakistanis decided they could do without a governor-general, so they did. The Australians and New Zealanders concluded a defence alliance with the United States, excluding Britain. In the United Nations the Commonwealth members voted against each other whenever they felt like it. "We want no unwilling partners," Attlee declared, so rather than have rules broken, the creators of the new Commonwealth did without rules.

But at least the development of this cloudy new brotherhood helped to muffle the breakdown of Empire. The British deluded themselves that it *was* the Empire, more or less, reconstituted in contemporary form—was not the Queen to be seen gracefully presiding over its assemblies, or sweetly chatting with the black and brown men who, more numerous with each year, soon came to sit in the front row of the group photographs, instead of standing self-consciously in the background?

As for the other members, most of them approached it with an ambivalent mixture of cynicism, respect and affection. Old habits die hard, even among militant nationalists, and it was still splendid after all to be honoured among the grave monuments of imperial London, and to be received by the Queen of England herself, in a diamond tiara and the Order of the Garter. Besides, there was still something to be gained from membership of the sterling area, the financial structure which underlay it, and which was still one of the great economic blocs of the world. There were many fringe benefits too, technical aid and economic perquisites, access to professional bodies or athletic competitions, even a sort of half-nostalgic bonhomie, like the comradeship of an old school tie.

Nobody aspired to much more. It did look comforting on the map, though: for even if the cartographers only striped the Commonwealth countries in red, at a cursory glance it looked as though a third of the world was still, in a manner of speaking, British. The Commonwealth was the last opaque reflection of the grand illusion.

But we must narrow our focus, for the British Empire was now something else. The Commonwealth countries became members of the wider world, and so slip away from our story: but in the 1950s there were still several million people, in four continents, directly subject to the rule of London. Towards them the Labour Government looked in an avuncular and improving spirit. Generally less worldly than their Conservative counterparts, less experienced in foreign affairs, they were if anything more paternalistic towards coloured peoples, and believed them to need, however shamefully they had been exploited in the past, several generations of kindly British socialist supervision. Giving the African colonies independence, said Herbert Morrison, the Home Secretary, would be "like giving a child of ten a latchkey, a bank account and a shotgun". Whatever had happened to the Dominions and India Offices, nobody suggested winding up the Colonial Office, and young men went out to Africa in the early 1950s looking forward with perfect confidence to a lifetime's useful career.

Much of the colonial Empire was derelict. The passing of the wartime Colonial Development Act, as much a propaganda gesture as a change of attitude, had been the very first time metropolitan Britain had agreed to pay for the economic and social progress of the colonies. Up until then it had been British policy always that each Crown Colony must pay its own way. And by now most of the tropical possessions were in a sorry state. Then in 1947, the Colonial Development Corporation came into being, publicly funded and charged with the creation of public utilities in the colonies—the roads, power stations, water supplies and irrigation works which would be the foundation of their progress.

Every month, it seemed, a new commission was established, a new inquiry was instituted, a new committee was assembled to discuss health services, legislative reform, educational priorities, the possibility of growing sugar beet on Ascension Island or the incidence of bilharzia in Dongola.

Never had the colonies been so elaborately governed. Everywhere local

The Commonwealth grew out of the old British Empire, as former colonies achieved their independence and joined together for consultation and cooperation. The British Commonwealth developed gradually between 1919 and 1949. The Statute of Westminster (1931) confirmed the self-governing dominions of Australia, Canada, New Zealand and South Africa as "freely associated members". In April 1949 membership was broadened to include republics acknowledging the British reigning monarch as head of the Commonwealth, and the word "British" was dropped from the title.

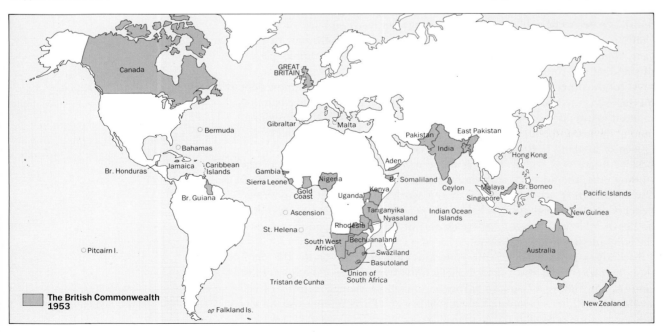

The British Commonwealth 1953

establishments were increased, sometimes tripled. In five years, six thousand five hundred new men were sent out to the colonies, six times as many as had administered the whole of British India in the heyday of Empire.

Money was poured out of Britain's denuded treasuries. The Colonial Development Corporation poured cash, men, tractors, test tubes and technicians into many a desolate tract of Empire, providing jobs for thousands of Britons otherwise difficult to employ in the office-like circumstances to which they had become accustomed, and plunging hosts of tribesmen bewilderedly into the deep end of Western method. Some of these activities were successful, some were famous fiascos, like the Groundnut Scheme for Tanganyika which sold not a single groundnut, or the Egg Scheme for Gambia which exported not an egg.

Earnest but over-sanguine, too, were the several schemes by which the British hoped to group their colonies into more rational political entities, ready to graduate in time into the ranks of the Commonwealth. They all made sense in theory. The West Indian islands, for example, could surely be united in a federation as a prelude to independence—they shared a common history, a common language, common customs and common problems: and so they were. In East Africa an old federal dream was revived, and Kenya, Uganda and Tanganyika were placed under a single East African High Commission. Farther south the plan was that Southern Rhodesia, Northern Rhodesia and Nyasaland should federate: the whites of Southern Rhodesia would supply the skills and the capital, the blacks of the other territories the labour and the mineral resources—a partnership, breezily suggested Godfrey Huggins, the Prime Minister of Southern Rhodesia, like that between a rider and his horse.

The official policy towards the colonies was perfectly clear: "It is," said Command Paper 7533, "to guide the colonial territories to responsible self-government within the Commonwealth in conditions that ensure to the people concerned both a fair standard of living and freedom from aggression from any quarter." Yet now as always, it seemed even the most liberal of the British did not really believe that the objective would ever be reached.

Almost opposite Westminster Abbey, in one of the finest sites in Europe, a German bomb had created a large empty space. There the British, in the last decades of their Empire, planned to build a new Colonial Office. It would be in the neo-Georgian mode, eight floors high, with the royal crest large above its symbolically decorated doors, twin flagstaffs on its roof and a façade facing across the square to the ancient purlieus of the Abbey. And it would represent everything frank and enlightened in contemporary colonial government from urban sewage to female education, Falklands seal-farming to East African Federation.

The brave new building was never even started. The last rally of colonial enthusiasm in the 1940s and 1950s was one of history's more endearing misjudgments. To almost everybody but the British activists themselves, all the signs and arguments were against it. Colonialism was excoriated in every corner of the world, and the growing power of African and Asian nationalism, openly backed now by the Soviet Union and certainly not discouraged by the Americans, was apparent for all to see.

So the new Colonial Office building was never begun, and the structural reforms of the Colonial Empire, too, were mostly aborted or abandoned. Throughout the 1950s the Empire continued to crumble. The West Indians,

Commemorative Independence stamps for Uganda (1962), Ghana (1957) and Nigeria (1960). All three independent nations were to remain within the Commonwealth.

THE WELFARE STATE

THE TERM "WELFARE STATE" began to be used generally for the first time after the Second World War when, with a Labour government in power with a large majority, a National Health Service was introduced in 1947, along with a comprehensive system of social security.

Yet the origins of the welfare state went back deeper into the past, and the people who fashioned it were by no means all Socialists. Churchill himself had been a member of the Liberal government which, between 1906 and 1916, introduced a wide range of welfare measures, including health insurance, in Lloyd George's 1909 Budget. And the politician who carried the legislation that broke up the Victorian Poor Law was a Conservative, Neville Chamberlain.

During the Second World War, Sir William Beveridge, a former civil servant, talked of attacking and defeating the five giants who had until now prevented ordinary people from fully enjoying their lives — want, disease, ignorance, squalor and idleness. Yet Beveridge did not want the state "to stifle initiative, opportunity responsibility". Like many other prophets of the Welfare State, he laid greater emphasis on its benefits for the individual citizen than on the extension of state power which it entailed.

Already by the time that the Labour Party lost power in 1951, there had been financial crises affecting the provision of welfare services. By the 1970s, however, it was clear that some of the new welfare structures created after 1945 were vulnerable, particularly when there was unemployment. Since 1979 the idea of the services provided by the welfare state being available to all at no financial cost has been abandoned by the government. As all institutions were brought under review, it became apparent that the National Health Service at least could not be spared.

DISPENSARIES IN THE DOCTOR'S SURGERY, like the one above, where the pharmacist made up the patients' prescriptions on the spot, were a familiar feature of life before the creation of the National Health Service. After 1948 there was a huge demand from those who had formerly been unable to afford medicine.

THE BEVERIDGE REPORT, published in December 1942, formed the basis of much welfare state legislation. Sir William Beveridge, an economist with wide experience in both government and university administration, campaigned for "cradle to grave benefits for all—from duke to dustman". The photograph (above) records Beveridge addressing a meeting. The inset cutting is from the front page of the December 2, 1942 edition of the Daily Mirror, announcing the publication of the Report. The plan was to be part of the country's postwar reconstruction. A Family Allowances Act of 1945 provided five shillings a week for the upkeep of all but the eldest child in a family. The following year saw the Industrial Injuries Bill, the National Insurance Act and the National Health Service Act. The last of these was regarded as the main foundation of the welfare state. Hospitals were transferred from local authorities and voluntary bodies and administered by regional hospital boards. The attendance of doctors and dentists was to be free and local authorities were to provide child welfare and home help services. Church and voluntary organisations continued to contribute much to welfare care.

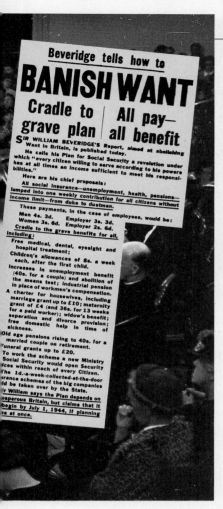

Beveridge tells how to

BANISH WANT

Cradle to grave plan | All pay— all benefit

SIR WILLIAM BEVERIDGE'S Report, aimed at abolishing Want in Britain, is published today.

He calls his Plan for Social Security a revolution under which "every citizen willing to serve according to his powers has at all times an income sufficient to meet his responsibilities."

Here are his chief proposals:

All social insurance—unemployment, health, pensions—lumped into one weekly contribution for all citizens without income limit—from duke to dustman.

These payments, in the case of employees, would be:

Men 4s. 3d. Employer 3s. 3d.
Women 3s. 6d. Employer 2s. 6d.

Cradle to the grave benefits for all, including:

Free medical, dental, eyesight and hospital treatment;

Children's allowances of 8s. a week each, after the first child.

Increases in unemployment benefit (40s. for a couple) and abolition of the means test; industrial pension in place of workmen's compensation.

A charter for housewives, including marriage grant up to £10; maternity grant of £4 (and 36s. for 13 weeks for a paid worker); widow's benefit; separation and divorce provision; free domestic help in time of sickness.

Old age pensions rising to 40s. for a married couple on retirement.

Funeral grants up to £20.

To work the scheme a new Ministry of Social Security would open Security offices within reach of every Citizen.

The 1d.-a-week-collected-at-the-door insurance schemes of the big companies would be taken over by the State.

Sir William says the Plan depends on prosperous Britain, but claims that it begin by July 1, 1944, if planning es at once.

FULL EMPLOYMENT *was seen by the government as the key to the welfare state. In 1933 one man in four of working age was unemployed. Many were well qualified, like the man in the photograph. Memories lingered, and it was thought that the economist J.M. Keynes was right: job-creation would increase spending-power, and thus full employment could be maintained. But Britain continued to depend on imports and there were recurrent balance of payments crises and subsequent cuts in government spending, which increased the number of unemployed again.*

NEW HOUSING *was a priority after the war, but despite the New Towns Bill of 1946 which transferred whole communities of people to spacious estates outside London's green belt, it was impossible to replace quickly all the dwellings that had been destroyed. This council flat (above) in Chelsea was built in 1948 and had three bedrooms, a living room, kitchen and bathroom. The rent was sixteen shillings and sixpence a week. A major housing drive, both public and private, was instituted by the Conservative government when they returned to power in 1951.*

THE NATIONAL HEALTH SERVICE *was launched on July 5, 1948. The Minister of Health for the 1945 Labour government which implemented the scheme was Aneurin (Nye) Bevan. The photograph above shows him touring the Park Hospital at Davyhulme in Lancashire on the first day of the new regime.*

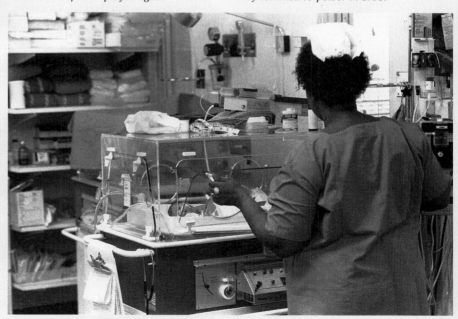

MATERNITY CARE *improved with the introduction of maternity benefits and the creation of well-equipped baby units in hospitals. The photograph above is of the premature baby* unit at the Royal Free Hospital in London. *The expectation of infant survival following birth has nearly doubled since the beginning of the twentieth century.*

being far less homogeneous than they looked on the map, and far more ambitious to be their own prime ministers, soon deserted their federation and split into petty autonomies. The East Africans, being of many different tribes, several different religions and three different colours, never were persuaded into unity. The blacks of the Central African Federation, rightly surmising that it would mean their indefinite subjection to white minority rule, demolished it as soon as possible. The hopeful departments of colonial development were dropped one by one, converted into organs of foreign aid, or silently dispersed.

CHAPTER 16

FAREWELL THE TRUMPETS

IT WAS IN PALESTINE THAT the British imperialists, for the first time, frankly abandoned the imperial responsibilities, and there the last retreat began. The withdrawal from India could be rationalised, even romanticised. The withdrawal from Palestine was without glory. The little country, hardly two hundred miles from north to south, sacred to three religions, had become materially the most advanced country in the Middle East. Britain's rule, however, had never been happy. It was a mandatory government, for one thing, so that in theory at least the British were not absolute masters. For another it was tinged with the suggestion of betrayal, since so many Arabs, and not a few Britons, believed that Palestine should properly have become part of an independent Arab kingdom. And it was embittered by the ambitions of the Zionists, who had professed to want only a national home within a multiracial Palestine, but who really aimed, it had long become apparent, at an independent Jewish state there.

Sometimes it was the Arabs who broke the peace, sometimes the Jews, and so inflammatory was the situation after the Second World War, when hundreds of thousands of European Jews desperately sought a new home, that the Holy Land became hardly more than an armed camp.

By now the Zionists, financed by Jews throughout the world, had rooted themselves in cities, farms and desert settlements all over Palestine. Though they were still only a third of the population, they were much better organised than the Arabs, and with their powerful supporters in America, far richer and more influential. The Arabs feared and loathed them, and the British by now, after fluctuations of sympathy, tended on the whole to agree. By 1947 the administration, though theoretically impartial, was virtually at war with the Jewish activists. Terrorists kidnapped and murdered British soldiers; there were ambushes and explosions and reprisals and threats; the whole country was in a state of fear, meshed with barbed wire, and patrolled always by the armoured cars of the Empire.

It had been the imperial intention to establish a self-governing Arab-Jewish state in Palestine, but even before the war a commission of inquiry had declared the idea unworkable, and had suggested partitioning the country into three—an Arab state, a Jewish state, a British enclave round the Holy Places. After the war the United Nations came to a similar conclusion, and in November 1947 voted for the creation of Arab and Jewish states. The Arabs rejected the plan, the Jews accepted it, the British refused all responsibility for it. Nagged by the United Nations, pestered by the Americans, bewildered by the Zionists, insulted by the Arabs, excoriated by world opinion, exhausted by the strain of it, impoverished by the cost, disillusioned, embittered, in December 1947 the British Government announced that, like Pilate before them, they would have no more of it. They washed their hands of the Holy Land. On May 14, 1948 the last British soldiers embarked on their troopships at Haifa: and even as they sailed away, behind them the disputing peoples of the Holy Land hurled themselves upon one another and, splitting the country furiously between them, prepared to live savagely ever after.

Palestine was a declaration. The British would no longer fight to the finish. For old hands this was a bitter realisation. Churchill, in Opposition, foresaw "a steady and remorseless process of divesting ourselves of what has been gained by so many generations of toil, administration and sacrifice."

Through the fifties and into the sixties, as people after people awoke to the realisation of patriotism, or were goaded into it by politicians, the imperial retreat continued. The barbed wire and armoured cars of Palestine were duplicated across the world, as successive colonies flared into revolt, and the British army, whose power had so stirred Macmillan at Tunis a decade before, was reduced to squalid duties of repression and withdrawal.

We see them in every climate and every landscape, always at their roadblocks, barricaded in their barracks, guarding post offices, escorting pale English children to school or squatting behind sandbags on the roofs of Government Houses. In Cyprus, which had never proved of the slightest use to the Empire, they struggle year after year against Greek guerrillas; in Kenya's White Highlands they fight the enigmatic and murderous Mau Mau; in Malaya they wearily stalk guerrillas through the jungle; in Egypt they run down young patriots across the battlefield of Tel el Kebir; in the Statt el Arab, the Royal Navy stands fruitless guard over the oil refineries of Abadan, soon to be nationalised by the Persians.

Often they succeeded, and curbing the impatient passions of the local patriots, managed to restore order in a colony before handing it over to

The British flag is lowered at Haifa, in Palestine, signifying the end of British influence in the Holy Land. The ceremony is watched by troops aboard the ship in the harbour, as they prepare to sail for home. In 1948 the United Nations divided Palestine into two separate states, Israel and Jordan. Arab-Israeli conflict has been continuous, as Arabs fight for a Palestinian homeland.

Jomo Kenyatta (1894-1978) acknowledges the crowds during the Independence Day celebrations in Kenya in 1963. Kenyatta had been suspected of being an organiser of the Mau Mau risings, and was imprisoned by the British (1952-61). He later became a major force in the independence negotiations and was subsequently elected Prime Minister. In 1964 Kenya became a Republic, with Kenyatta as its first President.

their successors. In Malaya a patient and methodical campaign finally contained the Communist guerrillas, and allowed the Malaysian Federation to get off to a peaceful start. In Kenya a ruthless and sometimes brutal operation subdued the rebellious Kikuyu, enabling Jomo Kenyatta, the most famous of the tribe, to become Prime Minister.

Elsewhere the withdrawal of British power, as in India, as in Palestine, left bloodshed behind. Hardly had the last aircraft withdrawn from the bases of Iraq than the young Harrovian king, with all his family, was murdered by the rebellious mob. And in Aden, the very first acquisition of Queen Victoria's Empire, the British left the city shooting to the last. Step by step they withdrew to the harbour and the airfield. The last commandos raced for their helicopters. The last flotilla of the Royal Navy sailed away into the Red Sea. Behind them rival groups of Arab guerrillas fell upon the abandoned stores and barracks, swarmed up the steps of Government House, and shot at each other from rooftops.

Far more often, though, the sequence of farewell was peaceful, and rather touching. The happiest of the imperial exits were stage-managed by Furse's protégés of the 1930s, now the governors and chief secretaries of their colonies, and they were characterised by the same tolerance and guileless optimism that Santayana had admired in them in their youth.

The bands played. Down came the flag, out rang the last bugles. The chief nationalist leader, lately released from detention and propelled into fame, wealth and power, found himself greeted by the retiring British governor with a comradely new bonhomie, and was saluted by white guards of honour as he arrived, dressed in his own ethnic fineries, at the Independence Day parade. Out from England had come some scion of royalty; at the Independence Day ball the new Prime Minister danced with Her Royal Highness; there were ceremonies of goodwill, a message from the Queen, a presentation of maces, crests, or Speaker's Chairs.

One by one they went, all through the 1950s and into the 1960s: Nigeria, Kenya, Ghana, the Sudan, Uganda, even the never-to-be abandoned Cyprus.

Sometimes sceptically, sometimes indulgently, the British observed all this. Progressives were delighted at the course of events, conservatives were saddened, the mass of the public seemed indifferent. A nation does not watch its power shrivel away, though, without some moments of bitterness, and as the great Empire dissolved a strain of resentment and self-pity fitfully entered British attitudes.

Only once did it flare into paranoia, as in a last impotent revival of the aggressive spirit the British tried to reverse the course of history. It was in 1956, and the last retreat was already precipitate. Anyone, it seemed, could now cock a snook at the British. There was no respect for The Flag anymore, no gratitude among the emancipated colonies; angry correspondents to the *Daily Telegraph* drew bitter conclusions from the decline of Empire, reminded the editor about the fate of Rome, and reproachfully quoted such poems as Tennyson's "Hands All Round":

> We sailed wherever ships could sail,
> We founded many a mighty State.
> Pray God our greatness may not fail
> Through craven fear of being great.

Even those less chauvinist or raucous in their patriotism felt, just the same, a sense of waste, unfairness and helplessness. Had they won the war simply to subside into the ranks of the minor powers? Was the whole imperial achievement a deception after all?

Among those most bitterly affected was Anthony Eden, who was born in the year of Victoria's Diamond Jubilee, and had succeeded Churchill as Conservative Prime Minister in 1955. Eden had spent his life close to the sources of British imperial power. The idea of a Britain to be defied with impunity by any impertinent sheikh or corruptible politician was not simply repugnant to him, but almost inconceivable. It was as if he stood at Churchill's shoulder still, next to President Roosevelt, beneath the gun turrets of the *Prince of Wales* deciding the future of the world.

Eden developed a particular and peculiar antipathy towards one of the most persistent of all the Empire's opponents, Gamal Abdul Nasser of Egypt. Nasser's revolutionary movement of army officers had deposed King Farouk in 1952, setting up a republic, and had obliged the British to give up their vast military base in the Suez Canal Zone. Then by intrigue and force of example Nasser had inflamed most of the Arab world against the British connection, effectively ending British suzerainty in the Middle East.

British troops dig in along the banks of the Suez Canal in 1956. Hostile world opinion soon forced them to withdraw and the British realised that they could no longer act as an imperial power.

In 1956 this ambitious dictator seized the Suez Canal, announcing that the Egyptians would henceforth run it for themselves. Nasser's action was not specifically directed against the British. But just as the assumption of British greatness was inherent to Eden's political thinking, so the Suez Canal remained an inescapable totem of it. A Suez Canal in unfriendly hands would mean, so British traditionalists cried, a Britain that had forfeited not merely her Empire, but her very freedom of action.

So Eden launched the last and most forlorn of all the imperial initiatives: the Suez adventure of 1956. It was also a cruel parody of the British imperial style. Eden cast himself as an elegant younger Churchill. Nasser he portrayed as a Muslim Hitler—"I want him destroyed!" cried the Prime Minister to one of his ministers. The ultimatum that was presented to the Egyptians, requiring them to restore the Canal to its rightful owners, rang with the righteous zeal of 1939. The invasion force that was assembled was like a punitive expedition of old. The Royal Navy mustered its ships and landing craft at Malta, jet bombers of the Royal Air Force were concentrated upon Cyprus, and in the streets of southern England convoys of army trucks, painted a desert yellow, hastened to the southern ports as in greater days before. And among the ageing imperialists in London clubs there was a general response to the theme of self-righteous retribution.

They were deluding themselves, however. Britain could no longer punish troublemakers as she pleased, with a resounding statement in the House of Commons and a brisk expeditionary force. Nothing was so simple now, in the complex world of the 1950s. A plan must be concocted with the French, who were in a similar mood of national frustration, and with the Zionists, who had now established their own state in Palestine, and considered the Egyptians their most threatening enemies. There were the Americans to consider—could they be trusted to help, or would they intervene to hinder? There was the now amorphous Commonwealth, some of its members reliable enough to be put in the picture, some more safely left in the dark. There was world opinion in general, as unsympathetic to British imperialism as ever it was in the Boer War. There was opinion at home, split furiously on the issue. And finally there was Russia, now the greatest imperial power.

Through this maze Eden and his advisers moved as in a dream, cunningly.

AUSTERITY AND AFFLUENCE

IN SPITE OF MARKED REGIONAL CONTRASTS, particularly between north and south, overall standards of living in Britain have risen dramatically in the twentieth century. Even before the Second World War, when there was heavy unemployment, the index of industrial production stood seventy-five per cent higher in 1935–38 than in 1910–13.

The Second World War brought a period of austerity and tough food-rationing, during which health standards improved, and this mood persisted after 1945. The people even accepted that bread, which had never been rationed during the war, should be rationed between July 1946 and July 1948, and potatoes at the end of 1947.

By the late 1950s, however, as world trading conditions improved, affluence became respectable. Between 1955 and 1960 there was an unparalleled consumer boom. The proportion of the population owning or hiring refrigerators, for example, rose from six to sixteen per cent, washing machines from twenty-five to forty-four per cent, and motor cars from eighteen to thirty-two per cent. The revolutionary car of the Sixties was the Mini, designed by Sir Alec Issigonis. Leisure became increasingly commercialised, a further move in a continuing process, and there was far more business sponsorship of sport and the arts.

In 1959 the Conservative Prime Minister, Harold Macmillan, "Super Mac", won a second term of office on the wave of prosperity, coupled with his promise that the standard of living would be further doubled within a generation. In 1979, a more radically-minded Prime Minister, Margaret Thatcher, also put her trust in the affluent, and encouraged the "enterprise culture". Yet with large-scale unemployment, contrasts persisted and although charitable activity increased, there was also a rise in crime and drug-taking.

THE POSTWAR YEARS accentuated the necessity for Britain to make her own way in a competitive world and the withdrawal of the American lend-lease agreement forced her to make an all-out export drive. Many people went straight from the grind of life in the ranks to that of life on the production line, as David Low's cartoon (above) illustrates. Clothes were still rationed until 1949 and food until 1953, and the government issued strict regulations over the design not only of clothes and furniture (so-called "Utility" patterns), but also of buildings. There was a nationalisation programme for coal, transport, gas, electricity, iron and steel, and the Tory government of 1951 did not reverse many of these measures

THE ECONOMIC RECOVERY of the 1950s brought a touch of affluence to the working people of Britain. Many controls were lifted, and in 1959 the Prime Minister, Harold Macmillan, could claim that Britons had "never had it so good". Full employment provided spending power, and luxury items were becoming available in the shops. The sale of television sets boomed, with nearly half the population watching 2.7 million television sets to see Elizabeth II being crowned on June 2, 1953. Many features in the photograph below, of an average family living-room in the 1950s, would rarely have been present in the previous decade: the TV, a fitted carpet, soft armchairs, a patterned tea service and even a box of sweets.

THE ARCTIC WINTER of 1947 caused further disruption in struggling Britain. Heavy snow blocked roads and railways so that people could not get to work and supplies of food could not get through. Fuel was limited; power cuts caused industrial and domestic chaos. When the thaw came, the land was so waterlogged that it could not be ploughed in time for a good harvest.

FOOD SHORTAGES led to long queues outside shops, as is evident in the photograph (below) of London's East End in March 1946. There were bombsites everywhere; shops and houses were dilapidated and thousands of people made homeless. Squatters occupied empty Nissen huts in army camps and the government speeded up plans to erect cheap houses known as "prefabs" and purpose-built new towns.

THE PERMISSIVE SOCIETY of the 1960s saw a revolution in dress, living styles and sexual conduct. British pop culture, spearheaded by the Beatles and such leading figures as the designer Mary Quant and the artist Peter Blake, set trends for the rest of the world. The publication of an unexpurgated edition of D.H. Lawrence's novel, Lady Chatterley's Lover, after a sensational trial in November 1960, set the trend for the new decade. Sexual liberation was advanced with the growing popularity of the Pill as a method of birth control. The death penalty for murder was finally abolished in 1970. The photograph (above) shows an open-air pop festival in the Isle of Wight in 1970.

They held secret meetings with the French and the Israelis. They told less than the truth to the Commonwealth, and actually lied to the Americans. While they pretended that they would occupy the Canal Zone only in order to pass the Canal into United Nations' care, they really planned the overthrow of Nasser himself. As the world watched aghast and unbelieving, the ultimatum was delivered to Nasser, requiring him to withdraw his forces from the Canal. Almost at the same time the Russians, invading Hungary with overwhelming force, and putting down the rising there with infinite cruelty, let it be known that if the Anglo-French invasion of Egypt were not aborted, Russian missiles might soon be falling upon London.

This was another world, beyond the capacity of the British imperialists. Of course the invasion was aborted—they had no choice. The invasion force, laboriously assembled and poorly equipped, did indeed invade Egypt, capturing Port Said and advancing down the Canal. The Egyptian air force was virtually destroyed by attacks on its airfields, the Israelis occupied the east bank of the Canal, the British and French pushed southward to occupy the west bank. But in no time the British lost their resolution, as the terrible truth dawned upon them that they could no longer behave imperially. The whole world was against them. Even a "wog", it seemed, had a voice in the United Nations. The invasion force was withdrawn, and the imperial ghosts turned uneasily in their graves.

The British were numbed by this unnecessary disaster, even those who had most passionately opposed the invasion. They did not like to talk about it, and a veiled reticence fell upon the subject. Eden himself, ill and distraught, retired from public life forever, handing over to Macmillan. It was as though a neurosis, erupting into a moment of schizophrenia, had subsided once again, this time forever.

It was nearly over now. Future historians may well say the British Empire ended at Suez, for there it was finally made plain that the imperial potency was lost. In the 1960s it became clear to the staunchest of the British imperialists that their Empire was gone, and in a frame of mind more bewildered than resentful their leaders half-heartedly set out to find a new role in the world—as mediators between east and west, as the ageing chatelaine of the increasingly skittish Commonwealth, or, as a last resort, as offshore islanders of a new Europe. Nostalgia set in, and while novelists and playwrights still made fun of the imperial postures, many other Englishmen looked back with wistful affection at the spectacle of their grandeur, fast dissolving into memory.

After Suez they recognised the tide of history, and bowed to it—or more pertinently, perhaps, they remembered that politics was only the art of the possible. In January 1960 Harold Macmillan set out on a tour of Africa. He was admittedly a man of the imperial age—for him the true Britain was still the Britain that had basked so expansively, so genially, in the flowered days of the Edwardian era. It was, after all, less than twenty years since, standing on the dais at Tunis while the Highlanders appeared over the crest of the road, he had believed the Empire to have the world at its feet.

He was a politician first, though; and in Cape Town in January 1960 it was he who formally recognised the end of the imperial idea. "In the twentieth century," he said, "and especially since the end of the war, the processes which gave birth to the nation-states of Europe have been repeated all over the world. We have seen the awakening of a national consciousness

Harold Macmillan (1894-1986), touring Africa in January 1960, during his term of office as Prime Minister, is met at Enugu airport in Nigeria by the Premier of eastern Nigeria, Dr Okpara, and his wife. Nigeria was to gain her independence in October of the same year.

in peoples who had lived for centuries in dependence upon some other Power." This was, Macmillan implied, something inevitable. It was not the work of agitators or false prophets. It was, he said, in the last of all the truisms and euphemisms that had enriched the vocabulary of imperialism, only the wind of change.

Let us end the story gently, on a loyal note, for not everybody saw the Empire as wicked—people all over the world admired it still, for all its weaknesses and excesses, as a force for good, a kindly force despite it all. Even in the 1960s many a possession and dependency preferred to stay within the old fold, remote, dreamy, contented or simply ill-informed, governed still by English gentlemen, and visited sometimes by the spick-and-span frigates of the shrunken Royal Navy.

Here and there they tried to stem the tide. The Maltese and the Seychellois unsuccessfully proposed integration with the United Kingdom itself, while the Falkland Islanders steadfastly preferred the rule of London, personified by a general-governor whose official car was a London taxicab, to the rule of the Argentine, personified as often as not by dictatorial criminals and military thugs. When the Gibraltarians held a referendum to decide whether to stay British or join Spain, forty-four voted for Spain, twelve thousand one hundred and thirty-eight for the Empire.

But the passion was spent, for or against Victoria's Empire, and so, except for these quaint or adamant anachronisms of loyalty, it came to an end calmly and almost apathetically, like an old soldier pacified at last by age, pain and experience. Abroad, the emancipated peoples soon adopted new styles and philosophies of government, or even acquired new overlords: at home a generation came of age which had never heard the trumpets.

In the winter of 1965 Sir Winston Churchill, aged, beloved, died at his home in London. He had by then passed beyond the bickerings of party politics, and had become the living exemplar of British glory. Reviled in earlier life, he was to be calumniated again after his death, in the way of legends: but for the moment, as he lay massive on his bed in death, ninety-one years old and the most universally honoured man on earth, he was beyond criticism. He was a dead spirit of grandeur, and for a day or two not only his own nation, but half the world paused wondering and reverent to mourn him.

For seventy years Churchill had lived the experience of Empire more intensely than any other man, through six reigns and many wars, from the climax of the old Queen's jubilee celebrations to the melancholy disillusionments of Suez. In him the lost Empire of the British, bad and good, had found its fallible embodiment—brave, blustering, kind, arrogant, blind in many things, visionary in others, splendid but often wrong, lovable but frequently infuriating.

In his rhetoric, his humour and his rotund prose Churchill had expressed the best and worst of imperial attitudes. He held no very strong moral views about Empire. It was the idea of it that he found exciting, the spectacle of that immense estate enhancing the grandeur of England. He was an imperialist in the classic High-Victorian mould, loving Empire for its own sake, for the swagger and the allegory.

Indeed, of all the charges of Empire, this dynamic had been the most consistent. Economics, strategy, world politics had all contributed to the British expansion, but the taste for glory had underpinned them all, still

Winston Churchill (1874-1965) died on January 24, 1965. His death was mourned throughout the world, and Queen Elizabeth accorded him the tribute of a State funeral, the first for a commoner since Gladstone's in 1898. With typical thoroughness Churchill had left instructions for his funeral: "I want lots of soldiers and bands." He is buried in Bladon churchyard, next to his parents and near Blenheim Palace. This wartime photograph is by Karsh of Ottawa.

recognisable in 1965 as the same atavistic tribal pride that animated the Diamond Jubilee.

To an astonishing degree the world had been changed by its drive. It had been the principal agent of an immense historical evolution, stirring dormant energies across the continents. Some of its achievements were indestructible, like the roads, railways and telegraph systems which provided the basis of the new industrial society, and which, though they would presently be superseded by more modern techniques, would leave their heritage of usefulness forever. It had given to the world its own language, English, one of the mightiest of all instruments of human intercourse. It had kindled the latent energies of many a people temporarily stagnant. It had done something to curb the worst cruelties of primitives, and for a century it had sustained, as the historian, Carlyle, said, "a mighty Conquest over Chaos". Through many generations, too, in many countries, it had been the peace-keeper and the lawmaker, generally fair by its own standards, generally humane, and except in its own interests, which were always paramount, as impartial as a judge ever is. Above all, it made the British, for better or for worse, one of those few peoples which, in the centuries of the nation states, were able to alter the face of the world—one of those peoples whose dust is left like a cloud in the air, as the Spaniard Miguel de Unamuno put it, when it goes galloping down the highroad of history.

They performed the Empire's obsequies, with Sir Winston's, on a grey London day in January, and for the last time the world watched a British imperial spectacle. Melancholy though the occasion was, the British did it, as Churchill wished, in the high old style. Big Ben was silenced for the day. Mourning guns were fired in Hyde Park. The great drum-horse of the Household Cavalry, drums swathed in black crepe, led the funeral procession solemnly through London to St Paul's, while band after band across the capital played the Dead March from *Saul* and the soldiers along the way reversed their arms.

The coffin, draped with the flags of the Cinque Ports and of the Spencer-Churchill family, was carried up the great steps into the cathedral. A hundred nations were represented there, and twenty of them had once been ruled from this very capital. A bugle played the Last Post in the Whispering Gallery, another answered with Reveille from the west door, and after the funeral service they took the coffin down to the River Thames. There, as the pipers played "The Flowers of the Forest", six tall guardsmen, their cold sad faces straining with the weight, carried it on board a river launch: and away up the London river it sailed towards Westminster, escorted by black police boats. "Rule Britannia" sounded from the shore, fighter aircraft flew overhead, farewell guns fired from the Tower of London, and as the little flotilla disappeared upstream, watched by the great mourning crowd below the cathedral, all the cranes on the riverside wharves were dipped in salute. Everyone knew what was happening, even the enemies of Empire. "The true old times were dead, when every morning brought a noble chance, and every chance a noble knight."

In the evening they put the old statesman's body reverently on a train, for he was to be buried in the family churchyard in Oxfordshire: and so as dusk fell, with white steam flying from the engines's funnel, and a hiss of its pistons through the meadows, it carried him sadly home again, to the green country heart of England.

EPILOGUE

Towards the Future

by Asa Briggs

SIR WINSTON CHURCHILL DIED IN JANUARY 1965, the middle of a decade of change, much of it exciting, most of it controversial. Those "swinging sixties" now seem almost as faraway as the "naughty nineties", with which Churchill concluded his *History*. Yet extraordinarily, apart from the brief premierships of Edward Heath from 1970 to 1974, and James Callaghan from 1976 to 1979, the next twenty-three years were divided between just two Prime Ministers, Labour's Harold Wilson and the Tory Margaret Thatcher.

Against a background of persistent East/West tension and an ever-accelerating growth in technology, their chief concerns were to break out from a cycle of recurrent sterling crises, to find a role for Britain in a post-imperial era, and to maintain industrial peace in the face of rising unemployment.

A year before Churchill's death, Harold Wilson had won the general election—if narrowly—on the slogan of "thirteen wasted years" of Conservative rule. The Labour Party polled 12,205,814 votes, the Conservative Party 12,001,369. The Liberal Party polled just over three million but won only nine seats out of six hundred and thirty. Wilson was to win the next general election which he called in 1966 by an increased majority—there were then three hundred and sixty-three Labour M.P.s as against three hundred and seventeen in 1964. Churchill had mentioned the Labour Party only once in his *History*. It was in a brief paragraph which described what proved with hindsight to be a historic meeting of trade unionists and Socialists in the Memorial Hall, Farringdon Street, London, on February 27, 1900. The purpose of the meeting had been to create "a distinct Labour group in Parliament who shall have their own whips and agree upon policy". In practice it was to prove easier—with indispensable trade union support—to create a "Labour group" in Parliament, and a party outside Parliament, than it was "to agree upon policy". Wilson himself had become leader of the Labour Party only after fierce internal debate and the death in 1963 of Hugh Gaitskell, the previous leader whose views on policy were radically different from his.

Earlier in the century, Churchill had predicted that if the Liberal Party lost its hold on the electorate the way would be open for "class politics". In fact, Wilson won the general election of 1966 on a national rather than on a class programme "a new deal for the scientist and technologist in higher education, a new status for scientists in government, and a

With little of the world left to be discovered, twentieth-century man set out to explore space. The first moon landing was made in July 1969 by members of the US Apollo 11 space mission, led by Neil Armstrong, who was the first man to walk on the lunar surface. Their achievement was heralded by Armstrong as, "One small step for man, one giant leap for mankind."

277

Harold Wilson (1916-   ) became Prime Minister of a Labour government in 1964, with a majority of only four seats. In the election of 1966, Labour increased its majority and remained in power until defeated by Edward Heath and the Conservatives in 1970. Wilson's third premiership ran from 1974 until his surprise resignation in 1976. Later that year he was created a life peer, Baron Wilson of Rievaulx.

Ian Smith, Prime Minister of Rhodesia, leaving Number 10, Downing Street after abortive talks with Harold Wilson over Rhodesian independence, in October 1965. Smith was determined to maintain white supremacy in Rhodesia although there was a large black majority.

new role for government-sponsored science in industrial development."

The appeal was well-timed, for the 1960s stand out even in retrospect as a period of unprecedented expansion in higher education, and once in power Wilson was to create a new Ministry of Technology with a well-known trade unionist, Frank Cousins, as first Minister. Yet, with or without the necessary technological drive to modernise British industry in the face of sharp foreign competition, not least from Japan, Britain faced serious financial difficulties throughout the Wilson years.

The first phase, Wilson's so-called "hundred days", was darkened by a major sterling crisis. Nor was that the end. The second Wilson government was dogged by financial problems. One phase in July 1966 was a six-month wage freeze, and it was followed by what was called a "period of severe restraint". The question of "prices and incomes" headed the agenda before sterling was belatedly devalued by 14.3 per cent in November 1967.

There were severe expenditure cuts after that and sharp increases in taxation. Moreover, the trade gap widened still more than it had done earlier in what had been a calamitous summer, and standby credits had to be secured from the International Monetary Fund. On the home front dental and prescription charges were reintroduced. The imposition of these charges in 1951 had led to the Bevanite revolt against Gaitskell in which Wilson had taken part, and they had been abolished in 1965. Not surprisingly, no fewer than forty-seven Labour M.P.s voted against the motion to reintroduce them in 1968, and there was party resistance to further "emergency measures" under the new Chancellor of the Exchequer, Roy Jenkins. Edward Heath, who had replaced Sir Alec Douglas-Home as leader of the Conservative Party in 1965, claimed that three years of Labour rule had "reduced Britain from a prosperous nation to an international pauper".

One implication of devaluation had important consequences internationally. As part of the cutbacks—a necessary word which was now as familiar as the overworked word "crisis"—all British forces in the Persian Gulf and in the Far East, except Hong Kong, were to be withdrawn by 1971. It was impossible, however, for the Wilson government to take any equally decisive step in relation to the most nagging imperial—or former imperial—issue of the 1960s, Rhodesia. In November 1965 Ian Smith, recently returned to power with a massive majority by a limited electorate, unilaterally declared Rhodesian independence, and Wilson, backed not only by his own party, but by the majority of the Conservative Party, itself divided on the issue, imposed a phased programme of economic sanctions.

The attempt to negotiate with Smith tested all Wilson's abilities, and neither much publicised talks on HMS *Tiger* in December 1966 nor more controversial talks on HMS *Fearless* off Gibraltar in October 1968—perfect imperialist settings—succeeded. It was to be a Conservative not a Labour government which disposed of the Rhodesian issue as a factor in British politics, at a Lancaster House Conference held in December 1979. By then the internal situation in Rhodesia had changed considerably, but it was largely thanks to the diplomatic skills of Mrs Thatcher's first Foreign Secretary, Lord Carrington, that rival black Rhodesian leaders, backed by guerrilla armies battling in Rhodesia, agreed to assemble at "collection points" after a cease-fire and accept an interim government under a British Commissioner who would prepare the way for full independence.

The Commissioner chosen for what at that time seemed to be the most challenging of imperial tasks—and, indeed, the last great task—was Churchill's son-in-law, Christopher Soames. Churchill might have been uneasy about the result—the first one-man one-vote elections in Rhodesia in 1981 which were won by Robert Mugabe—but he would have admired his son-in-law's performance and, not least, his style.

By the time that the first Rhodesian elections were held, it had become clear that Africa, over which Harold Macmillan's "winds of change" were still blowing, was not to provide the last scene for the playing out of the centuries-old imperial drama. Instead, the Falkland Islands, little known to most Britons, were to introduce not only a new setting and a new group of players but a new kind of plot.

The Falklands War began on April 2, 1982 when Argentine troops landed in remote islands eight thousand miles from Britain, where British colonists had landed in 1765 and where British settlers—there were now eighteen hundred of them—had lived continuously since 1833. The islands had been discovered, too, by an Englishman as early as 1592, and although the Argentinians, who called the islands the Malvinas, had claimed sovereignty since 1768, they had never been able to settle there. Under a dictator, General Galtieri, they now wished to put an end to British rule before any 150th anniversary celebrations of British occupation. Diplomatic talks failed, and when the Argentinians landed, the Governor, after a display of resistance by the Marines, was forced to surrender.

Lord Carrington, who had been concerned with the earlier abortive diplomacy, immediately resigned and Mrs Thatcher set about with vigour the organisation of a hastily improvised task force to displace the Argentinians. When the force eventually arrived on May 20–21, it was outnumbered by two to one. However, on June 14, after only one major campaign, the capital of the Falkland Islands, Port Stanley, was restored to British rule: two hundred and twenty-five British troops had been killed and seven hundred and seventy-seven injured. Mrs Thatcher's position as a national leader was now beyond contention, not least because her domestic critics, who complained in particular of the British sinking of the Argentinian battleship the *Belgrano*, were considered to be an "unpatriotic" minority. There was a daunting long-term financial cost, however, as the islands, which had previously been thought to be of little economic or strategic value, were turned into a "fortress", and as ships of the Royal Navy, the numbers of which had been cut before the action began, were diverted to the South Atlantic.

Between the failure of Harold Wilson to reach an agreement on Rhodesia with Ian Smith and the British victory in the Falkland Islands, which even critics, including some Argentinians, conceded was a victory over fascism, Britain had taken some of its most critical decisions in foreign policy—in Europe. It had been agreed, not without division, in 1966, that the Labour government should once more explore British entry into the European Community which a previous Conservative government under Harold Macmillan had failed to achieve (in face of de Gaulle's veto) in January 1963. There had always been a strong anti-Common Market section in the Labour Party, and not merely on the left, for Gaitskell, who preferred stronger Commonwealth links to stronger European links, had belonged to it. Yet Wilson, far less of a "European", at least on the surface, than some of his "pro-European" colleagues in the Cabinet, took the plunge in May

At the end of the Falklands War in 1982, the P. & O. liner Canberra *comes home to Southampton where she is welcomed by a helicopter display team, a flotilla of small boats and a jubilant crowd. The* Canberra *had been at sea for ninety-four days, having acted as troop carrier, hospital and prison ship during the crisis.*

British troops under attack in the streets of Northern Ireland. The province's traditional industries, shipbuilding and linen, have been in decline since the Second World War. Attempts by successive British governments to revive its economy have been hampered by the state of near civil war that has existed since 1969 between Protestant and Roman Catholic extremists.

1967 when he announced Britain's intention to apply for full membership. A further de Gaulle veto in May 1967 did not settle the issue this time, for de Gaulle himself was forced to resign in April 1969 after France had been profoundly shaken by internal political disturbances.

Before the Labour government could embark on what would have been complex and protracted negotiations about the conditions of entry, Wilson—against the predictions of the pollsters—lost office in May 1970 following a general election which he had expected to win and which was described at the time as "one of the most dramatic and unexpected turn-rounds of the century". The Conservative Party, led by Heath, secured 46.6 per cent of the vote with three hundred and thirty seats and the Labour Party only 43 per cent with two hundred and eighty-seven seats. The other parties outside Northern Ireland, already a storm centre in British politics, were effectively blotted out. Only six Liberals were returned—the 7.5 per cent vote was the lowest in the party's history—and there were no Plaid Cymru victors in Wales and only one Scottish Nationalist.

Heath, determined to change both the structure and the style of government, took up the European negotiations in June 1970. He himself had been the chief British negotiator in Brussels in 1961–63, and failure made him only more resolute in 1970. He had stated categorically when the earlier negotiations had broken down that Britain was not going to turn its back on "the mainland of Europe". Nor was he unduly perturbed by the fact that opinion polls showed that as late as 1970 only 16 per cent were in favour of entry as opposed to 61 per cent against. Indeed, there had never been a majority in favour.

The way ahead was not easy, however. Even in 1970, after Willy Brandt, a friend of Britain, had taken over in West Germany, and de Gaulle had been replaced by Pompidou, it still required a Heath/Pompidou summit to resolve difficulties faced by the negotiators. A white paper published in July marked agreement at last.

The final terms, which granted Britain a six-year transitional period before being fully drawn into the costs and responsibilities of membership, were not sufficiently generous to appeal to critics of entry either in the Conservative Party or the Labour Party. Despite support for the terms from Roy Jenkins and George Thompson, who would have been the Labour Party's negotiators, the National Executive of the party carried a resolution against entry in July as did the Party Conference in October. Wilson gave no lead. The House of Commons debated entry for five months, and it was clear that there were deep divisions inside the parties as well as between them. There were no fewer than a hundred and six divisions, and the third reading was carried on a rare free vote (the biggest issue on which there had been a free vote since the nineteenth century) by a majority of only seventeen, three hundred and one to two hundred and eighty-four on October 18, 1971. The Treaty of Accession was signed in Brussels in January 1972.

Wilson had once remarked in 1962 during the last uneasy years of the Macmillan government that "a dying government does not possess the right, constitutionally or morally, to take a divided nation into the Common Market". It was as a divided nation, however—or at least as a divided Parliament—that Britain formally entered the European Community, not without fanfares, on January 1, 1973.

The decision was ratified, however, by a substantial majority of the

THE MODERN WORLD

The twentieth century has been a century of headlong change — change that has now gathered pace with the passing of two world wars. In architecture, fashion, the arts and in our way of life, the "Modern World" is now outdated, updated every year.

COVENTRY CATHEDRAL, WARWICKSHIRE

THE FESTIVAL OF BRITAIN, *in 1951, not only celebrated the centenary of the Victorian Great Exhibition but was also a defiant gesture of optimism in an age of postwar austerity. It boasted many new buildings, of which only the central Royal Festival Hall (left), has been retained. New works of art were specially commissioned, such as these external sculptures by Richard Huws and Siegfried Charoux (below).*

IN 1953 THE CORONATION OF QUEEN ELIZABETH *(right) was seen as a new dawn for Britain. Austerity was ending. Fashion reflected the change with the return of glamour, style, and conspicuous expense, illustrated here by this evening dress (above) worn by the famous model, Barbara Goalen. The new Queen's father had been a symbol of stubborn courage in the Second World War. She was expected to preside over a second Elizabethan age of renewed power, glory and prosperity. In the event, she had a harder task — that of presiding over the end of the British Empire and of creating a new, less ceremonial, relationship between her subjects and members of the royal family.*

SUSSEX UNIVERSITY *(above) was designed by Sir Basil Spence, the architect of Coventry Cathedral, completed in 1962. It was one of eight new universities of the 1960s. The new universities and polytechnics made significant changes in the curriculum, breaking away from the pattern of single subject degrees, and also encouraging fashionable subjects such as sociology.*

*"*KING AND QUEEN*", (below) by Henry Moore, now dominates a hillside in Dumfries as its creator dominated British sculpture before and after the Second World War. Influenced by Mexican and Sumerian sculpture, Moore wrote: "A work must have a vitality . . . a pent-up energy, an intense life of its own, independent of the object it may represent."*

THE POST OFFICE TOWER, *(above) and* THE BARBICAN, *(right) symbolised the rebirth of London after the devastation of the Second World War. The former became a landmark of the new technology. It was built between 1960 and 1964 by a group led by Sir Eric Bedford, primarily to carry aerials to transmit and receive London's radio, television, and telephone signals. The Barbican, begun in 1957 to the design of Chamberlin, Powell and Bon, now provides housing for six thousand, two schools and an arts centre, on an area that was almost completely destroyed by wartime bombs.*

THE SWINGING SIXTIES *saw Britain unexpectedly set the pace in sport, fashion and pop music.* THE WEMBLEY WORLD CUP *in 1966, (top left) briefly restored Britain's dominance in football.* TWIGGY *(above), with her waif-like figure, established a new style in the world of fashion.* THE BEATLES *(top right) crowned their international top pop-star rating, with their "Sergeant Pepper's Lonely Hearts Club Band", its record cover designed by Peter Blake.* THE MINI, *here in 1960s' psychedelic colouring, (left) offered cheap, stylish mobility.* CARNABY STREET *(right) with its unisex boutiques became a mecca for youth.*

"MR AND MRS CLARKE AND PERCY", *by David Hockney, from the Tate Gallery, London. David Hockney has been one of Britain's most highly regarded painters since the 1960s, capturing everything from the mood of the moment to the people of the moment, such as the Clarkes, leading fashion designers of their generation.*

WESTMINSTER HALL, LONDON, *(left) the most ancient precinct of the Houses of Parliament, provided in January 1965 the ideal setting for the lying-in of its most distinguished statesman, Winston Spencer Churchill. For three days, in bitterly cold weather, queues of mourners stretched along the riverbank, and across Lambeth Bridge. More than twenty-five million watched from the streets and on television as a huge military procession accompanied his coffin to St Paul's Cathedral for his State funeral, and then as it left by river on his last journey to the graveyard of the little parish church at Bladon, close by his birthplace of Blenheim Palace.*

"SPAGHETTI JUNCTION", BIRMING-HAM, (above) was built in 1972 — the largest interchange in Europe, containing eighteen separate paths for traffic. Britain's transport network is still being transformed from a mixture of rail and narrow roads into a motorway system.

THE NATIONAL WESTMINSTER TOWER, LONDON, (left) was completed in 1980 to become the tallest building in Europe. It was designed by Richard Seifert, who has, it is said, changed London's skyline more than any architect since Wren.

THE NOTTING HILL CARNIVAL, LONDON, (below) has, since the 1970s celebrated the culture of one of the most recent waves of immi-grants that have combined to make and remake the British way of life.

THE THAMES BARRIER, THE LLOYD'S BUILDING, AND THE PRINCESS OF WALES CONSERVATORY, *are unique triumphs of British technology. The Barrier (above) spans five hundred and twenty metres. Built in 1982 to protect London from flooding, it can seal off the upper reaches of the river, in the event of a North Sea surge. The Lloyd's Building, in the City of London, (right) was designed by Richard Rogers in 1974, to provide the headquarters of British insurance with a computer-controlled building appropriate to the computer age. The Princess of Wales Conservatory, at Kew Gardens, (below) was opened in 1987. Built by Gordon Wilson, it contains in the one building ten distinct environments for its plants — from desert to rain forest.*

THE BURRELL COLLECTION BUILDING, GLASGOW, *(above) was designed by Barry Gasson in 1971, to contain one of the finest municipal art collections in Britain. Consisting of every kind of art treasure, the collection was gathered personally by Sir William Burrell over a period of eighty years, at the rate of two acquisitions a week.*

THE BRENT "C" OIL RIG, NORTH SEA, *(left) is one of the great islands built by man to extract mineral wealth from the sea. Western Europe — most especially Britain and Norway — first joined the major oil producers in the 1970s, and Britain now depends on revenue from the export of North Sea oil.*

THE LONDON DOCKLANDS DEVELOP-
MENT *is the largest urban regeneration project in Europe. Over eight
and a half square miles in extent,
by the year 2000 it will have created
over thirteen thousand new homes
(complete with their own social and
community facilities), and one and
a half million square feet of offices,
as well as its own international airport and light railway system. The
City's financial services are expanding to fill the gap left by the decline
of heavy industry and sea-borne
trade. Here another industrial revolution is in the making, reminding
us that our island's heritage must
always be a heritage of growth and
a heritage of constant change.*

electorate in the first—and so far only—referendum in British history in 1975. The idea of a referendum had been put forward by opponents of entry during the 1970–71 debates, and Wilson had agreed in March 1972 that if and when the Labour Party returned to power the government would insist not only on a referendum, which was strongly supported by Tony Benn and others on the left of the party, but on a renegotiation of the terms of entry. Renegotiation and the referendum were both items, therefore, in the Labour Party's manifesto at the election of February 1974. In June 1975 renegotiated terms, not significantly different from the old terms, were put before the electorate by a government which was itself sharply divided. Turnout was high, and by a majority of 67.2 per cent to 32.8 the electorate said yes to staying in the European Community.

On the other key issue of their time, however, that of industrial relations, neither Wilson nor Heath, with their different philosophies and styles of political leadership, had been able to establish a satisfactory relationship with the trade unions. This failure played a part not only in their two defeats in 1970 and 1974, but in the defeat of James Callaghan, Wilson's successor as Prime Minister, in 1979 after yet another winter of discontent.

In 1968 and 1969 Wilson and his energetic Employment Secretary, Barbara Castle, who was to the left of the party and among the most active anti-Marketeers, both favoured a reform of the trade unions, the Labour Party's ancient allies since 1900. It was on Wilson's initiative, indeed, that a Royal Commission under Lord Donovan had been appointed to look into the whole question of trade union organisation and power. Following the report of the Commission, the controversial white paper, *In Place of Strife*, was published in January 1969. Wilson thought it inadequately decisive in its recommendations, but it went further than the Donovan Report in recommending that a twenty-eight day conciliation period should be ordered in designated industrial disputes and a ballot of members required when a strike was threatened. Even more seriously, in the last resort it imposed "penal clauses" to ensure that the law would be enforced.

The trade unions were implacably opposed to the white paper and were backed by a large number of Labour M.P.s of various persuasions, including Callaghan who was at that time Treasurer of the Labour Party and knew at first hand that the party was just as dependent on trade union funds as it had been since its inception. As a result there was an inevitable compromise. The Trades Union Congress produced a *Programme for Action* which did not appeal to either Wilson or Mrs Castle, but when it became clear in June that a Bill containing penal clauses would face formidable difficulties in the House, the Government withdrew its proposals and the T.U.C. offered a "solemn and binding undertaking" that member unions would observe its own guidelines on regulating unofficial strikes. Since the T.U.C. had no penal clauses at its own disposal, the Labour Party had in effect capitulated to the trade unions.

They seemed, indeed, to be in an extremely powerful position in 1970, with over eleven million members, and with a number of leaders like Jack Jones and Hugh Scanlon who were well able to argue as well as to bargain. Their power was fully demonstrated during the Heath government when they ensured that a new Industrial Relations Act, of 1971, which went much further than Wilson's proposed legislation, was opposed not only in Parliament but in the streets.

The Act removed the immunity from suits by aggrieved employers that the unions had "enjoyed" since 1906, and established a new Industrial Relations Court of the standing of a High Court to deal with cases of breach of contract and "unfair practices". Far from reducing union pressure the Act increased it, for there was unprecedented violence in London and the provinces and in 1972 the number of days lost through strikes rose to twenty-four million, double the annual number in 1971 and more than four times the annual number during the 1960s.

The Act soon became as much of a dead letter as Wilson's proposed reform in 1969. Unions refused to register under it, the Government feared to take legal action, which on paper it could now do. The Labour Party itself moved to the left both in Parliament and above all in the constituencies, and when it returned to power after the fall of Heath in 1974 it granted the unions new privileges rather than curbing those which they already had. Inevitably this produced a move to the right within the Conservative Party. The way was being prepared for Mrs Thatcher, who under Heath was Secretary of State for Education.

The fall of Heath as Prime Minister, to be followed by his fall as party leader, was itself the result of confrontation. Faced with rising inflation and increasing unemployment, which seemed even to many professional economists reared on Keynes to be a most unlikely combination, the government found itself in confrontation with the most difficult of all Labour groups, the miners. Moreover, the timing of the miners' action against the government was extremely awkward. It coincided with an international oil crisis which once again—shades of Suez—began in Egypt, with an attack on Israel on October 6, 1973.

The Arab-dominated Organisation of Petroleum Exporting Countries (OPEC), with far more power at its disposal in these circumstances than any British trade union, announced the first of four upward price leaps which, taken together, raised the world price of oil in three months to four times what it had been before the Egyptian-Israeli War, and at the same time it cut shipments of oil to the Western nations by 24 per cent. The word "crisis" had been misused many times since 1961, but this was a real "crisis". It began in the deserts, but it soon moved to the mines and the factories. For a time it made Parliament look impotent and it accentuated every strain already present in a divided British society.

In the middle of the oil crisis the miners, who had won substantial wage increases in 1972 following their first national strike since the General Strike of 1926, demanded pay increases for some miners of as much as 47 per cent, meanwhile banning overtime; and the electric power-station workers and a section of the railway workers also chose this moment to go slow. On New Year's Day 1974, for the first time in British history, all national manufacturing and business firms were ordered to use electric power only three days a week. After various attempts at conciliation had failed, the miners stopped work completely.

The situation had a revolutionary element in it, or at least a revolutionary potential, but it was clear that even *in extremis* the miners, a far smaller group than they had been in the past, had a degree of public sympathy which was to be far less evident in a later miners' strike which Mrs Thatcher had to face in 1984. In January 1974 public opinion polls, themselves to become increasingly controversial before the end of the decade, suggested

The 1984 miners' strike was called by the militant president of the National Union of Mineworkers, Arthur Scargill. on the issues of pay and pit closures. But, unlike the strike of 1972, the miners faced a strong government and had little public support, and after a year of severe hardship they were forced back to work.

that 44 per cent of the public were prepared to support the miners and only 30 per cent the employers, and a month later 56 per cent believed that the government should give in to the miners and only 38 per cent believed that it should not.

Heath announced the dissolution of Parliament on February 7, 1974, although he still had a substantial majority there. "The choice before the nation today, as never before," he proclaimed, "is a choice between moderation and extremism." Much hinged in 1974, a year of two general elections, on what "moderation" actually meant. For example, during the first campaign, when Enoch Powell advised people to vote Labour in protest against Heath's European policies, the Director-General of the Confederation of British Industry complained that the Industrial Relations Act had "sullied every relationship at every level between unions and employers and ought to be repealed rather than amended." There was an atmosphere of great uncertainty in this grim year, grimmer for many people than any year of war when under Churchill the country had been united.

Heath and the Conservatives did badly in the first election of 1974, their share of the vote falling by 8.3 per cent, but the Labour Party did not do well either. Its share fell by 5.8 per cent, and the proportion of electors voting Labour (37.1 per cent) was lower than it had been in any general election since 1931. Faced with party confrontation as well as with employer union confrontation, 19.3 per cent of the electors chose in this election to vote Liberal, although only fourteen seats were won. Not for the first or the last time electoral reform seemed to be on the political agenda.

Wilson returned to power as leader of a minority government, and Labour increased its share of the poll by 2.1 per cent at the next general election of October 1974. More important, Wilson was in charge, now, of a majority government. The Conservatives lost twenty seats and the Liberals one. The Labour majority over the Conservatives was forty-three, but over all other parties only three.

There was a strange sense in 1974 and 1975, before and after the new Labour government overturned the trade-union policies of its predecessors

TOMORROW'S BRITAIN

THE PACE OF CHANGE in almost every sphere of life grows faster. Nevertheless, it is possible to identify several major features of today's society which will continue to affect the style and quality of life for years to come.

Firstly, since 1973, Britain has been a member of the European Economic Community, part of the third economic force in the world after the USA and the Soviet Union, with all the advantages and challenges which that inevitably implies.

Secondly, the computer revolution which has already put man on the moon is changing methods in offices and factories throughout the country. The immediate effects are redundancy and unemployment, but the hope is that, as people transfer to the new industries, there will be more opportunity for leisure and working at home.

Thirdly, Britain's resources of oil, so recently exploited, are running out. Alternative means of providing power for industry, housing and transport must be developed.

Fourthly, the countryside is changing; shrinking, both in size and population as the urban areas increase, and altering its appearance as new farming methods are adopted. Some forms of pollution have disappeared, but new hazards like acid rain take their place.

Fifthly, though motorways and airports are constantly built and enlarged, there are growing traffic jams and an increasing number of "near misses" in the air.

Sixthly, as a result of large numbers of immigrants (principally concentrated in the cities), Britain has become a multicultural society. Difficulties arise when attempts are made to integrate society and eliminate racialism, but these are now being tackled.

Lastly, day by day the media bring world events into British homes. This information explosion has influenced everybody's perception of the world and has provided an instant international platform for attention seekers, be they statesmen, terrorists, or multinational advertisers.

THE MEDIA *influence everybody's life, but whether for good or bad is a matter of constant debate. With at least twenty national newspapers, over one thousand five hundred established provincial newspapers and numerous specialist magazines, Britain is well served with instant reading material. Apart from the BBC, there are twenty-two commercial radio stations, and the introduction of satellite TV and the development of cable TV will hugely increase commercial programmes. Even now, few people can escape up-to-the-minute reports on major tragedies and disasters. Sometimes these reports can lead to amazing, positive responses such as when the singer, Bob Geldof, heard on BBC TV about the Ethiopian drought and organised such effective fundraising events as the Live Aid Concert at Wembley (above) in 1985.*

IMMIGRANTS *were encouraged to come to post-war Britain to swell the labour force. Workers from the West Indies, Africa, India, Bangladesh and Pakistan were welcomed, but the increase in immigration in the 1960s soon led to government restrictions. The 1962 Commonwealth Immigration Act's objective was to persuade more immigrants to apply for temporary work-permits, but instead many Asian families settled permanently. Race riots in Toxteth and Brixton in the 1980s have shown that Britain may be becoming less tolerant, especially when there is a high level of unemployment and crime. Yet there have been examples of constructive cooperation. The photograph below shows a multiracial London comprehensive school in the 1980s. Ethnic minorities are now represented in parliament, the police and the professions.*

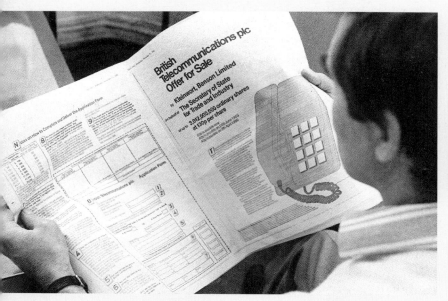

THE REGENERATION OF INNER CITIES *is a top world priority. In Britain, Glasgow has led the way and is becoming a showcase for architects, designers and sculptors. London's Docklands are being given a major face-lift, as is Merseyside's seven-mile waterfront and Bristol Quay, where Brunel's Great Eastern is now moored. New road, rail, air and water communications are being created to serve the thousands of new homes and offices which are being built in these and other areas. This futuristic light railway (above) links the redeveloped Docklands with the City of London.*

NATION OF SHAREHOLDERS *and home owners being created by Mrs Thatcher's Conservative governments. The sale of industries (above) which had been nationalised under state ownership has so far raised seventeen* billion pounds for the Treasury and tripled the number of shareholders to nine and a half million Britons. At the same time, the number of home owners has doubled from 32 per cent in 1938 to 64 per cent in 1987.

CHANNEL TUNNELS *have been dreamt of ever since Napoleon's invasion schemes of 1804. The construction of the Eurotunnel from Cheriton near Folkestone to Coquelles, just south of Calais, was the brainchild of Mrs Thatcher and President Mitterrand. The probable cost of nearly five billion pounds will be met by* private shareholders and loans arranged by the Banks. It is projected that the tunnel will carry two hundred cars and five hundred passengers in drive-on, drive-off trains scheduled to leave every seven minutes. A through train from London to Paris should take no more than three hours, and from Cheriton to Coquelles, about thirty-three minutes. Britain's links with the EEC will be further strengthened in 1992 when the current trade tariffs throughout the European Community will be abolished. The photograph above shows a detailed scale model of the Eurotunnel's proposed Folkestone terminal.

in the name of a "social contract", that Britain was in the grip of international forces that it could not control. Nor did the ratification of entry into the European Community resolve the doubts; it came at an unpropitious time in the affairs of Europe and the world. The rate of inflation in Britain which had been 9.2 per cent in 1972–73 had risen to 16 per cent between 1973–74 under a Heath government and reached 24.1 per cent under a Wilson government in 1974–75. Retail prices were now over 150 per cent higher than they had been when Churchill died, and in 1974–75 the balance of payments deficit on current account was the highest on record. At the same time unemployment had risen to over 700,000.

Had it not been for the fortunate discovery of North Sea oil in 1969 the economic record of the early and middle 1970s would have been one of almost unrelieved gloom. Moreover, there were many signs that Britain was becoming a more unpleasant country to live in; less tolerant, more bitterly divided on class lines, more prone to violence—and to crime. All the social effervescence which had permeated the 1960s had gone, indeed, there was a growing reaction against it.

That there could be political surprises was proved when Wilson suddenly and dramatically resigned in March 1976—he had announced his intention to do so to the Queen in the previous December—and was replaced by Callaghan. In that same year Jeremy Thorpe, who had been leader of the Liberal Party for nine years, went too, after a scandal. A year earlier Heath had been replaced as Conservative leader by Mrs Thatcher with one hundred and forty-six votes out of two hundred and seventy-one votes cast in the first Conservative leadership election of its kind.

Yet another sterling crisis in the summer of 1976 marked what seemed to be a low point in the economic history of the country and the assistance of the International Monetary Fund was once again called for at a high price. Unemployment continued to rise, reaching 1,400,000 in January 1977, but thanks to North Sea oil the economic position improved in 1977 and 1978. Surprisingly, Callaghan, whose political style was more reassuring than Wilson's, did not call a general election, and he faced an appalling winter of industrial disputes in 1978–79 which suggested that trade union

The large deposits of oil and natural gas discovered in the North Sea in the late 1960s have been a major factor in Britain's growing economic stability. This photograph shows the construction of an oil rig platform at Teesside, before it is towed out to sea and sited.

power, which he had always recognised, was capable of bringing down not only a Conservative government, but a Labour government as well.

There were other problems, some of which would have been familiar to Churchill, others not. The most familiar and the most intractable was that of Northern Ireland, where a new phase of unrest had begun as early as 1968. In April 1972 direct rule from London replaced rule by the Stormont Parliament in Belfast, but neither Heath nor Wilson had been able to improve the situation. Not only was Callaghan equally unsuccessful, he also faced demands for devolution, or increased self-rule, of powers to Wales and Scotland as well. His minority government, dependent on the votes of nationalist parties, was defeated more than once on issues of devolution in the House of Commons. Then on March 28, 1979 there came one of the most exciting votes in the history of Parliament. The government was defeated on a vote of confidence by three hundred and eleven votes to three hundred and ten. Had two Irish Catholic M.P.s voted with the government it would have won. Instead they abstained.

In the 1979 election which brought Mrs Thatcher to power the Conservatives polled 43.9 per cent of the votes and Labour only 36.9 per cent. There were significant differences, however, in the swings to the Conservatives in different parts of the country, a portent that suggested awkward times to come. Unlike all her predecessors, Mrs Thatcher did not appear to aim for a national consensus, although she was near to finding one during the Falkland Islands War. She demanded a break with the policies of the past and she proved that she had an indomitable will. She changed the terms of British politics. She was different from all her twentieth-century predecessors in one other respect also. She was to win three successive general elections in 1979, 1983 and 1987.

It is too early for a historian to place the record of her governments in perspective. In his history writing Churchill was wise to stop short before the immediate past, knowing that there can be sharp reactions in history as well as continuities, some inspiring, some depressing. Certainly, the problem phase of British history is not over. Nor is the future clear. However, if imperial days are over, as Morris believes, there are signs that we stand on the threshold of an age in which peace and indeed survival will depend on the leadership of power blocs greater even than the British Empire. Churchill believed passionately that the value of history was that it would equip his fellow-countrymen to make better choices than otherwise they might have done. It may well be that those choices must now be made by Britain as a leader within Europe, where she may yet have her most valuable—perhaps even Churchillian—role to play.

Margaret Thatcher (1925-), Britain's first woman Prime Minister, has won three successive general elections with the Conservative Party. Her indomitable will has earned her the nickname of "the Iron Lady".

BRITISH HISTORY		CIVILISATIONS AND EMPIRES		ECONOMICS	
BC					
55	Julius Caesar's first invasion of England		Decline of Greek culture and influence; rise of Rome from 1000 BC onwards; first as Republic then as Empire		Agrarian economies grow in size, productivity and power. Slavery as system of production widespread
0–1000					
43	Claudian invasion	23	Caesar Octavian inaugurates Roman Empire		Chinese silk trade with Rome well established over recognised routes
61	Boadicea's revolt crushed;	70	Jerusalem destroyed		Estate-based economy increases local autonomy in Europe and Asia
	Britain becomes a Roman province	200-600	Indian civilisation expands in S.E. Asia		
c.500	Saxon invasions and settlement	220	End of Han dynasty in China		Trade declines in volume as Roman Empire falls
789	Viking and Danish invasions begin	227	Persian Empire expands		
871-899	King Alfred	230	Sujin first known ruler of Japan		Paper money first used in China
980	Renewed Danish attacks	286	Division of the Roman Empire		Byzantine and Arab coinage becomes international trading currency of Middle Ages
		c.300	Mayan civilisation develops in America		
		330	Constantine reunites Roman Empire and founds Constantinople		In Europe, mining and weaving industries appear
		433-53	Attila the Hun		
		476	Rome falls to Barbarians		
		619	Tang dynasty in China		
		697	Arabs destroy Carthage		
		750	Islam spreads from Spain to China		
		800	Charlemagne crowned Holy Roman Emperor		
		907	Mongols begin capture of Inner Mongolia		
		920	Golden age of Ghanaian Empire		
		960	Sung dynasty in China		
1001–1400					
1066	Norman invasion under William	1189	Last known Norse expedition to North America		Feudal systems spread through Europe
1086	Domesday Book audit completed	1190	Genghis Khan		Agricultural yields improve through better land use and drainage
1154	Accession of Henry II whose marriage to Eleanor of Aquitaine had gained French land for England	1210	Genghis Khan invades China		Early establishment of regular trade links between Europe, Russia, China
		1240	End of Ghanaian Empire		
1170	Murder of Thomas Becket	1271	Marco Polo visits Kublai Khan		Annual trade fairs in Europe stimulate exchange of products
1175	Henry II claims "Lordship" of Ireland	1290	Ottoman Turk dynasty rises to challenge the Byzantine Empire		
1215	Magna Carta restricts royal absolutism				
1283	Edward I defeats Llewellyn	1307	The Empire of Mali succeeds that of Ghana in Africa		
	Conquest of Wales completed				
1314	Battle of Bannockburn	1325	Aztec Empire flourishes in Mexico		
	Scots secure independence	1363	Tamerlane advances through Asia		
1337	Beginning of Hundred Years' War	1370	French repossess much territory from English		
1346	Battle of Crécy	1400	Granada captured from Moors		
1349	Black Death				
1381	Peasants' Revolt				
1401–1603					
1415	Battle of Agincourt	1430s	Inca Empire at peak in Peru		Rise of towns boosts development of guilds and stimulates consumer market for goods and services
1453	End of Hundred Years' War; only Calais remains English possession in France	1450s	In Africa, the Benin and Zimbabwe civilisations flourish		Feudalism gradually weakens
1455-85	The Wars of the Roses	1453	Turkish capture of Constantinople ends the Byzantine Empire		European recession due to plague, land misuse, etc., provokes peasant unrest
1485	Battle of Bosworth Field; Tudor dynasty established		European maritime expansion		Italian commercial and financial dominance; Genoa, Florence, Venice become banking centres
	Accession of Henry VII	1520	Turkish power at height		
1534	England breaks with Papacy under Henry VIII	1526	Mogul dynasty founded in India—establishes Moslem India		
1558	Fall of Calais	1529	Ottoman Turks besiege Vienna		Economic power shifts north in Europe, to Antwerp, Bruges, then Amsterdam
	Accession of Elizabeth I	1533	Ivan the Terrible becomes Tsar in Russia	c.1500	Discovery of gold and silver by Spaniards in the New World
1588	Spanish Armada defeated			1575	Inflation leads to Spanish bankruptcy
1603	Elizabeth I dies and Tudor dynasty ends			1600	East India Company founded
1604–1700					
1605	Guy Fawkes' Gunpowder Plot foiled	1606	European settlement of N. America begins; Virginia founded as colony	1609	Modern deposit banking era starts with opening of Bank of Amsterdam
1640	Civil War breaks out between Royalists and Parliament	1620	Voyage of the *Mayflower*	1611	Amsterdam Stock Exchange opens
1649	Charles I executed	1640	Japan cuts itself off from contact with rest of world	c.1650	Dutch trading links with Japan and China bring new trade to Europe
1653-58	Oliver Cromwell as Lord Protector crushes Irish Catholics	1644	Dutch begin to chart Australia		Slave trade well established
1660	Restoration of monarchy; Charles II	1651	Anglo-Dutch rivalry deepens	1656	First European use of banknotes
1665	Great Plague in London followed by	1683	Turks repulsed from gates of Vienna	1688	Mr Lloyd's coffee-house becomes the forerunner of marine insurance
1666	Great Fire		Europe, freed from external threat, becomes preoccupied with internal rivalries until emergence of the USA and Soviet Union as superpowers in the twentieth century	1694	Bank of England established
1678	Habeas Corpus Act passed				Changes in European agriculture lead to increased yields
1685	James II, a Roman Catholic, becomes King				
1688	Glorious Revolution: William and Mary, both Protestants, replace James II			mid-1700s	The systematic analysis of the creation and distribution of wealth begins in France with the Physiocrats

RELIGION		SOCIETY AND CULTURE		DISCOVERIES	

BC

	Hinduism, Confucianism, Buddhism in the East; Zoroastrianism, Judaism in the West		Plato, Aristotle and other Greek thinkers debate the best model of society and political order		
4	Probable date of birth of Jesus Christ				

0–1000

30	Crucifixion of Jesus	6	Civil Service examinations start in China	c.160	Ptolemy draws 26 maps
40	Church built at Corinth	80	Colosseum completed in Rome	c.190	Galen's herbal medicines
58	Buddhism introduced into China	360	Books begin to replace scrolls	271	First use of compass in China
64-305	Persecution of Christians	413	Augustine of Hippo discourses on justice and the State	660	Woodblock printing used in China
73	Fall of Masada			700	Water mills appear in Europe
135	Dispersal of the Jews	425	Founding of University of Constantinople. Islamic cultural growth in art, architecture, literature, etc.		Flourishing of Islamic science—chemistry, astronomy and algebra
200	Revival of Hinduism leads to flourishing of Sanskrit learning			c.850	Advances in European navigational technology—the lateen sail and the astrolabe
570	Birth of Mohammed	c.600	Gregorian chants systematised		
590	Pope Gregory the Great	619	Tang dynasty in China establishes administrative system that lasts till twentieth century	890	Horseshoe in use
597	Augustine's Christian mission to England				Calibrated candles are used to tell time
624	Buddhism becomes the established religion of Japan	750	Spread of Islam from Spain to China influences art, architecture and science	1000	Chinese use gunpowder for firing rockets
632	Death of Mohammed	850	University founded at Salerno		Leif Ericsson discovers N. America
638	Muslims conquer Jerusalem	960	Art, science and manufacturing prosper during Sung dynasty in China		
663	English Church linked to Rome				
732	Defeat of Muslims at Tours				

1001–1400

1054	Roman and Eastern Churches split	1001-1200	Irrigation and flood control lead to centralised governments in Asia	1090	Water-driven mechanical clock
1096-99	First Crusade			1100	Islamic science enters its declining phase
1147	Second Crusade		Early polyphonic musical forms emerge and the troubadours grow in popularity	1125	Earliest mention of European use of compass
	Monastery system in Europe grows more influential in education, welfare, economics		Epic and religious poetry	1161	Chinese use explosives in warfare
1189-93	Third Crusade		Great age of Gothic building (European cathedrals) starts—Chartres, Paris, York, etc	1202	Arabic numerals introduced to Europe
1208	Albigensian Crusade (the first against the Christians)	1050-1123	Omar Khayyam—Persian poet, mathematician and astronomer		Compass comes into widespread use
1215	Medieval Church and Papacy at peak of power and influence	1119-1200	Universities of Bologna, Paris (Sorbonne), Oxford and Cambridge founded	1289	Block printing used in Ravenna, Italy
1252	Inquisition starts to use torture	1201-1400	Development of Gothic architecture	1290	Mechanical clock and spectacles in use
1290	Expulsion of Jews from England			c.1320	Innovations in archery: crossbow and longbow
1291	Fall of Acre ends Crusading in Holy Land	1350s	Beginnings of Italian Renaissance		
	Papal Schisms 1309-77 and 1378-1417	1353	Boccaccio's Il Decameron		
1380	Wyclif's translation of the Bible into English	1387	Chaucer begins The Canterbury Tales		
1400	Moors expelled from Spain				

1401–1603

1415	Church burns John Huss as heretic	1401-1603	Reformation provokes a religious and political debate over forms of authority	1454	Movable type printing introduced by Gutenberg
1517	Luther's theses start Protestant Reformation		Humanism weakens the intellectual authority of the modern Church		European voyages of discovery and exploration begin
1536	Calvin spreads Reformation to Switzerland	1440	Eton College founded	1488	Dias rounds Cape of Good Hope
1545	Church of Rome starts Counter-Reformation; establishes Order of Jesuits	1453	Scholars flee west from fallen Constantinople bringing new impetus to learning	1492	Columbus reaches W. Indies
1549	England becomes Protestant	1450-1500	Italian Renaissance flourishes under Medici patronage in Florence	1497	Cabot discovers Newfoundland
1553	Mary Tudor restores Catholicism in England			1498	Da Gama reaches India
1555	Knox takes Reformation to Scotland	1513	Machiavelli expounds theory of the modern State and its rulers	1522	Magellan circumnavigates globe
1572	St Bartholomew's Day Massacre of French Protestants	1516	Thomas More's Utopia published. Art and architecture achieve new heights—Michelangelo, Titian, Dürer	1569	Mercator's navigational map of the world
	Religious wars influence European rivalry		Literature and drama flourish. Shakespeare, Marlowe, Rabelais	1590-1608	Rapid development of precision instruments of observation and measurement—telescope, thermometer, microscope, clock

1604–1700

1611	King James Authorised Version of the Bible printed	1616	Shakespeare's plays	1609	Kepler's laws of planetary motion
1612	Last recorded burning of heretics in England	1630s	First newspapers published in France and Italy	1616	Harvey lectures on circulation of blood
	Baptist Church established in England		Art and literature flourish in Europe: Golden Age of Dutch painting—Rubens, Rembrandt, Vermeer, Van Dyck. Golden Age of French literature; Molière, Corneille, Pascal, Racine, La Fontaine	1661	Boyle defines chemical elements
1620	Christianity increasingly defensive against the onslaught of scientific and rationalist thought			1662	Foundation of the Royal Society
				1665	Newton experiments with gravitation
				1682	Halley observes comet named after him
		1641-1700	Descartes develops rationalist philosophy, influencing Spinoza, Leibniz	1687	Newton establishes basis of modern mathematics and laws of motion
		1660s	In England: Milton, Dryden, Pepys, Bunyan	1700	Leibniz founds Prussian Academy for the sciences
		1680s	Rise of instrumental music and opera—Purcell, Scarlatti, Corelli, Vivaldi		
		1690s	Rise of journalism and periodical literature		

BRITISH HISTORY		CIVILISATIONS AND EMPIRES		ECONOMICS	

1701–1815

1704-09	French defeated at Blenheim, Ramillies, Oudenarde and Malplaquet	c.1700	Peter the Great begins to modernise Russia and lay its foundations as a Great Power	1776	Adam Smith publishes *The Wealth of Nations*
1706	Act of Union with Scotland	1775	American War of Independence	1770s	Industrial Revolution shifts economic life to
1714	Hanoverian dynasty established	1776	American Declaration of Independence		factory system
1721	Sir Robert Walpole becomes the first Prime Minister	1783	End of American War of Independence	1771	Lloyd's form a society of underwriters
1745	Jacobite Rebellion defeated	1789	French Revolution starts; Ancien Régime challenged and overthrown	1790s	Canal-building fever in England
1756	Seven Years' War: Britain gains Canada		Declaration of The Rights of Man		
1774	Warren Hastings appointed Governor-General of India	1793	France declares war on Britain		
1793	Beginning of wars between Britain and France	1807	Peak of Napoleonic power		
		1810	Argentina becomes first independent South American state		
1805	Battle of Trafalgar	1812	Peninsular War		
1807	Parliamentary Act abolishes slave trade		Napoleon invades Russia		
1815	Battle of Waterloo ends wars with France	1815	Congress of Vienna		

1816–1901

1816-20	Social unrest caused by economic problems following French wars	1823	Monroe doctrine keeps Europe out of American affairs	1817	Ricardo publishes *Principles of Political Economy and Taxation* and founds classical economics
1819	Peterloo massacre	1848	Liberal and nationalist revolutions spread through Europe	1830s	Railway fever begins in England. Britain nears peak of manufacturing and industrial supremacy
1829	Catholic Emancipation				
1832	First Parliamentary Reform Act	c.1850s	Pax Britannica, the British Empire unrivalled and unchecked, but revolutions and nationalism in Europe sow seeds of future conflicts		
1833	Emancipation of slaves			1867	Walter Bagehot publishes *The English Constitution*
1834	"Tolpuddle martyrs"				
1837	Accession of Victoria	1853	Commodore Perry breaches Japanese isolationism after 200 years	1880s	World economy dominated by Europe
1845	Irish potato famine				
1846	Corn Laws repealed	1861-65	American Civil War		
1851	Great Exhibition	1870-71	Prussia defeats France		
1854	Outbreak of Crimean War against Russia	1879	German–Austrian alliance		
1867	Second Parliamentary Reform Act	1880s	German unification		
1884	Third Parliamentary Reform Act		Italian unification		
1886	Gladstone's Irish Home Rule Bill defeated		Europeans scramble for African possessions		
1899	Boer War breaks out	1895	Franco–Russian alliance		
1900	Mafeking relieved, Labour Representation Committee lays foundation of modern Labour Party				
1901	Victoria dies				

1902–1988

1906-14	Liberal government introduces welfare reforms	1904	Entente Cordiale between Britain and France	1909	Ford's first assembly-line production of cars
1909	Old-age pensions introduced	1905	"Dress rehearsal" revolutions in Russia	1925	Return to gold standard
1914-18	Britain in First World War	1911	Nationalist revolution in China	1929	Wall Street stock-market crash starts world slump and recession until late 1930s
1922	Irish independence	1914-18	First World War		
1924	First Labour government in Britain	1917	Bolshevik revolution in Russia	1930s	Growth of Keynesian policies which stimulate demand and lower unemployment
1926	General Strike	1919	Failure of revolution in Germany		
1931	Political crisis: "National government"		League of Nations established	1931	Britain goes off gold standard
1936	Abdication of Edward VIII; accession of George VI	1922	Italian fascism triumphs under Mussolini	1936	Keynes's *The General Theory of Employment, Interest, and Money*
		1933	Hitler becomes Chancellor in Germany		
1939-45	Britain in Second World War	1936	Civil War in Spain. Fascist expansionism continues until end of Second World War	1944	Bretton Woods Agreement sets up postwar economic system; establishes World Bank and International Monetary Fund
1945	Sweeping Labour victory; extensive "welfare state"	1939-45	Second World War		
1951	Conservatives return to government	1941	Germany attacks Soviet Union, Japan attacks USA	1947	Marshall Plan: USA invests heavily in post-war European recovery
1952	Accession of Elizabeth II				
1956	Suez Canal crisis	1945	End of European and Japanese Wars United Nations established	1950	Diners' Club introduces credit card in USA
1964-70	Wilson's Labour governments			1958	Original six members establish the European Economic Community
1969	Beginning of protracted difficulties in Northern Ireland	1947	Indian Independence		
		1950s	Cold War begins	1973	OPEC price-rise fuels inflation
1970	Conservatives regain power under Heath	1950-53	Korean War	1974	UN Resolution on New International Economic Order—fairer deal for developing countries
1973	Britain joins the EEC	1953	Arab nationalism grows		
1974	Two general elections: return of Labour government	1956	Soviet Union crushes Hungarian regime		
		1960	Sharpeville Massacre in S. Africa Nkrumah becomes President of Ghana		Rise of monetarism which stresses control of inflation at expense of unemployment
1979-88	Thatcher wins three successive elections, 1979, 1983, 1987	1961	Cuban missile crisis		Asian industrial capitalism enters dynamic phase—Japan, Taiwan, Hong Kong, S. Korea, etc., outpace Western economies
1982	The Falklands War	1968	Soviet Union crushes Czech regime		
		1970s	USA withdraws from Vietnam; superpower détente, political importance of the "Third World" grows. Japan, China, Australasia become more strategically important	1980	Brandt Report calls for shift in terms of trade between rich north and poor south Europe
				1980s	Debt crisis as poorer countries cannot repay loans; loans rescheduled
		1979	Soviet Union occupies Afghanistan		
		1980	Mugabe becomes President of Zimbabwe	1982	World recession as unemployment rises and industrial production falls
		1983	USA invades Grenada		
		1987	USA and Soviet Union agree to reduce nuclear armaments	1987	Stock-market slump, dollar weakens
		1988	Soviet Union agrees to end hostilities in Afghanistan		

RELIGION

1738	Methodist ministry begun by John Wesley—an optimistic, socially engaged version of Protestantism

SOCIETY AND CULTURE

DISCOVERIES

1701-1800	Age of Enlightenment. European critique of accepted, especially religious, belief
	Enlightened despotism. Age of Revolution
	Rousseau: Social contract
1706	Flourishing of English art, letters and science; a period of financial growth and prosperity
1709	First piano built
	Bach, Handel
1785	*The Times* starts publication
	Mozart, Haydn, rise of symphony
1801-1900	Romanticism—reaction to technology influences poetry, prose, music and art
1807	Slave trade abolished in British Empire

1704	Newcomen's steam engine
1709	Smelting of iron ore with coke
1714	Fahrenheit develops thermometer and scale
1733	Kay's flying shuttle begins innovation in textile industry
1764	Hargreaves' spinning jenny
1769	Arkwright's water frame
	James Watt's steam engine
1774	Oxygen discovered
1783	Montgolfier brothers' hot-air balloon ascent in France
1790	Lavoisier's table of chemical elements
1792	First semaphore system links Paris—Lille
1796	Jenner's smallpox vaccination
1800	Volta's electric battery

1830	Mormons founded by Joseph Smith in USA, and expanded by Brigham Young
1863	Birth of the Bahai religion in Persia; emphasis on spiritual unity of all mankind
1870	Papal infallibility doctrine proclaimed
1897	Zionism gains ground

1828	The founding of London University opens higher education to nonconformists
1830s	Early social science seeks the laws of social behaviour
1833	Emancipation of slaves
1839	Fox-Talbot develops photography
1848	Marx and Engels publish *Communist Manifesto*
1861	Abolition of serfdom in Russia
1864	*The First International* founded by Marx and Engels
1869	Darwin's *On the Origin of Species* influences social and political thought
1870	English Education Act establishes universal primary education. Rise of popular culture.
1870s	Universal male suffrage was established in many industrial societies
	Impressionism
1883	National Insurance introduced in Germany
1895	Freud publishes work on psychoanalysis

1819	Steamship *Savannah* crosses Atlantic
1825	Stockton and Darlington Railway opens
1831	Faraday's dynamo and transformer
1837	Telegraph patented
1844	Morse code
1845	R.W. Thompson patented pneumatic tyre (not adopted until 1888)
1856	Bessemer method of steel production
1858	Singer's sewing machine
1860	Winchester repeating rifle
1867	Nobel invents dynamite
1869	Transcontinental railway completed in USA
	Suez Canal opened
1876	Bell patents telephone
	Otto develops internal-combustion engine
1878	Edison's phonograph
1879	Edison's electric light bulb
1888	Pneumatic tyre was improved by Dunlop
1898	Radium discovered by the Curies
1899	Marconi's wireless experiments

1900s	Theosophy attracts more followers—a blend of Eastern and Western religious ideas
1950s	Revival of Western interests in Eastern religions—especially Buddhism
1960s	"Liberation theology" grows in Third World countries—a radical interpretation of Christianity as the Creed of the Oppressed
	Many new cults emerge in Western societies—Scientologists, Moonies, Hare Krishna, etc.
1970s	Christian revivalism in the USA
1979	Islamic fundamentalism plays a major part in the overthrow of the Shah of Iran
1980s	Hindu-Sikh conflicts in India, Catholic-Protestant conflicts in Ireland, Sunni-Shiah conflicts in Middle East

1902-1988	Expressionism and Cubism in art
1902	Education Act establishes secondary education
1920s	European imperialism challenged by American doctrine of self-determination
	Soviet communism, Italian, German and Spanish fascism all stress pre-eminence of the State over the individual
	Rise of jazz
	Growth of cinema
1936	Scheduled TV starts in England
	Surrealism, existentialism, and post-modernism in art and literature
1944	Education Act establishes free secondary education for all
1946	UNESCO established
1948	Chinese revolution led by Mao
1949	Apartheid policy introduced in S. Africa
1954	Independent Television Act
1960s	Black civil rights movement in USA
	Robbins Report expands British higher education
1969	Open University founded
mid-1960s to 70s	Student unrest. Hippie and "Flower Power" movements in industrial societies
mid-1970s	Environmental—"Green" politics direct attention to pollution, conservation and finite resources
1980s	Spread of AIDS affects moral thought and behaviour

1903	Powered flight—the Wright brothers
1908	Discovery of Bakelite, the first plastic
1915	Einstein's theory of relativity
1925	Baird invents television
1928	Fleming discovers penicillin
1930	Whittle invents jet engine
1935	Watson-Watts develops radar
1941	First jet fighter flies in Germany
1942	First atomic reactor in USA
1943	Biro invents ballpoint pen
1944	Digital computer developed
1945	Atomic bomb tested then used against Japan
1953	Genetic code (DNA) cracked
1954	First nuclear power station (Soviet Union)
1955	Oral contraceptives developed
1957	Soviet Union launches *Sputnik 1*
1961	First manned space flight (Soviet Union)
	Silicon chip patented in USA
1969	First men on moon (USA)
1970s	Satellite technology for surveillance communication
1974	Mars landing (Soviet Union)
1976	Mars landing (USA)
1978	First test-tube baby born
1981	First re-usable space shuttle flies

PREHISTORIC TIMES

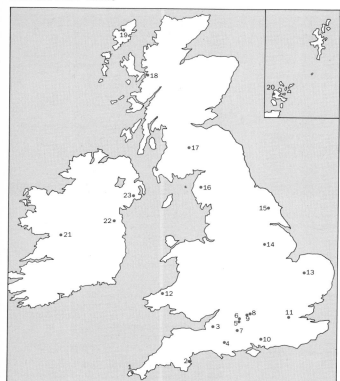

THE YEARS OF THE INVADERS

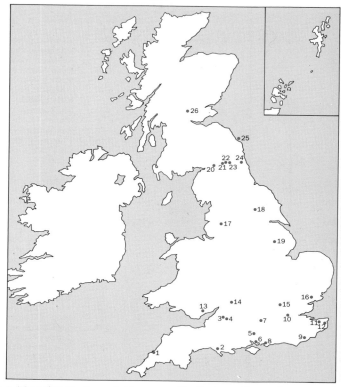

1. Chysauster, Cornwall (3 miles N of Penzance off B3311). Iron Age village, remarkably well-preserved.

2. Kent's Cavern, Torquay, Devon (in Ilsham Rd.). Remains of early British cavemen. Relics in Torquay Museum.

3. Cheddar Gorge, Somerset. Stone Age weapons and a 12,000-year-old skeleton in Gough's Cave Museum.

4. Hambledon Hill, Dorset (5 miles NW of Blandford Forum off A350). A spectacular Iron Age fort.

5. Silbury Hill, Wilts (5 miles W of Marlborough by A4). The largest, most puzzling, neolithic structure in Europe.

6. Avebury, Wilts. Largest European stone circle – 450 yards across.

7. Stonehenge, Wilts (8 miles N of Salisbury off A344). Part temple, part observatory, perhaps even a prehistoric calculator.

8. The Uffington Horse, Oxon (6 miles W of Wantage off B4507). The most famous of the chalk-cut horses, this overlooks the Ridge Way, the Iron Age route across the Berkshire Downs.

9. Wayland's Smithy, Oxon (7½ miles W of Wantage off B4507). A huge neolithic burial chamber.

10. Butser Farm, Hants (4 miles S of Petersfield off A3). Working reconstruction of an Iron Age farm.

11. London. The British Museum has the body of Pete Marsh, 2,500 years old, found in Lindow Moss, Cheshire. It also holds a collection of prehistoric art, including the treasure from Snettisham,

Norfolk. The Natural History Museum has the oldest British human skull fragments from Swanscombe, Kent.

12. Pentre Ifan, Dyfed (10 miles E of Fishguard off A487). A massive bluestone burial chamber.

13. Grime's Graves, Norfolk (7 miles NW of Thetford off A134). The earliest major industrial site in Europe – flint mines of 2300 BC.

14. Creswell Crags, Derbys (1 mile E of Creswell). Caves occupied by Early Stone Age hunters.

15. Duggleby Howe, N. Yorks (7 miles SE of Norton off B1248). One of Britain's biggest round barrows.

16. Castlerigg, Cumbria (1½ miles E of Keswick). Major stone circle.

17. Arbory Hill, Strathclyde (1 mile E of Abington). Iron Age fort.

18. Dun Telve, Highland (10 miles W of Shiel Bridge). The best-preserved of the mainland brochs (towers dating from about 100 BC).

19. Callanish, Lewis, W. Isles. The most northern of the stone circles.

20. Skara Brae, Orkney. A 4,500-year-old village preserved by the sand.

21. The Turoe Stone, Galway (4 miles NE of Loughrea off R350). Celtic stone with *La Tene* (Swiss) decoration.

22. Brugh na Boinne, Meath (5 miles W of Drogheda). Prehistoric cemetery.

23. Legananny Dolmen, Down (10 miles SE of Ballynahinch, on the slopes of Slieve Croob). A dolmen with a rare coffin-shaped capstone.

1. Tintagel Castle, Cornwall. The starting point of Arthurian legend.

2. Maiden Castle, Dorset (2 miles SW of Dorchester off A354). Where the Romans crushed the Celts in AD 43.

3. Bath, Avon. A city where Roman baths and buildings stand intact.

4. Bradford-on-Avon, Wilts. The 8th-century Church of St Lawrence.

5. Winchester, Hants. King Alfred's capital; Saxon tombs in the cathedral.

6. Portchester Castle, Hants. A fort used successively by Romans, Saxons and Normans, largely intact.

7. Silchester, Hants. The houses and town walls of Roman Calleva can still be traced; also a museum.

8. Fishbourne, W. Sussex (1½ miles W of Chichester on A27). Superb remains of a Romano-British palace.

9. Battle, E. Sussex. The abbey marks the site of the Saxons' last stand at the Battle of Hastings.

10. London. The British Museum has the Mildenhall (Romano-British) and Sutton Hoo (Saxon) treasures, the *Lindisfarne Gospels*, and Roman statuary. The Museum of London also has Roman relics, and a rare Danish tombstone.

11. Canterbury, Kent. Roman pavements, the Roman Church of St Martin, Saxon graves and stones in the old abbey and the cathedral.

12. Richborough, Kent. Where the Romans probably came ashore in AD 43, they built a fort to repel the Saxons.

13. Caerleon, Gwent. An excavated Roman amphitheatre seating 6,000.

14. Chedworth Roman Villa, Glos. Beautifully preserved mosaics and baths.

15. St Albans, Herts. The Roman town of Verulamium, its walls and theatre lying to the west of the town.

16. Colchester, Essex. Sacked by Boadicea in AD 60, rebuilt by the Romans, its walls survive today.

17. Blackstone Edge, G. Manchester (5 miles NE of Rochdale on A58). A fine stretch of Roman road.

18. York. The Viking Museum, based on new excavations, giving a superb picture of the Viking way of life.

19. Lincoln. Once a Roman fortress, it still has in Bailgate a Roman arch in use today, and relics in the City Museum.

20 to 24. Hadrian's Wall, Cumbria, Northumberland, and Tyne and Wear. Originally the wall stretched from coast to coast. It can still be followed for much if its length, or seen to good effect from Birdoswald (20–26 miles NE of Brampton off B6318) and the forts to its east: Housesteads, Carrawburgh and Chesters (21, 22 and 23 – also off B6318). There is a major collection of inscriptions at 24 – the Museum of Antiquities at Newcastle University.

25. Holy Island, Northumberland. The stones of the Saxon Priory can still be seen in Lindisfarne Castle's walls.

26. Ardoch Fort, Tayside (12 miles N of Stirling off A822 at Braco). The Romans' Antonine Wall has almost disappeared, but this outpost has survived.

MEDIEVAL BRITAIN

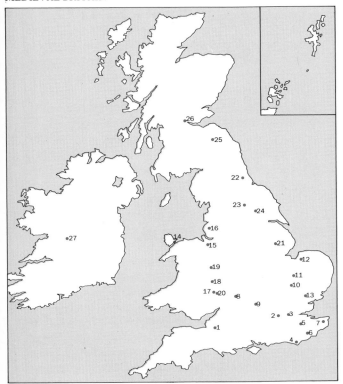

TUDOR AND STUART TIMES

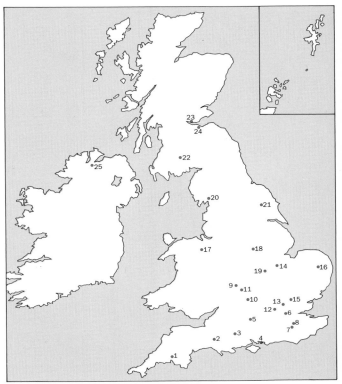

1. Wells, Somerset. The first entirely Gothic English cathedral.

2. Windsor Castle, Berks. William I's Norman castle, expanded, decorated and furnished in every style since.

3. London. From 1066 the undisputed capital city, with its royal fortress (the Tower), coronation church (Westminster Abbey), law courts (Westminster Hall).

4. Alfriston, E. Sussex. The 14th-century Old Clergy House.

5. Old Soar Manor, Kent (6 miles NE of Tonbridge off A227). The original chapel and private living quarters of a 13th-century private house.

6. Bodiam Castle, E. Sussex. Built in the 14th century, for comfort and strength. Spectacularly intact.

7. Canterbury, Kent. England's premier cathedral, with the tombs of Becket and the Black Prince.

8. Chipping Campden, Glos. St James's Church and Woolstaplers' Hall recall Cotswolds' wool-trade wealth.

9. Oxford. Medieval architecture everywhere. See especially Merton, Magdalen, New and Worcester Colleges.

10. Cambridge. Fine medieval building at the Colleges of King's, Queens', Corpus Christi and Peterhouse.

11. Ely, Cambs. Norman cathedral built on the site of a Saxon abbey.

12. Castle Rising, Norfolk. Spectacular 12th-century Norman castle.

13. Castle Hedingham, Essex. One of the best preserved examples of Norman military architecture.

14. Beaumaris Castle, Anglesey. The finest of our concentric castles.

15. Chester, Cheshire. Buildings in every style from Roman days, with medieval galleried streets, The Rows.

16. Rufford, Lancs. The Old Hall is almost unchanged in 500 years.

17. Weobley, Hereford and Worcs. Famous for its wealth of medieval timber-framed buildings.

18. Stokesay, Salop. Its "castle" is a preserved fortified manor house.

19. Shrewsbury, Salop. A border town with many fine medieval buildings.

20. Hereford. In the restored cathedral: a fine Lady Chapel, and Britain's largest chained library, including the Mappa Mundi, c. 1300.

21. Lincoln. The Norman cathedral, and the medieval Jew's House.

22. Durham. The most spectacularly powerful of the Norman cathedrals.

23. Fountains Abbey, N. Yorks (4 miles SW of Ripon off B6265). One of the most complete sets of abbey buildings.

24. York. Clifford's Tower, and the Norman Minster with Britain's best display of medieval stained glass.

25. Melrose Abbey, Borders. The great abbey, now ruined, where the heart of Robert Bruce was buried.

26. Stirling, Central. Rebuilt in the 15th century, the fortress symbolised resistance to the English.

27. Clonfert Cathedral, Galway. 12th-century cathedral, once part of St Brendan's monastery.

1. Buckland Abbey, Devon (11 miles N of Plymouth off A386). The home of Francis Drake, and of his drum.

2. Montacute House, Somerset. A great Elizabethan mansion, with a collection of Armada portraits.

3. Wilton House, Wilts. The beautifully furnished centre of Stuart culture.

4. Portsmouth, Hants. The home of Henry VIII's flagship, the *Mary Rose*.

5. Donnington, Berks. A castle and superb 17th-century almshouses.

6. London. The centre of Tudor and Stuart trade and fashion, containing: Wolsey's Hampton Court; Inigo Jones's Greenwich and the Banqueting House, Whitehall; Wren's St Paul's; Ham House and Kew Palace. The major museums, especially the Victoria and Albert, have fine period collections.

7. Hever Castle, Kent. Where Henry VIII courted Anne Boleyn.

8. Knole, Kent. One of the biggest Stuart private houses, needing 119 servants and craftsmen to run it.

9. Stratford-upon-Avon, Warks. Shakespeare's birthplace, the church where he is buried. Anne Hathaway's Cottage is one mile away, at Shottery.

10. Blenheim Palace, Oxon. Britain's gift to the Duke of Marlborough; birthplace of Winston Churchill.

11. Compton Wynyates, Warks (10 miles W of Banbury off B4035). Superb Tudor house and gardens.

12. Chalfont St Giles, Bucks. Milton's Cottage, where he wrote *Paradise Lost*.

13. Hatfield House, Herts. Childhood home of Elizabeth I.

14. Burghley House, Cambs (1 mile SE of Stamford off B1443). The Elizabethan mansion of the Cecil family.

15. Thaxted, Essex. Houses of several periods, especially Queen Anne's.

16. Elm Hill, Norwich. A street of 17th-century and medieval houses.

17. Erddig, Clwyd (1 mile S of Wrexham). A 17th-century house, still maintained in working order.

18. Hardwick Hall, Derbys (6 miles NW of Mansfield off A617). Fine Tudor house, with superb furniture and pictures, and collections of tapestry and needlework.

19. Market Harborough, Leics. The 17th-century timbered grammar school and the market.

20. Levens Hall, Cumbria. Topiary gardens as they were designed in 1690.

21. Castle Howard, N. Yorks. Vanbrugh's magnificent mansion, with picture gallery and costume collection.

22. Drumlanrig Castle, Dumfries and Galloway. Scotland's first and finest Renaissance mansion.

23. Culross, Fife. A town built on coalmining, in the 17th century, with many of the original houses.

24. Edinburgh. The palace of Holyroodhouse, John Knox's house, and Gladstone's Land — all from this period.

25. Londonderry. City walls that survived the siege of 1688/89.

GEORGIAN BRITAIN

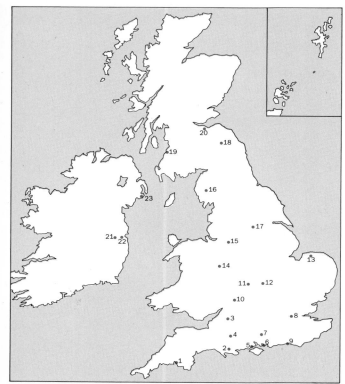

MODERN TIMES

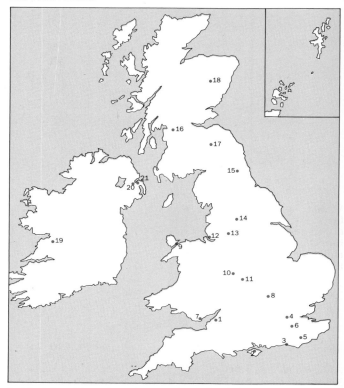

1. Plymouth, Devon. The Georgian Devonport dockyards, Eddystone Lighthouse, and the fine City Museum.

2. Milton Abbas, Dorset. A village moved out of sight by the landlord.

3. Bath, Avon. The Roman town that became the smartest Georgian spa.

4. Stourhead, Wilts. (3 miles NW of Mere off B3092). Palladian house, with one of the finest landscape gardens.

5. Buckler's Hard, Hants. A shipyard of the Napoleonic Wars.

6. Portsmouth, Hants. The home of Nelson's flagship, HMS *Victory*.

7. Chawton, Hants. The home of novelist, Jane Austen, now a museum.

8. London. Palladian Chiswick House, Gothic Strawberry Hill at Twickenham, and Nash's Regent's Park. The great British painters are to be seen in the National and Portrait Galleries, and relics of Waterloo in Apsley House.

9. Brighton, E. Sussex. The Royal Pavilion, the Prince Regent's palace, largely built by John Nash.

10. Cheltenham, Glos. The Pump Room, elegant Regency terraces and decorative balcony iron work.

11. Napton Lock, Warks. An old lock on the picturesque Oxford Canal, one of the first industrial waterways.

12. Althorp House, Northants (5 miles NW of Northampton off A428). The family home of the Princess of Wales, with fine private art collection.

13. Holkham Hall, Norfolk. Lavishly furnished Palladian house, once home of

agriculturalist, Thomas William Coke.

14. Coalbrookdale, Salop. The birthplace of the Industrial Revolution, with the first iron bridge, and restored workshops and cottages.

15. Styal, Cheshire. Quarry Bank cotton mill preserved as it was in the 18th century, with textile machinery museum.

16. Grasmere, Cumbria. Dove Cottage where Wordsworth lived and wrote.

17. Nostell Priory, W. Yorks (6 miles SE of Wakefield on A638). A fine house containing a superb collection of Chippendale furniture.

18. Mellerstain House, Borders (8 miles NW of Kelso off A6089). Begun by William Adam, completed magnificently by his son, Robert.

19. Culzean Castle, Strathclyde (12 miles S of Ayr off A719). A 16th-century tower converted by Robert Adam into a beautiful country house.

20. Edinburgh. The 18th-century "New Town". No. 7 Charlotte Square is decorated in period style.

21. Celbridge, Kildare. Castletown, the largest and most influential 18th-century house in Ireland.

22. Dublin. Trinity College, rebuilt in the Palladian style (with its great library containing *The Book of Kells*), and fine squares, churches and public buildings from the Georgian period.

23. Strangford, Down. Castle Ward, a bizarre 18th-century house, on which the owner and his wife could not agree. One front is Gothic, the other Classical.

1. Bristol, Avon. Home of Brunel's great masterpiece: the SS *Great Britain*.

2. Osborne House, IOW (1 mile SE of E. Cowes off A3021). Built by Thomas Cubitt for Queen Victoria.

3. Brighton, W. Sussex. Sussex's outstanding postwar university building.

4. London. From the neo-Gothic St Pancras, Law Courts, Houses of Parliament, Natural History Museum, and Albert Memorial, on to Battersea Power Station, the Lloyd's Building, the Thames Barrier and Docklands. In Kew Gardens, great glasshouses in both Victorian and 1980s' style. In the Tate Gallery pictures from Turner to Lowry.

5. Bateman's, E. Sussex (1 mile S of Burwash off A265). Rudyard Kipling's house and relics.

6. Chartwell, Kent (2 miles S of Westerham off B2026). From 1924 to 1965 Winston Churchill's home, and now a museum to his memory.

7. Cardiff. Despite its Roman fort and Norman castle, chiefly a 19th-century city, with the impressive 20th-century National Museum of Wales.

8. Milton Keynes, Bucks. The classic new town of the 1960s.

9. Menai Bridge, Gwynedd. Telford's suspension bridge of 1826.

10. Birmingham, W. Midlands. A great modern city, with Pugin's Catholic cathedral, superb Pre-Raphaelite pictures in the City Museum — and, of course, Spaghetti Junction.

11. Coventry, W. Midlands. Former

bombed cathedral now rebuilt by Sir Basil Spence.

12. Liverpool, Merseyside. A city built on ocean trade, with the Victorian classical St George's Hall, two 20th-century cathedrals, and a wealth of galleries.

13. Manchester, Lancs. The Town Hall, symbol of Victorian civic pride, built by Alfred Waterhouse.

14. Haworth, W. Yorks. The bleak parsonage where the Brontë sisters wrote, now a museum.

15. Beamish, Durham. North of England Open Air Museum, with Victorian colliery, shops, trains.

16. Glasgow, Strathclyde. Contains many historic buildings, but known especially for its School of Art, and the Burrell, Britain's finest city art collection.

17. Abbotsford, Borders. The house built for Sir Walter Scott, in which he wrote the Waverley novels.

18. Balmoral Castle, Grampian. The royal family's holiday estate, built in baronial style by the Prince Consort. Only the gardens are open to the public.

19. Gort, Galway. Ballylee Castle, where Yeats lived and wrote, now restored as a museum to him.

20. Belfast. Essentially a 19th-century city, with fine Victorian buildings, many of them by Sir Charles Lanyon. Also the 20th-century cathedral, town hall and the Parliament House at Stormont.

21. Holywood, Down. Cultra Manor Folk Museum, with traditional Irish buildings, crafts, and furniture.

Index

D

L

M

N

O

P

Y

Z

Acknowledgments

Cover illustrations: Brian Delf

The publishers acknowledge their indebtedness to the following for permission to use their photographs:

VOLUME ONE: 8 Michael Holford; 11 British Museum; 12 bottom Kenneth Scowen; 13 British Museum; 14 top Reader's Digest; centre and bottom British Museum; 15 top left British Museum; top right Paul Joyce; bottom left British Museum; bottom right Georg Gerster/Magnum/John Hillelson Agency; 16 top George Gerster/Magnum/John Hillelson Agency; bottom Vatican Museum, Rome/Mansell Collection; 18 British Museum; 20 Paul Joyce; 21 C.M. Dixon; 22 top Museum of London; bottom Royal Museum of Scotland; 23 Museum of London; 24 top British Museum; bottom Museum of London; 25 Museum of London; 26 top Susan Griggs; centre Museum of London/Ikon; bottom Reading Museum and Art Gallery; 27 top left and right Ashmolean Museum, Oxford; bottom left Reader's Digest; bottom right British Museum; 28 top British Museum; bottom Aerofilms; 29 Aerofilms; 30 British Museum/Bridgeman Art Library; 31 British Museum; 32 Trinity College Library, Dublin; 33 Skyscan; 34 top left Vision Bank; top right Mayotte Magnus and Jorge Lewinski/*English Heritage* published by Queen Anne Press; bottom left C.M. Dixon; bottom right Susan Griggs/Adam Woolfitt; 35 top Aerofilms; bottom Susan Griggs/Michael St Maur Sheil; 36 top Georg Gerster/Magnum/John Hillelson Agency; centre C.M. Dixon; bottom Angelo Hornak; 37 C.M. Dixon; 38 top left and bottom Ancient Art and Architecture Collection; top centre Michael Holford; top right Fred Mayer/John Hillelson Agency; bottom right Michael Holford; 39 top British Library; bottom left Bridgeman Art Library; bottom right Ashmolean Museum, Oxford/Bridgeman Art Library; 40 top left, bottom right and top right Michael Holford; lower top right and bottom right Colourcentre; centre right British Museum/Colourcentre; 41 Michael Holford; 42 British Museum; 43 Arthur Lockwood; 44 British Museum/Arthur Lockwood; 45 Arthur Lockwood; 46 Reader's Digest; 47 British Museum; 48 English Heritage; 49–50 British Museum; 51 Bodleian Library, Oxford/E.T. Archive; 52 Werner Forman Archives; 53 English Heritage; 54 top University of Cambridge Committee for Aerial Photography; bottom British Museum/Arthur Lockwood; lower top left British Library/Arthur Lockwood; top right Reader's Digest; bottom left Mansell Collection; bottom centre and right British Museum; 56 National Museum of Ireland, Dublin; 57 British Museum/Arthur Lockwood; 58 *The Independent*; 59 Georg Gerster/Magnum/John Hillelson Agency; 60 Dean and Chapter Library of Durham; 61 Mansell Collection; 63 Royal Museum of Scotland; 64 Statens Historika Museer/Antikvarisk-topografiska arkivet, Stockholm/Sören Hallgren; 65 British Museum/Michael Holford; 66 The Masters and Fellows of Corpus Christi College, Cambridge; 67 The Masters and Fellows of Corpus Christi College, Cambridge/Bodleian Library, Oxford; Ms. 183, fol. 1v; 69 Mansell Collection; 70 Paul Joyce; 71 A.F. Kersting; 72–73 British Museum; 75–79 Michael Holford; 80 top Michael Holford; bottom National Portrait Gallery; 81 Aerofilms; 82 A.F. Kersting; 83 top Victoria and Albert Museum; bottom A.F Kersting; 84 top Public Records Office; bottom The Masters and Fellows of Trinity College, Cambridge; ref. R.17.1. folio 283; 85 top right British Library/Arthur Lockwood; centre left English Heritage; bottom left Michael Holford; bottom right Aerofilms; 86 Reader's Digest; 87 A.F. Kersting; 88 British Museum/*History Today;* 89 A.F. Kersting; 90 British Museum; 91 E.T. Archive; 93 A.F. Kersting; 95 BBC Hulton Picture Library; 97 British Museum/*History Today;* 98 top A.F. Kersting; bottom Arthur Lockwood; 99 top left British Library; top right A.F. Kersting; bottom left Reader's Digest; bottom centre British Library; bottom right Bodleian Library, Oxford; Ms. Ashmole 1431; 100 British Museum/Arthur Lockwood; 101 Paul Joyce; 102–103 Arthur Lockwood; 104 Crown Copyright: Public Records Office/Godfrey New; 105 Michael Holford; 106 Aerofilms; 107 top Bridgeman Art Library; centre Susan Griggs/Adam Woolfitt; bottom Ancient Art and Architecture Collection; 108 Department of the Environment; 109 top and centre left Susan Griggs/Adam Woolfitt; centre right Angelo Hornak; bottom Picturepoint; 110 top left Michael Holford; centre left Vision Bank; bottom left Sonia Halliday; right Michael Holford; 111 top Vision Bank; bottom C.M. Dixon; 112 S & O Mathews; 113 Bodleian Library, Oxford; Ms. Ch. Oxon, 58; 114 Crown Copyright: Public Records Office/Godfrey New; 116 top British Museum/Weidenfeld and Nicolson; bottom A.F. Kersting; 117 Victoria and Albert Museum; 118 Arthur Lockwood; 119 The Masters and Fellows of Corpus Christi College, Cambridge/Arthur Lockwood; 120 British Museum/Ikon; 121 Lefevre-Pontalis/© Arch. Phot, SPADEM; 122 British Museum; 125 British Museum/Weidenfeld and Nicolson; 126 Mansell Collection; 128 top British Library; centre British Museum/Arthur Lockwood; bottom Mansell Collection; 129 left Guildhall Library/Godfrey New; top right Douglas Dickens; bottom right Reader's Digest; 131 National Portrait Gallery; 132 The Masters and Fellows of Corpus Christi College, Cambridge; 133 A.F. Kersting; 135 Arthur Lockwood; 136 Paul Joyce; 137 Ikon; 139 The Masters and Fellows of Corpus Christi College, Oxford; 141 British Museum; 142 A.F. Kersting; 143 Crown Copyright: Public Records Office/Ikon; 144 British Museum/Arthur Lockwood; 145 Arthur Lockwood; 146 British Museum/Weidenfeld and Nicolson; 147 top British Museum/Diagram; bottom Photosource; 148 top BBC Hulton Picture Library; bottom Glasgow Museums and Art Galleries, Burrell Collection; 149 top left E.T. Archive; top right Board of Trustees of the Armouries; centre left John Freeman; bottom left Board of Trustees of the Armouries; bottom right The Masters and Fellows of Magdalene College, Cambridge; 150 BBC Hulton Picture Library; 151 Scottish Development Department, Edinburgh; 152 Reader's Digest; 153 top Scottish Development Department, Edinburgh; bottom British Museum/Weidenfeld and Nicolson; 154 Scottish Development Department, Edinburgh; 155 top British Museum/Reader's Digest; bottom The Masters and Fellows of Corpus Christi College, Cambridge; 156 Michael Holford; 157 top Mansell Collection; 158 top British Museum/Pitkin Pictorials; bottom Reader's Digest; 159 Crown Copyright; 160 National Museum of Ireland, Dublin; 161 top Tony Stone; bottom National Library of Ireland, Dublin; 163 top Bodleian Library, Oxford/Arthur Lockwood; bottom National Portrait Gallery; 164 British Museum; 165 top BBC Hulton Picture Library; bottom National Monuments Record; 166 Bibliothèque Nationale, Paris; 167 Paul Joyce; 168 top *The Independent*; bottom Ikon; 169 top left Reader's Digest; top right Bodleian Library, Oxford; Ms. Douce 203, fol. 103v; centre left Courtauld Institute/Civic Library, Bergamo; centre right Reader's Digest; bottom Arthur Lockwood; 171 British Museum/Arthur Lockwood; 172 Paul Joyce; 173 Arthur Lockwood; 174 Mansell Collection; 176 BBC Hulton Picture Library; 177 John Hillelson Agency; 178 top and bottom left Picturepoint; bottom right Mayotte Magnus and Jorge Lewinski/*English Heritage* published by Queen Anne Press; 179 top Mayotte Magnus and Jorge Lewinski/*English Heritage* published by Queen Anne Press; bottom National Trust; 180 top Image Bank; centre British Library; bottom left E.T. Archive; bottom right Adam Woolfitt/*Britain on View*; 181 Susan Griggs/Adam Woolfitt; 182 top left Sonia Halliday; top right Susan Griggs/Julian Nieman; centre British Library; bottom National Gallery; left and top right Michael Holford; bottom right Reader's Digest; 184 Michael Holford; 185 British Library/Arthur Lockwood; 186 National Portrait Gallery; 187 Aerofilms; 188 BBC Hulton Picture Library; 189 Michael Holford; 190 Victoria and Albert Museum; 191 British Museum; 193 Bodleian Library, Oxford; Ms. Douce 195, fol. 105; 194 top Ikon; centre National Trust/Petworth House; 195 top left National Portrait Gallery; top right Ikon; centre C.M. Dixon; bottom left Ikon; bottom right Mary Evans Picture Library; 196 Ikon; 197 National Gallery; 198 British Museum; 199 Michael Holford; 200 BBC Hulton Picture Library; 201 British Museum; 202 A.F. Kersting; 203 top National Portrait Gallery; bottom John Freeman; 204–205 BBC Hulton Picture Library; 206 Sonia Halliday; 207 National Portrait Gallery; 208 BBC Hulton Picture Library; 209 Giraudon; 210 BBC Hulton Picture Library; 211 top Bibliothèque Nationale, Paris; bottom BBC Hulton Picture Library; 212 A.F. Kersting; 213 BBC Hulton Picture Library; 214 Paul Joyce; 215 Victoria and Albert Museum; 216 A.F. Kersting; 217 BBC Hulton Picture Library; 220 top Paul Joyce; centre BBC Hulton Picture Library; bottom Medieval Players; 221 top left Bodleian Library, Oxford; Ms. Douce 208, fol. 120v; top right and bottom left Guildhall Library; bottom right John Freeman/The Worshipful Company of Barber-Surgeons; 222 Victoria and Albert Museum; 223 National Portrait Gallery; 224–225 BBC Hulton Picture Library; 226 top BBC Hulton Picture Library; bottom John Freeman; 227 The Masters and Fellows of Queens' College, Cambridge; 228 Bodleian Library, Oxford; Ms. Douce 365, fol. CXV; 229–232 BBC Hulton Picture Library; 233 Aerofilms; 234 National Monuments Record; 235 Giraudon/Musée Condé, Chantilly; 236 National Portrait Gallery; 237 British Museum/Weidenfeld & Nicolson; 238 top BBC Hulton Picture Library; bottom Department of the Environment; 239 Paul Joyce; 240 Victoria and Albert Museum; 241 top left British Museum; top right Bridgeman Art Library; centre left BBC Hulton Picture Library; centre right John Freeman; bottom Ikon; 242 E.T. Archive; 243 H.M. The Queen; 244 top Paul Joyce; bottom John Freeman; 245 National Portrait Gallery; 246 Susan Griggs; 247 top The Masters and Fellows of St John's College, Cambridge; bottom Reader's Digest; 248 Devonshire Collection, Chatsworth, Reproduced by permission of the Chatsworth Settlement Trustees/Weidenfeld and Nicolson; 249 top National Monuments Record; bottom BBC Hulton Picture Library; 250 La Pensée Universitaire, Aix-en-Provence; 252 National Portrait Gallery; 253 Victoria and Albert Museum; 254–255 National Portrait Gallery; 257 BBC Hulton Picture Library; 258 top Michael Holford; bottom left Susan Griggs; bottom right Victoria and Albert Museum; 259 top left Bridgeman Art Library; top right Reader's Digest; centre E.T. Archive; bottom right Michael Holford; 260 top Michael Holford; bottom Paul Joyce; 261 BBC Hulton Picture Library; 262 National Portrait Gallery; 263 top A.F. Kersting; bottom BBC Hulton Picture Library; 265 National Portrait Gallery; bottom John Freeman; 267 top left Mary Evans Picture Library; top right National Monuments Record; bottom left Bridgeman Art Library; bottom right Michael Holford; 268 National Portrait Gallery; 269 Mansell Collection; 270–271 BBC Hulton Picture Library; 272 Board of Trustees of the Armouries; 273 A.F. Kersting; 274 Victoria and Albert Museum; 275 E.T. Archive; 276 National Portrait Gallery; 277 top A.F. Kersting; bottom John Freeman; 278 top The Louvre, Paris; bottom A.F. Kersting; 280; National Portrait Gallery; 281 Skyscan; 282 top left Susan Griggs/Adam Woolfitt; top right Thyssen-Bornemisza Collection, Lugano, Switzerland/Bridgeman Art Library; bottom H.M. The Queen; 283 top National Trust; centre left British Tourist Association; centre right National Trust; bottom Victoria and Albert Museum; 284 top left National Portrait Gallery; top right National Trust; centre left Reader's Digest; bottom left National Portrait Gallery; upper bottom right *Mary Rose* Trust; bottom right Susan Griggs/Adam Woolfitt; 285 top Michael Holford; bottom Susan Griggs/Adam Woolfitt; 286 Bridgeman Art Library/John Bethell; bottom Robert Harding; 287 top left, right and lower right Susan Griggs/Adam Woolfitt; bottom left Victoria and Albert Museum/Bridgeman Art Library; bottom centre Susan Griggs/Jurgen Schadeberg; bottom right Victoria and Albert Museum/Michael Holford; 288 Courtesy of the Marquis of Salisbury/John Freeman; 289 National Portrait Gallery; 290 BBC Hulton Picture Library; 291 Susan Griggs; 292 National Monuments Record; 293 BBC Hulton Picture Library; 294 National Portrait Gallery; 295–296 BBC Hulton Picture Library; 297 top BBC Hulton Picture Library; bottom National Portrait Gallery; 298 John Freeman; 299 top Susan Griggs; bottom John Freeman; 300 top Guildhall Library; centre British Library; bottom Mary Evans Picture Library; 301 top right BBC Hulton Picture Library; bottom left Mary Evans Picture Library; centre John Freeman; centre left Dulwich Picture Gallery; 302 Susan Griggs; 304 top National Portrait Gallery; bottom BBC Hulton Picture Library; 305 Reader's Digest; 307

John Freeman; 308 Victoria and Albert Museum; 309 BBC Hulton Picture Library; 310 top Mary Evans Picture Library; bottom left Michael Holford; bottom right John Freeman; 311 top left City of Plymouth Museum and Art Gallery; top right John Freeman; centre BBC Hulton Picture Library; bottom Library of Congress, Washington; 312 BBC Hulton Picture Library; 313 National Portrait Gallery; 314 BBC Hulton Picture Library; 315 British Library; 316 top Mary Evans Picture Library; bottom BBC Hulton Picture Library; 317 National Portrait Gallery; 318 top Board of Trustees of the Armouries; 318–319 bottom Robert Harding; 320 National Portrait Gallery.

VOLUME TWO: 7 National Portrait Gallery; 8 British Museum; 9–12 John Freeman; 13 top H.M. The Queen; bottom Mansell Collection; 14 top National Portrait Gallery; bottom Reader's Digest; 15 Ashmolean Museum, Oxford; 16 Peter Newark's Western Americana; 17 Beken of Cowes; 18 Enoch Pratt Free Library, Baltimore; 19 National Portrait Gallery; 20 BBC Hulton Picture Library; 21 National Portrait Gallery; 22 top A.F. Kersting; centre Victoria and Albert Museum; bottom Devonshire Collection, Chatsworth. Reproduced by permission of the Chatsworth Settlement Trustees/Courtauld Institute; 23 top The Masters and Fellows of Magdalene College, Cambridge; centre Devonshire Collection, Chatsworth. Reproduced by permission of the Chatsworth Settlement Trustees/Courtauld Institute; bottom A.F. Kersting; 24 John Freeman; 25 Mansell Collection; 26 BBC Hulton Picture Library; 27 The Masters and Fellows of Worcester College, Oxford/Conway Library, Courtauld Institute; 28 National Maritime Museum; 29 By permission of the Archbishop of Canterbury; copyright reserved to the Church Commissioners and Courtauld Institute of Art; 30 John Freeman; 31 Barnaby's Picture Library; 32 BBC Hulton Picture Library; 33 National Gallery/Ikon; 34 top Kenneth Scowen; bottom Angelo Hornak; 35 top Victoria and Albert Museum/Bridgeman Art Library; bottom left and right Angelo Hornak; 36 A.F. Kersting; 37 top left Kenneth Scowen; top right Tate Gallery; bottom left British Tourist Association; bottom right Bridgeman Art Library; 38 top Fred Mayer/John Hillelson Agency; bottom left Kenneth Scowen; bottom right Woodmansterne; 39 top left Kenneth Scowen; bottom left Bodleian Library, Oxford; Ms. Ashmole 1461, fol. 47r; right Reader's Digest; 40 Kenneth Scowen; 41 BBC Hulton Picture Library; 42 Country Life; 43 John Freeman; 44 BBC Hulton Picture Library; 45 John Freeman; 46–47 National Trust/Dunster Castle; 48 Mansell Collection; 49 National Portrait Gallery; 50 John Freeman; 51 Church Missionary Society; 52 National Portrait Gallery; 53 Roundwood Press/John Wright Photography; 55 National Museums and Galleries on Merseyside (Walker Art Gallery); 56 John Freeman; 57 National Portrait Gallery; 58 top A.F. Kersting; bottom BBC Hulton Picture Library; 59 Cromwell Museum, Huntingdon; 60 British Museum; 61 John Freeman; 62 Cromwell Museum, Huntingdon; 63 National Army Museum; 64 National Portrait Gallery; 65 Barnaby's Picture Library; inset Mary Evans Picture Library; 66 National Portrait Gallery; 67 Aerofilms; 68 John Freeman; 69 Museum of London; 70 Mansell Collection; 71 John Freeman; 72 top H.M. The Queen; bottom National Army Museum; 73 BBC Hulton Picture Library; 74 Mary Evans Picture Library; 75 top and centre BBC Hulton Picture Library; centre right Barnaby's Picture Library; bottom National Army Museum; 76 BBC Hulton Picture Library; 77 National Portrait Gallery; 78 BBC Hulton Picture Library; 79 top Mansell Collection; bottom John Freeman; 80 National Maritime Museum; 82 BBC Hulton Picture Library; 84 Mary Evans Picture Library; 85 Mansell Collection; 86 top BBC Hulton Picture Library; bottom National Army Museum; 87 BBC Hulton Picture Library; 88 top Sotheby's; bottom Ham House/National Trust; 89 top National Portrait Gallery; bottom left BBC Hulton Picture Library; bottom right John Freeman; 90 H.M. The Queen; 92 National Monuments Record; 93 Mary Margary; 94 Victoria and Albert Museum; 95 top A.F. Kersting; bottom John Freeman; 97 National Portrait Gallery; 99 BBC Hulton Picture Library; 101 Mansell Collection; 103 Mansell Collection/Wallace Collection; 104 Michael Holford; 105 John Freeman; 107 Mansell Collection; 109 Courtesy of the Verney Collection, Claydon House; 111 National Portrait Gallery; 112 H.M. The Queen; 113 Patrick Thurston; 114 top BBC Hulton Picture Library; bottom left Ann Ronan Picture Library; bottom right BBC Hulton Picture Library; 115 top left E.T. Archive; top right Angelo Hornak; bottom left and right Ann Ronan Picture Library; 116 BBC Hulton Picture Library; 117 Ikon; 119 National Portrait Gallery; 120 H.M. Tower of London; 121 John Freeman; 122–123 BBC Hulton Picture Library; 124 Bristol City Art Gallery; 126 John Freeman; 127 Mansell Collection; 128 top British Library; bottom Mary Evans Picture Library; 129 top Mary Evans Picture Library; bottom left National Monuments Record; bottom right Reader's Digest; 130 Museum of London; 131 Mansell Collection; 132–133 John Freeman; 134 Glasgow Art Gallery; 135 National Portrait Gallery; 136 Mansell Collection; 137–138 Angelo Hornak; 139 top Bridgeman Art Library; bottom left National Portrait Gallery/Woodmansterne; bottom right Angelo Hornak; 140 top National Trust; bottom left Kenneth Scowen; bottom right David Hurn/Magnum; 141 top left and bottom Bridgeman Art Library; top right National Portrait Gallery/Bridgeman Art Library; 142 Aerofilms; 143 top Susan Griggs/Adam Woolfitt;

centre Ancient Art and Architecture Collection; bottom left Michael Holford; bottom right National Trust; 144 Angelo Hornak; 145 Aerofilms; 146 National Portrait Gallery; 147 Ikon; 148 Mansell Collection; 150 Aerofilms; 151 National Portrait Gallery; 153 John Freeman; 154 A.F. Kersting; 155 John Freeman; 156–157 Mary Margary; 158 Thomas Photos; 159–160 Mary Margary; 161–163 Jeremy Whitaker; 164 BBC Hulton Picture Library; 165 Mansell Collection; 166 top left Ann Ronan Picture Library; top right Royal College of Physicians; bottom Mansell Collection; 167 UMDS, Guy's Hospital; 168 Paul Mellon Centre; 169 Robert Harding; 170 Jeremy Whitaker; 171 British Museum; 172 Jeremy Whitaker; 173 National Portrait Gallery; 175 John Freeman; 176 A.F. Kersting; 177 Ikon/Diana Phillips; 178 John Freeman; 179 Robert Harding; 180 British Museum; 181 BBC Hulton Picture Library; 183 Mansell Collection; 184 Mary Evans Picture Library; 186 top BBC Hulton Picture Library; centre National Portrait Gallery; bottom BBC Hulton Picture Library; 187 top Tate Gallery; bottom left and centre National Portrait Gallery; bottom right BBC Hulton Picture Library; 189 BBC Hulton Picture Library; 190 Department of the Environment/Diagram; 191 National Portrait Gallery; 193 National Army Museum; 194 Paul Bartlett; 195 National Portrait Gallery; 196 Patrick Thurston; 197 National Library of Scotland; 198 National Maritime Museum; 199 John Freeman; 200–201 Colonial Williamsburg Foundation, Virginia; 202 John Freeman; 204 BBC Hulton Picture Library; 205 top Mansell Collection; bottom left and right BBC Hulton Picture Library; 206 BBC Hulton Picture Library; 208 top National Gallery of Canada; bottom National Portrait Gallery 209 Woodmansterne; 210 top left Bristol Art Gallery; bottom left Angelo Hornak; bottom right Royal Collection; 211 top left Michael Holford; top right Bridgeman Art Library; bottom Sir John Soane Museum/Bridgeman Art Library; 212 top Manchester City Art Gallery/Bridgeman Art Library; centre left Bridgeman Art Library; centre right Kenneth Scowen; bottom left Bridgeman Art Library; bottom centre Harewood House, Yorks/Bridgeman Art Library; bottom right National Gallery/Bridgeman Art Library; 213 A.F. Kersting; 214 top Susan Griggs/Nathan Benn; bottom left A.F. Kersting; bottom right National Trust for Scotland/Woodmansterne; 215 top Tate Gallery/Bridgeman Art Library; bottom left National Museums and Art Galleries on Merseyside (Walker Art Gallery); bottom right Waterways Photo Library; 216 Waterways Photo Library; 218 National Army Museum/Ikon; 219 Mary Evans Picture Library; 220 National Portrait Gallery; 221 National Army Museum; 224 H.M. The Queen; 226 John Freeman; 227 National Portrait Gallery; 228 top John Freeman; bottom Mansell Collection; 229 top left National Trust; top right A.F. Kersting; bottom left Bradford Art Gallery; centre right Sir John Soane Museum; 231 top Colonial Williamsburg Foundation, Virginia; bottom Peter Newark's Western Americana; 233 Peter Newark's Western Americana; 234 BBC Hulton Picture Library; 235 Peter Newark's Western Americana; 237 BBC Hulton Picture Library; 238 Library of Congress, Washington/Ikon; 239 British Museum; 240 Ikon; 243 top Tate Gallery; bottom Reader's Digest; 244 National Portrait Gallery; 245 Military Collection/Brown University Library, USA; 246 Peter Newark's Western Americana; 247 John Freeman; 249 BBC Hulton Picture Library; 250 E.T. Archive; 251 National Portrait Gallery; 252 top Mansell Collection; bottom Douglas Dickens; 253 top National Portrait Gallery; bottom left and right John Freeman; 254 British Museum; 256 English Heritage; 257 Mary Evans Picture Library; 258 John Freeman; 259 National Portrait Gallery; 260 top BBC Hulton Picture Library; bottom Mansell Collection; 261 top left The Wedgwood Museum; top right John Freeman; bottom left Museum of London; bottom right The Wedgwood Museum; 262 Barnaby's Picture Library; 263 National Portrait Gallery; 264–267 John Freeman; 268 BBC Hulton Picture Library; 269–270 Bulloz; 271 BBC Hulton Picture Library; bottom Bulloz; 272–275 Bulloz; 276 BBC Hulton Picture Library; 277 Michael Holford; 278 National Portrait Gallery; 279 National Maritime Museum; 281 Angelo Hornak; 282 top and centre left National Trust for Scotland/Woodmansterne; centre right Angelo Hornak; bottom left Susan Griggs/Adam Woolfitt; bottom right Ancient Art and Architecture Collection; 283 Angelo Hornak; 284 top left Michael Holford; top right Reader's Digest; bottom left Woodmansterne; bottom right Susan Griggs/Ian Yeomans; 285 top Earl Spencer Collection, Northampton/Bridgeman Art Library; bottom left Tate Gallery; bottom right E.T. Archive; 286 top left National Portrait Gallery/John Freeman; top right Reader's Digest; centre Wellington Museum/Woodmansterne; bottom left National Gallery; bottom right National Maritime Museum/E.T. Archive; 287 Robert Harding; 288 National Gallery/Bridgeman Art Library; 289 BBC Hulton Picture Library; 291 Bulloz; 292 Skyscan; 293 top left Ann Ronan Picture Library; top right National Portrait Gallery; centre Mansell Collection; bottom Ann Ronan Picture Library; 294 John Freeman; 295 Bulloz; 297–298 John Freeman; 299 National Portrait Gallery; 301 BBC Hulton Picture Library; 302 Bulloz; 303 Mary Evans Picture Library; 304 Victoria and Albert Museum/Ikon; 306 John Freeman; 308–314 BBC Hulton Picture Library; 316 Mary Evans Picture Library; 317 National Army Museum; 318–320 BBC Hulton Picture Library.

VOLUME THREE: 7 Mansell Collection; 8 National Portrait

Gallery; 9 BBC Hulton Picture Library; 11 John Freeman; 12 top and bottom BBC Hulton Picture Library; centre Ikon; 13 top National Museums and Galleries on Merseyside (Walker Art Gallery); centre Tate Gallery/E.T. Archive; 14 Mansell Collection; 15 Wallace Collection; 16–19 National Portrait Gallery; 21–23 BBC Hulton Picture Library; 25 top John Freeman; bottom BBC Hulton Picture Library; 27 National Portrait Gallery; 28 top Windsor Castle Royal Library © 1988 Her Majesty The Queen; bottom BBC Hulton Picture Library; 29 top left BBC Hulton Picture Library; top right Aerofilms; bottom left, centre and right BBC Hulton Picture Library; 31 John Freeman; 32 BBC Hulton Picture Library; 33 Victoria and Albert Museum/Bridgeman Art Library; 34 top Derek Widdicombe; bottom left Brian Seed/John Hillelson Agency; bottom right National Portrait Gallery; 35 top Tate Gallery/E.T. Archive; centre Woodmansterne; bottom Scottish Tourist Board; 36 Woodmansterne; 37 Museum of London/Bridgeman Art Library; bottom left Photosource; bottom centre and right Angelo Hornak; 38 top Tate Gallery; centre left and right Bridgeman Art Library; bottom E.T. Archive; 39 top left Ian Bradshaw; top right Tate Gallery; bottom National Gallery/Bridgeman Art Library; 40 Woodmansterne; 41 The Wedgwood Museum; 42–44 BBC Hulton Picture Library; 45 top Mansell Collection; bottom Topham Picture Library; 46–47 BBC Hulton Picture Library; 48 E.T. Archive; bottom BBC Hulton Picture Library; 49 top left and bottom right BBC Hulton Picture Library; top right Ikon; bottom left National Monuments Record; 50–51 BBC Hulton Picture Library; 52 top BBC Hulton Picture Library; centre Picturepoint; bottom Victoria and Albert Museum; 53 top and bottom right BBC Hulton Picture Library; bottom left Mansell Collection; 54 Mary Evans Picture Library; 55 National Portrait Gallery; 57 BBC Hulton Picture Library; 58–59 Mansell Collection; 60–61 BBC Hulton Picture Library; 63 Victoria and Albert Museum/Ikon; 65 Mary Evans Picture Library; 66 top Sheffield City Museum; bottom National Museums and Galleries on Merseyside (Walker Art Gallery); 67 BBC Hulton Picture Library; 69–71 Mansell Collection; 72 Stanley Gibbons Ltd; 73 Picturepoint; 74 BBC Hulton Picture Library; 76 Mansell Collection; 77 BBC Hulton Picture Library; 78 top State Library for New South Wales/Ikon; bottom Mitchell Library, Australia/Ikon; 79 Mary Evans Picture Library; 80 top State Library of Victoria/Ikon; bottom State Library for New South Wales/Ikon; 81 BBC Hulton Picture Library; 82 Alexander Turnbull Library, Wellington, New Zealand/Ikon; 83 Mansell Collection; 84 BBC Hulton Picture Library; 85 Ikon; 86 Mansell Collection; 87 Wellcome Museum/Ikon; 88 top and bottom right BBC Hulton Picture Library; bottom left Ikon; 89 top John Freeman; bottom left UMDS, Guy's Hospital/Ikon; bottom right BBC Hulton Picture Library; 90–91 BBC Hulton Picture Library; 92 John Freeman; 93 Mary Evans Picture Library; 94 top and bottom right BBC Hulton Picture Library; bottom left Michael Freeman; 95 top Harrogate Art Gallery; bottom BBC Hulton Picture Library; 96 Mansell Collection; 97 top BBC Hulton Picture Library; bottom Mansell Collection; 98 Colorsport; 99 Mansell Collection; 101 Mary Evans Picture Library; 102 Topham Picture Library; 103 BBC Hulton Picture Library; 105 Guildhall Art Gallery/Bridgeman Art Library; 106 Birmingham Art Gallery/Bridgeman Art Library; 107 top left E.T. Archive; top centre Picturepoint; top right and centre E.T. Archive; bottom left Barnaby's Picture Library; bottom right SS Great Britain Project; 108 top left Bridgeman Art Library; top lower left National Portrait Gallery; right Erich Lessing/John Hillelson Agency; bottom left Crown Copyright reproduced with the permission of the Controller of Her Majesty's Stationery Office/Woodmansterne; 109 top Picturepoint; centre left Angelo Hornak; centre right Picturepoint; bottom Angelo Hornak; 110 top Angelo Hornak; bottom left E.T. Archive; bottom right Photosource; 111 top left E.T. Archive; top right Angelo Hornak; bottom left Mansell Collection; bottom right Bridgeman Art Library; 112 Susan Griggs; 113–115 BBC Hulton Picture Library; 116 top John Freeman; bottom Trades Union Congress; 117 top Transport and General Workers' Union; centre left Ironbridge Museum; centre bottom and right BBC Hulton Picture Library; 118–120 BBC Hulton Picture Library; 121 Mansell Collection; 122–123 BBC Hulton Picture Library; 124 John Webb/Ikon; 125 BBC Hulton Picture Library; 126 National Army Museum/Ikon; 127 Royal Commonwealth Society; 128 Topham Picture Library; 129 BBC Hulton Picture Library; 130 Topham Picture Library; 131 Ikon; 132 British Library; 134–136 BBC Hulton Picture Library; 137 Mansell Collection; 138 John Freeman; 139 BBC Hulton Picture Library; 140 GEC-Marconi Company; 141 BBC Hulton Picture Library; 142 top BBC Hulton Picture Library; centre Mansell Collection; 143 top left and right, bottom left BBC Hulton Picture Library; centre right London Transport Museum; 144 Mansell Collection; 145 Tate Gallery; 146 top left Victoria and Albert Museum/Bridgeman Art Library; top right Tate Gallery; centre left Tate Gallery/E.T. Archive; bottom right Manchester City Art Gallery/Bridgeman Art Library; 147 Woodmansterne; bottom left Bridgeman Art Library; bottom right Angelo Hornak; 148 top Imperial War Museum/Bridgeman Art Library; bottom centre E.T. Archive; bottom right Imperial War Museum/E.T. Archive; 149 top Imperial War Museum/Bridgeman Art Library; centre Bridgeman Art Library; bottom Imperial War Museum/Bridgeman Art Library; 150 top left Photosource; top right P & O; centre left Tate Gallery; bottom Daily Telegraph Colour Library;